THE FUTURE OF ANTHROPOLOGY
ITS RELEVANCE TO THE CONTEMPORARY WORLD

The Future of Anthropology

*Its Relevance
to the Contemporary World*

Edited by
Akbar S. Ahmed and Cris N. Shore

ATHLONE
London & Atlantic Highlands, NJ

First published 1995 by
THE ATHLONE PRESS
1 Park Drive, London NW11 7SG
and 165 First Avenue,
Atlantic Highlands, NJ 07716

British Library Cataloguing in Publication Data
*A catalogue record for this book is available
from the British Library*

ISBN 0 485 11445 3   hb
0 485 12105 0   pb

Library of Congress Cataloging in Publication Data
The future of anthropology : its relevance to the contempo-
rary world / edited by Akbar S. Ahmed & Cris N. Shore.
    p.   cm.
Includes bibliographical references and index.
ISBN 0-485-11445-3 (hb). -- ISBN 0-485-12105-0 (pbk.)
1. Ethnology--Philosophy.   2. Ethnology--Methodology.
I. Ahmed, Akbar S.   II. Shore, Cris, 1959–
GN345.F87   1995
305.8′001--dc20   95-34567
                                                          CIP

Typeset by
Bibloset, Chester

Printed and bound in Great Britain by
WBC, Bridgend, Mid Glam.

Contents

Contributors   vi

Foreword: From Self-Applause through Self-Criticism to
  Self-Confidence   *Jonathan Benthall*   1
1 Introduction: Is Anthropology Relevant to the Contemporary
  World?   *Akbar S. Ahmed and Cris N. Shore*   12
2 The Rise and Fall of Scientific Ethnography
  Anna Grimshaw and Keith Hart   46
3 Anthropology: Still the Uncomfortable Discipline?
  Susan Wright   65
4 Anthropologists for Sale?
  I.M. Lewis   94
5 Learning from AIDS: The Future of Anthropology
  Ronald Frankenberg   110
6 Feminist Anthropologies and Questions of Masculinity
  Andrea Cornwall and Nancy Lindisfarne   134
7 Tourism, Modernity and Nostalgia
  Nelson H.H. Graburn   158
8 Prospects for Tourism Study in Anthropology
  Dennison Nash   179
9 Lost Horizons Regained: Old Age and the Anthropology
  of Contemporary Society
  Haim Hazan   203
10 Cultural Imperialism and the Mediation of Otherness
  David Morley and Kevin Robins   228
11 After Emotion: Ethnic Cleansing in the Former Yugoslavia,
  and Beyond
  Stjepan G. Meštrović   251
12 Epilogue: Notes on the Future of Anthropology
  Anthony Giddens   272

Index   278

Contributors

Akbar S. Ahmed is a distinguished anthropologist, writer and commentator on Islamic affairs. His book *Discovering Islam: Making Sense of Muslim History and Society* (1988) was widely praised by Muslim and Western commentators alike, and has been translated into many languages, including Turkish and Indonesian. The book was the inspiration for the television series *Living Islam* of which he was chief consultant. He also wrote a book of the series *Living Islam*. He has written numerous articles for journals and newspapers, and many books, including *Postmodernism and Islam: Predicament and Promise*, published in 1992.

He is Fellow of Selwyn College at Cambridge University and has been Visiting Professor at the Institute for Advanced Study, Princeton, and at Harvard University, and was the Allama Iqbal Fellow at Cambridge. He is the first Pakistani to have been elected a member of the Council of the Royal Anthropological Institute and has been awarded the Star of Excellence (*Sitara-i-Imtiaz*) for academic distinction by the Pakistani Government. In 1995, he was awarded the Sir Percy Sykes Memorial Medal by the Royal Sociey for Asian Affairs.

Jonathan Benthall is Director of the Royal Anthropological Institute and Editor of *Anthropology Today*. He was awarded the Anthropology in Media Award by the American Anthropological Association in 1993, and is currently an Honorary Research Fellow in the Department of Anthropology, University College London. His recent publications include *Disasters, Relief and the Media* (I.B. Tauris, London, and St Martin's Press, New York, 1993).

Andrea Cornwall is based in the Anthropology Department, School of Oriental and African Studies, University of London. She is conducting research in Southwestern Nigeria on processes of gendering over the life course. Her previous work has been on participatory research methodology and reproductive health. She has published on both gender and development topics.

Ronald Frankenberg is Professor Emeritus of Sociology and Social Anthropology at the Keele University where until this year he taught a Master's Programme as founder-director, ten years ago, of the Centre for Medical Social Anthropology. He is currently Professor Associate in the *Centre for the Study of Health Sickness and Disablement* at Brunel University in West London where teaches on the M.Sc Programme in Medical Anthropology. His writings include *Village on the Border* (1957 and 1989) *Communities in Britain* (1966 and 1994), and the edited volumes *Custom and Conflict in British Society* 1982 and *Time, Health and Medicine*, 1990. He has worked on health care in Lusaka, Zambia and in Italy. His current research interests are epidemics including AIDS/HIV, the cultural performance of sickness, temporality in Biomedicine, and narrative dialogues of chronic suffering.

Anthony Giddens is Professor of Sociology and Fellow of King's College, Cambridge University. He has written extensively on social theory, sociology, the nation-state and modernity. His most recent books include *Modernity and Self-Identity* (Polity and Stanford University Press 1991; 1994), *Beyond Left and Right* (Polity and Stanford University Press, 1994), and *Politics, Sociology and Social Theory* (Polity Press, 1995).

Nelson Graburn has carried out field research among the Inuit (Eskimo) of the Canadian Arctic since 1959, and in Japan since 1974. He has taught anthropology at the University of California, Berkeley, since 1964; he has also served as a visiting scholar at the National Museum of Ethnology, Japan, and the Centre des Hautes Etudes Touristiques, Aix-en-Provence.

His publications include *Circumpolar Peoples* (1973), *Ethnic and Tourist Arts* (1976), *To Pray, Pay and Play: the Cultural Structure of Japanese Domestic Tourism* (1983) and *Anthropological Research on Contemporary Tourism* (1988).

Keith Hart is Director of the African Studies Centre and lecturer in Social Anthropology, Cambridge University. He is co-founder of Prickly Pear Press and author of *The Political Economy of West African Agriculture* (1982) and co-editor, with Joanna Lewis, of *Why Angola Matters* (African Studies Centre, 1995). He is best known for having invented the concept of the 'informal economy'.

Haim Hazan is a professor of social anthropology at Tel-Aviv University. Among his writings are: *The Limbo People* (1980), *A Paradoxical*

Community (1990), *Managing Change in Old Age*, and *Old Age: Constructions and Deconstructions* (1994).

Anna Grimshaw PhD is Lecturer in Visual Anthropology at the Granada Centre for Visual Anthropology, University of Manchester. She has edited four volumes of the writings of C.L.R. James and is author of *Servants of the Buddha* (1992). She is also co-founder of Prickly Pear Press.

Ioan Lewis is Emeritus Professor of Anthropology at the London School of Economics and Chairman of the African Educational Trust. He was formerly Director of the International African Institute (1981–88) and Editor of *Man* (1969–72). He has conducted extensive field research in Somalia since the 1950s, and shorter spells of field work in Central Africa and Malaysia. He has worked on 'applied' projects for ActionAid, the ODA, FAO, USAID, ILCA, UNHCR and the EC.

Nancy Lindisfarne is Senior Lecturer in the Anthropology of the Arab World at the School of Oriental and African Studies, University of London. She has done fieldwork in Iran, Afghanistan, Turkey and Syria. She has published numerous articles on gender, marriage and Islam in the Middle East and, as Nancy Tapper, is the author of *Bartered Brides: Politics, Gender and Marriage in an Afghan Tribal Society* (1991).

Stjepan Mestrovic is Professor of Sociology at Texas A&M University, College Station, Texas. The author of numerous scholarly articles, his most recent books include: *Habits of the Balkan Heart* (1993), *The Road From Paradise* (1993), *The Barbarian Temperament* (1993), and *The Balkanization of the West* (1994).

David Morley is Reader in Communications, Goldsmiths' College, University of London. He is the author of *Television, Audiences and Cultural Studies*, (Routledge 1992), with Kevin Robins of *Spaces of Identity* (Routledge 1995), and with Kuan Hsing Chen, the editor of *Stuart Hall: Critical Dialogues in Cultural Studies* (Routledge 1995).

Dennison Nash is Emeritus Professor of Anthropology and Sociology at the University of Connecticut, USA. He has conducted field research in the Caribbean, Europe and the US. He is author of *A Little Anthropology* (Englewood Cliffs, N.J. 1991), 'An Exploration of Tourism as a Kind of

Superstructure' (in R. Butler and D. Pearce eds., *Changes in Tourism: People, Places and Processes*, Routledge), and co-editor (with Valene Smith) of 'Tourism as an Anthropological Subject' *Annals of Tourism Research* (1991, No. 15).

Kevin Robins is Reader in Cultural Geography at the University of Newcastle upon Tyne and a researcher at the Centre for Urban and Regional Development Studies. He is author, with David Morley, of *Spaces of Identity* (Routledge, 1995), and of *Into the Image* (to be published by Lawrence and Wishart in 1996).

Cris Shore lectures in Anthropology at Goldsmiths College, University of London and is former editor of the journal *Anthropology in Action*. He has written extensively on the European integration and the European Union. He is author of *Italian Communism. The Escape from Leninism* (Pluto, 1990), and editor (with Victoria Goddard and Josep Llobera) of *The Anthropology of Europe: Identities and Boundaries in Conflict* (Berg, 1994), and, with Susan Wright, of *The Anthropology of Policy* (to be published by Routledge, 1996).

Susan Wright (D.Phil. Oxon) is lecturer in social anthropology at the University of Sussex. After studying people's relations with the state in Iran and Britain, she became involved in doing participant observation in state organisations themselves. Recent books are *Anthropology of Organizations* (1994, Routledge) and, co-edited with Nici Nelson, *Power and Participatory Development* (1995, Intermediate Technology Publications).

From Self-Applause through Self-Criticism to Self-Confidence
Jonathan Benthall

This book is intended to argue the relevance of socio-cultural anthropology – too often stereotyped as the study by Europeans of non-Europeans – to central issues of the contemporary world.

Neither of its two editors fits the traditional mould of anthropologist. Akbar Ahmed is a Pakistani who has held senior posts as a government official in his own country, and he is a practising Muslim. As well as writing extensively about Pakistan, Muslim societies and relations between Muslims and other societies, especially the British, he has considerable experience of working with television and radio. Cris Shore is a young British anthropologist who has specialized in research on various European issues such as Italian communism and the harmonization of nation-states within the European Community, and who has also played a leading part in activating a more public-spirited kind of anthropology than the academic mainstream prefers, especially through his editorship of the new journal *Anthropology in Action*.

I believe and hope that the editors are pushing at an open door. Having been working for some time towards broadly similar ends as director of the Royal Anthropological Institute (RAI) and editor of its bimonthly *Anthropology Today*, I have felt the task to be a little easier in recent years. In one field, for instance, of which I have special knowledge, the work of humanitarian and development agencies, there is no doubt that the contribution of anthropology to clarifying their problems is now widely recognized. When the RAI organized a conference called 'The Refugee Experience' in 1980, I was rebuked by a prominent anthropologist on the grounds that it was irresponsible to suggest that anthropology had anything useful to say about refugee issues. There is now a thriving Refugee Studies Programme at Oxford University, well supported by the various agencies, and similar initiatives in many other places.[1] We should work towards the extension of such a contribution to literally *all* areas of public debate. Tourism (discussed in this book by Graburn), the media (by Morley and Robins) and medicine and health (an aspect of which is treated by Frankenberg), are just three areas that seem specially promising.

This is of course an ambitious programme. The American anthropologist Roy Rappaport has well summarized anthropology's great strength as its siting of value, meaning and information at the *centre* of whatever models of social and economic and ecological reality we may devise, rather than as peripheral add-ons.[2]

Rather than attempting to pre-empt what the editors will say in their introduction, I venture to assume that the reader of this book is, if not necessarily fully convinced at the outset, at least sympathetic to their intent. I shall use this space to explore some aspects of the self-image of contemporary socio-cultural anthropology, and in particular its penchant for an uneasy self-criticism which in my opinion could sometimes be more rigorously aimed. By approaching the topic from an oblique angle, through reference to some literary as opposed to academic material, I hope to delineate some elements in what might be called a specifically anthropological identity. If these elements are properly recognized, they ought to help the discipline move forward with more self-confidence to undertake some of the programme that Akbar Ahmed and Cris Shore have in mind for it.

Socio-cultural anthropology has engaged in the therapy of a searching self-examination for some twenty years. Little has been left unexamined: from intellectual origins to sources of funding. At its most negative, a casual reader of this auto-critique might come away with a pitiable impression: an impression of a discipline with lofty aspirations which allegedly compromised with the civil powers, exploited indigenous informants and the subjects of research, connived in the manipulation of oppressed peoples, and propagated stereotypes which are not so different in kind from those put about by the popularizers and romantic novelists whom anthropology affects to despise. Are we really to think of traditional unreconstructed anthropology as Pope's goddess, Dullness?

> She, tinselled o'er in robes of varying hues,
> With self-applause her wild creation views;
> Sees momentary monsters rise and fall,
> And with her own fools-colours gilds them all.[3]

The phase of auto-critique is indeed a reaction against an excessive sac-ralization of the discipline by an earlier generation. As a quasi-religious movement, anthropology has had its ancestor-worship, its demanding initiation rites, its conference-hopping swamis, its long-bearded world-renouncers, its rapt novices. Other excessively sacralized professions have benefited from pressures to acknowledge that their histories and established institutions are not without flaw. The Christian churches, for instance, have been familiar with these pressures for longer than anthropology; most recently, perhaps, it is the turn of humanitarian charities.

Auto-critique is healthy for anthropology, but 'the lady does protest too much, methinks'.

It is possible to draw up a persuasive credit balance in favour of the socio-cultural anthropology which has been bequeathed to us. I think of Robertson Smith and Frazer with their challenges to Victorian religious dogmatism; Boas decisively refuting racism; Mauss's studies of gift-giving and of the 'techniques of the body', which still read so freshly today; Redfield's demonstration of the complex interactions between 'world religions' and their countless local variants; Stanner's promotion of Aboriginal land rights in Australia; the generation of Malinowski's students attempting to convince sceptical colonial administrators that indigenous ceremonies were not wickednesses to be stamped out; Oscar Lewis's attention to the lives of impoverished townspeople, even though his findings on the culture of poverty have since had to be much qualified; Margaret Mead's early engagement with the challenges of environmentalism; Gluckman's comparison of Western law with customary systems of dispute settlement; Audrey Richards and Phyllis Kaberry focusing in their ethnographies on the life cycles of girls and women; Margaret Read's pioneering of health education in Africa; Victor Turner's demonstration that shamanistic therapy in West Africa can succeed by uncovering the sources of tension in a village which come to a head in an individual patient's symptoms; Lucy Mair's attention to the unintended consequences of often well-meaning schemes for national development; Godfrey Lienhardt exploring the subtleties of the religious experience of a Sudanese people; Leach's demonstration that simple equilibrium models are not adequate to explain the complexities of the relationship between ideology and 'real life'; the sustained intellectual opposition to apartheid carried on for many years by anthropologists in South Africa such as David Webster, who gave his life for human rights in 1989; the revolution in the conception and design of museums which was led in France by Georges-Henri Rivière; John Blacking's commitment to the idea of innate human musicality; Anthony Forge's study of the pictorial art of New Guinea as a language-like style with its own aesthetic criteria.

The list is somewhat arbitrary, excludes anthropologists who are still alive at the time of writing, and is also confined to Euro-American scholars. Any such roll-call prepared in ten or twenty years' time is likely to include a larger proportion of women as well as a wider range of national origins. It should also be noted that anthropology has contributed significantly to intellectual movements of various kinds: anti-racism, multiculturalism, black studies, cultural studies, feminism, minority rights, structuralism, and so forth; but it consistently tends to be cast off as not sufficiently radical.

Furthermore, there is a wing of socio-cultural anthropology which is more closely interested in various aspects of biological science than is suggested in the above roll-call. I shall do no more here than point to the existence of a whole realm of biological, evolutionary and ecological anthropology towards which some socio-cultural anthropologists are actively concerned with building academic bridges.[4]

An undoubted *faiblesse* of anthropology, which has been relatively little emphasized during the process of auto-critique but which I am relieved to see diagnosed by a number of contributors to the present collection, is one which it shares with most other academic disciplines, and that is a certain clannishness and intellectual presumption.

Ahmed and Shore note for instance, in their introduction, the tendency of anthropologists of the older generation to treat 'my village' as an exclusive personal territory; the status hierarchy which still sets 'pure' theoreticians above 'applied' anthropologists who earn their living outside the university (a state of affairs also commented on by Lewis and by Wright); and the slowness of the discipline to appreciate its full cosmopolitan potential and give adequate recognition in its hall of fame to non-Western scholars. It might be further noted that those anthropologists who write in languages other than English, French, German and Spanish tend to be virtually ignored by the metropolitan anthropology journals.[5]

Grimshaw and Hart observe that academics in general have lost some of the respect that they used to be accorded. Furthermore, say Grimshaw and Hart, the culture of academia has dictated for anthropologists a spurious intellectual distance between the study and the 'field'; individual subjects have been gaining celebrity by writing about anonymous collective objects; but now, the knowledge gained by fieldworkers is increasingly subject to challenge by articulate 'natives'. Frankenberg quotes a gay and lesbian activist T-shirt slogan, 'These natives can speak for themselves'.

Grimshaw and Hart may be exaggerating for effect when they say that the famous kinship algebra developed by anthropologists was largely a device to impress the laity; yet there is a serious point here. Today, kinship algebra is out of fashion, but an anthropologist applying for a job, or submitting an article or book for publication, can sometimes be at a disadvantage if he or she is not familiar with the latest buzz-words.

Even the more politically sophisticated anthropologists of our day sometimes have difficulty in accepting the criticism that they have become much better at communicating with their colleagues than with others. For instance, in a recent issue of the journal *Current Anthropology*, Orin Starn of Duke University contributes a combative article attempting to show what was wrong, particularly, with the anthropology of the Andes.[6] While accepting that some undoubtedly innovative thinkers tend to write in murky prose, Starn deplores that 'over the past 50 years, the appeal of anthropologists to wider audiences has shrunk with the increase in the number of practitioners. Ramified into subfields with their own debates, jargons, journals, and conferences, anthropologists have grown increasingly removed from the public sphere'. Why are there not more books that reach 'with graceful prose to lay readers without any sacrifice of empirical detail or theoretical sophistication'?

To this, in the usual *Current Anthropology* 'Comment' format, Olivia Harris replies that 'one of the reasons anthropology does not make the sort of interventions into public debate that Boas, Mead, and [Ruth] Benedict did is surely our refusal to simplify and our commitment to the complexity of lived reality'. Stephen Nugent questions Starn's 'preoccupation with readership, reader-friendliness, and the market/audience. While this may be read as a desire to reinsert anthropology (if it was ever effectively inserted) into the wide cultural domain, it could just as easily indicate acquiescence in the market's demand for relevant commodities'.

Both Harris and Nugent make valid points. Their position would probably be supported by many a student who has taken anthropology courses and has been impressed by the refusal of contemporary anthropologists to make glib and simplified generalizations. But they ignore the observation – embarrassingly patent as it is to people outside academia – that academics love to step the catwalk of *haute couture universitaire.*

Anthropology in the future is more likely to live up to its undoubted promise if it conducts itself with modesty and remains as permeable as possible to other fields of study. This might equally be said of all the social sciences. To illustrate this point I shall show that a guiding idea of social science over the last 25 years – incidentally, one that fits in happily with the rhetoric of this foreword – was foreshadowed 40 years beforehand by a novelist who seems to have thought it out with only slight help from the social science of the day. If social science had been more permeable, it might have picked up these thoughts sooner. Those anthropologists today with a curiosity that extends outside their specialist journals – and there are fortunately many such – are most likely to be alive to guiding ideas in the social thought of tomorrow.

The idea I refer to is that the experiences of different kinds of repressed groups or minorities can be analytically superimposed on one another. Most would say that this idea emerged in the 1960s in the United States. A key text is Erving Goffman's *Stigma: Notes on the Management of Spoiled Identity*,[7] published in 1963, in which he wrote: '[I]n an important sense, there is only one complete unblushing male in America: a young, married, white, urban, northern heterosexual Protestant father of college education, fully employed, of good complexion, weight and height, and a recent record in sports'. There followed the heyday of Black Power, the Gay Liberation Front, together with the realization that women, though numerically more or less equal to men, nonetheless constitute a minority in terms of influence and power. By 1972, it was possible for the dependably with-it Institute of Contemporary Arts in London to put on a multi-media season, 'The Body as a Medium of Expression', in which the expressive practices of blacks, male homosexuals and deaf people were compared, with the indication that women, female homosexuals, artists, lunatics and children might soon be brought into the net.[8] Since then, minorities have sprouted on every side: from children in care to Grey Panthers, diabetics to the 'diagnosed mentally ill'. As Goffman noted, we are all members of minorities of one kind or another, we all bear a stigma.

The idea of the transposability of minority experience became a commonplace among progressives, and before long was taken over by reactionary elements of various kinds: for instance, by disgruntled professions such as prison officers, and by *dominant* political minorities such as the Ulster Orangemen and the Afrikaner Broederbond. The latest banalizations of the idea may be found in the Men's Movement, which is dissected in this book by Lindisfarne and Cornwall, or in the decisions of certain local authorities in England a few years ago that all ethnic minorities including Gypsies should be designated in their own interest as 'black'.

But if we think back to the first quarter of the century, this was not an idea that had currency in social science, let alone in the political discourse of everyday life. It took a novelist of extraordinary intuition, not a social scientist, to develop the idea.

From the many themes in Marcel Proust's novel *Remembrance of Things Past* (1912–27)[9], I single out here his drawing of a parallel between the predicament of homosexuals and Jews in a Catholic country, France, which showed intolerance towards both minorities. The conviction and imprisonment of Oscar Wilde in 1895 in England, and the Eulenburg scandal of 1907–9, in which an aristocratic diplomat was disgraced in Germany, were dramatic instances of the downfall which could result from imprudent homosexual behaviour. Anti-semitism pervaded French institutions and its most prominent victim was Albert Dreyfus, the French Jewish army officer who was convicted for treason in 1894 and later cleared after many years of passionate divisive controversy. Proust happened to be both homosexual and Jewish himself, and this provoked one of the most searching investigations into the question of identity that any writer has achieved. In particular, his examination of how a minority's stigmatization and repression can lead to perverse forms – the Jewish anti-semite, Albert Bloch, and the homosexual homophobe, the Baron de Charlus – is markedly subtle. 'Sodom and Zion contaminate one another and become confused' writes Julia Kristeva in her study of Proust;

> It is not a question of describing the sociological reality of a Jew or his community, nor even of mastering the psychological reality of the invert. By knocking the two marginalities against each other, by accumulating the criticisms and backbiting to which they are subjected by 'good society', Proust turns the calumny back.[10]

Proust's concern with the themes of identity and clannishness extends to the whole of his social experience. He likens the clannishness of homosexuals to that of freemasonry, hobby and collecting clubs, vegetarianism or political leftism;[11] these are all communities which do not necessarily love their fellow members so much as they are drawn by a charm in common. For 'A snob is not a man who likes snobs, nor is an invert a man who likes inverts, but a snob cannot see a duchess, an invert cannot see a handsome boy, without feeling drawn to them'.[12]

Proust is still seen by many readers as the minute but limited analyst of a particular plutocratic milieu. However, he was one of the signatories of the first manifesto protesting against Captain Dreyfus's conviction. He quickly became disillusioned with political activism. His ideas on minority consciousness make him, as Kristeva claims, in many ways a contemporary of the present day.[13] There is no more pressing political issue today than that of identity and clannishness. In Kristeva's words,

> Every group congregates around beings who are not like others and then lives, with them and against them, in the logic of sadomaso-chism: love of hatred, hatred of love, persecution, humiliation, delectable grief. There is no social outcome to this: all of the social, the whole of the social, is comprised in it.[14]

Just as we are all members of cross-cutting minorities, so we all have recourse to a kind of mental perversion, or what the existentialists were to call 'bad faith' (*mauvaise foi*), as the price of living in society.

Proust's merciless satire of art-world groupies who meet in the salon of Madame Verdurin is well enough known. But he does not let intellectuals and academics off the hook either. In one throwaway simile, he compares a solitary homosexual who has to make do with rent-boys with a professor of Sanskrit at the Collège de France whose only listeners are ragamuffins who have come to get warm.[15] Devoted scholars are like other people driven by a specialized desire.

> In every clan – whether worldly, political or literary – people contract a perverse facility for discovering in a conversation, in an official speech, in a piece of fiction, in a sonnet, everything that the honest reader would never have dreamt of finding there.[16]

Anthropologists of all people should be the most tolerant and appreciative of other people's intellectual desires and traditions. But elements of the profession itself are not without their share of sectarianism. Anthropology has had most success by remaining relatively small and impressing other disciplines with its reach and persuasiveness. It is likely to prosper if it offers consultation and cooperation to other, larger disciplines,[17] in the confidence that these will always have to rely on anthropology as the *only* social science which is consistently committed to countering the ethnocentrism inherent in all discourse about society. Anthropology should never contend for academic hegemony. It should be happy with remaining what Firth calls 'the uncomfortable science' (as enlarged on by Sue Wright in her essay in this collection).

The charge that anthropology was a handmaiden of power was always one-sided. It can be argued just as convincingly that anthropologists have an elective affinity for a critical stance. Yet much of the subject-matter of anthropology, as this collection of essays shows, is anything but marginal; and the vast majority of professional anthropologists in the West are now employed in universities or other large bureaucratic organizations. Somehow – and without lapsing into quixotry – anthropology needs to conserve the spice of marginality.[18]

Finally, as Western technological rationality allied to consumerism spreads all over the planet, it is likely that anthropology will seek to maintain its independence of approach through refreshing itself more open-mindedly from non-Western intellectual sources. A hint of this trend is given by Mondher Kilani,[19] who looks to Islam as an alternative universalism, for this kind of critical stimulus; but Veena Das, for instance, has been inspired by the Sanskritic tradition,[20] and a number of well-known anthropologists either are Buddhists or have been influenced by Buddhist thought. Kilani's point applies to the availability of all these non-European traditions:

> It is not a question of repudiating anthropological knowledge, which arose with the extension to a planetary scale of European consciousness, but of showing that it must never stop tearing itself from particular systems of thought, whatever they are or wherever they derive from, including those which are at the origins of its own conditions of existence: in other words, universalistic authority and the modern ideology which accompanies it.[21]

NOTES
I am grateful to Gustaaf Houtman, Stephen O. Murray and Jean-Yves Tadié for stimulus towards the writing of this preface. It represents a personal view only. Translations from the French are by the author.
 1 A report on the RAI/ESRC exploratory workshop held on 9 January 1995, 'International NGOs and Complex Political Emergencies: Perspectives from

Anthropology', organized by the author and Mark Duffield, is published by the Royal Anthropological Institute (ISBN 0 900632 41 0).

2 Roy A. Rappaport, Distinguished Lecture in General Anthropology, 'The anthropology of trouble', *American Anthropologist*, June 1993.

3 *The Dunciad*, I:80ff.

4 For an excellent and up-to-date introduction to general anthropology from Darwin to the present day, see Adam Kuper, *The Chosen Primate: Human Nature and Cultural Diversity* (Harvard UP, 1994).

5 David Scheffel, 'The domestication of the "science of man"', *Anthropology Today*, 4.6, December 1988.

6 'Rethinking the politics of anthropology: the case of the Andes', *Current Anthropology*, 35, 1, February 1994.

7 Prentice-Hall, 1963.

8 Jonathan Benthall, 'A prospectus as published in *Studio International*, July 1972', in *The Body as a Medium of Expression*, ed. J. Benthall and T. Polhemus (Allen Lane and Dutton, 1975).

9 Proust died in 1922 and the last three volumes of the seven-volume work (French title, *A la Recherche du Temps Perdu*) were published posthumously.

10 Julia Kristeva, *Le temps sensible: Proust et l'expérience littéraire*, Gallimard, Paris, 1994, p.190. It seems that, in his understanding of what we would now call minority consciousness, Proust may have got some help from a prominent French sociologist of the day, Gabriel Tarde, who Kristeva argues was a major influence on his novel. Tarde was concerned with 'imitation' and 'desire' as social forces; this led him to see conformism as an essential fact of human life, but as an extreme individualist (sharply opposed to Durkheim's 'collective representations') he believed freedom could only come through 'disassimilation' from the group. (Ibid., pp.325ff., and see Gabriel Tarde, *Les Lois de l'Imitation*, 1895.)

11 Part I of *Sodome et Gomorrhe* (1921), translated in English as *Cities of the Plain*, is the key text for this discussion. Pléiade edition, Gallimard, 1988, vol. III, pp.19ff.

12 Pléiade edn, III, p.1284 (notes).

13 Stephen O. Murray, commenting on a draft of this foreword, points out correctly that Proust may have foreshadowed, but did not actually articulate any social *theory*. My suggestion however is that if social scientists before the 1960s had been more alive to ideas that were in the air, they might have developed their understanding of the dynamics of minorities earlier. They might even have done more to mitigate the oppressions of many minorities during the twentieth century.

14 Kristeva, ibid., p.197.

15 Pléiade edn, III, p.28.

16 Pléiade edn, III, p.340.

17 As has been suggested over many years by Mary Douglas, Ronnie Frankenberg and others.

18 It has often been noted that many anthropologists have been ethnically marginal, but as we have seen above there are numerous other forms of marginality. Organizations like the Centre for Cross-Cultural Studies of Women, University of Oxford, have been important in mobilizing the contribution of women anthropologists, who were until recently marginal, though now women are in the majority among anthropology students. The contribution of gay anthropologists is one aspect of this topic which has as yet been hardly explored. Cf. Stephen O. Murray, 'Writing with others', paper presented at American Anthropological Association Annual Meeting, Washington, DC, November 1993.

19 Mondher Kilani, *L'invention de l'autre: Essais sur le discours anthropologique* (Editions Payot, Lausanne, 1994).

20 Veena Das, 'The anthropological discourse on India: reason and its other' in *Assessing Cultural Anthropology*, ed. R. Borofsky, McGraw-Hill, New York, 1994.

21 Kilani, *L'invention de l'autre*, p.298.

CHAPTER 1

Introduction: Is Anthropology Relevant to the Contemporary World?

Akbar S. Ahmed and Cris N. Shore

So streetwise historians were announcing the End of History, journos like me were noting the close of the Cold War, politicians everywhere were talking of the New World Order – especially in the New World. Marxism and the command economy were plainly dying of terminal exhaustion. On the other hand liberal capitalism wasn't doing so very well either. There was a budget crisis in Washington, high-street recession in Britain, fiscal jitters in Tokyo, and bank fraud all over the place. In Brussels Napoleonic dreamers were reinventing Europe, if they could just find out where its edges started and stopped. There was conflict in Yugoslavia, independence rioting in the Baltics, ethnic and tribal tension everywhere . . . . To a nice upstanding young fellow like myself, in my green shellsuit and Reebok trainers, these were troubling days. They were also my days.

(Malcolm Bradbury, *Doctor Criminale*, 1992).

Academic disciplines are murderers of curiosity and breeders of cultism.

(Robin Fox, *The Red Lamp of Incest*, 1980).

As the end of the twentieth century draws closer it is becoming increasingly apparent that the world is changing, not just incrementally but also qualitatively. Human societies are moving into a new phase of history. Economic and technological developments are giving rise to ever greater cultural diversity, fragmentation and differentiation in place of the homogeneity and standardization that were once the hallmarks of modernism and mass society (Hall and Jacques, 1989: 11–12). Flexible specialization, de-industrialization, time–space compression, the decentring of the human subject, discontinuity, and the 'end of history' – these processes are said to characterize the condition of postmodernity in the world today (Harvey, 1989; Hebdige, 1989). At the same time, however, there appear to be contradictory tendencies within the process of globalization. On the one hand, there is an increasing centralization of power in high-level planning and decision-making and the emergence of what the international business press calls a 'de-facto world government' with its own institutions: the International Monetary Fund (IMF), World Bank, G-7, the General Agreement on Tariffs and Trade (GATT). As Noam Chomsky says (quoting the *Financial Times*), 'these are becoming the governing institutions of a "new imperial age"' (Chomsky, 1993: 1). On the other hand, however, these tendencies have been matched by a revival of localism and ethnic chauvinism and an increase in xenophobia and nationalism throughout Europe and beyond (cf. Hobsbawm, 1992). At the same time there is talk of a 'global culture' – increasing supranationalism, multinational corporations and globalized consumerism (epitomized in the seemingly ubiquitous presence of MacDonald's, Mickey Mouse, commercial video, Japanese electronics and so forth). Revolutions in information and communications technologies, mass consumption and the globalization of capital appear to be contributing to a fundamental dislocation of everyday working practices and social relations (Beck, 1992; Robertson, 1992; Ahmed and Donnan, 1994).

These contradictory developments are often seen as symptoms of a profound 'crisis of identity' afflicting individuals in the modern world. As Stuart Hall sums it up:

> For those theorists who believe that modern identities are breaking up, the argument runs something like this. A distinctive type of structural change is transforming modern societies in the late twentieth century. This is fragmenting the cultural landscape of class, gender, sexuality, ethnicity, race and nationality which gave us firm locations as social individuals. These transformations are also shifting our personal identities, undermining our sense of ourselves as integrated subjects (Hall, 1992b: 274–5).

More to the point, this pattern of economic restructuring, rationalization, migration and mobility is resulting in the emergence of new identities – consumer and media-oriented, ethnic, regional, national and migrant – and new subjectivities. As Boissevain (1994) notes, these processes are everywhere creating new communities of 'insiders' and 'outsiders', new patterns of inter-ethnic relations and new hybrid cultures.

The problem confronting those trying to make sense of these developments is that 'postmodernism' and 'postmodernity' (the former the critique of the grand narratives, the latter the condition of globalization, information technologies, the decline of established nation-states, the new world order) are themselves elusive and difficult to define. Are we talking of a 'style' (the former) or of an historic period (the latter)? Are we discussing literature, architecture or philosophy? Is this a Western (i.e. industrialized, developed nation) phenomenon or truly global? Moreover, not everyone is convinced that we have entered a new phase. 'Postmodernism' has already become suspect as a term; a highly fashionable cliché during the 1980s (which in many respects reflected the politics of that decade), but increasingly *passé*. Giddens instead talks of a continuity of modernity and prefers to call this period the Late Modern Age or High Modernity (Giddens, 1990; 1991). For other analysts the distinction is between modern culture as elitist and inaccessible and postmodernism as popular and accessible (Jencks, 1984). Nonetheless, many observers would agree that it is 'a moment of gentle apocalypse' (Barthes, 1989: xxii). Postmodernity, they find, is 'enigmatic and troubling' (Foucault, 1984: 39). For some it is 'panic' culture – 'panic sex, panic art, panic identity, panic bodies, panic noise, and panic theory' (Kroker and Cook, 1988: 1). For others it is simply the 'cultural logic of late capitalism' (Jameson, 1984). Whatever term we use to describe this phenomenon (and 'rupture', 'fragmentation' and 'dislocation' are among the most common), the point is that the cultural landscapes of the (post)modern world are changing, and our experience of ourselves – and of our societies – as unified and stable entities has become increasingly problematic.

The question is where does all this leave anthropology today? How is it responding to these changes and how relevant is it to understanding those key issues confronting the modern world as it enters the next millennium? According to some contemporary social theorists postmodernism has led to a profound 'crisis of representation' in the human sciences. Within anthropology this has been attributed to a growing 'uncertainty about adequate means of describing social reality' (Marcus and Fischer, 1986: 8; see also Ahmed, 1992, and Turner, 1994); an acute loss of confidence in existing scientific paradigms and a deepening sense of incredulity and disbelief towards those 'meta-narratives' (liberalism, Marxism, Freudianism, etc.) that have come to characterize the human sciences for most of this century.

This loss of confidence – which reflects a more general dislocation in the discourses of Enlightenment rationalism – was heightened by powerful critiques of the discipline's colonialist legacy, most notably from Asad (1973) and Said (1978; 1993), both scholars with 'Third World' backgrounds but situated in Western universities, and by feminist writers (cf. Cornwall and Lindisfarne, this volume). Confronted with this paralysing uncertainty, the response of some anthropologists has been to turn their gaze inwards, towards reflexivity, selfhood and the literary analysis of social scientific texts, particularly ethnographic writing, as the central problem of the discipline. Others have pursued this literary turn still further, raising the philosophical question of whether anthropologists can ever truly 'represent' a foreign culture, or whether anthropological discourses are not ultimately condemned to redundancy, the prisoners of their own authoritative images and linguistic protocols from which they can never escape (cf. Clifford and Marcus, 1986). The postmodernist current has thus provoked a chronic sense of insecurity and self-doubt about the legitimacy of the anthropological enterprise. As Ivan Karp (1986: 132) puts it, 'in their anxiety to deny the privileged stance of ethnographers as knowers of cultural Others, many postmodern writers resolve their epistemological angst by privileging the experience of the ethnographer over the experience of the subjects of ethnographic research.' The result is often a descent into solipsism – or worse, a retreat 'from a consideration of the power relations in which knowledge is constituted toward an egocentric and nihilistic celebration of the ethnographer as author, creator and consumer of the Other' (Pollier and Roseberry, 1989: 246). The merits and weaknesses of these arguments have been amply detailed elsewhere so it is unnecessary to rehearse the debates here (cf. among others, Scholte, 1986; Sangren, 1988; Pool, 1991).

Our own perspective on the predicament of modern anthropology differs in a number of critical ways. First and foremost, we suggest that it is not a crisis of *representation* which now threatens our discipline but a problem of *relevance*. Social anthropology as we have known it is in danger of becoming marginalized and redundant unless it adapts to the changing world which now threatens to undermine its cherished theories, methods and practices. This means, above all, re-evaluating its conventional objects of study and developing new domains and methods of enquiry that are commensurate with the new subjects and social forces that are emerging in the contemporary world. It also means engaging with contentious issues and problems of wider public concern, and communicating with a wider audience than the restricted community of academics that has hitherto been its arena. In short, anthropology's image as a discipline still primarily concerned with exotic, small-scale, disappearing worlds must be complemented – perhaps even supplanted – by greater concern with 'emerging worlds', the cultures of the 'colonizers' as well as those of the colonized, and on subject areas that cannot be defined by traditional fieldwork methods alone.

This is not a new argument. Since the 1970s there have been many urgent calls within the discipline for new methods and concepts to deal with the 'complexity' of non-tribal, non-peasant societies (Boissevain, 1975), and for anthropology to 'reinvent itself' with a more critical and analytical orientation (Hymes, 1972), or 'recapture' its intellectual high ground (Fox, 1991). We would add our voice to this call. The question, however, is how exactly is this to be achieved, what do we mean by 'relevance', and what kind of anthropology is this likely to result in? As the different topics and approaches adopted by the contributors to this volume suggest, these issues are open to wide interpretation.

ANTHROPOLOGY'S CURRENT PREDICAMENT

To a large extent, the contemporary problems of anthropology can be traced to developments from the 1940s onwards – the period *after* Malinowski, the Boasians, Benedict and Mead. While Grimshaw and Hart (this volume) locate the root of the problem in the breakdown of anthropology's central paradigm of 'scientific ethnography', we suggest that the growing institutionalization of anthropology as a university-based discipline during and after this period is also of critical significance. Bronislaw Malinowski, Margaret Mead and Alfred Reginald Radcliffe-Brown may well have established 'scientific ethnography' as a defining feature of their recently institutionalized profession. However, they were all public figures who spoke to, and wrote for, a national and international audience – beyond the insularity of the academy. The same cannot be said of most of their successors. Laura Nader made similar observations in the early 1970s:

Many of our brighter students look at the anthropology journals of recent times and conclude that anthropology appears to be phasing out, content to make a living for the most part by rediscovering what has been discovered or by selling our wares to other disciplines and professions. The audience is too narrow, the nitpicking too precious. Making a living by selling one's wares is not an inappropriate way to subsist; it is however, in this case, symptomatic that a talent, the perspective for a *Mirror for Man*, is being under-used (Nader, 1972: 284–5).

The editor of that same volume, Dell Hymes, wrote somewhat prophetically that the future of anthropology in the United States 'is thus a question of whether its present institutional context, essentially the graduate department, will prove to have been chrysalis or coffin' (Hymes, 1972: 6–7). If anthropology remains confined there, he added, it is likely to wane into irrelevance. For various reasons, including the pressures on university-based anthropologists to meet 'performance targets' and tailor their research to suit increasingly draconian research selectivity exercises and audits, and the increasingly constraining 'factory-like' conditions under which anthropological research work is now conducted (Fox, 1991: 9), this dilemma has grown more acute, particularly in the UK.

What follows is a rough and somewhat arbitrary periodization, setting out four phases in the development of the discipline, using British anthropology as our main exemplar. It should be stressed that this schema, which doubtless will be criticized for its over-simplicity and anglo-centric bias, is intended purely as an outline and context for discussing the current state of anthropology, rather than an attempt to chart a detailed history of the discipline.

Anthropology in the last century effectively began as a kind of Victorian exercise, practised in the main by gentlemen scholars, amateurs, anti-slave campaigners, Christian philanthropists and social reformers (Evans-Pritchard, 1962; Lienhardt, 1964). This period saw not only the great armchair anthropologists and evolutionists such as Herbert Spencer, Lewis Henry Morgan, J. F. McLennan, Sir Henry Maine, Sir James Frazer, Sir Edward Tylor, James Hunt and Emile Durkheim, but also the adventurer-scholars; people like A.C. Haddon, W.H.R. Rivers, Franz Boas and Edward Westermarck and Captain Richard Burton; the swash-buckling traveller, explorer, translator and chronicler, writing often highly personalized ethnography, but addressed to the reading public in general as well as an audience of scholars and professionals.

The second phase witnessed the ascendancy of the classic anthropologists: Malinowski and Radcliffe-Brown in the UK, and Kroeber, Mead and Benedict in the USA, were the forebears of what was to become a new 'generation' of anthropologists composed primarily of their students. For British anthropology these included Evans-Pritchard, Firth, Fortes, Richards, Leach and many others. But the work of this pioneering group of scholars was bound up, to greater or lesser degrees, in the colonial enterprise. Whether it was Leach in Burma, Malinowski in Melanesia, Haimendorf in India, or Evans-Pritchard in Africa, their research foci were inextricably related to colonial administration, and this naturally influenced the perspectives or paradigms they operated as fieldworkers (Asad, 1973).

The third phase, that of the Cold War, witnessed the ascendancy of the American and Soviet superpowers and their division of the globe into two blocs: the Western and Communist worlds. Despite the climate of polarization and censorship this generated, a small number of anthropologists working in the West during this period were nonetheless influenced by Marxism, whose imprint can be clearly seen in the work of some of the discipline's most distinguished writers. Among the best examples in British anthropology are Worsley's *The Trumpet Shall Sound* and Asad's *Anthropology and the Colonial Encounter*.[1] In America, J. Steward and Leslie White were among the few anthropologists to risk being associated with a Marxist perspective during the Cold War era. As Bloch (1983: 128) notes, 'White was seen by many American anthropologists as a dangerous subversive because of his earlier contact with Soviet anthropologists' and was for a long time isolated and ignored. It was not until the 1960s, with the work of anthropologists such as Sydney Mintz and Eric Wolf, and later Dell Hymes' collection, *Reinventing Anthropology*, that a radical perspective gained a measure of respectability in American anthropology. In France, by contrast, Marxism had a far greater impact on the discipline through the influence of Althusser and the development of his ideas by writers such as Godelier, Terray and Rey.[2]

The fourth phase is what concerns us. This post Cold War phase into which the world has entered since 1989 still does not have a proper name to describe it: post-communist, post-industrial, post-colonial, post-modern or whatever, but 'post' something. It is a new phase, whose social and cultural features we believe necessitate a volume of this kind. Our goal as anthropologists, therefore, is to identify those defining characteristics and organizing principles which give shape and meaning to this new phase into which we are entering, and to try to map out the implications of these changes for anthropology as a discipline.

ANTHROPOLOGY AND THE CHALLENGE OF THE PRESENT

A key feature of the modern era with far-reaching implications for anthropological theory and method has been the disappearance of the 'primitive' and the 'savage'. In the second phase of anthropology – its high noon – authors like Malinowski (1967) perhaps quite innocently referred to native peoples as 'savages' and 'primitives' and gave prominence to these terms in the titles of their books.[3] Indeed, the study of native (usually tribal) peoples – later broadened to 'other cultures' – became the central object of anthropological enquiry. Following Malinowski's example, this involved a long-term participatory fieldwork experience – a year or two years living in the community under study – followed by an intensive period writing up one's ethnographic notes into a fieldwork monograph. Here the authorial voice of the anthropologist would assume a tone of detached scientific impartiality; the expert presenting an objective account of native life for a predominantly middle-class and university-educated Western audience. Today this kind of anthropology is increasingly untenable, not least because 'native peoples' exist in very changed circumstances. Many developments have occurred which now complicate the traditionally unquestioned relationship between anthropologists and their 'objects' of study. The natives are likely to be educated, often with a university degree or PhD from a Western university. They are increasingly likely to be members of the anthropologist's own society. As Frankenberg points out (this volume), the slogan 'these natives can speak for themselves' is being taken up by an increasing number of marginalized groups, from women, gay men and HIV sufferers to the physically disadvantaged and the homeless. These natives are capable of creating a political storm if something that is politically incorrect is sensed. If there is an imagined slight it may attract negative publicity in the media, local protests and organized responses, which in turn may precipitate wider political action. Formerly natives could do none of that. In short, Western scholars writing about the 'Other' can now be held to account and may find their writings challenged by natives who may also be anthropologists.[4]

The momentous developments in media, communications and information technology over the last decade also have major implications for anthropology. For example, a Bedouin tribesman with satellite television or a factory worker in Thailand may be as familiar with *Dallas* or other Western soap operas as a family from Texas (cf. Morley and Robins, this volume); Kayapo Indians in Brazil are making video documentaries about themselves which are then screened at anthropological conferences and Western film festivals; curators of ethnographic museums receive faxes from hitherto remote New Guinea highland tribesmen demanding information about the current exhibition of their artefacts; or take the example given at a recent School of American Research seminar of the anthropologist 'who heads half way around the world to India only to find that the Hindu priest who is his chief informant has departed to serve parishioners (and to encounter other anthropologists?) in Houston, Texas' (Fox, 1991: 4).[5]

All these developments sound the death knell of classical anthropology with its implicit assumption that the anthropologist was studying a fairly simple and remote society, relatively unchanged by time, the essence of which could be grasped after a year or two of fieldwork and then transcribed, unproblematically, into text. It also challenges the traditional role of the anthropologist as undisputed 'expert' and authority on the culture of this or that group of people, able to speak for and about those people while remaining largely unaccountable to them or to others. This in turn leads to a healthy undermining of the old tendency, still prevalent among some anthropologists, to treat ethnographic subjects as exclusive personal territory: what has been dubbed the 'in my village' syndrome which allowed anthropologists to build their careers as champions and spokespersons for a particular tribe or neighbourhood.

These developments also undermine two other key assumptions implicit in classical anthropological theory and method. First, the idea that cultures are bounded wholes which can be treated as discrete units of study and analysed 'holistically', and in relative isolation from other more global influences has become more and more questionable. Second, the idea that insights gained from in-depth micro-studies of one village or neighbourhood can be used to make generalizations about the wider society has become increasingly problematic. The uncritical assumption that small communities somehow serve as exemplars (or 'synecdoches') for an entire culture looks steadily more implausible as so-called 'traditional' societies become ever more heterogeneous and fragmentary. While some regions of the world have long been colonized and creolized (the Mediterranean and Latin America being two obvious cases in point, though migration and cultural linkages over the centuries have resulted in hybridization and heterogeneity in most regions of the world), even those societies that have traditionally been defined as relatively stable and culturally homogenous have had to accept a reclassification of themselves as multicultural and ethnically fragmented. The idea of 'tradition', always a rather ambiguous and constructed notion, has itself become commoditized (cf. Graburn, this volume). Furthermore, the capitalist-led mass migrations across the globe this century have everywhere created new kinds of ethnic enclave. These have given rise not only to new patterns of *residence*, but to a new politics of *belonging*: what Benedict Anderson (1992) calls the phenomenon of the 'long-distance nationalist'. Tamils in Melbourne, Jews and Irish in America, Kurds in Paris, Croats in Sydney, Ukranians in Canada, Palestinians in Tunisia, Jamaicans in London – all of these new ethnicities are linked to nationalism, but often in explosive ways. As Anderson says, we are faced with a new kind of nationalist:

> For while technically a citizen of the state in which he comfortably lives, but to which he may feel little attachment, he finds it tempting to play identity politics by participating (via propaganda, money, weapons, any way but voting) in the conflicts of his imagined *Heimat* – now only fax-time away (Anderson, 1992: 13).

These developments have serious implications for anthropological method. The traditional practice of going out into the 'field', finding a community to study and writing an interpretative account of that society based on ethnographic insights becomes increasingly untenable if the society in question has no unified or bounded centre, and if our unit of study no longer even approximates the social reality as it is lived and experienced by our ethnographic subjects. Anthropology has yet to develop a new methodological toolbag to cope with the complexity of this increasingly fluid 'new world order'.

CHALLENGES FROM JOURNALISM AND LITERATURE

Another development is the emergence of journalists with strong anthropological interests: sophisticated and highly analytical writers and reporters who address those social and cultural issues that fall squarely within the anthropological domain. George Orwell and J. B. Priestley, in their day, were writers of this kind. So too, perhaps,

were Charles Dickens, Jane Austen, Walter Bagehot, E. M. Forster
and John Steinbeck. In our own times one might also include writers
such as Michael Ignatieff, Neil Ascherson, Germaine Greer and Beatrix
Campbell (Britain), or M. J. Akbar, Ashis Nandy or Mark Tully
(India), and perhaps, among many others, Arthur Hailey and Mario
Puzzo (USA). These writers are also popular on the academic circuit
and pose a healthy challenge to anthropologists and sociologists. For
example, Ignatieff's recent BBC series on ethnic violence, entitled
Blood and Belonging, fell squarely within the domain of anthropology.
Similarly, three of the most widely read and informative of recent books
on Pakistani and Indian society – however much they may be lacking
in ethnographic sophistication – have been written by journalists rather
than anthropologists (Duncan, 1989; Lamb, 1991; Tully, 1991).

Martin Woollacott of the *Guardian* newspaper, whose articles helped
bring to the world's attention the plight of the Kurds in northern
Iraq, provides another exemplary case in point. These were excellent pieces of almost ethnographic writing, complete with accounts
of local leadership structures, patterns of social organization, tribal
configurations, a brief history of the Kurds and their relationship
to the state and an analysis of core–periphery relationship. In short,
there was much here that a traditional anthropologist would have
looked for and, more to the point, taken several years to look at
before publishing a single research finding. Similarly, some of the
most powerful and perceptive accounts of life in war-torn Bosnia
came from journalists such as Maggie O'Kane and Ed Vulliamy.

Despite efforts by several of its professional bodies to address a wider
audience (most notably the increasingly media-conscious American
Anthropological Association and the Royal Anthropological Institute),
and notwithstanding the excellent contributions by journals such as
Anthropology Today, *Anthropology in Action*, *Current Anthropology*
and *Critique of Anthropology* to broaden the discipline's agenda and
engage with a wider public, anthropology has contributed relatively
little to public debates on the most controversial – and therefore most
widely discussed – issues of our times, including 'ethnic cleansing',
fundamentalism and war. This is not because anthropology has nothing
to say about such themes: on the contrary, culture, folklore, language,
religion, myth and local history – the fabric from which ethnicity is
constructed – lie at the heart of the discipline. Nor is it because there
is a shortage of anthropologists actively engaged with contemporary
problems, as the contributors to this volume illustrate, and as Wright's

overview of anthropology in policy and practice clearly demonstrates. But again, journalists and media experts have commented freely on topics such as famine, drought, modern warfare and religious fundamentalism, and with few exceptions – at least in Britain (cf. Ahmed, 1992; 1993; Benthall, 1993; de Waal, 1993; and Gellner, 1992) – have edged out the arguably more authoritative voice of anthropologists.[6] This is not to say that anthropologists are not concerned with the key issues of our times, only that the anthropological voice tends not to be heard beyond the domains of the university campus or refereed journal.

The conclusion one might draw from this is that given the same time and resources as the anthropologist, a good journalist could produce what anthropologists produce, only more cheaply, better and faster – and in a format calculated to reach a far wider audience. Indeed, it is journalists – not anthropologists or social scientists – who have led the field in describing and analysing the conflict in Bosnia, not only in newspaper articles, but also in literature and broadcasting (cf. Glenny, 1990; Scott and Jones, 1993). If this trend continues, grant-giving agencies might well begin to question the logic of channelling their diminishing resources to fund leisurely academic ethnographic studies. It is salutary to remember that Martin Woollacott and Maggie O'Kane are not anthropologists. Neither is Edward Said, yet all are successfully encroaching upon anthropological terrain, and their writing is increasingly anthropological in its focus. Similarly, in the case of modern literature, it is often novelists, such as Salman Rushdie, Gabriel Garcia Marquez, or Isabel Allende who have made their mark as critics and commentators on their particular societies, capturing the intellectual high ground as far as cultural critique is concerned. Anthropologists – with a few historical exceptions such as Malinowski, Mead and Leach – appear to have largely abdicated that public position.

There is also a growing challenge to traditional anthropology from other disciplines, particularly from the media and from 'cultural studies', the expansion of which is seen as a threat by some anthropologists – especially in the United States (Handler, 1993: 991; Rosaldo, 1994: 529). How should anthropologists respond to this competition? The response has usually been to retreat behind the walls of academia and dismiss journalists and other writers as dilettantes and poachers whose descriptions rarely do justice to the fine-grained, three-dimensional intricacy and complexity of social relationships in a community – which only a professionally trained anthropologist with intimate personal knowledge of the society can provide.

It is a sad irony that while some novelists have become more 'anthropological' in orientation and outlook, many anthropologists, following Geertz, have abandoned their social science heritage and have tried to become quasi-novelists, arguing that anthropological accounts are forms of writing not altogether very different from fiction. It is also ironic that while writers of fiction are often praised and emulated by anthropologists,[7] other more professional writers such as journalists, are usually held in low esteem. In academic discourse 'journalistic' is virtually a term of abuse: a synonym for the hastily written, superficial and trivial rather than 'concise', 'informative' and 'accessible' – which is perhaps a more accurate definition of the term. Journalists, it seems, even more so than sociologists and psychologists, have become part of the professional 'other' against which anthropology as a discipline defines itself. But this stereotype ignores the fact that many journalists and foreign correspondents are long-term residents in the countries they report – often spending more years in the 'field' and acquiring greater expertise than do anthropologists. This is particularly true of those beyond-the-community domains (including the money markets, the state, agencies of government, the European Community (EC), multinational corporations and so forth) that anthropology must turn to explore if it wishes to understand the complexity of the contemporary world. Moreover, there is something curiously ethnocentric about the academic use of the term 'journalistic'. As Nader wrote:

> work that is considered in the objective social science mode, when carried out abroad might well be dubbed 'journalistic' by the subjects. Telling it like it is may be perceived as muckraking by the subjects of study (Oscar Lewis's work on Mexico was so viewed), *or* by fellow professionals who feel more comfortable if data is presented in social science jargon which would protect the work from common consumption (Nader, 1972: 305).

In a climate of economic stringency and increasingly blurred boundaries, where people are asking sharp questions and expecting prompt answers, anthropology's patrician defence and its claim to privileged knowledge is likely to be greeted with scepticism. Outside of the discipline, most anthropologists command little public attention and are seldom called upon by the media for their views, however knowledgeable they may be in their particular field.

In part, this cynicism towards anthropology derives from its continuing association in the public mind with the upper-class, Anglo-Saxon image of its high noon phase. Anthropologists from Africa, Asia and Latin America cannot fail to note that the big prizes, distinguished awards and honorific lectures are from the Anglo-Saxon world. We see relatively few Latin Americans, Arabs, Africans or Japanese in anthropology's hall of fame. Whatever the explanation for this, be it for reasons of language, culture, history or academic priorities, its effect is to demarcate this discipline clearly as elitist and restricted to a certain part of the world. This is an important point and one that may explain why critics still accuse anthropology of being neo-colonial and utilizing a discourse of power. Anthropologists in the West are not entirely aware of how sharply this is felt.

ANTHROPOLOGY AND CURRENT AFFAIRS

Another area where anthropology is failing to come to terms with events in the modern world is its inability to deal with current affairs. This has not been helped by its tradition of lengthy fieldwork, usually carried out alone, in difficult circumstances, and the often painfully slow process of writing up, where, until recently, students would spend anything from five to ten years completing their doctorate. As a result, it is sometimes up to a decade before the results of ethnographic studies find their way into print, by which time the findings may have lost their immediacy and public interest. While anthropologists continue to break new ground in a variety of areas of public interest and concern – some quite controversial, such as famine, disasters, political ritual, new reproductive technologies, citizenship, and the issues discussed in this volume – the discipline has been less successful (and often rather reluctant) to address controversial topics in the public domain. The reasons for this may be linked in some cases to political expediency: a fear of losing respectability and a concern not to court the displeasure of its government sponsors,[8] or it may be explained by the slow mechanism by which anthropological knowledge is produced and disseminated. However, another problem embedded deep within the discipline, which helps explain the missing areas of study, is that anthropology has allowed fieldwork to dictate its theoretical content. What cannot be studied empirically and by participant observation has tended to be treated as non-anthropological and simply ignored (cf. Wolf, 1982; Llobera, 1986).

This failure to engage with current affairs and contemporary social and political issues is a damning indictment of anthropology. We have seen examples of this recently in Britain over the Gulf War,[9] Bosnia, the fate of the Marsh Arabs in Iraq and acts of near genocide in East Timor. Anthropological analysis of, or involvement in, these episodes of human misery compares rather poorly with the contribution of charities, aid workers, pressure groups, political scientists and journalists. Similarly, the voice of anthropology has been characteristically silent or muted in a vast range of contemporary social issues, from racism, education and public health to debates about poverty, crime, overseas aid, single mothers and government policies aimed at restoring 'traditional' family values. Is it because these areas no longer fall within the domain of anthropological enquiry? Is it because others – sociologists, pressure groups, politicians or whoever – put the arguments so much better than anthropologists can? Or is it because anthropology as a discipline is uneasy about handling controversial topics that are potentially divisive and would bring them face to face with other professions? Whatever the reason, this absence of anthropologists from public debates serves to emphasize anthropology's marginal status and lack of relevance to most people's lives. As a professional body we need to be much more responsive to immediate, urgent developments and be able to comment on them, not necessarily as journalists, but certainly via newspaper articles and televised debates.

There are a number of other reasons why anthropologists are failing to engage with the key problems of the contemporary world. One is the character of the discipline itself and the way it has traditionally drawn a boundary between the notions of 'pure' (i.e. academic and theoretical) and 'applied' research. Applied anthropology is still regarded as the ultimate sin: a second-division league for failed scholars unable to find 'proper' (i.e. university) jobs. Since its consolidation as a *discipline* (i.e. a university-based profession) there has been a similar tendency to construct a hierarchical dichotomy between the 'popularization' of anthropology (which is, almost by definition, deemed to be vulgar), and 'serious scholarship' – as though these positions were mutually exclusive.

Another reason for many of the apparent shortcomings of British anthropology lies in its traditional image of itself as non-political, its reluctance as a profession to be associated with overtly critical standpoints, and its notion that one can only speak after many years of research – and even then, only on the specific area of one's specialism. These shortcomings do not necessarily arise from the peculiar class character of English society and the influence this has exerted over the development of the discipline. However, British anthropology still has the image of an arcane discipline, dominated by the privileged classes and students of Oxbridge colleges – even if this is no longer the reality. Much of the media, for its part, exhibits a characteristically British attitude of anti-intellectualism, which only serves to reinforce the stereotypes of the anthropologist as eccentric boffin. Yet many anthropologists, in turn, exhibit an almost reflex reluctance to take the non-academic media seriously, either as a channel for popularizing anthropological ideas, or as an object of anthropological investigation – despite the fact that television has become a key feature of the contemporary cultural landscape. Some attempts have been successfully made, for instance the anthropologists involved in Granada Television's *Disappearing World* series. But as Morley and Robins point out (this volume), on the whole few anthropologists have tried to study the way audiences receive or interpret television images. The idea that 'real' anthropology is primarily about the study of exotic peoples overseas (preferably tribal and non-literate) has acted as a brake on this kind of research. While this image is gradually waning, it nevertheless continues to have its supporters in many university departments. However, this notion is being progressively undermined as anthropological research is increasingly conducted 'at home', not only among the marginal groups and minorities that exist within Western societies (who for some constitute anthropology's new 'primitives'), but also into the mainstream cultures of Western societies themselves (cf. Barley, 1990; Jackson, 1986).

THE FUTURE OF ANTHROPOLOGY?

The aim of this book is to try to map out key aspects of the cultural landscape that will be confronting anthropologists as we enter the next millennium. In doing so, we hope to be able to point out some of the more profitable directions in which anthropologists might move. Broadly speaking, the contributors to this volume have taken up this challenge in two different ways. Some of them, like Meštrović, Grimshaw and Hart, Frankenberg, and Cornwall and Lindisfarne, pursue the question in terms of current dilemmas in social theory, and argue for a greater degree of reflexivity and new theoretical approaches that might transcend the traditional subject–object dualism of anthropology's positivistic legacy (which has denied subjectivity and emotion). Others suggest that changes in perspective should proceed from a shift in the focus of anthropological research. Here it is argued that we need to address ourselves to new areas of knowledge by embracing a wider set of concerns, particularly contemporary social issues. Many of the themes explored in this volume, such as old age, tourism, heritage, masculinity, policy, war, and the problems associated with HIV/AIDS research, reflect a shared concern among our contributors to expand the frontiers of what has traditionally been thought of as the field of anthropology's subject-matter. It is for this reason, and in the interest of transcending unhelpful disciplinary boundaries, that we have also invited contributions from non-anthropologists (Morley and Robbins, Meštrović, Giddens). Evidence of a shift towards more policy- and problem-oriented anthropological research concerning issues of contemporary public concern in the anthropologist's own society as well as abroad can be detected elsewhere in a variety of new areas, for example, in the study of public policy (Donnan and MacFarlane, 1989), new reproductive technologies (Rivière, 1985; Cannell, 1990; Strathern, 1991; Shore, 1992; Edwards *et al.*, 1993), child abuse and images of 'youth' (Ennew, 1986; 1994; La Fontaine, 1990), socialism (Hann, 1992), environmentalism (Milton, 1993), organizations (Wright, 1944), computing (Fischer, 1994), science (Woolgar, 1991), institutions and policies of the European Union (Abélès, 1992; Shore, 1993), and the human genome project (Rabinow, 1993). It can also be detected in the increasing anthropological interest in the policy dimensions of a host of topics such as education, management, bureaucracy, community care, health and medicine, youth, and the rights of indigenous peoples, all of which have been a focus of particular interest for the journals *Human Organisation* and *Anthropology in Action* (cf. Wright, this volume). Each of these issues also obliges the anthropologist to enter into dialogue with other disciplines. While some anthropologists see this as a threat to the purity of anthropology and its disciplinary boundaries, we see it as a highly profitable arena for intellectual cross-fertilization. Indeed, like Wright, we believe that new theoretical approaches will emerge almost by necessity from the challenge of confronting new domains of policy and practice. The problem for anthropology is to identify those domains towards which it wishes to turn its expertise.

The world as it stands in the 1990s and for the foreseeable future is likely to be one of emerging or re-emerging nationalism and ethnic identification, leading in many cases to confrontation and violence. It is in this context that anthropological knowledge can be of particular help in explaining the cultural differences and the rival interpretations of history that so often provide the backbone to such conflicts. And it is in this field that the failure of anthropology is really felt. For example, the Caucasus and south and central Asia have once again become major theatres of social and ethnic upheaval, but there is little commentary from anthropology. Meštrović's argument (this volume) is that social scientists in general are failing to make sense of events surrounding the Balkanization of Eastern Europe and the former USSR. Instead, their role has been usurped by right-wing philosophers like Fukuyama, and various postmodernist writers.

Yet anthropologists do have a role to play in our world. For example, it was anthropologists such as Geertz (1968) or Gellner (1981), writing in Morocco, who were among the first to comment on the staying power of Islam in an increasingly secular world. By contrast, right up until the 1970s the political scientists were speculating about the continuity of the Shah, the fading of Islam, and predicting that Iran would become the fifth largest power in the world (cf. Thaiss, 1978).

In a very practical sense the findings of anthropology also link up with aid. What kinds of aid to send? How to send it? Who to send it to? Each of these questions requires an accurate understanding of leadership patterns, family structures, cultural values and political organization. Without such knowledge the result is often disastrous – as in the case of the 1970 flood in Bengal where American relief aid resulted in tins of ham and heavy winter coats being airlifted for a Muslim population that does not eat swine and lives in tropical country that has never seen snow (Ahmed, 1980: 7–8).

Anthropologists are also often ideally placed to act as a link between the local society or group and the Western media: to act as interpreter of the one to the other, or simply to explain what the media wants. Television crews and journalists when they arrive in a foreign country are there to look for their story, and are under pressure to finish it and leave as quickly as possible. But in their own way they often want to do some good for the situation they encounter. And the anthropologist can, if he or she is on that squad, assist in this enterprise of intercultural communication by bringing the different parties together facilitating mutual understanding. This again has been a marked feature of the recent crises in which the anthropologists have been absent. As Gellner remarked recently at a press conference organized to mark the 150th anniversary of the Royal Anthropological Society, in a world where the political scientists and the economists have been unable to deliver, perhaps it is time to let the anthropologists have a hearing. This is not to suggest that we should seek to substitute the expertise and authority of the economist or politician with that of the anthropologist. Anthropology has no easy panaceas, and it would be a misleading hubris for the discipline to claim otherwise. But it can contribute something of value to public debates, particularly when it engages in a critical reflexive commentary that engages with a wider audience and transcends the narrow confines of academic discourse.

Anthropologists since Malinowski and Mead have often used apparently innocent descriptions of other cultures and lifestyles to reflect critically upon their own societies. Herein lies a major role for the future of anthropology. Serious cultural critique requires that anthropologists, whether American, Indian or African, turn their professional gaze towards a better understanding of their own societies. Most anthropologists are not particularly well equipped to do this, having been trained in the study of 'other' cultures, but not necessarily in the study of their own. A truly reflexive, holistic and critical anthropology must 'study up' as well as 'studying down'. As Wright says, echoing Donnan and MacFarlane (1989), it must analyse the 'culture of policy professionals' as well as the objects of such policies, or as Nader put it, 'the colonizers rather than the colonized, the culture of power rather than the culture of the powerless' (Nader, 1972: 289). The implications of this are that anthropology must strive to become what it has always claimed to be: the study of *all* of humanity and not just 'Other' cultures. Moreover, it suggests that, like charity, anthropological analysis also begins at home in so far as contextualizing knowledge is concerned.

Detailed personal knowledge and a wider socio-cultural perspective on the societies they study does give anthropologists a particularly useful lens onto the problems facing a specific group of people, though it is perhaps the secondary insights and elaborations that can be made from this that matter more than the raw data. In the case of some of the non-anthropological writers mentioned earlier, some of these features are also in evidence, although many journalists are restricted, because of newspaper schedules, to brief stints.

Perhaps more importantly, the interest and focus of anthropologists allows them to say things about ritual, customs and cultures which, during the Cold War era, had become secondary to the analysis of politics and economics. Anthropological expertise on matters such as marriages, rituals and customs, or how people define themselves, tended to be perceived as esoteric and irrelevant to the needs of governments and non-governmental organizations whose primary interest lay in blueprints for stimulating growth and development. Here the emphasis lay on more 'practical' matters, such as ideas on bridges and highways, winning contracts, or canvassing the opinions of military strategists on the geopolitical implications of development in a particular region. Today, as ethnicity has become central to geopolitical conflict, anthropological expertise has become highly relevant and even practical as 'culture' (understood in terms of history, language, religion or class), lies at the heart of ethnic identifications. There is a parallel here with Frankenberg's observations (this volume) about the relationship between anthropology and HIV research. Whenever the problem is defined as being a 'cultural' phenomenon (as in the case of 'drug cultures', 'youth sub-cultures', 'culture of poverty', 'culture of crime' and so forth), wisely or otherwise, governments turn to anthropologists for answers – though they may not like the answers they obtain. In the case of ethnicity and ethnic violence anthropology has a great deal to offer and, perhaps more than most other disciplines, has demonstrated an understanding of and sensitivity towards the way ethnic boundaries are created and maintained through the mobilization of history, language and other cultural variables. The question, as always, is how such knowledge is used. Understanding the causes of phenomena such as ethnicity or racism does not necessarily lead people to want to reduce ethnic or racial tensions. Indeed, in the case of ethnos theory in the former Soviet Union, or the Afrikaner version of ethnology, knowledge of ethnicity has been used not to ameliorate conflict but to bolster ethnically oppressive regimes. As several of the contributors to this volume illustrate (cf. Frankenberg; Wright; Lewis), anthropologists need to be aware of the different ways – and the different social and political contexts – in which anthropological ideas and concepts are used by non-anthropologists.

THE CONCEPT OF 'RELEVANCE' IN ANTHROPOLOGY

A central question that arises in the light of this discussion is what is meant by 'relevance'? As a cultural concept this term has ambiguous meanings. One definition, much favoured by government, equates relevance with the idea of utility and economy in the sphere of production, wealth creation and marketable skills. In Britain and elsewhere the argument that the education system is failing the economy has prompted the idea of government initiatives towards creating an 'enterprise culture' (cf. Keat and Abercrombie, 1991; Selwyn and Shore, 1992). The increasing pressure that has been brought to bear on academic institutions to demonstrate their relevance according to market principles has prompted a major shift in the context in which anthropology operates, and particularly the way it is funded. In the 1990s, to take but one example, the success of a university vice-chancellor or principal – traditionally one of the most privileged and isolated of national institutions – is now determined predominantly by how much money he or she can raise for the college.

Anthropology cannot ignore the fact that it exists in a market-oriented society; indeed, market ideologies, management cultures and state institutions must themselves become subjects of anthropological research if the discipline is serious about understanding the context in which anthropological knowledge is produced (cf. Dilley, 1993). But the idea of anthropology's 'relevance' needs also to be understood in terms of human societies passing through a phase in global history. Ecologists might claim to be spokespersons of the modern era because of their message about the destruction of the planet's fragile ecosystems. But how are the anthropologists addressing this and other key issues?

A second definition of 'relevance' is in terms of anthropology's explanatory power. It has been fashionable in recent debates to suggest that the postmodern condition has rendered all attempts at scientific-like explanation futile and obsolete. Some anthropologists argue that we should therefore content ourselves with deconstruction, abandon any attempt at discovering 'truth' as this notion simply perpetuates the myths and authoritarianism of Enlightenment grand narratives, and instead celebrate the poetics and aesthetics of our own literary creation as an end in their own right (cf. Tyler, 1986; Crapanzano, 1986). It is this retreat from society and the idea of 'reality' towards a preoccupation with text, writing and selfhood that has led critics to describe postmodernism as an expression of exhausted progressive impulses and moral bankruptcy. Our approach to anthropology is explicitly anti-postmodernist in this sense. While we may share its scepticism about the claims and methods of science (or any philosophy which purports to offer the truth), for anthropology to have explanatory power we believe that it must continue to adhere to the principles of social science. It must also therefore resist the temptation of defining itself as an interpretive quest in search of meaning, whose interpretations, like those of the novelist, are mere 'fictions'.

A third definition of 'relevance', closely related to this, is in terms of the discipline's 'moral significance'. This concerns the way knowledge is used (or misused) and its ethical and political value. Anthropology has enormous potential for understanding, defining, bringing people together, and creating some harmony in a world riven with conflict and hatred. To put it simply, it is a discipline that is capable of doing some good – although this term may evoke church, clergy and religious preaching and antagonize academics trained in a secular tradition of scientific detachment. But without that moral dimension it is reduced to being neither a science nor part of the humanities. Nader pointed the way when she wrote about anthropology's 'democratic relevance', the need for 'studying up', and the service function anthropologists could provide if they were to write ethnographies for the 'natives' rather than for themselves or for the interests of the powerful (Nader, 1972: 293).

The problem with much of the postmodernist current in contemporary social science is that its attempts to transcend morality and politics have left it with no moral centre; at the heart of deconstruction there is an ethical vacuum. Relevance in this sense, therefore, implies that anthropologists should situate themselves in relation to the issues they write about, be it gender, ethnicity, racial violence or government policy. In this respect the traditional methodology of intensive ethnographic fieldwork will continue to play a central role, if not in guaranteeing anthropology's moral integrity, then at least in making sure that the discipline does not stray too far from the world in which real people live and work.

Understanding the nature of that world and its changing cultural landscapes at the close of the twentieth century may seem to be an awesome and daunting task, but it is a goal worth pursuing. Some of the more visible trends emerging in Africa, Asia and across Europe, for example – such as globalization, industrialization and de-industrialization, commercialization, religious fundamentalism, bureaucratization, ethnic conflict, famine, urbanization, unemployment, homelessness and the transformation of family and kinship patterns – are concerns which relate directly to anthropology. The question is what contribution can the anthropologist make to understanding these processes that is different from, or better than, that of the politician, the historian or the journalist?

THE SCOPE OF THIS VOLUME

This volume sets out to answer some of these questions in a way that is, we hope, open and exploratory rather than prescriptive. Contributors were invited to respond to the question of whether the anthropological endeavour has been rendered obsolete by changes in the modern world, drawing upon their own areas of research. In a spirit of ecumenicism, several non-anthropologists working in the fields of Cultural Studies and Sociology were invited to set out their views on the debate. The result was a wide-ranging set of responses. Not every author discusses explicitly the problems for anthropology posed by the challenge of postmodernity. But the problems are present in all the essays. Most authors agree that anthropology has reached, if not a 'crisis point', then certainly a major crossroads in its development. Most also share the view that a greater degree of anthropological engagement with issues affecting the contemporary world is both necessary and desirable, though their approaches to the idea of 'relevance' differ. While acknowledging the contribution made by postmodernist critiques to contemporary debates about the authority of anthropological writing, most authors are highly critical of the postmodernist literary turn in anthropology, particularly its neglect of the social and political context in which anthropologists carry out their work.

These criticisms are developed by Grimshaw and Hart who use an historical overview of the development of British anthropology to trace the origins of the current crisis in 'scientific ethnography'. But while critical of positivist anthropology – particularly its objectivizing, intellectual elitism and its inability to treat the objects of anthropological study as creative subjects – they also criticize the romantic, anti-science branches of post-colonial anthropology for failing to situate themselves within their wider social and historical context and for maintaining the polarization between creative subjects and collective objects. The problem of transcending the subject–object dualism entails finding an analytical framework that can simultaneously accommodate both agency and structure: the living subject and the impersonal forces driving world history. One possible solution they suggest lies in the development of a 'dialectical' rather than a 'dialogic' approach – the dialectic in this case referring to what Leach called an 'ethical engagement' between anthropological self and society. Elements of such a perspective are identified in the work of a number of recent feminist writers.

For some writers (and, increasingly, many governments and funding bodies) 'relevance' suggests practising and applied anthropology. But as the essays of Wright and Lewis show, the nature and scope of what might be termed 'applied anthropology' varies considerably. Drawing on his experience in overseas development work, Lewis gives a robust defence of the need for anthropological professionalism and expertise in development projects, particularly as an antidote to the limited perspectives and technocratic solutions offered by the 'development set'. He cites the World Health Organization, the Food and Agricultural Organization, the Overseas Development Agency, USAID and Oxfam as examples of some of the national and international agencies that use anthropological expertise. Against the current vein of deconstruction he calls for more 'objective research' by qualified, technically competent and 'impartial' anthropological experts, arguing that ethnographic accounts 'can achieve standards of accuracy and authenticity which transcend the subjectivity of the individual anthropologist'.

Wright assesses the application of anthropology to practical problems. taking as a case study the development of anthropology in policy and practice in Britain. Her historical overview of the rise of applied anthropology as a branch of general anthropology has a secondary function, however: it provides the springboard for a powerful critique of the politics and ideology that have come to shape British anthropology. Foremost among these are the status divisions between (sic) 'pure' and applied anthropology and the discipline's characteristic stance of political and ethical impartiality. Following Raymond Firth, she argues that the role of anthropologists is also to confront contentious social and political problems and to communicate their findings to those who frame policy. Unlike Firth, however, she suggests that the cultures of policy professionals themselves might also be regarded as a fertile field for anthropological research. Using ethnographic insights from her own work, she explores this theme by examining some of the corporate strategies used by a local council in northern England to tackle the social consequences of high unemployment. Her conclusion, which closely supports our own, is that the shift from the study of peoples to the study of 'policy' and state institutions is a trend that should be encouraged in anthropology. Moreover, this shift towards greater political reflexivity (where reflexivity is understood in terms of cultural critique rather than deliberations on the nature of oneself) has profound implications for the way anthropologists 'engage' with their fields of study.

Wright's message that anthropology should remain an 'uncomfortable discipline' – both for those with institutional power and for anthropologists themselves – by becoming actively engaged with issues of power and its own position within the context of government rationality, is echoed in Frankenberg's study of anthropology and HIV/AIDS research. Like Lewis, he notes the way that anthropologists are sometimes recruited to provide legitimacy for government initiatives and 'to give scientific validity to socially constructed stereotypes'. In the case of AIDS, anthropologists were invited to contribute to policy-making as consultants on the assumed 'cultures' of so-called 'high risk groups'. But this seems to have had a traumatic effect on anthropologists' use of their core concept of culture. Frankenberg suggests that in order to please those who have appealed to their expertise, anthropologists have intensified their tendency to reify culture in the vain attempt to 'discover' fictitious entities such as the 'cultures' of intravenous drug users, gay men and prostitutes. For Frankenberg, the encounter between the cultures of biomedicine, anthropology and patients is structurally similar to that which existed, in colonial days, between colonial administrator, anthropologist and native subjects. Overcoming this particular subject–object dualism for Frankenberg entails taking sides and working *with* (rather than attempting to act *on*) other people.

The relevance of anthropological studies of tourism is the theme explored by both Nash and Graburn. Indeed, given its increasing size and influence in the world economy today, tourism deserves to be high on the anthropological agenda, though as a topic of serious research it is still in its relative infancy. As Urry (1990) has noted, not only is it one of the world's fastest growing industries and perhaps the largest source of employment worldwide, but it has also played a key role in intercultural communications, in restructuring urban and rural landscapes, and in establishing heritage sites and leisure activities throughout the globe. In reviewing the literature on tourism and its relevance for anthropology, Nash identifies three main themes in tourism research; 'acculturation' (or development), personal transition (or tourism as a personal rite of passage), and tourism as a kind of superstructure. While the first two themes have made some theoretical advance in recent years, Nash suggests that the study of tourism as a social process generated by, and specific to, certain kinds of economy and society offers a far richer field for anthropological study. Above all, Nash argues that we shift our attention towards the 'tourist generating' end of the tourist process, rather than simply the destination areas.

Graburn, by contrast, explores the relationship between tourism and modernity, asking to what extent can the study of tourism shed light on wider contemporary cultural processes? He argues that postmodernism poses a paradox. It is said to promote economic fragmentation, social diversity and dislocation, and cultural hybridity, but from a touristic perspective the world appears to be growing more homogenous because 'the *same kinds* of mixtures, blends and incongruities can be found almost anywhere, channelled by the same sorts of techno-bureaucratic institutions'. Like Harvey (1989) and Jameson (1984), Graburn sees postmodernism as 'the cultural logic of late capitalism', it's impulse is to 'promote endless consumerism by proliferating product differentiation'. The effect of this has been to stimulate not only widespread concern with authenticity (which is seen as fast receding from the modern world), but a burgeoning commercial sector geared towards meeting tourist demands by manufacturing heritage and tradition. As Harvey (1989: 62–3) observed, the growth of a museum culture and heritage industry has simply added a populist twist to the commercialization of history and cultural forms over the past two decades. For Graburn, while 'heritage' undoubtedly represents one of the most powerful of all modern tropes of attraction, 'nostalgia' is the force that drives this kind of touristic enterprise. However, unlike those critics who deplore the commodification of culture and the homogenizing effects of commercialization and globalization, Graburn comes to the surprising conclusion that the spread of metropolitan institutions in this way may actually benefit people in Third World countries and elsewhere by making it easier for them to adapt to living in the metropolis.

Postmodernism also poses problems for feminist analysis, as Cornwall and Lindisfarne point out. Their essay focuses on some of the issues of gender raised by feminist and postmodernist theory. By deconstructing the fundamental categories upon which Western social theory resides, postmodernist writing also undermines the old certainties of feminism as a political project. To put it simply, if there is no such thing as 'woman' – if our basic categories and concepts are all just fictions of discourse – then how can 'women' be oppressed? If everything is relative, feminist critiques of social theory become irrelevant. In addressing these questions, Cornwall and Lindisfarne suggest that finding a new basis for making moral judgements about sexual inequality and power has become the central postmodern problem for feminists. The solution they propose is found using Foucault's work on power and Strathern's writings on 'agency', 'replication' and the production of gendered difference. They claim that both these writers transcend conventional dualistic analyses and pave the way for a new 'feminist politics of location' which does away with essentialist notions of 'women', 'men' or 'masculinized power'. How this analysis translates into feminist praxis is, perhaps, another matter.

Hazan's chapter takes a different direction. He argues that the study of old age can serve as a way of exploring the nature of contemporary living. Unlike the rest of our contributors, most of whom take issue with the style and politics of postmodernism, Hazan claims that a 'postmodernist perspective' on ageing provides an important new domain for anthropology and raises insights into various theoretical issues. He sets out to demonstrate this by identifying six major current problems in anthropology and their relevance for the study of ageing. Each of these six problems is related to the predicament of postmodern culture: the blurring of boundaries and the fragmentation of those 'bounded units' that once provided anthropology with a focus of study; the breakdown of the notion of 'holism'; confusion in the social reckoning of time; difficulties in coming to terms with the relationship between 'self' and society when in place of the 'self' we are confronted with multiple, fractured 'selves'; the need for a new conceptual language to analyse postmodern society, and the problem of representing the 'Other'. For Hazan, all of these issues are highlighted in the anthropology of ageing. The elderly seem to epitomize the postmodern condition. As Hazan concludes, theirs is a kind of looking-glass reality; the anthropologist is confronted with fragmentary identities, partial memories, multiple selves and a host of alternative personal narratives. In this sense he suggests, echoing one of the recurring themes of postmodernist writers, 'texts' assume more importance than context. He ends with the idealistic, if dubious, plea that anthropologists join forces with 'postmodern humanism' in order to rehumanize our perception of the elderly.

The chapter by David Morley and Kevin Robins develops the theme of cultural imperialism in a postmodern world, exploring both the effects of Western media on 'foreign' audiences, and the effects of communications systems on media audiences in the West. Rejecting as over-simplistic the conventional assumption about Western television's automatic and hegemonic influence over non-Western viewers (the 'hypodermic model' of media imperialism), they provide powerful illustrations of the ways in which audiences in different cultural settings invariably 'read' television programmes and images through the prism of their own cultures. The effects of the media in ordering our own experience, however, is a question they take up in the second half of their essay. They argue that media technologies have profoundly restructured our perception of place and space. Television, they contend, has created new imagined communities of spectators in a mediated, electronic, 'virtual' world; it has transformed our experiences of geography, allowing us to share vicariously the literal time of persons who are elsewhere. Through this process, they suggest, television is transforming us into 'armchair imperialists'. This point is illustrated by reference to the Gulf crisis and to the war in Bosnia. In both these cases, rather than bringing its audience *closer* to the human tragedy involved in these violent events, television screening of the war became a key mechanism through which an important process of psychological *distancing* was achieved. The TV audience is invited to *gaze* at the Bosnian Other, but from a safe distance, and from the comfort of their living-rooms. The result of this 'mediation' of experience is a detachment which serves to protect us (emotionally and psychologically) from the full horrors of such wars.

Western responses to the war in Bosnia is an issue also explored by Meštrović. Like Morley and Robins, he accuses the West of voyeurism and hypocrisy in its policies towards the former Yugoslavia. But Meštrović's aim is more than simply policy critique. His goal, as a social scientist, is both to make sense of the Balkan war and to use it as a vehicle for discussing the 'Balkanization' of Western societies more generally. Part of the reason why the Western media appears to be mesmerized by the Bosnian conflict, he suggests, is because it touches on issues of collective guilt, ethnic apartheid and religious intolerance that lie at the heart of many Western societies. Drawing on a synthesis of work by Simmel, Durkheim and the Frankfurt school, he proposes a new sociological concept as an alternative to the sterile textuality of postmodernism: 'post-emotionalism'. Post-emotional politics, he argues, are characterized by nostalgia, sentimentality and kitsch (the same ingredients, incidentally, that Graburn identifies in the modern heritage industry) .

In many respects Meštrović's chapter takes up the challenge posed by Grimshaw and Hart: it is a subjective and emotional account (written by an American Croat) harnessed to a rigorous sociological analysis. The result is a moving and reflexive analysis that alerts us in a highly critical way to some of the problems of representation in the modern age. Yet what is interesting about the chapters of both Meštrović and Morley and Robins is the way they engage with the modern media. Newspapers and television – which are two of the most important instruments through which modern collective identities are constructed and maintained – are treated both as objects of analysis and as sources of data.

As Giddens notes in his epilogue, none of the topics dealt with in this book has much to do with anthropology as traditionally conceived, nor does long-term fieldwork appear to have any special relevance for them. This, of course, is no bad thing. Anthropology's traditional domain is evaporating and, like the other social sciences, it is obliged to broaden its horizons and develop common areas of interest with other disciplines. On one point, however, Giddens is adamant: anthropology has little to gain from succumbing to postmodernism. The term itself, he suggests is fairly meaningless, or rather, it is an approach based on a defective theory of meaning, one that ignores the context of practical experience.

We share Giddens' scepticism and suggest that rather than adopting the tropes and strategies of postmodernist writing and joining forces with its philosophical nihilism, anthropologists would do better to reflect critically on the circumstances that have brought about this tendency so that they might work out strategies for mounting a counter-challenge to the threat of postmodernism and take advantage of its promise. Situating knowledge and cultural phenomena in their full social contexts remains essential to this task. We believe that the future of anthropology as a generalizing social science is more promising than its critics and detractors have led themselves to think. The task is to make it relevant to its audiences as well as to its practitioners.

NOTES

1   As Worsley commented recently, being a member of the Communist Party from 1942 to 1956 'certainly limited my academic opportunities' (Worsley, 1993: 11). It not only disqualified him from gaining a university post in anthropology, but also resulted in his being banned from entering New Guinea to carry out fieldwork.

2   Cf. Bloch (1983) for a succinct account of anthropology and Marxism in France and elsewhere.

3   These include, most notably, *The Sexual Life of Savages* and *Sex and Repression in Savage Society*.

4   For a recent example of this (billed as 'a "native" strikes back'), see Hong's critique of anthropology in Taiwan (Hong, 1994) and the polemic this generated in subsequent issues of the journal *Anthropology Today*.

5   Yet another new development which complicates the relationship between Western anthropology and its traditional objects of enquiry is that anthropologists from the former colonies, many of whom have long been critical of the bias and power relations implicit in Western anthropology, are now turning their critical gaze towards Western societies themselves (cf. Ahmed and Mynors, 1994).

6   According to Alex de Waal (1994), media coverage of the conflict in Rwanda during the critical early phase of the war was fundamentally flawed, and this actually inhibited the kind of international response that might have helped prevent the subsequent carnage.

7   This tendency can also be traced to Malinowski, the founder of scientific

ethnography. As Barnard (1994: 242) reminds us, one of Malinowski's most revealing remarks was 'Rivers is the Rider Haggard of anthropology; I shall be the Conrad'.

8 This was a fate which befell sociology in Britain during the early 1980s with adverse consequences for jobs. Sociology was often singled out as 'academic socialism' and therefore treated as a legitimate target for attack by members of Margaret Thatcher's Conservative Government.

9 In Britain one of the exceptions to this pattern was *Anthropology in Action* (formerly the Newsletter of the British Association of Social Anthropology in Policy and Practice, or BASAPP) which published a special issue on Anthropology and the Gulf Crisis (BASAPP Newsletter, nos. 9 and 10, 1990).

REFERENCES

Abélès, M. (1992) *La vie quotidienne au parlement européenne*, Paris: Hachette.

Ahmed, A.S. (1980) 'How to aid Afghan refugees', *RAIN*, 39 (August).

—— (1992) *Postmodernism and Islam: Predicament and Promise*, London: Routledge.

—— (1993) *Living Islam*, London: BBC Books.

Ahmed, A.S. and H. Donnan (1994) *Islam, Globalization and Postmodernity*, London: Routledge.

Ahmed, A.S. and J. Mynors (1994) 'Fowlmere', *Anthropology Today*, 10, 5 (October), pp.3–8.

Anderson, B. (1992) 'The new world disorder', *New Left Review*, 193 (May/June), pp.3–14.

Asad, T. (1973) *Anthropology and the Colonial Encounter*, London: Ithaca.

Barley, N. (1990) *Native Land*, Harmondsworth: Penguin.

Barnard, A. (1994) 'Tarzan and the lost races: parallels between anthropology and early science fiction' in E. Archetti (ed.) *Exploring the Written: Anthropology and the Multiplicity of Writing*, Oslo: Scandinavian University Press, pp.231–57.

Barthes, R. (1989) *Barthes: Selected Writings*, ed. Susan Sontag, London: Fontana.

Beck, U. (1992) *Risk Society: Towards a New Modernity*, London: Sage.

Benthall, J. (1993) *Disasters, Relief and the Media*, London: Taurus.

Bloch, M. (1983) *Marxism and Anthropology*, Oxford: OUP.

Boissevain, J. (1975) 'Towards an anthropology of Europe' in J. Boissevain and J. Friedl (eds) *Beyond the Community: Social Processes in Europe*, The Hague: Department of Education and Science.

—— (1994) 'Towards an anthropology of the European Communities?' in V. Goddard, J. Llobera and C. Shore (eds) *Anthropology of Europe: Identities and Boundaries in Conflict*, Oxford: Berg, pp.41–56.

Cannell, F. (1990) 'Concepts of parenthood: The Warnock Report, the Gillick debate and contemporary myths', *American Ethnologist*, 17, pp.667–86.

Chomsky, N. (1993) 'Nationalism and the new world order: an interview with Takis Fotopoulos', *Society and Nature*, 5, pp.1–7.

Clifford, M. and G. Marcus (1986) *Anthropology as Cultural Critique*, Chicago: University of Chicago Press.

Crapanzano, V. (1986) 'Hermes dilemma: the masking of subversion in ethnographic description' in J. Clifford and G. Marcus (eds) *Writing Culture: The Poetics and Politics of Ethnography*, University of California Press, pp.51–76.

De Waal, A. (1993) 'In the disasters zone: anthropologists and the ambiguity of aid', *Times Literary Supplement*, 4711 (16 July), pp.5–6.

—— (1994) 'Meta-conflict and the policy of mass murder', *Anthropology in Action*, 1, 3 (n.s.), pp.8–11.

Dilley, R. (ed.) (1993) *Contesting Markets. The Anthropology of Ideology, Discourse and Practice*, Edinburgh: Edinburgh University Press.

Donnan, H. and G. MacFarlane (eds) (1989) *Social Anthropology and Public Policy in Northern Ireland*, Aldershot: Avebury.

Duncan, E. (1989) *Breaking the Curfew*, London: Michael Joseph.

Edwards, J. *et al.* (1993) *Technologies of Procreation: Kinship in the Age of Assisted Conception*, Manchester: Manchester University Press.

Ennew, J. (1986) *The Sexual Exploitation of Children*, Cambridge, Polity.

—— (1994) 'Less bitter than expected: street youth in Latin America', *Anthropology in Action*, 1, 1 (n.s.), pp.7–10.

Evans-Pritchard, E. (1962) *Essays in Social Anthropology*, Oxford: Oxford University Press.

Fischer, M. (1994) *Applications in Computing for Social Anthropologists*, London: Routledge.

Foucault, M. (1984) *The Foucault Reader*, ed. P. Rabinow, Harmondsworth: Penguin.

Fox, R. (1991) 'Introduction: working in the present' in R. Fox (ed.) *Recapturing Anthropology*, Santa Fe: School of American Research Press, pp.1–16.

Geertz, C. (1968) *Islam Observed: Religious Developments in Morocco and Indonesia*, New Haven and London: Yale University Press.

Gellner, E. (1981) *Muslim Society*, Cambridge: Cambridge University Press.

—— (1992) *Postmodernism, Reason and Religion*, London: Routledge.

Giddens, A. (1990) *The Consequences of Modernity*, Cambridge: Polity.

—— (1991) *Modernity and Self-Identity: Self and Society in the Late Modern Age*, Cambridge: Polity.

Glenny, M. (1990) *The Fall of Yugoslavia*, Harmondsworth: Penguin.

Hall, S. (1992a) 'Our mongrel selves', *New Statesman and Society*, (special issue on 'Borderlands'), 5, 207 (June), pp.6–9.

—— (1992b) 'The question of cultural identity' in S. Hall, D. Held and T. McGrew (eds) *Modernity and Its Futures*, Cambridge: Polity Press and Open University Press, pp.273–326.

Hall, S. and M. Jacques (1989) 'Introduction' in S. Hall and M. Jacques (eds)

New Times: The Changing Face of Politics in the 1990s, London: Lawrence & Wishart, pp.11–22.

Halliday, F. (1991) 'Why I backed the war: the left and the war', *New Statesman and Society*, 8 March.

Handler, R. (1993) 'Anthropology is dead! Long live anthropology!', *American Anthropologist*, 95, 4, pp.991–9.

Hann, C. (ed.) (1992) *Socialism: Ideals, Ideologies and Local Practice* (ASA Monograph no.31), London: Routledge.

Harvey, D. (1989) *The Condition of Postmodernity*, Oxford: Blackwell.

Hebdige, D. (1989) 'After the masses' in S. Hall and M. Jacques (eds) *New Times: The Changing Face of Politics in the 1990s*, London: Lawrence & Wishart, pp.76–93.

Hobsbawm,E. (1992) 'Ethnicity and nationalism in Europe today', *Anthropology Today*, 8, 1 (February) pp.3–8.

Hong, K. (1994) 'Experiences of being a 'native' while observing anthropology', *Anthropology Today*, 10, 3 (June), pp.6–8.

Hymes, D. (ed.) (1972) *Reinventing Anthropology*, New York: Random House.

Jackson, A. (ed.) (1986) *Anthropology at Home*, London: Tavistock.

Jameson, F. (1984) 'Postmodernism, or, The cultural logic of late capitalism', *New Left Review*, 146 (July–August), pp.65–88.

Jencks. C. (1984) *The Language of Post-Modern Architecture*, New York: Rizzoli.

Karp, I. (1986) 'Agency and social theory: a review of Anthony Giddens', *American Ethnologist*, 13, 1 (February), pp.131–7.

Keat, R. and N. Abercrombie (eds) (1991) *Enterprise Culture*, London: Routledge.

Kroker, A. and D. Cook (1988) *The Postmodern Scene: Excremental Culture and Hyper-aesthetics*, London: Macmillan Education.

La Fontaine, J. (1990) *Child Sexual Abuse*, Cambridge, Polity.

Lamb, C. (1991) *Waiting for Allah*, Harmondsworth: Hamish Hamilton.

Lienhardt, G. (1964) *Social Anthropology*, Oxford: Oxford University Press.

Llobera, J. (1986) 'Fieldwork in southern Europe', *Critique of Anthropology*, 6, 2, pp.25–33.

Lyotard, J. (1984) *The Post-Modern Condition: A Report on Knowledge*, Minneapolis: University of Minnesota Press.

Malinowski, B. (1967) *A Diary in the Strict Sense of the Term*, London: Athlone.

Marcus, G. and M. Fischer (1986) *Anthropology as Cultural Critique*, Chicago: University of Chicago Press.

Milton, K. (ed.) (1993) *Environmentalism: The View from Anthropology*, (ASA Monograph 32), London: Routledge.

Nader, L. (1972) 'Up the anthropologist – perspectives gained from studying up' in D. Humes (ed.) *Reinventing Anthropology*, New York: Random House.

Pollier, N. and W. Roseberry (1989) 'Tristes tropes: post-modern anthropologists encounter the other and discover themselves', *Economy and Society*, 18, 2, pp.245–64.
Pool, R. (1991) 'Postmodern ethnography', *Critique of Anthropology*, 11, 4, pp.309–31.
Rabinow, P. (1993) 'Studies in the anthropology of reason', *Anthropology Today*, 8, 5, pp.7–10.
Rivière, P. (1985) 'Unscrambling parenthood', *Anthropology Today*, 1, 4, pp.2–7.
Robertson, R. (1992) *Globalisation: Social Theory and Global Culture*, London: Sage.
Rosaldo, R. (1994) 'Whose cultural studies?', *American Anthropologist*, 96, 3 (September) pp.524–8.
Said, E. (1978) *Orientalism*, London: Routledge & Kegan Paul.
—— (1993) *Culture and Imperialism*, London: Chatto & Windus.
Sangren, S. (1988) 'Rhetoric and the authority of ethnography: "Postmodernism" and the social reproduction of texts', *Current Anthropology*, 29, 3 (June), pp.405–35.
Scholte, B. (1986) 'The literary turn in contemporary anthropology', *Critique of Anthropology*, 7, 1, pp.33–47.
Scott, N. and E. Jones (eds) (1993) *Bloody Bosnia: A European Tragedy*, London: *The Guardian* and Channel 4 Television.
Selwyn, T. and C. Shore (1992) 'Education, markets and managers: a clash of cultures?', *Reflections on Higher Education*, 4 (November) pp.88–95.
Shore, C. (1992) 'Virgin births and sterile debates: anthropology and the new reproductive technologies', *Current Anthropology*, 33, 3 (June), pp.295–314.
—— (1993) 'Inventing the "People's Europe": critical perspectives on European Community cultural policy', *Man*, 28, 4 (December), pp.779–800.
Strathern, M. (1991) *Reproducing the Future: Anthropology, Kinship and the New Reproductive Technologies*, Manchester University Press.
Thaiss, G. (1978) 'Religious symbolism and social change: the drama of Husain' in N. R. Keddie (ed.) *Scholars, Saints and Sufis*, Berkeley: University of California Press.
Tully, M. (1991) *No Full Stops in India*, Harmondsworth: Viking Penguin.
Turner, B. (1994) *Orientalism, Postmodernism and Globalization*, London: Routledge.
Tyler, S. (1986) 'Post-modern ethnography: from document of the occult to occult documentation' in J. Clifford and G. Marcus (eds), *Writing Culture: The Poetics and Politics of Ethnography*, Berkeley: University of California Press, pp.122–40.
Urry, J. (1990) *The Tourist Gaze: Leisure and Travel in Contemporary Societies*, London: Sage.
Wolf, E. (1982) *Europe and the People Without History*, Berkeley: University of California Press.

Woolgar, S. (1991) 'What is "Anthropological" about the anthropology of science?', *Current Anthropology*, 32, 1.

Worsley, P. (1993) 'Give me a place to stand and I'll change the world! An interview with Peter Worsley', *European Association of Social Anthropologists Newsletter*, 10 (August).

Wright, S. (ed.) (1994) *The Anthropology of Organisations*, London: Routledge.

CHAPTER 2

The Rise and Fall of
Scientific Ethnography
Anna Grimshaw and Keith Hart

ANTHROPOLOGY AND THE CRISIS OF THE INTELLECTUALS

The notion that anthropology is in crisis, or at least faces a major turning-point, has become commonplace. It is easy for middle-aged academics, secure in their tenure, to argue that the perception of crisis is perennial, that there has never been agreement on what anthropology really is or where its future lies. And it is true that the discipline has lacked a unified sense of purpose for a full three decades now, ever since the collapse of empire. But the questions posed today by young newcomers to the subject do seem to have an urgency which is new. Students want to know what the point of anthropology is; and they are highly sceptical of the answers they are usually given. They look to anthropological knowledge as a possible bridge between themselves as individuals and the world they live in; and for the most part they are disappointed. Their teachers seem old and out of touch; the discipline's models of enquiry and its canonical texts belong to a previous era.

The roots of anthropology's malaise can be traced to the breakdown of its central paradigm, scientific ethnography. The intellectual authority of modern social anthropology in the beginning rested on objective reporting of first-hand experience gained with exotic peoples through the practice of 'fieldwork'.[1] Nowadays the truth claims of these monographs are viewed with much suspicion. Ethnography is seen more often as a species of creative writing than as science; and the realism of conventional accounts is considered to be as limited in its formal scope as its content is often deceptive. Moreover, objectification of other people is linked to political hierarchy, an uncomfortable reminder of anthropology's affinity for the world's dominant classes, beginning with its association with European colonial rule.

If one event summarized the recent challenge to anthropology's scientific paradigm, it was the publication in 1986 of *Writing Culture* (edited by J. Clifford and G. Marcus). Here a number of American anthropologists sought to subvert the old division between the thinking subject and a passive social object, replacing it with a number of devices indicative of a more equal and engaged relationship. Specifically, they advocated the adoption of experimental writing strategies aimed at incorporating the objects of fieldwork into ethnography as active human subjects. This 'literary turn' has since gathered momentum, even in Britain, where feminist anthropologists in particular have exploited the cracks in a dominant paradigm to which they already felt marginal as women.

Although there are several features of anthropology which make it special, the phenomenon of disciplinary confusion is widespread in academic circles. Everywhere the foundations of expert knowledge are being undermined; and this reflects a general crisis in the relationship between intellectuals and society in the late twentieth century.[2]

The problem is that people today either no longer trust the professionals whose impersonal knowledge governs so much of their lives or they have learned how to bypass dependence on experts by acquiring relevant knowledge in their own way. In either case, they are increasingly sceptical of authority claims made by intellectuals whose activities may be perceived as being at best irrelevant, at worst actually harmful. Bodies of specialized knowledge have to be stable to be useful; but the rapid movement of the modern world subverts any intellectual strategy based on fixed rules. Global movements of people, goods, money and information make it hard to maintain local monopolies of any sort, especially monopolies of ideas. In consequence, popular resistance to dominance by intellectuals is manifested in negative beliefs which bid fair to replace their legitimating predecessors as common currency – that scientists endanger the environment, doctors are bad for your health, economists' predictions are wrong, the law is an expensive farce, and so on. Professors, who have long been known to be inarticulate and incompetent, are now suspected of having nothing to say at all. Certainly, the number of people who depend on humanist intellectuals as the arbiters of civilization and taste is dwindling.

Anthropologists suffer most acutely from their own variant of this dilemma; for they have always derived their intellectual authority from direct experience of social life. Their claim to special expertise traditionally rested on reporting unknown peoples to both lay and academic audiences at home. That is, they knew the exotic Other and their readers did not. Within that framework of bridging the gap between civilized and primitive, they emphasized the salience of the everyday, the ordinary. It is true that they did play up an arcane algebra of kinship as their unique professional tool of analysis; but in general ethnographers traded in common sense, relying on the unchallengeable monopoly afforded by fieldwork in foreign places.

The accelerated integration of world society since the Second World War has severely embarrassed this project. Apart from political difficulties which have rendered many former colonies less accessible, the knowledge of fieldworkers is increasingly subject to challenge from a wide variety of sources, not least the people studied themselves. Moreover, artless communication of commonsense knowledge can be derided as mere gossip or dismissed as redundant.[3] In a world of television, credit cards and mass travel, the idea that genealogical charts offer a sure guide to social structure is, to say the least, unconvincing. It is, therefore, not surprising that anthropologists today, even more than most other branches of the academic division of labour, find themselves in a quandary when asked to explain how they contribute to understanding the world we all live in.

The contributors to *Writing Culture* grasped the essence of this issue when they attacked anthropology's pretension to be a scientific discipline. Clearly a preference for pinning people down to rigidly objective social codes is not the best way of coming to grips with the fluidity of a world in movement. But their perspective was limited. In common with most writing on anthropology's current predicament, they failed to locate the crisis – and their own response to it – in an adequate conception of social history. If the scientific paradigm of ethnography is in trouble, we need to ask what social conditions have made this so now. We also need to go back to the origins of anthropology's modern phase, in order to discover both what was right with the discipline at the time of its foundation and what went wrong later. Nor should such an enquiry treat anthropology in isolation from the broader historical question of the place of intellectuals in twentieth-century society.

For the sake of tracing specific historical relationships and because it still stands as the most illustrious example of the genre, the following discussion of scientific ethnography and its aftermath will focus on the British school of social anthropologists. There is a sense in which the kind of cultural anthropology advocated by *Writing Culture* is a direct challenge to the Malinowskian paradigm of ethnography which still underpins a British school whose members are on the whole rather defensive in the face of this American trend. This is, moreover, the specific institutional framework within which we now work and received our training as anthropologists.[4] It is consistent with the approach we advocate that we first seek to place ourselves self-consciously inside the social history of which we are a part.

THE RISE OF SCIENTIFIC ETHNOGRAPHY

Scientific ethnography was born out of a rejection of Victorian evolutionary racism. That is, it was the negation of anthropology's previous, nineteenth-century stage. Anthropology began in the seventeenth and eighteenth centuries as philosophical speculation about human nature. The social conventions of the old regime were discredited and liberal democrats sought a universal basis for human society, largely through theoretical speculation informed by the discovery of the New World. The American and French Revolutions made theory into history, thereby paving the way for a second stage of anthropology in which humanity was conceptualized as the outcome of a progressive process of world history.

Britain's industrial revolution and the consequent emergence of a world market divided between imperial powers supported a vision of global society as an association of unequally developed races. Only some sections of Western civilization had attained the full rational development of which human beings were capable. The rest – women, children, the lower classes, madmen, criminals, savages, orientals, the darker races – were held to be backward and in need of guidance. Anthropology, after Darwin had destroyed the biblical creation myth, thus became in the nineteenth century the secular search for mankind's primitive origins and a celebration of Victorian civilization's rational achievements in contrast with those of the world's inferior races.

This version of anthropology was undermined in the decades leading up to the First World War, an event whose shattering barbarity finally put paid to the evolutionary model and prepared the way for anthropology's third, twentieth-century stage. Scientific ethnography was, at first, in the hands of Rivers or Boas, a way of escaping from prevailing prejudices. The so-called 'functionalist' revolution, completed in Britain by Malinowski and Radcliffe-Brown, substituted for reconstruction of the human past an emphasis on the coherence of what people did here and now, as revealed by fieldwork in specific remote locations.[5] In place of a global racial hierarchy these ethnographers offered a plural and relativistic model of self-sufficient primitive societies, each with its own reasons for existence. By emphasizing what made sense in these societies, they extended the conception of rational humanity, simultaneously questioning Western arrogance and demanding intellectual respect for 'primitives'.

It is hard to imagine, given the sour pessimism of our own day, that ethnography based on fieldwork once evoked a vision of science harnessed to social progress. Science, the disciplined pursuit of secular knowledge, has long been regarded as indispensable to the political goal of democracy.[6] Ideally, science extends human capacities; it is egalitarian in its effects; and it ruthlessly exposes mystical grounds for the maintenance of social inequality.

Malinowski's version of scientific ethnography began as a moment of personal freedom; but its social impact was amplified by the democratic impulse of the twentieth century. Certainly, it replaced myths of racial inferiority with a broader conception of human equality. It rejected official narratives of power in favour of an emphasis on people's capacity for self-organization. Having exposed existing categories of knowledge as mere prejudice, it placed what people really do in the world above what others think about them. By abolishing the gap between the library and life (ethnographers were both theorists and fieldworkers at the same time), it enabled humanist intellectuals to join the people on terms (almost) of the latter's making. Finally, the new ethnography stressed what matters to ordinary people – the everyday, the mundane – over the extraordinary and the fabulous, the real over the spiritual; and this too is central to the historical project of building democracy.

The method of scientific ethnography required the invention of a new literary form; and here too Malinowski's lead was decisive, with Evans-Pritchard following close behind as a formative master of the type of fieldwork-based monograph associated with the British school in its classical phase (roughly speaking, 1920–1960).[7] Like the novel in its heyday, the fieldwork-based monograph adopted the style of realism, of being close to life; but, unlike the novel, it abjured any fictional devices, claiming to be an objective, factual report and explicitly engaging in analytical argument. Thus, the empirical circumstances of an exotic people, described in some detail bv an anthropologist who had lived with them for at least a year, were used to illustrate ideas of general theoretical interest to audiences in the English-speaking world.

The distinctive innovation of scientific ethnography was to make ideas seem to emerge from descriptions of real life, as when Fortes and Evans-Pritchard, claiming that their model of *African Political*

Systems (1940) was discovered in the field, refused to acknowledge their intellectual debt to Morgan, Durkheim and many others. We may call this innovation the 'synthetic *a posteriori*', being a hybrid construct of Kant's famous distinction between the mental forms we bring to an enquiry, the synthetic *a priori*, and the empirical inferences we make subsequently, the analytical *a posteriori*. The habit of deriving concepts from specific field locations meant that the epitome of gift-exchange became the Trobriand *kula* or the Northwest Coast *potlatch*, and politics without the state was embodied in the lineages of the Nuer or the Tallensi. The intellectual authority of these anthropologists, therefore, rested on their ability to make interesting theoretical arguments (about rationality, kinship, politics, etc.) through convincing accounts of their own extensive empirical observations.

It is now widely recognized that Malinowski was much less successful in putting into practice his scientific principles than he was in expounding them. His texts have been exposed as modernist collages, in contrast to his own description of them as objective accounts of social reality. His claims to be a dispassionate, objective observer convince no one, especially since the publication of his fieldwork diaries revealed the strain between his professional and private personalities.[8]

From the above we can begin to see how the spirit of scientific democracy, embodied in fieldwork, might be transformed under the social conditions of academic production back home. If exposure to exotic places enabled anthropologists to claim that having 'been there' was what mattered and that the ideas of intellectuals are simply an extrapolation from the real world, true academic respectability came from their contribution to a cumulative body of scientific doctrine, to 'theory'; and it is this pursuit of intellectual credibility within the academy which produced rather less impressive results in hindsight.

It is now clear that the ethnographers' texts were literary productions as much as scientific reports; and that authors often made misleading claims about ideas and facts designed to enhance their own reputations. Attempts to establish specialist expertise, for example, through developing an esoteric jargon and algebraic notation for kinship studies, now seem spurious; as does the category of 'primitive' societies which became the discipline's academic specialism.[9] The banality of common-sense reports was obscured by the exoticism of remote ethnographic locations; so that monographs often lacked the depth we associate with serious investigations of more familiar phenomena. Moreover, whatever its virtues as propaganda, the habit of deriving ideas from ethnographic facts, rather than acknowledge the influence of Western traditions, made the task of intellectual reproduction virtually impossible.

The division between fieldwork and writing was so huge that British anthropologists have long preserved a dual image of their foundation as a distinctive school. Although both men united fieldwork and theoretical writing in practice, Malinowski is celebrated as the inventor of the empirical tradition, while Radcliffe-Brown is seen as the author of the social theory ('structural-functionalism') which gave the school a rationalist foundation. The worlds of the field and the study were truly separate, allowing the equality and reciprocity of social life 'out there' to be replaced with the objectifying hierarchy and intellectual distance on which academic authority depends.

If fieldwork encouraged isolated and vulnerable individuals to join the people they studied and to explore the possibilities for intersubjective exchange, writing up encouraged detachment and a one-sided objectivity. It is, of course, an axiom of scientific method that replicable knowledge of the world is more attainable if the investigator's particular subjectivity is repressed; but the price to be paid for bringing such an attitude to reports based on human encounters is great indeed. By making shared social life conform to a model of representation in which individual subjects wrote about anonymous collective objects, ethnographers reproduced the class inequality not only of colonialism, but also of universities at home. Moreover, as the specialist science of primitive societies, anthropology had nothing to say directly about home society; and this lent support to its identification with Western civilization's imperialist drive to control the rest of the world.

Against this, the ethnographers' practice of assuming that the small-scale communities they studied were both culturally homogeneous and territorially self-sufficient replicated the nationalist consensus which prevailed in their home societies. Certainly, Radcliffe-Brown's theories of social integration reflected the ideology of a harmonious division of labour to which the rulers of industrial states often appealed in the first half of this century.[10] Perhaps most damaging of all, however, the ethnographic model of static, isolated societies denied the participation of colonial peoples in the movement of world history; and it was this error which came to haunt the profession most vividly when the European empires collapsed soon after the Second World War.

Science thus has two faces: it is an agent of freedom and equality in human affairs, extending knowledge and powers in ways that can enhance democracy, if the scale and perspective of ordinary people's lives are respected; yet it is also a means of concentrating power and knowledge into the hands of an exclusive elite, making the rest feel powerless and dependent. When science is subordinated to the needs of a power elite (including the scientists themselves), it tends to become closed and atrophied, shutting itself off from the sources of its own renewal in human creativity.

When this happens, as it has in many university disciplines including anthropology since the Second World War, science loses its progressive momentum, becoming a conservative vehicle for the reproduction of narrow professional expertise, less open to eclectic working methods and insights based on diffuse personal experience. Indeed, by the mid-point of this century, science had come to embody for many an oppressive, impersonal force in society, leading to a stark polarization between objective scientists who were allegedly indifferent to human concerns and specialists in the arts whose focus on individual creativity ignored what scientists knew.

British social anthropology's expansive phase could thus be viewed as a creative moment when, under the collective banner of a new science, but with the benefit of individual inspiration, intellectual enquiry followed the liberating movement to establish the equality of all human beings. The story of the twentieth century has largely been one of the betrayal of that early promise, and anthropology is no exception. If the discipline is to be renewed at this time, we should reflect on the positive forces which gave it impetus in the first half of this century; for much that has happened since represents a move backwards to the kind of remote intellectual elitism which scientific ethnography was originally designed to overthrow.

ANTHROPOLOGY'S RECENT LITERARY TURN

The erosion of scientific ethnography's premises has been long drawn out and multifarious; but the most striking evidence of its deteriorating position within British social anthropology has been a recent trend to view ethnography as a species of creative writing. This 'literary turn' is in many ways the negation of an objectivism which represented anthropological monographs as factual reports of phenomena observed scientifically in the field. For, in order to maintain the purity of an objective stance, the founders of modern ethnography felt obliged to exclude any positive role for subjectivity, metaphor, fiction and rhetoric. Their accounts were definitely not 'stories', travellers' tales to be disparaged by the practitioners of other academic disciplines.

Diffuse dissatisfaction with what such a position left out led eventually to an attempt to restore the perspective of creative writing to the theory and practice of ethnography. This movement originated in the United States, most notably through the work of Clifford Geertz from the 1970s;[11] but it is epitomized by the publication of *Writing Culture* in 1986. Although this collection is often seen as the romantic antithesis of scientific ethnography, emphasizing as it does creative subjectivity, its authors claimed only to seek to extend ethnography beyond the rigidities of an undialectical objectivism. To this end, they advocated a more fluid and two-sided approach to anthropological practice, recasting subject–object relations in new ways not envisaged by the traditional, authoritarian model.

The contributions to *Writing Culture* are various and of unequal value, while James Clifford's introduction reflects his own background in textual scholarship rather than anthropological fieldwork. Nevertheless, some generalizations can be made. The volume seeks to restore the art of writing to the centre of the ethnographic enterprise. It sees ethnography as an interdisciplinary affair, a 'hybrid textual activity', which has won a measure of autonomy out of the ruins of anthropology's breakdown as a unitary field. Ethnographic truth is always partial. It combines the poetics and politics which are intrinsic to all human endeavours. The ethnographer is a social agent with an imagination; and this should be explicitly recognized.

At the core of *Writing Culture* is an attempt to link meaning on the human scale of action to 'the modern world system'.[12] This is joined to a critique of anthropology's complicity with imperialism which had previously peaked in the 1960s. Now it was reinforced by an argument, derived from Foucault and others, that the claim to objectivity as a means of asserting intellectual authority normally rests on unequal power relations. Against this contributors suggested experimental methods for establishing more two-sided, egalitarian relations with the subjects and readers of ethnography. Stephen Tyler's essay on 'postmodern ethnography' went furthest in exploring the potential for intersubjective exchange between all parties; but reflexivity, dialogue and reciprocity emerge as the general watchwords of what was clearly intended as a new movement for anthropology.

Despite disclaimers to the contrary, *Writing Culture* comes across as anti-scientific, within the recent tradition of symbolic, interpretive anthropology associated with Geertz. Its emphasis on experimental writing as a solution to anthropology's problems ties the enterprise precisely to those old forms of intellectual authority which were identified as the chief obstacle to progress. If ethnography as a form of 'textual activity' is to be separated logically from the lived experience of fieldwork and indeed from the anthropological tradition, as Clifford implies, this too suggests an intellectualism which has removed itself from social life. The restriction of participation in what was billed as an advanced seminar on textual theory to a homogeneous group of male professors betrays a similarly limited conception of the political issues involved. And this reflects the main failing of *Writing Culture*: its inadequately dialectical conception of the self as an historical subject in society, whether this be the concrete conditions of the world at large or, more narrowly, the institutions of academic life.

The reception of *Writing Culture* in Britain was mixed. It is widely referred to here, more often negatively than positively, as a landmark text in social anthropology's recent development.[13] As such it has become a symbol of the challenge to scientific ethnography posed by the discipline's literary wing. But British social anthropology had already been open for some time to an emphasis on subjective meaning through assimilation of the interpretive or symbolic school of anthropology; and French critical thought made substantial inroads in the 1980s. So it would be wrong to overstate *Writing Culture*'s influence. Yet it is indisputable that the opposition between science and literature, which may be said to have underpinned anthropology's modern paradigm, has come under a sustained critique in the last decade.

It is a remarkable fact that Britain's version of the literary turn in anthropology comes largely out of the work of feminist writers, in ironic contrast with the exclusively male composition of the *Writing Culture* seminar. Women have played the leading role in reinventing British anthropology since the mid-1970s and Marilyn Strathern (who sees feminism and anthropology as related but distinct enterprises) is the most prominent of these. Her Frazer lecture (Strathern, 1987) used the contrast between Malinowski and the author of *The Golden Bough* to explore the issue of anthropology as a form of writing; and in several works, notably *The Gender of the Gift* (1988), she attacks the objectivism of scientific ethnography through deconstruction of the basic categories or 'fictions' which organize anthropological understanding: culture/nature, individual/society, etc.

In the course of the 1980s, it became increasingly common for anthropologists to refer to their ethnographic sources (and not just their own writings) as 'texts': making the experience of life in the field a kind of reading. Henrietta Moore's study of the Marakwet of Kenya, *Space, Text and Gender* (1985), combines feminist and post-structuralist theory in a sophisticated example of this new ethnographic style. Judith Okely's pioneering critique of ethnographic objectivism, 'The self and scientism' (1975), owed much to her carrying out fieldwork as a woman in her own society. Since then she has focused her attention as an anthropologist on the historical construction of the human subject, through a biography of Simone de Beauvoir and a collection of autobiographies written by British ethnographers.[14]

A number of ethnographies, written self-consciously in opposition to the old scientific paradigm, have begun to appear in the early 1990s. Helen Watson's *Women in the City of the Dead* (1991) seeks to give a voice to the subjects of ethnography by retelling the stories of women migrants in Cairo, juxtaposing proverbial narratives with individual life histories. Katy Gardner's *Songs at the River's Edge* (1991), produces a narrative of rural Bangladesh, with the ethnographer herself as a prominent actor, in a style reminiscent of realist fiction. Finally, Anna Grimshaw's *Servants of the Buddha* (1992) is an imaginative memoir of her stay in a Himalayan nunnery which seeks to undermine the realist conventions of anthropological writing while renewing the ethnographic tradition as a self-consciously literary enterprise.[15]

For these women anthropologists the literary turn is a means of exploiting the contradictions in a paradigm which expresses the authority claims of dominant, white male intellectuals. Their experience of society precludes identification with such a model, not least because they have often been placed at a disadvantage by the institutions that it reflects. Feminists undermined scientific ethnography in two principal ways. First, by revealing the 'invisibility' of women in previous ethnographic reports, they subverted the latter's claim to objectivity. Second, as we have seen above, they tested the limits of ethnographic conventions by exploring new forms capable of giving expression to new content.

This new ethnography, and the theoretical argument underlying it, constitutes the most progressive feature of British social anthropology in recent years; and as such it represents the most concrete evidence that the days of the old scientific ethnography paradigm are numbered. But a similar claim might have been made three decades ago, in the aftermath of decolonization. It is one of the limitations of the literary turn that its exponents have not yet sought to place themselves explicitly within the social and intellectual history of the twentieth century. With such an objective in mind, we now examine developments in British anthropology since the colonial heyday of its founding generation.

What is remarkable about social anthropology's paradigm of scientific ethnography is not the challenge posed to its centrality in the 1980s, but the fact that it survived for so long at the core of the discipline. For at the moment of anthropology's professional consolidation after the Second World War the very idea of 'primitive society' was rendered obsolete by the achievement of independence by colonial peoples; and science as a progressive project became deeply compromised by the superpower rivalry of the Cold War.

Adjustments to this new situation were clearly evident in the work of postwar anthropologists. But there had also been an implicit recognition of impending political transformation in the writings of many of the classical ethnographers. For example, in the 1930s Malinowski was preoccupied with what he called 'the dynamics of culture contact' and he financed the fieldwork of some of his most notable students (Fortes, Nadel and others) through a Rockefeller Foundation grant to study 'social change in Africa'.[16] Evans-Pritchard explicitly dealt with historical questions in much of his work; and Firth saw individual choice as a key to the analysis of social change.[17]

All these uncoordinated attempts to reconcile stable ideas with a moving reality culminated in the collective efforts of the Manchester school under Gluckman to address class and racial conflict in central/southern Africa during the 1950s.[18] But if the model of scientific ethnography had begun to be adapted piecemeal to historical processes of integration and transformation under colonialism, the end of empire opened the floodgates. As a consequence, younger anthropologists working in the period after 1960 pushed British social anthropology in new directions.

On the one hand, some anthropologists sought to connect the subjects of ethnography to world society through a version of evolutionary history reflecting the development aspirations of newly independent nations;[19] and on the other there was a shift away from direct engagement in society into a search for subjective meaning through the study of culture.[20] Jack Goody and Clifford Geertz owe their prominence in part to the fact that they came to epitomize these two contrasting responses to the post-colonial situation.[21]

Although these innovations opened new horizons for exploration, and the legitimacy of much established theory and practice came to be questioned, the work of British anthropologists did not abandon or even seriously challenge the centrality of the scientific ethnography paradigm. Moreover, the idea of anthropologists as academic specialists whose professional expertise is manifested in objective reports of fieldwork carried out among an identifiable, exotic people was now underpinned by an unprecedented institutional expansion. During the 1960s the numbers of university lecturers in social anthropology multiplied across the country. In the context of such expansion, research and teaching obligations required further consolidation of the discipline's intellectual foundations, a move enhanced by anthropologists' need to demarcate their distinctive practices from the other expanding sciences of society (especially sociology). These factors, combined with the prominence of anthropologists from the British school's classical phase as heads of departments, helped reinforce an ideological attachment to the old methods.

At one level, then, the two directions in which British anthropology moved in the wake of independence (the one reflecting the integration of global society, the other an increased awareness of the cultural forces shaping individual consciousness) may be understood as positive responses to a changed world. But, at another level, they tended to separate the two functions unified by Malinowski in the shape of the fieldworker-theorist.

In most general terms, this had been an attempt to bridge the growing gap between subject and object, between a class of thinkers ('intellectuals') whose knowledge and decisions affect the rest of society and the anonymous mass of doers ('the people') whose work for society is not held to be self-conscious. Scientific ethnography had originally brought intellectuals and the people together 'in the field' as subjects who think (or see) and objects who do – even if the institutional dominance of home-based universities restored the primacy of theory, and this in turn took the unusual form of ideas being drawn from life.

The later polarization of anthropology's development towards culture and history only served to fracture the creative connection between ideas and social life. And by separately pursuing the creative subject and the collective object, these branches of post-colonial anthropology reproduced the contradiction which lies at the heart of modern human experience – namely, the absence of a meaningful connection between living persons and the impersonal forces driving world history.

The wave of nationalism, imperialism and bureaucratic centralization which ushered in the twentieth century gave scientific ethnography its social impetus. For half a century now the world has been turning against that model of society. The issue, though, is far from being settled. The question is whether humanity will invent social forms conducive to its continuing integration as a world civilization or dissolve into barbaric fragmentation.[22] Anthropologists, by endorsing a fractured vision of society, have hitherto failed to resist the divisive nationalist forces which have so marked our twentieth-century world. Today, more than ever, we must find the energies to renew our discipline as a force for internationalism and democracy.

This is anthropology's predicament: the institutions which once gave it life now obstruct its capacity to grow. Whatever the original merits of scientific ethnography as a model of anthropological enquiry, it no longer represents an adequate strategy for coming to grips with the progressive movement of our world. This is widely recognized in anthropology today. The response, however, has so far largely remained at the level of individual innovation, setting up contradictions within the discipline as a whole. For if the Malinowskian model has continued to provide the formal basis for the British school's coherence in a post-colonial world, individual anthropologists have increasingly felt free to respond to new circumstances in their own way, crossing disciplinary boundaries at will. The result has been a widening gap between what particular individuals do and the professional model they continue to uphold to students and those outside the discipline.

This contradiction between the individual and collective needs of anthropologists is a central thread running throughout *Writing Culture*. The book suggests that in contemporary anthropology 'anything goes', encouraging individuals to explore their own creative subjectivity as idiosyncratically as they like. The social context for such activity is, however, left vague. *Writing Culture*'s contributors make few references to the institutional realities of life in anthropology departments and express a pretty abstract idea of society as 'the modern world system'. Hence Paul Rabinow's uneasy joke that the methods advocated in *Writing Culture* are best carried out by professors with tenure.[23]

Herein lies the nub of anthropology's dilemma. *Writing Culture* can only offer a subjective counterpart to scientific objectivity; and its failure to make an effective connection between individual subject and social object is reflected both in the lives of most professional anthropologists and in the British school's post-colonial split between culture and history. If the discipline is to reinvent itself as a project in the late twentieth century, it has to find new ways of integrating individual creativity with social life.

This imperative was recognized as early as 1967 by Edmund Leach. In his Reith Lectures, *A Runaway World?* (1968), Leach argued that contemporary culture was incapable of responding adequately to the pace of change in the modern world. He recognized the central problem to be the dialectical relationship between thinking and doing, ideas and social context, intellectuals and the lay public; and he developed a devastating critique of the prevailing ethos of scientific detachment which fixed thought outside the movement of social life. Against the search for moral absolutes sustained by the mental habit of separation and division, Leach advocated ethical engagement with a complex world whose most salient feature was the interconnectedness of people and things. Thus, instead of opposing a subjective idealism to scientific objectivism, Leach pointed the way towards an intellectual practice based on the integration of subject and object as a single living whole.

Although Leach did not present his Reith Lectures as an explicit commentary on anthropology, they clearly were relevant to the methodological confusion which was endemic in the discipline at the time.[24] *A Runaway World?* was something of a *succès de scandale*, provoking much discussion among its public radio audience; but the lectures were largely ignored by the profession. The British school was not ready to examine the roots of scientific ethnography in the 1960s; and even less was it willing to conflate the discipline's problems with the general shortcomings of intellectuals in modern society. Moreover, Leach himself later turned away from his radical vision and embraced a version of structuralism founded on the same Cartesian divisions which *A Runaway World?* had disparaged.[25]

Perhaps anthropologists today would be more likely to acknowledge themselves as 'petrified observers of a runaway world'.[26] Established forms, both concepts and practices, no longer seem adequate for engaging with the shifting complexity of contemporary society. But the uncertainties which beset the discipline are a reflection of the much wider crisis facing intellectuals in the late twentieth century, a crisis which is particularly acute for anthropology. For, from the beginning of the modern phase, anthropologists have straddled a divide between a commitment to engaging directly with people in society and a desire to find acceptance within established structures of academic bureaucracy. Over the course of the last half-century the balance between these two sides of the project has shifted decisively towards the second; and, as a consequence, the new and radical impulse which inspired modern anthropology has been slowly dissipated.

The mistake of Clifford and Marcus lay in supposing that anthropologists' problems could be fixed by drawing on the existing repertoire of forms available to intellectuals (forms with a strong literary bias), without altering their relationship to society. But anthropology as a project will not be saved by formal innovation alone, by literary devices dreamt up by isolated intellectuals in the seclusion of their studies. Rather, its renewal depends upon a more active, dialectical relationship with society. New forms will emerge in the context of that engagement, reflecting the dynamic of the modern world itself.

In particular, anthropology needs to discover a new notion of science, one which integrates the subject–object pair rather than being opposed to art and human creativity. This is the impulse of our age. For while people everywhere are seeking to break down the existing social categories which have fragmented and confined their lives, stifling their individuality, so too are they urgently seeking more effective knowledge of the world at large. Anthropologists have no privileged perspective on that world; but we can and should seek to incorporate into our work an expanded conception of humanity appropriate to our age. Then perhaps anthropology will be a means of building bridges between the infinite particularity of individual existence and the emergent expression of human unity and social interdependence.

NOTES

1 Haddon (1905) coined the distinction between the old 'armchair' anthropology and a new one based on 'fieldwork'.

2 By 'intellectuals' we mean the broad class of professionals who live by selling their specialized knowledge, not just the guardians of high culture. The freethinking individual was the hero of the early modern age; but the intellectual role in our society has been transformed by bureaucracy and mass communications.

3 Trinh Minh-ha (1989: 67–8).

4 We were both educated at Cambridge, being supervised for our doctorates by Edmund Leach and Jack Goody respectively. We now teach anthropology at Manchester and Cambridge Universities. Our approach owes a great deal to C.L.R. James, whose *American Civilisation* (ed. Grimshaw and Hart, 1993) we edited together. James's critique of modern intellectuals in that volume underlies much of what we say here. A wide range of James's writings may be found in *The C.L.R. James Reader*, ed. A. Grimshaw (James, 1992).

5 Evans-Pritchard (1962).

6 This was the basis of Keith Hart's speech proposing the motion 'Social Anthropology is a Generalizing Science or it is Nothing' in the first meeting of the Group for Debates in Anthropological Theory (Ingold (ed.) 1989). The motion was defeated. Boas claimed to have been formed politically by the revolutions of 1848 and Rivers was adopted as a Labour candidate for Parliament; for both of them anthropological science served democracy.

7 The paradigmatic texts were Malinowski (1922) and Evans-Pritchard (1940a).

8 See Malinowski's *A Diary in the Strict Sense of the Term* (1967). Clifford (1988: ch. 1) offers an elegant deconstruction of the ethnographic authority which Malinowski strove so successfully to attach to himself.

9 Kuper (1988) offers a recent critique.

10 Kuklick's (1992) history of British social anthropology up to 1945 makes much of the state's influence on the discipline's theoretical outlook.

11 Geertz (1973, 1988).

12 Clifford and Marcus (1986), following Wallerstein (1974).

13 Pool, 1991; Ulin, 1991; Kuper (1993); Spencer (1989).

14 See Okely 1975, 1989; Okely and Callaway, 1992.

15 Shortly to be published in the United States by Pilgrim Press, the book is now distributed by Prickly Pear Press, 6 Clare Street, Cambridge CB4 3BY, United Kingdom.

16 Malinowski (1945) and Mair (ed.) (1938).

17 Evans-Pritchard's monographs on the Anuak (1940b) and the Sanusi of Cyrenaica (1949) as well as his later essays (1962); Firth (1939, 1951, 1959).

18 See the essays by Gluckman and Mitchell in Southall (ed.) (1960) *Social Change in Modern Africa*, London: Oxford UP.

19 Neo-evolutionism took the successive forms of Modernization, Marxism and Development, culminating in the sort of Grand History practised by Goody (see note 21), Macfarlane (1978) and Gellner (1988). See also Hart (1982).

20 At first this stream was informed by Lévi-Strauss's structuralism; but from the 1970s the dominant focus has been on symbolic or interpretive anthropology, emphasizing the individual subject as an actor in particular cultural settings.

21 Goody moved from African history (1971) to global comparison, always with a strong historical or evolutionary slant (1976 and many subsequent volumes); Geertz (see note 11 above) has been a more influential source for cultural anthropology in Britain than the nearest home contenders, such as Douglas.

22 This is a pervasive theme of James's work (e.g. Grimshaw and Hart, 1993).

23 Rabinow (1986) and Clifford (1988: 21n).

24 Leach (1954, 1961) had already attacked the narrow empiricism of scientific ethnography in his earlier work.

25 Especially in his textbook, *Culture and Communication* (Leach 1975).

26 See two contrasting essays on the Reith Lectures by Grimshaw (1989–90) and Strathern (1989–90) in a special edition of *Cambridge Anthropology* commemorating Leach.

BIBLIOGRAPHY

Clifford, J. (1988) *The Predicament of Culture*, Cambridge, Mass.: Harvard UP.
Clifford, J. and G. Marcus (eds) (1986) *Writing Culture*, Berkeley: University of California Press.
Evans-Pritchard, E.E. (1940a) *The Nuer*, Oxford: Clarendon.
—— (1940b) *The Political System of the Anuak*, London: London School of Economics and Political Science.
—— (1949) *The Sanusi of Cyrenaica*, London: Oxford UP.
—— (1962) 'Anthropology and history' in *Essays in Social Anthropology*, London: Routledge.
Firth, R. (1939) *Primitive Polynesian Economy*, London: Routledge.
—— (1951) *Elements of Social Organisation*, London: Watts.
—— (1959) *Social Change in Tikopia*, London: Allen & Unwin.
Fortes, M. and E.E. Evans-Pritchard (1940) *African Political Systems*, London: Oxford UP.
Frazer, J.G. (1890) *The Golden Bough*, London: Macmillan.
Gardner, K. (1991) *Songs At The River's Edge*, London: Virago.
Geertz, C. (1973) *The Interpretation of Culture*, Chicago: Chicago UP.
—— (1988) *Works and Lives*, Oxford: Polity.
Gellner, E. (1988) *Plough, Sword and Book*, London: Harper Collins.
Gluckman, M. (1960) 'Anthropological problems arising from the African industrial revolution' in A. Southall (ed.) *Social Change in Modern Africa*, London: Oxford UP.
Goody, J. (1971) *Technology, Tradition and the State*, London: Oxford UP.
—— (1976) *Production and Reproduction*, Cambridge: Cambridge UP.
Grimshaw, A. (1989–90) 'A runaway world? Anthropology as public debate', *Cambridge Anthropology*, 13, 3.
—— (1992) *Servants of the Buddha*, London: Open Letters.
Grimshaw, A. and K. Hart (1993) *Anthropology and the Crisis of the Intellectuals*, Cambridge: Prickly Pear pamphlet no. 1.
Haddon, A.C. (1905) 'Presidential address to section H of the British Association for the Advancement of Science', *Reports of the British Association for the Advancement of Science*, 75: 512.
—— (1910) *History of Anthropology*, London: Watts.
Hart, K. (1982) *The Political Economy of West African Agriculture*, Cambridge: Cambridge UP.
Ingold, T. (ed.) (1989) *Social Anthropology is a Generalising Science or it is Nothing*, Manchester: Group for Debate in Anthropological Theory.
James, C.L.R. (1992) *The C.L.R. James Reader*, Oxford: Blackwell.
—— (1993) *American Civilisation*, ed. A. Grimshaw and K. Hart, Oxford: Blackwell.

Kuklick, H. (1991) *The Savage Within*, Cambridge: Cambridge UP.

Kuper, A. (1988) *The Invention of Primitive Society*, London: Routledge.

—— (1993) 'Postmodernism, Cambridge and the great Kalahari debate', *Social Anthropology*, 1, 1A.

Leach, E.R. (1954) *Political Systems of Highland Burma*, London: G. Bell.

—— (1961) *Rethinking Anthropology*, London: Athlone.

—— (1968) *A Runaway World?* London: BBC..

—— (1975) *Culture and Communication*, Cambridge: Cambridge UP.

Macfarlane, A. (1978) *The Origins of English Individualism*, Cambridge: Cambridge UP.

Mair, L. (ed.) (1938) *Methods of Study of Culture Contact in Africa*, London: International African Institute.

Malinowski, B. (1922) *Argonauts of the Western Pacific*, London: Routledge.

—— (1945) *The Dynamics of Culture Change*, New Haven: Yale UP.

—— (1967) *A Diary in the Strict Sense of the Term*, London: Routledge.

Minh-ha, T. (1989) *Woman, Native, Other*, Bloomington: Indiana UP.

Mitchell, J.C. (1960) 'Social change and the stability of African marriage in Northern Rhodesia' in A. Southall (ed.) *Social Change in Modern Africa*, London: Oxford UP.

Moore, H. (1985) *Space, Text and Gender*, Cambridge: Cambridge UP.

Okely, J. (1975) 'The Self and Scientism', *Journal of the Anthropological Society of Oxford*, 6, 3.

—— (1989) *Simone de Beauvoir*, London: Virago.

Okely, J. and H. Callaway (eds) (1992) *Anthropology and Autobiography*, London: Routledge.

Pool, R. (1991) 'Postmodern Ethnography?' *Critique of Anthropology*, 11, 4.

Rabinow, P. (1986) 'Representations are social facts: modernity and post-modernity in anthropology' in J. Clifford and G. Marcus (eds) *Writing Culture*, Berkeley: University of California Press.

Sangren, P.S. 'Rhetoric and the authority of ethnography: 'postmodernism' and the social reproduction of texts', *Current Anthropology*, 29, 3.

Scholte, B. (1987) 'The literary turn in contemporary anthropology', *Critique of Anthropology*, 7, 1.

Spencer, J. (1989) 'Anthropology as a kind of writing', *Man* (n.s.) 24.

Strathern, M. (1987) 'Out of context: the persuasive fictions of anthropology', *Current Anthropology*, 28.

—— (1988) *The Gender of the Gift*, Berkeley: University of California Press.

—— (1989–90) 'Stopping the world: Elmdon and the Reith lectures', *Cambridge Anthropology*, 13, 3.

Ulin, R.C. (1991) 'Critical anthropology twenty years later', *Critique of Anthropology*, 11, 1.

Wallerstein, I. (1974) *The Modern World System*, New York and London: Academic Press.

Watson, H. (1992) *Women in the City of the Dead*, London: Hurst.

CHAPTER 3

Anthropology: Still the Uncomfortable Discipline?
Susan Wright

I have taken my title from Firth's (1981) article which surveys the history of applying anthropology to practical problems from the 1930s to 1970s. My aim in this chapter is to ask how, in the subsequent period from the late 1970s to early 1990s, has anthropological work in policy and practice developed in relation to the rest of the discipline and in relation to changes in the wider political context within which we are working? What does this suggest for future developments in anthropology? And if anthropology is still to be called an 'uncomfortable discipline', would it be for the reasons attributed by Firth for the earlier period?

Firth concluded his article:

> We need to focus our work more on social problems, and on communication with those already engaged on such problems, as well as with the general public.
>
> But the very nature of anthropology as an inquisitive, challenging, uncomfortable discipline, questioning established positions and proclaimed values, peering into underlying interests, and if not destroying fictions and empty phrases . . . at least exposing them – all this poses difficulty for its application to practical problems (Firth, 1981: 200).

He argued that the strength of anthropology is in description and analysis. Anthropology can explore paradoxes; it can expose contradictions, conflicts of interest, and verbal smokescreens: it is an uncomfortable discipline. Firth agreed with Malinowski that anthropologists 'have the right and duty to formulate their conclusions in a way in which they can be seriously considered by those who frame policy and carry it out' (ibid.: 195). But, Firth argued, anthropologists should not become involved in framing and implementing solutions – making decisions and handling practical affairs are outside our competence (ibid.). Making suggestions about how to get people to change their behaviour he considered 'chancy', and where politics are dominant, protest may alienate the anthropologist from influence of any kind. The ability to analyse, describe and trace out possibly unpalatable findings relies on distance. He sets out his position:

> My own reaction to problems of applied anthropology has not been one of detachment. But it has been one of engagement rather than commitment – a conviction of the importance of problems rather than an assurance as to the nature of the solutions or of my own role in relation to them (ibid.: 196).

While I agree that one of the great strengths of anthropology is in analysing situations, developing concepts and exposing contradictions, Firth's account raises issues about the way anthropologists position themselves in relation to their 'subjects' and in relation to the policy and institutional context within which they are working. It provokes the question whether the 'distance' needed for critical academic analysis also implies distance from political processes. Is it still possible or acceptable to think of anthropologists hovering hesitatingly in some neutral space at the edge of or above politics and the handling of practical affairs? On the issues of distance, commitment and politics there have been considerable changes in the last 15 years. Partly these arise from changes in the institutionalized structure of the discipline, with the development of a strong organization for anthropologists involved in policy and practice. Partly they arise from changes in the way anthropologists conceptualize the field of research and their location within it; and partly they come from changes in the state in Britain and its relation with academics. I will argue that it is important for the mainstream of the discipline of anthropology not to marginalize involvement in practical affairs but to examine theoretical issues arising from 'engagement' rather than 'commitment', and in doing so to address politically contentious issues.

CHANGING INSTITUTIONALIZATION OF THE PURE AND APPLIED DIVIDE

Firth's distinctions between 'detached', 'engaged' and 'committed' anthropology betray a continuing professional concern with boundary maintenance between pure and applied anthropology. Since the early years of the discipline a divide has been established between a 'pure' centre to the discipline and an 'applied' penumbra around it.[1] There is also a third category, that of 'no longer anthropologist' in which a person, however well trained in anthropology, is deemed to be too much involved in policy or administration and loses the designation 'anthropologist'. Precisely where the boundaries are drawn between these three categories varies. In Firth's terms it is proper for (pure) anthropologists to 'engage' with pressing issues of the day, but anthropologists should not cross from description and analysis into saying what is the solution, or becoming the person who administers decisions. Similarly, new university departments of social anthropology gave colonial administrators a training in the discipline but they did not become 'anthropologists': anthropology was a skill for them to apply. Grillo draws the boundaries differently. He refers to the pure and applied divide and in place of the latter details nine kinds of 'practical anthropological activity'. This includes participating in policy formation as a policy professional, which in other formulations is placed in the 'no longer anthropologist' category (1985: 6–7). In the United States the categorization and labelling is more standardized. First are the unmarked (pure) academic anthropologists. 'Applied' anthropologists are also employed in universities but undertaking contract research. Those who have an anthropological training but are employed in firms or agencies, and who are the 'no longer' category in Britain, are called 'practising anthropologists' in the United States (van Willigen, 1987: 1).

In Britain the boundary around 'pure' anthropology was institutionalized through the conditions for membership of the professional body, the Association of Social Anthropologists. Firth (1986) explains that the ASA was formed to promote 'a new order in anthropology' infused with the social theory of Malinowski and Radcliffe-Brown (as against the wider range of branches of anthropology represented by the Royal Anthropological Institute). Membership was by invitation and unanimous approval of the members, and the Association's particular concern was to influence 'the creation of new teaching posts and appointment of research workers' (ibid.: 5). Grillo records Leach's view that the original role of the ASA in 1946 was to 'prevent the Universities from employing unqualified refugees from the disappearing Colonial Service to teach "applied anthropology"' (1984: 310). Until 1983 membership was restricted to those in Commonwealth universities with a postgraduate degree in anthropology and a teaching or a research appointment. 'Application' was marginalized and others, the 'no longer' category, were sloughed off.

In the early 1980s this institutional boundary came under pressure. As the expansion of the university sector came to an end, anthropologists with doctorates were far in excess of the number required to reproduce the departments. They began to find ways to use their anthropology in employment outside the universities. There was reluctance to lose their anthropological identity, but there was no institutionalized way of keeping in contact with the discipline. A very few university-based anthropologists saw employment prospects of graduates outside the academy as a matter of professional concern. Other members of the ASA 'strongly dissented' from this view (ASA, 1983: 10). Those academics, led by Paul Stirling, who were concerned about the future employment of their graduate students and some anthropologists who were working outside universities came together when the United States-based Society for Applied Anthropology held its 1981 annual meeting in Edinburgh. Initially the name Applied Anthropology Group was mooted but at a well-attended follow-up meeting held at the Royal Anthropological Institute, the name Group for Anthropology in Policy and Practice (GAPP) was decided upon (Stirling and Wright, 1988). The name was chosen specifically to avoid the language of pure and applied, to indicate to people working in policy that they could retain an identity as anthropologists, and to point to the 'gap' that needed to be bridged between anthropologists working in universities and those working in other fields. Group rather than society or association was chosen to convey an accessible and unhierarchical ethos. Membership was open to anyone with a background or interest in anthropology. Nearly all had at least undergraduate and most had postgraduate qualifications in anthropology and were working outside the universities. GAPP had 150 members in two years.

GAPP had three aims: to create a network among anthropologists using their discipline in policy and practice; to make their experience available to students, faculty, and people in the public, private and voluntary sectors, thereby promoting the teaching and use of anthropology in policy and practice; and to provide training for students to help them use their anthropology in employment outside the academy (Stirling and Wright, 1988).

Immediately, GAPP started holding meetings to create networks of anthropologists working in similar areas and to inform students about the ways they used their anthropological knowledge and skills in employment. These anthropologists displayed an ability to enter a surprising range of fields and roles. Anthropological involvement in overseas development had withered in the 1950s and 1960s (Grillo, 1985: 16). Now anthropologists began the long haul of getting 'the social' taken into account in development procedures dominated by economic and technical paradigms. There was an equally strong commitment to using an anthropological perspective to make real contributions to the operation of the welfare state and to the direction of cultural, political, social and economic transformations in the United Kingdom (Donnan and MacFarlane, 1989: 2). Whether in the United Kingdom or in overseas work, relatively few had permanent employment, for example in consulting firms, community work, journalism, health or housing authorities. Most were building a career out of a sequence of short-term contracts from the public and voluntary/NGO (non-governmental) sectors and consultancies. The roles varied from training in multicultural awareness, evaluating projects, researching different perceptions of a problem for an agency (especially when 'people' were not reacting to a policy in the expected way), making needs assessments and acting as advocates. Whether in Britain or overseas, they tended to be located in the disjunctures between the state and the people or between management and workers.

Through the late 1980s regular GAPP Talks were held four times a term in London.[2] People in fields as wide apart as gender planning, rapid rural appraisal, disaster relief, financial institutions, drama therapy and various aspects of health care explained to a mainly student audience how they used their anthropology and what additional skills they had needed to acquire in their work. Major conferences were held on Information Technology (1987), Ethnography of the North of England (1988), Tourism (1988), Organizations (1990 and 1991) and Participatory Development (1992).[3] These not only brought together the latest work by scattered and isolated anthropologists, but also, sometimes successfully, demonstrated the benefits of their perspectives to non-anthropologist practitioners in the field.

From its inception, GAPP also experimented with workshops simulating the conditions for working in overseas development, industry, and the public and voluntary sectors in Britain. They were facilitated by anthropologists employed in the actual projects on which the modules were based. Four one-day workshops were held in different parts of the country. A working party of the ASA with nominees of the Royal Anthropological Institute (RAI), GAPP and coopted experts, produced a report on the curriculum changes needed to equip postgraduates for employment outside the academy (Grillo, 1984). This report endorsed and lent authority to GAPP's training methods and recommended they be developed into a week-long Vocational Practice in Anthropology course. This received Social Science Research Council funding and was held in 1985. Training on ethical issues, of pressing concern in this new context, was helped by the production of guidelines by the ASA (Akeroyd, 1987). While the ethical guidelines were used by departments, the ideas and methods developed in the GAPP Vocational Training Course in 1985 were not adopted into university curricula.

In the late 1980s, the production of anthropology graduates went from boom to bust. Reductions in research funding generated a fear that there would be insufficient doctorates for university departments to reproduce themselves, let alone be available for other employment.[4] However, GAPP continued with its networking and training so as not to lose the experience of the last generation of students in gaining employment outside the academy. There was a danger that by the time of the next boom, their tracks would have grown over and a new set of graduates would have to start at the machete stage again. At the same time, the Economic and Social Research Council (ESRC)'s Collaborative Awards in the Social Sciences, which funded doctoral projects linking university departments with outside organizations, opened up new areas of work on housing, social services, and especially care in the community. MAs were also now available in the Anthropology of Development, Health, Community Work and Tourism. However, postgraduate training still did not equip students with the additional skills needed for work in policy and practice. Therefore from 1989 GAPP established the Vocational Practice Course with a distinctive pedagogy and agenda: learning experientially from simulations of real projects, working in teams, assessing the time, resources and costs involved, deciding on research strategies and methods of data collection and analysis (including using computers), presenting results in oral and written reports, and assessing ethical and policy issues (Mascarenhas-Keyes, 1989). Under the leadership of Stella Mascarenhas-Keyes, this became an annual event with ESRC support and sponsorship of places by the ASA. The course became highly regarded and most departments regularly sent their students as part of their postgraduate training. In the 1990s, reflecting the changing labour market, some of the course content and students have been drawn from other European countries.

Another feature of the 1980s was a proliferation of organiza-tions concerned with anthropology in practice. Although GAPP was a generic organization and had already held a meeting discussing community work, the ASA working party recommended setting up a separate organization for anthropologists in social and community work (Grillo, 1994). This led to the formation of SASCW (Social Anthropology: Social and Community Work) and a series of meetings mainly exploring anti-racism, concepts of community, and especially care in the community. A new Anthropology Training and Education (ATE) group formed out of an RAI committee on that topic. The British Medical Anthropology Society (BMAS) which had formed in 1976 was joined by a new Anthropology and Nursing Association (ANA).

In 1988 with the help of grants from the Wenner-Gren Foundation, the different applied anthropology organizations, GAPP, Social and Community Work (SASCW) and Anthropology, Training and Education (ATE), but unfortunately not the medical and nursing associations, BMAS or ANA, came together as the British Association for Social Anthropology in Policy and Practice (BASAPP) (Lloyd, 1988). The aims of BASAPP were to network the overlapping memberships of the various organizations, and to employ a part-time administrator to produce a membership register and a high quality newsletter, later called *Anthropology In Action*, three times a year. As intended, this streamlining of the administration released the energy of the organizers for more activities. In addition, BASAPP made international links, both in Europe and through helping to set up an International Commission on Anthropology in Policy and Practice (under the auspices of the International Union of Anthropological and Ethnographic Sciences (IUAES)). Reflecting a shift from its British focus, in December 1993 BASAPP was renamed Anthropology in Action.

By the early 1990s Anthropology in Action was securely established. It was solvent, and the newsletter was turned into a journal which looked professional and raised challenging issues. The committee worked well, with smooth transitions from one convenor to the next and an annual influx of young and energetic committee members. At least four major events were held each year on different fields of policy and practice including an annual meeting attracting 40–60 members. Anthropologists from both the 'applied' and 'no longer' categories were able to retain their identity and connections with the discipline in a recognized institution alongside the 'professional' Association of Social Anthropologists. In 1983 the ASA widened its definition of 'professional' anthropologists to include some using their anthropology in 'non-academic employment' and those who were 'unavoidably unemployed' a year after completing their training (ASA,

1983: 12). Although there was some overlap in committee membership to facilitate communication between the two organizations,[5] they still had very different memberships and interests. In 1991 Anthropology in Action/BASAPP had 308 members, of whom only 21 per cent also appeared in the ASA register for 1992 (Grillo, 1994: 311). In 1993 out of 361 ASA members with UK addresses 204 were in departments of anthropology or sociology, 76 were in other university departments, and only 81 (22 per cent) gave non-university addresses (some of these were retired faculty). The discreteness of the memberships could either indicate a sensible division of labour between the ASA and Anthropology in Action, or that the discipline was still quite clearly divided.

Although relations between the two wings of the discipline were much improved, a sense of hierarchy persisted between them, based on the evaluative connotations of pure and applied. Grillo, in his review in the mid-1980s, discerned a 'persistent distinction between research which is applied, practical or engaged and that which is pure, abstract and theoretical' (Grillo, 1985: 8). The remark of Malinowski to Mair continued to be quoted, that applied anthropology is 'an occupation for the half baked' (Mair, 1969: 8). 'Pure' still implied pure theory, pure intellect, and (a spurious) moral and political purity, whereas 'applied' was assumed to be not only less demanding but tainted. Moreover, as Donnan and MacFarlane said in their review of applied research in Northern Ireland, there was still a feeling that this kind of work was parasitical on the theories of the discipline (1989: 13). This point reveals how the division was impeding the intellectual development of the discipline. Discussions in BASAPP had begun to identify issues which were arising from the new anthropological work in policy and practice that pertained to the theoretical core of the discipline. However the separate memberships and perceived differences in the cultures of the two organizations meant that, apart from a few individuals who spanned the gap, there were not the necessary institutional mechanisms for an intellectual interchange.

Rather than thinking of applied as a 'polluting drain' on the 'pure' theoretical core, it is time to extend the plumbing metaphor. The introduction of a feedback mechanism between the two sides of the discipline would enable ideas to flow in a circuit so that the pure/applied distinction can be dissolved. This aims for theoretical issues arising in policy and practice to influence the agenda of work in universities. A current issue on which anthropologists involved in practical work are trying to develop a sharper theoretical analysis is the context within which policy is formulated and of the discourses through which power and knowledge are articulated (Shore and Jöhncke, 1992). University-based research on discourse, knowledge and power in a policy context would advance our understanding of these central theoretical concepts in the discipline. In return, this theoretical work would assist those anthropologists who raised the issue because they are trying to be more critically aware of the terms through which they intervene in policy-making and practice. Institutional mechanisms are needed if theoretical issues arising from practical work are to enter university research agendas and if in return their development of ideas is to influence practice.[6] Such exchange would enable anthropologists to dissolve the pure and applied divide and to consider themselves part of the discipline 'as a whole'.

FROM 'STUDYING DOWN' AND A DISTANCED STUDY OF 'A PEOPLE' . . .

This expansion of anthropological work in the 1970s and 1980s coincided with widespread methodological and ethical debates in the discipline. These concerned the appropriate unit of research, the location of the researcher in the study, and questions about the politics of knowledge production. This section traces the transformation of anthropology in all three of these respects during the last two decades. Parallel debates went on among university-based and practising anthropologists. Firth's distinctions began to be dismantled, making anthropology more committed and beginning to dissolve the divide between pure and applied. The most tangible, but not the only outcome was a refocusing of the unit of study from a distanced study of 'a people' to a committed study of 'policy'.

From the 1960s there was a criticism of early modern anthropology in the discipline as a whole for taking its unit of study as 'a people', a bounded entity, dislocated from historical context and wider economic, social and political systems, with attitudes and behaviour generalized into homogeneity. Even after anthropologists had begun to conceptualize 'people' in a wider context, this way of thinking continued to inform much policy-making. It was built into contracts asking 'What do the people need?' or "What is the view of the community?' My account of a parish (Wright *et al.*, 1980) which stressed the great variety of backgrounds, perceptions, problems and ideas of the residents, with hardly any informal day-to-day contact let alone formal arenas for exchanging ideas, was received by a seminar of senior local government officials with 'That's no use, we can't do anything if a village doesn't have a view.' Similarly, in a hamlet with a highly polluted and unreliable water supply, but where there was no consensus among residents about the causes or possible solutions, the council refused to act as the community 'did not have a view' (Wright, 1992). Admittedly these examples are both from Britain where the idea that a homogeneous 'people' is essential for administration is heightened by imagery of 'community'. Moreover, these examples date from the time when public administration was concerned with 'collective' (generalized) solutions for 'groups' (really categories), before Thatcherism swung to the other extreme with an emphasis on 'the individual'. However, in the Third World anthropologists were having to be equally careful not to accept such homogenizing questions at face value and at least to discriminate the different experiences and interests of men and women, young and old, richer and poorer.

However nuanced the account, this kind of contract positioned the anthropologist in a disjuncture between administrative powerholders and marginalized people. If anthropologists 'should invariably be on the side of the planned for and the administered, i.e. the people' (Donnan and MacFarlane, 1989: 5), such a contract offered the opportunity to act as mediator or advocate. However, these roles and this positioning in an administrative structure evoked a strong ethical debate. Was it 'right' to collect information on people who have been marginalized and to pass it up to those who administer and control them? Some argued that this was acceptable if the latter were well intentioned. Others replied that this was to support the very system which had made the people powerless and had caused their voices to carry no weight, a relation of domination which would not be dinted by giving powerholders more information.

This framing of the issue in terms of personal ethics echoed the concurrent debate about anthropologists under colonialism. Generalizations abounded, despite differences in colonial situations, periods and theoretical persuasions (Loizos, 1977). Arguments that anthropologists had connived with the colonial system of domination were countered by evidence that individual anthropologists had made themselves unpopular by lobbying for culturally sensitive and better-informed administration of 'their' people. James argued that they were moral (if not political) radicals (1973: 44–5). Moreover, she argued that they only claimed anthropology to be extremely useful when seeking funding for research access; when asked to give policy advice, they distanced themselves from the system by claiming freedom to pursue an objective science which produced general statements of no direct value to administrators (ibid.: 49). Grillo argued in a similar fashion that anthropology provided very little of value to colonialists, and that they distanced themselves from 'application' as that meant intervening in a society or culture on behalf of a system whose values they did not share or wish to sustain (1985: 16). This attempt to resolve a debate about personal probity in terms of research pragmatics in the colonial era had limited applicability for anthropologists in the 1980s who were committed to using their discipline to make an active contribution to overseas development or domestic policy.

In the USA the terms of a debate which also started with personal ethics were shifted to question the research paradigm. It was revealed that the State Department and the Pentagon had tried to recruit anthropologists and use anthropological knowledge for counter-insurgency in South America and South-East Asia. Gough (1968) and colleagues in *Current Anthropology* argued that anthropology's construction of the unit of research and of the location of the researcher within the study lent itself to this kind of manipulation. The study of communities which were as small, remote and pristine as possible, and their analysis in terms of very general concepts like 'culture contact', 'modernization' and 'social change', from which force, suffering and exploitation tended to disappear, did not aid our critical understanding of the international systems of domination in which they were located. They argued that the aim should not be to understand the organization of small-scale societies in isolation, but through them to understand the operation of national and international systems of capitalism and governance. Nor could the anthropologist pretend to stand outside those systems, claiming some neutral ground necessary for 'scientific objectivity': the construction of anthropological knowledge was located within systems of domination. To avoid manipulation, it should address those systems. Gough argued for conceptualizing localities within 'big systems' as a means of recapturing academic freedom of enquiry and action.

This debate often is regarded now, in Britain at least, as a moment of overheated excitement by a minority interest in the discipline that calmed down eventually and went away. However, a figure of the stature of Malinowski (1961)[1945] had argued for a similar change in the unit of research. When the Pax Britannica in Africa began to break down and a gulf opened up between the colonial administrators' claims of good faith in maintaining a just political order and the arguments of African nationalism, socialism and autonomous churches,

Malinowski argued for a widening of the anthropological unit of study, taking into account economic and imperial issues of Western rule,

> the whole range of European influences, interests, good intention, and predatory drives must become an essential part of the study of African culture change (Malinowski, quoted in James, 1973: 67).

It was no longer possible, he continued, to treat the situation as one 'well integrated whole', as the dynamism of the process was one-sided, with African people not given the instruments of physical power (guns, planes, poison gas), the instruments of political mastery or a share in economic wealth. To ignore this 'distorts the evidence, and this is a sin against science' (James, 1973: 68).

Asad agreed. By trying to make a value-free study of 'other cultures' without analysing the colonial system and the unequal world it represented, anthropological knowledge was 'malformed'.

> For any object which is subordinated and manipulated is partly the product of a power relationship, and to ignore this fact is to miscomprehend the nature of that object (1973: 18).

Asad pitched the 'colonial encounter' debate at a more conceptual and ideological level. He examined the imagery of politics and power in Western accounts of 'the other'. The partial imagery of *African Political Systems* (Fortes and Evans-Pritchard, 1940) presented small homogeneous tribal societies as integrated and ordered and did not include in the picture their subjection to colonial rule imposed by force. This he contrasted with the equally partial Orientalist images of Middle Eastern political systems as disrupting a wider Islamic society and therefore based on tyranny and arbitrary cruelty (rather than Islamic populism). Each of these images was consonant with the different colonial projects in the two areas. Asad argued that anthropology was rooted in the unequal power encounter between the West and the Third World, and the way anthropology chose its topics, defined its field and objectified its knowledge confirmed the powerful in their world. This argument has been taken much further by Said (1978). Whilst colonialism did not depend on anthropology, as J. Marcus says (1990: 5, 10), the discipline 'trafficked' in the images of 'the primitif other', the mirror to modernity, through which the West knew itself and justified its 'responsibility' to control and administer 'the other'. These images were therefore part of the mechanics of domination – even if anthropology did not invent them in the first place (Fox, 1991: 10).

The colonial critique and the debate in the United States about anthropology and imperialism were both read for their significance to the renewed British work in policy and practice. They not only changed the unit of study 'inventing a representation of a larger order' (G. Marcus, 1986: 173), but made central the concepts of domination, power and ideology. One new approach was to analyse Third World locations, especially those involved in commodity production, within an analytical framework of the historical development of world systems of capitalism. For example, Wolfe (1977) analysed Congo mining operations within world systems. Nash (1979) and Taussig (1980) studied cultural constructs and material conditions of Bolivian tin mines in the context of national and international political and economic processes. Mintz (1985) traced different facets of the sugar industry.

Some anthropologists used this approach to try and reverse the traditional relations in the production of anthropological knowledge. Gedicks (1979) aimed to make available to residents an understanding of links between international mining corporations' operations in South America and their impoverishment of mining communities in the USA. Huizer (1979), taking 'a view from below and within', derived his agenda from peasants and did research on the landowners and administrators, giving the results to the peasants to use in their strategies to improve their conditions. This he called participatory or liberation anthropology. Schrijvers (1989), in a dialogic approach, developed a critical understanding of gender ideology whilst enabling poor Sri Lankan women to determine and organize ways to earn an income more regularly and autonomously and gain respect. Her approach first focused on change, and, second, involved establishing a dialogue or exchange of ideas which relied on acute awareness of inequalities which otherwise inhibited the researcher from taking on the perspective of less powerful people. Third, it entailed sharing the power to define the objectives, analytical concepts and outcomes of the research. It was easier to achieve a dialogic relationship with farmers, as it was the researcher who was committed to conceding power, than with bureaucrats who do not readily concede the power to define. Feminists have continued through the 1980s to integrate a critical approach to knowledge production with action. In a way akin to Harding's (1987: 184) 'standpoint research' and Mies' 'conscious partiality' (1983), Schrijvers argues that in each research situation it is necessary to choose for whom, through whom, and how the research is being done, and what changes you want to support with knowledge (1993:

38). This recognizes that the anthropologist is participating in, in order to analyse, a system of domination, and can no longer rely on a rational, objectifying gaze from some supposedly apolitical position outside society and free of power (J. Marcus, 1990: 12). Once the 'objective scientific' status of anthropology is questioned by the recognition that all research is located within systems of domination, and that no knowledge is 'pure' in the sense of 'free of power', the distinction between pure and applied is unsustainable.

... TO 'STUDYING UP' AND A COMMITTED STUDY OF 'POLICY'

A second response to the debates about the role and conduct of anthropology was to turn attention from the Third World and to 'study up'. That is, to study people in First World industrial organizations, state and international institutions who are more powerful than the anthropologist, and through whose actions systems of domination are maintained. This shifted the subject of study from a dominated 'people', and a strand of anthropology in the United States and Britain explored different ways of conceptualizing and analysing organizations (Britan and Cohen, 1980; Wright, 1994). As Donnan and MacFarlane say, through

> analysing the cultures of the policy professional, in penetrating and uncovering the perceptions of those who seek to make their definitions of the world and its problems stick (1989: 6).

anthropology itself became a policy science.

One problem was a tendency to treat organizations as bounded entities and lose sight again of the processes of domination in which they were involved. Nader (1980) proposed a solution which connected 'people' and 'policy' through what she called 'the vertical slice'. For example, starting with children in the United States, instead of just concentrating on families as the site of child development, she traced the hidden hierarchies of industry and government which shaped their food, health and housing:

> corporations feed our children, clothe our children, and help determine their genetic legacy. The important link is between the child and General Foods, Gerber, and Beech Nut, as well as the Food and Drugs administration. These are but facets of the hidden hierarchies (1980: 37).

Nader had an avowedly political agenda. How could democracy work if people in the First World knew so little about organizations affecting their daily lives and if they had so little ability to cope with their manipulation? (1972: 294). This research studied 'the culture of power' (ibid.: 289), the ways these hierarchies remained hidden, their distancing mechanisms, the cultural constraints members of organizations felt in dealing with the public, and the ways clients were manipulated.

The 'vertical slice' was particularly useful when anthropologists were asked to reconceptualize a field, which, as Donnan and MacFarlane say, was one of the roles anthropologists played in the 1980s. Nader used it to rethink what was involved in child policy. I was asked to rethink 'rural policy' in Britain, and to bring all the relevant agencies between selected rural communities and central government into the analysis in order to see whether processes of decision-making at the 'top' or 'middle' were causes of, rather than solutions to some of the problems 'on the ground' (Wright, 1984). Only a minor component of a vertical slice was the social organization of face to face communities – the traditional ethnographic 'people'. It involved multi-site ethnography and traced policy connections between different organizational and everyday worlds, even if the actors did not know each other.

A similar methodology was proposed in overseas development by focusing on a 'policy or programme community'. That is, an intervention was evaluated by studying all the people and organizations involved in the development – the international aid agency, international NGOs, state institutions, local organizations, programme staff and various categories of local residents. The 'world view' of each of these is explored so as to identify their different understandings of 'the problem' and how to solve it. While fracturing 'reality' into a 'prism of perceptions' (Salisbury, 1977), the aim is not, as in some 'postmodern' texts, to produce a bricolage of interpretations as multiple and open-ended alternatives, offering spurious equality to disenfranchised voices (J. Marcus, 1990). This 'policy community' is not a rhetorical but a political space. The point is to examine how these differently situated discourses are contested: whether intended beneficiaries are able to define their own reality and influence the design of the intervention and its outcomes; or, as is more often the case, how despite the good intentions of their rhetoric (e.g. about empowerment and participation), certain voices have recourse to institutional power to make their definitions of the situation authoritative. In Asad's terms this means an 'authoritative discourse' is produced which, founded in material conditions, 'seeks continually to pre-empt the space of radically opposed utterances and so to prevent them from being uttered' (Asad, 1979: 621).

This kind of cultural critique, which exposes relations of power that are embedded in culture, can be deployed to evaluate development interventions without simply replicating the hierarchical assumptions of dominant voices and the structures of domination they encode. It is with the aim of not just considering the point of view of the dominated, but to analyse the process of domination, that anthropologists have been devising qualitative and interpretive indicators to assess development interventions. These indicators are interpretive in that they are embedded in the context of the social and cultural processes involved in a project. This contrasts with traditional methods of evaluation based on products of development rather than processes of intervention. Interpretive indicators can be quantitative as well as descriptive; but they are not measurements which are 'objective' in the sense of dissociated from the development process and collected by a detached scientist (Marsden and Oakley, 1990).

This is the theoretical framework which I adapted to a British context when asked to evaluate the corporate strategy of a council which aimed to tackle social effects of high levels of unemployment by becoming an 'enabling state' through empowerment and community development (Wright, 1991/2). The policy community extended from intended beneficiaries (residents in 'action areas' and especially unemployed people), to field staff, middle-tier officers, senior officers and politicians of the council. Also included was a study of central government discourse, as it was in response to the Thatcherite 'individual' whose freedom was to be achieved through 'rolling back state' that this Labour-controlled council was attempting to muster a defence of public services through a resurrected metaphor of community.

A prism of perceptions has also been taken by a number of members of Anthropology in Action on the central government policy for 'Care in the Community'. These researchers have been differently situated within the policy community, studying aspects of the de-institutionalization of care for people who are elderly, have disabilities or learning difficulties. Cohen has studied legal aspects of the pseudo-market between service providers and purchasers; for a national voluntary organization Collins (1992, 1993) evaluated the way the management of closure of long-stay institutions and the changes to established ways of working affected people with learning difficulties; Dalley, after analysing gendered concepts of community involved in the policies (1988), engaged with bureaucratic procedures to implement the policy by working for a health authority; Lloyd

(1993; 1994) studied whether different kinds of care for the elderly in rural areas were empowering, and questioned to what extent residents in sheltered housing organized themselves as a community: Meethan (1995) monitored procedures for determining packages of care for individuals and attempts by different service agencies to collaborate with each other and with voluntary sector and informal carers; McCourt-Perring (1994) studied the effect of closing a psychiatric hospital in order to understand in which respects 'patients' were or were not freed from institutionalization when they became 'residents' of community homes. Policy studies such as these raise three questions pertaining to the theoretical core of the discipline.

First is the need to problematize 'policy'. This is a major institution of Western and international governance, on a par with other ideological and politicized concepts like 'family' and 'society', yet one which has received scant attention from anthropologists. 'Policy' can refer to three different aspects of institutions: a written statement of a problem and how it is to be ameliorated; unwritten assumptions and images of policy professionals about 'the people' and 'the problem' which inform their actions but may differ from the written statement; and procedures followed by street-level (and field-level) bureaucrats (Lipsky, 1980) whose detail may produce results very different from those intended in the written statements or the shared images of the policy professionals.

Apthorpe called written policy a 'mode of thinking-wording-willing' (1985: 91) and identified the characteristics of written policy as 'sloganic brevity, seemingly firm resolution, little if anything to do with either abstract theory or troublesome practice' (ibid.: 98–9). It rarely spells out what action is to be achieved or how it is to be assessed. However, written policy can also have the opposite characteristics. It can contain no briefly stated aims, but many proposals for action. It can rely for coherence on the second aspect of policy: the sharing among officers of unwritten anecdotes or metaphors for the kinds of social relations the policy should achieve. For example, in the council policy that I evaluated, the policy document had been written by officers from different departments and resembled a portmanteau of their different approaches to ideas of empowerment, decentralization and client-centred service delivery. The document contained several specific proposals for action but it lacked the sloganic brevity of an overall statement of intent. When it came to be implemented, different officers constructed different lists of policy aims from the document. Throughout the first year there was a debate about whether intended beneficiaries were only unemployed people or everyone in communities with high levels of unemployment. Many of those closely involved in the policy's formation shared an image of 'the people' and 'the problem' that the policy addressed in the form of an anecdote about an unemployed man. He sat in front of his television all day, too poor to go to the pub or club where his social and political contacts had been based, and he did not get involved in voluntary activities to improve his community whose physical fabric and social conditions deteriorated around him. In interviews, this anecdote was recited to explain that the aim of the policy was to mobilize the unemployed into community action, to 'take more control of their lives', reinvigorate local politics and defend public services in the process. (This image ignored the continuous involvement of women in community organizing in what were often highly gendered divisions of public spaces, contrary to the usual assumption of a division between male/public/political and female/private/domestic). This anecdote did not amount to a clear metaphor of the kind of social relations between people and with the local state that the council was trying to achieve. 'Community' had multiple referents. This made the policy weak as a means of contesting central government policies which were informed by a clear image of 'the individual'; and it meant that those who devised the policy did not have a shared imagery to mobilize officers throughout the council, let alone the public, in support of the policy. In evaluating the policy it was therefore important to resurrect and record the original cluster of ideas and to document how they had been changed. This became the main critical analysis of the political culture of the authority (Wright, 1991/2, paper 2). It revealed a disjuncture between the senior officers and politicians who lost sight of the policy's aims, and the increasingly isolated 'street-level' community action teams whose practices continued to be in keeping with the original cluster of ideas.

Similar contradictory images of community and individual, of informal reciprocal networks and markets have been identified in discussions of Care in the Community (Lloyd, 1990). Fairclough (1985) has considered some aspects of the role of discourse in organizations. However, the style of written documents, the role of orally conferred anecdotes, how contradictory images are kept in play, the problems of constructing mobilizing metaphors or symbols of intended changes to social relations, and the discourse envisaging certain political actions and behaviour (and closing off others) have not been developed sufficiently in a critical analysis of 'policy' as an institution.

The second question raised by anthropological work on policy which has relevance to the discipline as a whole is the analysis of formal organizations and organizational change. Our speciality is still processes of organization informally articulated through communal relationships with overlapping kinship, economic, political and religious content supported by moral imperatives, rather than associative forms based on formal contract (Cohen, 1993: 83). It was in finding this 'informal' organization within formal institutional settings like workplaces and bureaucracies that anthropology made its first contribution to organizational studies (Wright, 1994). Bastide said we should analyse organizations as the 'old anthropology analysed kinship systems, economic and political institutions, spontaneous processes of change and with exactly the same techniques of approach' (1973: 180–1). However, new 'techniques of approach' have come from interpretive anthropology. No longer are organizations seen as having two separate spheres, the managers' rational systems of formal rules and procedures and the workers' informal (irrational) relationships. As Donnan and MacFarlane say,

> Out have gone the models of the world of the policy maker. . . . The formal rules or the organisational blueprints are not principles for actions, but are rather principles which people appeal to, or which people ignore or otherwise play with as practical exigencies dictate (1989: 9).

All aspects now tend to be viewed as part of continual processes of organizing, that is, processes by which people of every status in the organization use institutionally sited discourses within a policy field to negotiate meaning through symbols, stories and anecdotes.

Organizational studies attribute 'the culture concept' to anthropology. However, anthropology has to reassert its meaning of culture as an analytical concept derived initially from the kinds of organisation Cohen (above) described as communal. That is, as Street says, in his paper 'Culture is a Verb': 'culture is an active process of meaning making and contestation over definition, including of itself' (1993: 25). Borrowing from a distinction made by Smircich (1983: 347), there is a tendency in organizational studies to lose sight of culture as something an organization *is* and to treat culture as something an organization *has*. This can take the form of a checklist of characteristics of the old bounded entity. Culture then becomes a tool of management, trying to introduce a new set of preferred characteristics throughout the organization's operations.

A distinction between culture as a property of an organization, with the meanings of symbols defined by management, and culture as a continual process of negotiating meaning, often through contested symbols, has to be carefully made and reasserted by anthropologists. In the implementation of Care in the Community policies, both Dalley and Meethan identified that organization culture was being used by bureaucrats as an instrument for centralizing power whilst propounding a rhetoric of decentralization and empowerment of clients (Fleming, 1993: 4–5). Meethan has contrasted this organization culture with the very different cultures of field staffs of statutory and voluntary organizations. They are meant to be coordinating closely but have problems reaching agreement over the design of common assessment forms which are replete with material for symbolizing their differences (1995). This work is making progress in seeing how one of our central analytical concepts, culture, can illuminate a much wider range of forms of organization than it was originally devised for, and this is a second area of future work in anthropology.

A third area of work arising from anthropological studies of 'policy' and organizations concerns political discourse. Care in the Community policies provoked a contest between different meanings of 'culture' with implications for different systems of management. This is one of many areas of current policy change involving major restructuring of public organizations and redefinition of the roles of public, private and voluntary sectors. Each change involves the transformation of meanings of key words such as 'client', 'citizen', 'customer', 'individual', 'community', or 'society' (Strathern, 1990). Each assertion of a new meaning for a key word draws on layers of meaning from previous moments of contestation. The assertion of a new meaning as authoritative in one discourse draws in its train transformations in associated discourses, revealing the way in which an ideological shift is achieved.

Two issues, one theoretical and the other methodological, need addressing to advance analyses of political discourse and policy change. The theoretical issue concerns the analysis of process. There is a tendency to examine political discourse at a particular moment and not to trace how it is transformed through time. For example, van Dijk (1993) reveals the modes of argumentation of dominant political language in the late 1980s but treats that period as static. What is important is to explain the processes of transformation by which some forms of argumentation became authoritative and others not. The methodological issue is linked to this: processes of ideological transformation are Political (with a capital P). In studying policy it is often only with policy professionals that anthropologists have contact. It is they who commission studies and receive reports. It is easy to fall in with policy professionals' attempts to maintain their conceptual separation between 'administration' and 'politics'. However, focusing on processes of contestation among policy professionals may blinker the anthropologist from the more ideological aspects of power and domination which are accessible if politicians are included in the field.

A number of doctoral students at Sussex have been studying the political processes of transformation of dominant ideologies in Western and Third World countries, often involving an interchange between academic and policy discourses. For example, Mackey (1995) has examined how the Royal Ontario Museum used an ironic postmodern discourse on colonialism drawn from anthropology and feminism in its 'Into the Heart of Africa' exhibition. This was an important reformulation of the concept of 'multiculturalism' central to the ideology of the Canadian state. But when challenged by African Canadians, the Museum used its institutional power to reassert an authoritative discourse.

Reinhold's (1994) policy ethnography traces the dispute over 'positive images' in Haringey Council in London and the passage of Section 28 of the Local Government Act through Parliament, which prohibited local government from 'promoting' the acceptability of homosexuality as a 'pretended family relationship'. Her work draws together the issues raised in this chapter. Hers is not only a multi-site ethnography; it is not based on a 'community' at all. She is not analysing 'the other' as a gay community, but the processes by which the other is constituted: 'gay' whilst being marginalized is shown to be symbolically central to the construction of dominant ideology in Britain. Reinhold is certainly not 'studying down'; she seems at last to have found a way of 'studying up', by focusing centrally on policy-makers and activists without a referent subordinated 'people'. She herself claims she is 'studying through' (ibid.: 477–9), that is, analysing a cultural process of domination by ranging back and forth across the different sites of her ethnography.

Through an ethnography of the local dispute and how it intersected with the parliamentary debate, Reinhold shows how the discourse shifted through time. 'Promoting' which was at first associated with 'positive images', was appropriated by those with greater 'agentive power' and turned into 'promoting' homosexuality. 'Promotion' came to mean seduction of 'normal' children, and equated with an attack on 'the family', the basis of order in the state, and thus with subversion. This shift in one key term drew in a trail of transformations of associated terms in five overlapping discourses until a new ideology, asserted as 'real', with the power to mobilize politically, was made authoritative through state legislation. In a way relevant to studies of black and other minorities, she shows how this process of manufacturing revulsion, marginalizing, excluding, and dehumanizing an 'enemy within' is central to the process of continually transforming and asserting a dominant ideology in Britain (ibid.: 471–2).

In tracking the shift from studying 'a people' to 'studying up' and studying policy, three issues have been identified from work in policy and practice which refer to core theoretical concerns of the discipline: the problematization of policy as an institution; the study of a wider range of organizations than hitherto; and the analysis of transformations of discourses of power. This introduces 'commitment' to politically contentious issues into the core theoretical development of the discipline.

AN UNCOMFORTABLE AND COMMITTED DISCIPLINE?
Firth suggested two ways in which anthropology was an uncomfortable discipline. First, it was uncomfortable for those with institutional power on the occasions when anthropology challenged their assumptions, their established positions and contradictions. Second, it was uncomfortable for anthropologists themselves, engaged with 'their' people but trying to maintain distance from them and from policies affecting them, hesitating, uncertain how to intervene without supporting with their knowledge regimes for which they lacked sympathy. I have argued that the researcher maintaining a position engaged but distanced both from 'the people', who in administrative terms are also 'the problem', and from decision-making, is a particular model of cultural politics. The shift to include policy and state institutions in the field of study makes anthropology more uncomfortable in the first respect. It also changes the nature of the discomfort for anthropologists themselves, enabling them to resituate themselves in the field of study and to take a standpoint in Harding's terms, engage in dialogic research in Schrijver's terms, or be committed in Firth's terms.

The changed model of cultural politics involved in this shift from studying 'people' to 'policy' has to take into account changes in the way the state is thought about. When anthropologists were establishing their discipline in the 1930s, the state was conceptualized as a benign and neutral administration for the public good. The quality of decision-making was thought to depend on the availability to administrators of objective factual information – provided by experts or by 'the people' themselves. This was one source of disagreement between anthropology and two other contemporaneous movements in Britain, Mass Observation (an anthropology for the people by the people) and the Social Documentary Film Movement. Despite disagreements, all shared Grierson's view that accurate documentary information would enable otherwise ill-informed administrators to improve their decision-making.

This way of thinking was radically changed by Miliband's (1969) analysis of the state not as neutral to competition between pluralist elites but as a site of class struggle, a means through which the ruling class maintains inequalities. Thus in the 1970s there was a much more politicized view of relations between 'people' and 'the state' and of the impossibility of anthropologists standing in some neutral or objective location outside these relations. This became even clearer in the 1980s in Britain when 'the state' became politically equated with 'government' and the ideology of a new fraction of the bourgeoisie (Elliott and McCrone, 1987). These changes also disrupted the categories used for much academic analysis. The boundaries between and content of 'state', 'civil society' and 'domestic organization' were debated and variously redrawn. In their place, Foucault's concept of 'governmentality' seems to be gaining ground (Foucault, 1991; Gordon, 1991). This is the idea that institutions of the state are derived from practices of governing. These practices in turn derive from a rationality of government, that is a system of thinking about the nature and control of a 'population' and an 'economy'. Anthropological knowledge is part of a system of documentation, analysis and evaluation essential to governmentality. This rationality for governing pervades the population and all institutions, both internal and external to the state.

Foucault (Gordon, 1991) depicted late twentieth-century governmentality informed by liberalism as simultaneously totalizing and individualizing. State institutions are reduced to a minimum, and functions of governance are delegated to private and voluntary organizations outside the state. Whilst proclaiming the freedom of individuals, this practice requires the highly intrusive collection of 'intelligence' on hitherto private aspects of life to evaluate the efficacy of these delegated interventions for the management of the population. This liberal state is both more remote and more intrusive.

This helps explain why anthropologists, although located within this system of governmentality, in the 1980s and 1990s have felt increasingly distanced from the state. Thatcherite policies to replace 'public service' with privatization, the transfer of some state roles to the voluntary sector, and the responsibility for each individual to help themselves, regardless of structural disadvantage, have broken up the postwar political consensus. Not only have welfare state professionals been marginalized, but academic policy studies have been displaced to an outer periphery (Pollitt, 1989). Increasingly academics of all disciplines who study the social impact of these changes no longer have an *entrée* through policy professionals into political decision-making. From a highly marginal position they now have to negotiate to be heard directly by politicians. A good example is Collins's work, located in a voluntary organization called Values into Action, on the impact of Care in the Community policies on people with learning difficulties. Her reports (1992; 1993) have been launched in the House of Commons and she has appeared on all the main television and radio news programmes. Policy research has become a highly politicized process. Whilst standards of accuracy and reliability of course have to be maintained, 'objectivity' can no longer be confused with 'value free' research; nor can a research relationship in society be neutral or free of power.

If anthropologists are implicated in a pervasive system of governmentality, they also have the potential to contest the rationality from which government practices and institutions derive. All anthropologists, whether labelled 'pure', 'applied' or 'no longer', are, and always have been, implicated in power relations: the basis for these divisions is dissolved. For a committed stance within a system of governmentality a conception of 'the discipline as a whole' is required with better institutional links between its parts. This is so that as anthropologists working in policy and practice raise issues which are of central theoretical concern to the discipline, they can be taken up by anthropologists working in the universities. Seeing the discipline critically located within governmentality makes it impossible to consider anthropologists as apolitical observers on the edge of society and free of power. It provokes us to resituate ourselves in the field of study in a new cultural politics in which the process of knowledge production persists in being 'uncomfortable' for both those 'studied up' and for the researchers themselves.

ACKNOWLEDGEMENTS
Earlier versions of this chapter were given at Brunel and Cambridge Universities, where questions and comments were very helpful. I am grateful to Eva Mackey for her perceptive and stimulating comments on an earlier draft, and to Sue Reinhold for responding with a long and helpful letter. I am thankful to Henrietta Moore and Ursula Sharma for helping to research changes in ASA membership rules, and to Ralph Grillo for being one of seemingly very few people with a set of ASA Annals.

NOTES
1   Van Willigen (1987) argued that the pure/applied distinction was not present at the beginning of modern anthropology because the classic texts were funded for reasons of policy to examine areas defined as problems in colonial terms. This is to ignore how anthropologists handled that relationship culturally. It seems that a boundary was drawn around engaged but pure anthropology in the new university departments to keep them 'uncommitted' and separate from administrators who might use anthropological knowledge in their practice.

2   GAPP Talks were organized by Nici Nelson of Goldsmiths' College and reported in *BASAPP News*, no. 2: 12; no 3: 7; no. 9: 2–7; no. 11: 4.

3   These conferences were organized respectively by Sarah Ladbury, Sarah Southwold, Tom Selwyn (Selwyn, 1988), David Marsden, Mark O'Sullivan and Sue Wright (Wright, 1994), and Nici Nelson jointly with Sue Wright (Nelson and Wright, 1995).

4   In the USA in contrast there has been a steady increase in the numbers of graduates employed outside the academy. In the early 1970s, 1 in 40 of new anthropology PhDs went into business, industry or consulting (Baba, 1986: 1). In the mid-1980s the numbers were 1 in 10 (ibid.: 2). By 1993 it was expected that 50 per cent of all new anthropology PhDs would be working outside the academy (ibid.: 10) .

5   As Convenor of GAPP and co-founder of BASAPP, I was asked to join the ASA Committee to make links between the organizations. In 1993 Cris Shore, Editor of *Anthropology in Action* was elected to the ASA committee and Sandra Wallman, one of the founders of GAPP, became chair of the ASA.

6   One such mechanism would be arrangements for anthropologists working in practice to have sabbatical periods attached to a university department so as to exchange ideas with colleagues, reflect critically on their work and write for journal publication. It is possible for university-based anthropologists to work in overseas development or policy evaluation in Britain for periods of time, but the opposite is rarely if ever possible.

REFERENCES

Akeroyd, A. (1987) *Ethical Guidelines for Good Practice*, Association of Social Anthropologists.

Apthorpe, R. (1985) 'Pleading and reading agricultural development policy: small farm, big state, and the 'case of Taiwan', in R. Grillo and A. Rew (eds) *Social Anthropology and Development Policy*, London: Tavistock.

ASA (Association of Social Anthropologists) (1983) *Annals of the Association of Social Anthropologists of the Commonwealth*, 4.

—— (1991) *Annals of the Association of Social Anthropologists of the Commonwealth*, 12.

Asad, T. (ed.) (1973) *Anthropology and the Colonial Encounter*, London: Ithaca.

—— (1979) 'Anthropology and the analysis of ideology', *Man* (n.s.), 14: 607–27.

Baba, M. L. (1986) *Business and Industrial Anthropology: An Overview*, NAPA Bulletin no. 2. Washington DC: National Association for the Practice of Anthropology.

Bastide, R. (1973) *Applied Anthropology*, London: Croom Helm.

Britan, G. M. and Cohen, R. (eds) (1980) *Hierarchy and Society: Perspectives on Bureaucracy*, Philadelphia: Institute for the Study of Human Issues.

Cohen, A. (1993) *Masquerade Politics: Explorations in the Structure of Urban Cultural Movements*, Oxford: Berg.

Collins, J. (1992) *When the Eagles Fly: A Report on Resettlement of People with Learning Difficulties from Long-Stay Institutions*, London: Values Into Action.

—— (1993) *The Resettlement Game: Policy and Procrastination in the Closure of Mental Handicap Hospitals*, London: Values Into Action.

Dalley, G. (1988) *Ideologies of Caring*, Basingstoke: Macmillan Education.

Donnan, H. and MacFarlane. G. (eds) (1989) *Social Anthropology and Public Policy in Northern Ireland*, Aldershot: Avebury.

Elliott, B. and McCrone. D. (1987) 'Class, culture and morality: a sociological analysis of neo-conservatism', *Sociological Review*, 35, 3: 485–515.

Fairclough, N. (1985) 'Critical and descriptive goals in discourse analysis', *Journal of Pragmatics*, 9: 739–63.

Firth, R. (1981) 'Engagement and detachment: reflections on applying social anthropology to social affairs', *Human Organization*, 40: 193–201.

—— (1986) 'The founding and early history of the ASA', *Annals of the ASA*, 7: 4–10.

Fleming, S. (1993) 'Reconciling anthropologies: knowledge, policy and practice', *Anthropology in Action*, 16: 4–5.

Foucault, M. 'Governmentality' in G. Burchell, C. Gordon and P. Miller (eds) *The Foucault Effect: Studies in Governmentality*, London: Harvester Wheatsheaf.

Fortes, M. and E. E. Evans-Pritchard (eds) (1940) *African Political Systems*, Oxford: Oxford University Press.

Fox, R. G. (ed.) (1991) *Recapturing Anthropology*, Sante Fe, New Mexico: School of American Research Press.

Gedicks, A. (1979) 'Research from within and below: reversing the machinery' in G. Huizer and B. Mannheim (eds) *Politics of Anthropology*, The Hague: Mouton.

Gordon, C. (1991) 'Governmental rationality: an introduction' in G. Burchell, C. Gordon and P. Miller (eds) *The Foucault Effect: Studies in Governmentality*, London: Harvester Wheatsheaf.

Gough, K. (1968) 'New proposals for anthropologists', *Current Anthropology*, 9: 403–7.

Grillo, R. (1984) 'Working Party report on training for applied anthropology', Association of Social Anthropologists.

—— (1985) 'Applied anthropology in the 1980s: retrospect and prospect' in R. Grillo and A. Rew (eds) *Social Anthropology and Development Policy*, London: Tavistock.

—— (1994) 'The application of anthropology in Britain 1983-1993' in C. Hann (ed.) *When History Accelerates: Essays on Rapid Social Change, Complexity and Creativity*, London: Athlone.

Grillo, R. and Rew, A. (eds) (1985) *Social Anthropology and Development Policy*, London: Tavistock.

Harding, S. (ed.) (1987) *Feminism and Methodology*, Milton Keynes: Open University Press.

Huizer, G. (1979) 'Research through action: some practical experiences with peasant organization' in G. Huizer and B. Mannheim (eds) *The Politics of Anthropology: From Colonialism and Sexism to a View from Below*, The Hague: Mouton.

James, W. (1973) 'The anthropologist as reluctant imperialist' in T. Asad (ed.) *Anthropology and the Colonial Encounter*, London: Ithaca.

Lipsky, M. (1980) *Street-Level Bureaucracy: Dilemmas of the Individual in the Public Services*, New York: Russell Sage.

Lloyd, P. (1988) 'Birth of BASAPP', *BASAPP News*, 1: 1.

—— (1990) 'SASCW annual conference', *BASAPP News*, 5: 7.

—— (1993) *Community Care in Rural Areas: Approaches to the Problem*, Research Paper, Lewes: Sussex Rural Community Council.

—— (1994) 'Participation in sheltered housing management', paper presented at British Society of Gerontology Conference, Royal Holloway College, Egham, Surrey (September).

Loizos, P. (1977) 'Anthropological research in British colonies: some personal accounts', *Anthropological Forum*, 4.

Mackey, E. (1995) 'Postmodernism and cultural politics in a multicultural nation: contests over truth in the *Into the Heart of Africa* controversy' *Public Culture*, 7, 2: 403–31.

Mair, L. (1969) *Anthropology and Social Change*, LSE Monographs on Social Anthropology 38, London: Athlone.

Malinowski, B. (1961)[1945] *The Dynamics of Culture Change: an Inquiry into*

Race Relations in Africa, edited by P. Kaberry, New Haven: Yale University Press (1st edition 1945).

Marcus, G. E. (1986) 'Contemporary problems of ethnography in the modern world system' in J. Clifford and G. E. Marcus (eds) *Writing Culture*, Berkeley: University of California Press.

Marcus, J. (1990) 'Introduction: anthropology, culture and postmodernity', *Social Analysis*, 27: 3–16 (special issue *Writing Australian Culture: Text, Society and National Identity*).

Marsden, D. and Oakley, P. (eds) (1990) *Evaluating Social Development Projects*, Oxford: OXFAM.

Mascarenhas-Keyes, S. (1989) 'GAPP vocational training for anthropologists', *BASAPP News*, 2: 8–9.

McCourt-Perring, C. (1994) 'Community care as de-institutionalization? Continuity and change in the transition from hospital to community-based care' in S. Wright (ed.) *Anthropology of Organizations*, London: Routledge.

Meethan, K. (1995) 'Service led or needs led care for older people?' in N. Nelson and S. Wright (eds) *Power and Participatory Development*, London: Intermediate Technology.

Mies, M. (1983) 'Towards a methodology for feminist research' in G. Bowles and R. Duelli-Klein (eds) *Theories of Women's Studies*, London: Routledge & Kegan Paul.

Miliband, R. (1969) *The State in Capitalist Society*, London: Weidenfeld & Nicolson.

Mintz, S. W. (1985) *Sweetness and Power: The Place of Sugar in Modern History*, Harmondsworth: Penguin.

Nader, L. (1972) 'Up the anthropologist – perspectives gained from studying up' in D. Hymes (ed.) *Reinventing Anthropology*, New York: Random House.

Nader, L. (1980) 'The vertical slice: hierarchies and children' in G. M. Britan and R. Cohen (eds) *Hierarchy and Society*, Philadelphia: Institute for the Study of Human Issues.

Nash, J. (1979) *We Eat the Mines and The Mines Eat Us*, New York: Columbia University Press.

Nelson, N. and S. Wright (eds) (1995) *Power and Participatory Development: Theory and Practice*, London: Intermediate Technology.

Pollitt, C. (1989) 'Ethnography in social policy research', *BASAPP News*, 2: 16-17.

Reinhold, S. (1994) 'Local conflict and ideological struggle: "Positive Images" and Section 28', unpublished D. Phil. thesis, University of Sussex.

Robertson, A. F. (1984) *People and the State: An Anthropology of Planned Development*, Cambridge: Cambridge University Press.

Said, E. (1978) *Orientalism*, Harmondsworth: Penguin.

Salisbury, R. (1977) 'A prism of perceptions: the James Bay hydro-electricity project' in S. Wallman (ed.) *Perceptions of Development*, Cambridge: Cambridge University Press.

Schrijvers, J. (1989) 'Dialectics of a dialogical ideal: studying down, studying sideways and studying up', *Kennis en Methode* 13: 344-61, reprinted in L. Nencel and P. Pels (eds) *Constructing Knowledge: Authority and Critique in Social Science*, London: Sage.

—— (1993) *The Violence of Development: A Choice for Intellectuals*, Institute for Development Research, Amsterdam. Utrecht: International Books.

Selwyn, T. (1988) 'Anthropology of tourism: conference report', *BASAPP News*, 1: 9–10.

Shore, C. and Jöhncke, S. (1992) 'Reassessing "applied anthropology" in Europe', *European Association of Social Anthropologists Newsletter*, 8: 11–12.

Smircich, L. (1983) 'Concepts of culture and organizational analysis' *Administrative Science Quarterly*, 28: 339–58.

Stirling, P. and Wright, S. (1988) 'Past, present and future. Group for Anthropology in Policy and Practice' *BASAPP News*, 1: 2–5.

Strathern, M. (1990) 'The concept of society is theoretically obsolete' in T. Ingold (ed.) *Group for Debates in Anthropological Theory*, Manchester.

Street, B. V. (1993) 'Culture is a verb: anthropological aspects of language and cultural process' in D. Graddol, L. Thompson and M. Bryman (eds) *Language and Culture*, Clevedon, Avon: British Association for Applied Linguistics in association with Multilingual Matters.

Taussig, M. (1980) *The Devil and Commodity Fetishism in South America*, Chapel Hill: University of North Carolina Press.

Van Dijk, A. (1993) *Elite Discourses and Racism*, London: Sage.

Van Willigen, J. (1987) 'Becoming a practising anthropologist: a guide to careers and training programmes in applied anthropology', *NAPA Bulletin* no. 3, Washington: National Association for the Practice of Anthropology.

Wenger, G. C. (ed.) *The Research Relationship*, London: Allen & Unwin.

Wolfe, A. W. (1977) 'The supranational organization of production: an evolutionary perspective' *Current Anthropology*, 18: 615–35.

Wright, S., Smart, G. and Hursey, C. (1980) *Decision Making for Rural Areas: West Dorset Study*, Report to the Department of the Environment. London: University College, London.

Wright, S. (1982) *Parish to Whitehall: Administrative Structure and Perceptions of Community in Rural Areas*, Papers in Local and Rural Planning no.16. Gloucester: GLOSCAT.

—— (1984) 'Rural communities and decision makers', *Royal Anthropological Institute News* no. 63: 9–13.

—— (1991/2) *Evaluation of the Unemployment Strategy*, series of 7 papers. Middlesbrough: Research and Intelligence Unit, Cleveland County Council with Sussex University.

—— (1992) 'Community development: what sort of social change?' *Journal of Rural Studies*, 8: 15–28.

Wright, S. (ed.) (1994) *Anthropology of Organizations*, London: Routledge.

CHAPTER 4

Anthropologists for Sale?
I.M. Lewis

There is a growing demand for applied anthropologists to work in the field of development in the Third World, and in Europe and America in such not entirely unrelated areas as ethnic relations and refugee problems. The demand for anthropological expertise here exists on the part of such international organizations as the Food and Agricultural Organization (FAO), World Health Organization (WHO), International Livestock Centre for Africa (ILCA), etc., as well as on that of such bilateral aid organizations as the United States Agency for International Development (USAID), the British Overseas Development Administration (ODA) and the Swedish equivalents, SIDA and SAREC. Private firms in America and Europe, competing for aid contracts, are also increasingly encouraged to include a social anthropological or sociological component in their planning and implementation missions. Oxfam, Help the Aged, Survival International, and other voluntary (development and relief) agencies now likewise regularly recruit social anthropologists. 'Applied' or 'development' anthropology thus offers an important and rapidly expanding source of work opportunities for trained social anthropologists of all nationalities.[1]

APPLIED ANTHROPOLOGY IN THE COLONIAL PERIOD

This boom in applied anthropology – for that is what it amounts to – makes a paradoxical, and interesting, contrast with the earlier colonial context in which so many of us older European anthropologists carried out our first fieldwork.[2] As we all know, particularly through Malinowski's illuminating analysis of myths, the past is constantly viewed and reinterpreted through the distorting lenses of the present. Particularly in America, the vast contemporary expansion of applied anthropology and its use sometimes for politically dubious ends,[3] has promoted the generalized myth that all anthropology in the period of European colonial rule was politically motivated in the interests of the colonial authorities (see Asad, 1973; Hymes, 1973; Lewis,

1985). This is a distorting mystification. In reality the practice varied considerably under different colonial regimes. I think it is true, but I may be wrong, that the French and Belgians tended to make more use of applied anthropology in the service of their interests than the British, and that this in many cases involved colonial administrators becoming professional anthropologists – sometimes distinguished ones. In this sense they could be said to have partly 'colonized' African and oriental studies – by transforming administrators into academics.

Again, the practice varied in time and place, under the same colonial power. In relation to Britain I think that a persuasive case could be made for the development of anthropology under the colonial aegis in India and South Africa. However, in the latter case, it has at once to be said that anglophone South African social anthropology has consistently tended to be associated with subversion and dissidence in relation to white supremacist 'apartheid' associated with Afrikaans ethnology.[4] In India under the British *raj*, social (or cultural) anthropology was actually taught by *Indian scholars at Indian universities* as early as 1920 (see Vidyarthi, 1980) and administrative 'applied' anthropology seems initially to have been mainly linked with the monumental census of Indian castes and tribes.

Elsewhere in British Africa, on the other hand, in the few cases where colonial administrations directly employed anthropologists, or established local social science research centres such as the justly famous Rhodes-Livingstone Institute in Zambia (then Northern Rhodesia) (Brown, 1973; 1979), they tolerated a remarkable degree of academic independence and often outright political criticism. Thus the Rhodes-Livingstone Institute's directors included such committed 'left-wing' Africanists as Godfrey Wilson and Max Gluckman, a member of the Communist Party. British social anthropologists often sought to impress the practical utility they claimed for their subject on governments, usually in order to secure financial support for research. But, paradoxically, when they achieved some success in this endeavour they were apt to find that while paying some lip-service to the value of applied anthropology, administrators in general did not have much time (or respect) for long-winded 'academic egg-heads' whose learned disquisitions tended to be couched in abstruse jargon and concentrated on exotic 'theoretical' problems rather than important, practical issues. Actually this probably suited both parties: certainly it helped the anthropologists to maintain their independence.

To this day, although there are always exceptions (Lord Malcolm

Hailey was a notable one),[5] there is a strong vein of philistinism in official British circles where, as in British politics, far less attention and deference are paid to academics than is the case in the United States, for example. Thus, for instance, while the American State Department will send its ambassadors to consult foreign experts, British Foreign Office diplomatic briefings often take little account of relevant academic expertise. I mention these differences because they are significant and are regularly obscured in ethnocentric presentist generalizations, which interpret the anthropological *past* in terms of the *present* pattern of applied anthropology. It is also worth mentioning that many devoted colonial officials were deeply suspicious of the motives of anthropologists whom they saw, not entirely unjustly, as exploitative opportunists who were more interested in using the local population as material for PhD theses, to advance their personal careers, than in the latter's long-term problems and welfare.

THE 'HUMAN FACTOR' EXPERT

However, my object here is not to defend the anthropology practised in the Third World prior to its independence. Drawing on personal experience in a number of applied projects with different international and bilateral agencies, I want to focus attention on some of the problems which the present opportunity for applied anthropology presents. Let me begin by noting that this demand for anthropologists in development work arises from a growing recognition and conviction that material technology is not enough to achieve effective development. It is becoming increasingly obvious that, however sophisticated and well planned technologically, development plans are ultimately hostage to a refractory residual problem, usually referred to as 'the human factor'. Reflecting this belated acknowledgement, a growing proportion of development projects, large and small, include in their design and organization a role described as 'rural sociologist' or 'social anthropologist' to deal with this recalcitrant 'human problem'.

This has in fact led to the formation of a new category of international 'expert' – the 'Human Problem' expert. Not all those recruited under this banner, however, are fully qualified, professionally recognized social anthropologists or sociologists. By academic criteria, some of those appointed to this position seem under-qualified. Yet they do usually possess that basic feature which is an essential precondition for serving as international 'expert'. Such an 'expert', like the proverbial prophet, is by implicit definition one who works 'outside his own country', and who is thus a professional alien. This, of course, is a role ideally suited to social anthropologists since it corresponds so closely to the traditional concept of the Eurocentric anthropologist as one who studies '*other* cultures' outside his own European tradition. It is thus not surprising that anthropologists should so readily join the swelling ranks of development 'experts' so brilliantly satirized in Ross Coggins' lines on what he calls 'The Development Set':[6]

Excuse me, friends, I must catch my jet,
I'm off to join the Development Set;
My bags are packed, and I've had all my shots,
I have traveller's checks and pills for the trots!
The Development Set is bright and noble,
Our thoughts are deep and our vision global;
Although we move with the better classes,
Our thoughts are always with the masses.
In Sheraton hotels in scattered nations
We damn multi-national corporations;
Injustice seems easy to protest
In such seething hotbeds of social rest.
We discuss malnutrition over steaks
And plan hunger talks during coffee breaks.
Whether Asian floods or African drought,
We face each issue with an open mouth.
We bring in consultants whose circumlocution
Raises difficulties for every solution –
Thus guaranteeing continued good eating
By showing the need for another meeting.
The language of the Development Set
Stretches the English alphabet;
We use swell words like 'epigenetic'
'Micro' 'Macro' and 'logarithmetic',
It pleasures us to be esoteric –
It's so intellectually atmospheric!
And though establishments may be unmoved,
Our vocabularies are much improved.
When the talk gets deep and you're feeling dumb
You can keep your shame to a minimum:
To show that you too are intelligent
Smugly ask, 'Is it really development?'

Or say, 'That's fine in practice, but don't you see:
It doesn't work out in theory!'
A few may find this incomprehensible,
But most will admire you as deep and sensible.
Development Set homes are extremely chic,
Full of carvings, curios, and draped with batik.
Eye-level photographs subtly assure
That your host is at home with the great and the poor.
Enough of these verses – on with the mission!
Our task is as broad as the human condition!
Just pray Good the biblical promise is true:
The poor ye shall always have with you.

Although it has certainly been overdone, some would say prostituted, the concept of such an external 'expert' is, or course, by no means indefensible. There are many delicate problems, involving conflicts of interest at a local and/or national level, and issues which a particular country may not find it easy to have explored and analysed by its own nationals. An outsider, with no local, vested interests or commitments, may therefore be in a better position to offer an impartial assessment of sensitive problems. Local nationals can paradoxically also sometimes be too unsympathetic to 'traditional' issues: they are sometimes apt to over-identify with foreign technology and may seek to distance themselves from 'backward' local practice. To be properly effective, however, the advantages of this detached, but sympathetic perspective assumed by a harmless outsider, require technical competence, self-awareness, and moral integrity. Ethical considerations are inescapable here.

As I have explained elsewhere (Lewis, 1985: 364–70), I take a robust view of the validity of ethnographic reporting and regard 'postmodernist' deconstruction as a largely unproductive distraction in social anthropology. It is abundantly obvious that ethnographic accounts can achieve standards of accuracy and authenticity which transcend the subjectivity of the individual anthropologist. The most impressive endorsement of the fidelity of the foreign fieldworker's reportage is that provided by native 'auto-anthropologists' whose negative assessment must be correspondingly devastating. I certainly feel particularly sensitive to criticism from professional Somali anthropologists and historians and relieved and gratified when their research confirms my own studies and interpretations of Somali society.

HOW LEGITIMATE IS APPLIED ANTHROPOLOGY?

Because such work obviously raises moral problems this does not, in my view, mean that they are so overwhelming that they make any applied anthropology a questionable exercise. At least in England, those academic social anthropologists who see their work as centred on 'theoretical' problems tend to be contemptuous of colleagues who enter the applied field. Applied anthropology is subject to considerable discrimination and regarded as appealing particularly to those professional lesser breeds who cannot quite make it in the elitist academic world. As I have indicated, it is easy to find some justification for this disparaging view in the frequent employment of poorly qualified sociological and anthropological 'experts'. But it is also partly a case of giving a dog a bad name here. This negative image is sometimes even extended to those interested in 'social change'. I recall a purist (and evidently anti-empiricist) colleague objecting that studies of change would have to wait on the development of an acceptable general theory of social change!

My own view, which is shared by a growing number of British social anthropologists now, is very different. It seems to me that those of us who, as professional social anthropologists, depend primarily on the resources of the Third World have a moral duty to try to contribute positively to its development. 'Development', of course, as is very clear now, is not an unambiguous or unproblematic concept. What does a given development programme actually provide in tangible benefits and enhancement of the quality of life for the target (a significant expression) population? Who in theory, and who in practice, actually benefits – the rich or the poor? How is the promised progress to be measured and assessed? Measures of gross national product or diminished infant mortality or general longevity are supremely unenlightening. What, moreover, are the costs, and how are they apportioned? Sometimes, perhaps often, the 'cost' seems to fall most heavily upon a particular local community which a high-principled, concerned, anthropologist has closely studied and identifies with strongly. Yet it may transparently be in the wider national interest to build a dam, or exploit mineral resources, in just such a site causing inevitable disruption to the local residents. The problem of the potential conflict between parochial local and national interests is widespread and naturally by no means limited to the Third World. But when it occurs in such a setting, surely the least that an informed and sympathetic anthropologist can do is to try to find ways of limiting and ameliorating the ensuing dislocation.

Equally anthropologists should have scruples about contributing, in however insignificant a fashion, to 'development' which seems likely to conflict with the interests of a significant constituency of have-nots – unless there are extraordinarily compelling counter-arguments.

A case in point concerns the eradication of tsetse fly along the banks of the two main rivers of the Somali Republic. The immediate aim here, which on the face of it seems eminently desirable, was to make these riverine grazing areas available to livestock in the dry seasons, thus extending pasture resources. However, an unanticipated consequence would be to increase the pressure on the existing riverine cultivators who have far less 'political' muscle than the numerically much stronger pastoralists. Theoretically, such potential conflict over land rights could be regulated and minimized by a rational management system: but such an enlightened administration does not exist in this particular instance.

The growing practice of applying anthropology makes all these moral issues all the more acute. Although it will not automatically solve such ethical problems, it is necessary, I believe, to insist on a clear perception and definition of the anthropologist's role and upon high professional standards. The recruitment of unqualified people who masquerade as 'anthropological experts' should be discouraged. At the same time, qualified social anthropologists should be careful not to exceed their competence. There are limits to the transfer of intellectual technology, and social anthropologists are obviously best-qualified to offer advice on cultures, modes of livelihood and projects involving theoretical problems in which they specialize. Although most social anthropologists have their specializations in terms of culture area and research interests, they tend at the same time also to think of themselves as omnicompetent generalists. It is therefore necessary for us social and cultural anthropologists to remember the old saying: jack of all trades and master of none.

FROM LEGITIMACY TO LEGITIMATION

This cautionary note is all the more important in view of the increasing use of anthropologists to *legitimate* development projects. Agencies such as ILCA and SIDA and SAREC wisely now include anthropologists in project identification, feasibility studies, implementation and monitoring retrospective assessment. I have myself participated in an ILCA assessment of the workings of grazing reserves and watering facilities in north-eastern Kenya, and have also been involved in a long-term Swedish research training project in Somalia. This scheme financed primarily by the Swedish agency, SAREC,[7] included trilateral collaboration with the Somali National Academy (which coordinated research in Somalia) and Somali National University, various Swedish universities and research institutions and the Department of Anthropology, London School of Economics (LSE), where Somali personnel from a variety of ministries (including the Ministry of Agriculture and Livestock) studied for our master's degree in anthropology. This training project was initiated by an enlightened former head of the Somali Academy who told me that she had chosen our anthropology department because she knew how to 'handle' me and was confident that she would get what she wanted. The intention was to prepare research staff for work in such fields as: fishing cooperatives (for ex-nomads); agricultural settlements; rural community health; camel-husbandry; traditional medicine; the production and exporting of precious gums (myrrh and frankincense) on which one of these graduates wrote his PhD at LSE.

As we have found, the careful selection of personnel is vital if social anthropologists are to make a serious, positive contribution. Here the anthropological presence is not simply a concession to the current vogue for socially appropriate development. This, however, is in danger of becoming so when anthropological assessments are institutionalized in the development aid process. In such circumstances the very desirable formal recognition of the 'human factor' in development risks degenerating into a mere cypher – manipulated as required by powerful economic and political interests.

Without necessarily implying any generalized negative criticism, let me illustrate by reference to the operation of USAID. With, no doubt, the best of intentions, legislation in the US Congress requires all USAID projects to satisfy criteria of 'environmental and social soundness' before they are implemented. This reflects concern for ecological resources, for the interests of women and for those described in the cliché as 'the poorest of the poor'. Development should cause as little environmental and social disruption as possible and be of maximum benefit to deprived sections of the population concerned. These seem unexceptionable objectives and their elevation into legal requirements which are formally assessed, appears imaginative and forward-looking.

How does this work in practice? Here, I speak from my own limited experience. First, a Third World government requests American aid in a variety of fields. Several possible areas are identified and emphasized – e.g. rural health; farming extension and improvement; rural water supplies; minimum housing in farming settlements for marginalized ex-nomads. USAID commissions a feasibility study by a team of US 'experts' who come out to the country and after a short visit of two weeks or so, prepare a 'project identification document' (PID). If this is favourable, and it is likely to be so, since those preparing it may have further interests in securing work in its implementation, another – usually separate – team of foreign (ideally US) experts is commissioned to make a more detailed and extended study. Here the aim, with the help of the local USAID office, is to produce a formal and quite elaborate Project Paper (PP) including budgetary costings for the proposed development project. Ideally all the 'experts' involved in preparing this document should be in the country at the same time so that the resulting report is an integrated affair, offering considered and fully discussed judgements on all aspects of the proposal. In practice, however, the various individuals who contribute to this Planning Paper may not all arrive together, and parts of the document may be written and rewritten on an *ad hoc* basis without the overall cohesion that is theoretically required.

It is this document with its vital components on environmental and social soundness (the latter written by someone described as a social scientist/social anthropologist) that is our primary concern here. The official guidelines for the 'social roundness analysis' include the follow-ing headings: 'socio-cultural context'; 'beneficiaries' (direct, indirect, 'disbeneficiaries' (!)); 'participation' (in design, implementation, evalu-ation); 'socio-cultural feasibility'; 'impact' (including replicability); 'issues' (women, minorities, etc.). These carefully rendered components form an integral part of the document, and are written by commissioned 'experts' or USAID field staff if they possess appropriate expertise. The Project Paper is now sent or taken to Washington for approval and is open to Congressional scrutiny which, of course, involves various potentially vested interests in relation to the implementation of the proposed development under the official Project Agreement binding the US and host governments. In practice, this Paper, with its built-in certificates of environmental and social soundness, is actually an application to Congress for aid funds which may, or may not be forthcoming. The USAID interest, naturally, is to secure the aid, and those responsible for editing and presenting the Project Paper speak of 'selling the project'. If this is achieved, the 'social soundness' expert will have fulfilled his role in contributing a persuasive assessment.

Without questioning the competence or *bona fides* of the social anthropologists involved, it is clear that this kind of assessment which is, in effect, *part of the grant application* is very different from an independent external assessor's appraisal of a project application. In practice, the process described is apt to amount to a form of automatic approval, a kind of self-certification or legitimation. Of course, this is not the end of the story. Once the USAID Project Paper is presented in Washington, it is likely to stimulate the proliferating development-agency market and attract competing bids for the implementing contracts. Some Congressional lobbies may indeed have sufficient muscle to significantly modify the project in the interest of one of their constituents – for example a powerful Tropical Agriculture Faculty. It may, indeed, be argued that the project is too complex and technical to be left to AID personnel to implement, requiring specialized expertise only possessed by a particular US university or research station. We should not be too horrified by all this since the finance involved is, naturally, American, and if they choose to see that a substantial part of the budget (possibly over 70 per cent) is used to pay expatriate Americans and purchase American equipment, who are we to complain? It is, after all, a 'gift' and gifts are proverbially 'poison'.

My main point here, however, is that in the process described above the role of the social scientist (in our case anthropologist) risks being transformed from detached social soundness investigator to partisan social soundness certifier. It is of course not only USAID which thrusts this legitimizing role on (presumably) well-intentioned social anthropologists. Nor is it extended only to anthropologists working for multinational companies. It is significantly also, sometimes, required by the recipients of aid themselves.

This can be seen negatively as well as positively, in the sense that such social science expertise is expected to endorse existing government policy, not to question or subvert it. Let me give one example with which I am familiar. A small international agency was requested to undertake a social survey of the social implications of the increased provision of wells in an arid pastoralist area in an African state. This was in the context of a World Bank scheme to develop rural water supplies. The fully qualified anthropological researchers discovered that there were already more than enough water points, and that the local population did not want more wells. They also discovered that a third of the population consisted of people who, though not directly incorporated in the local government structure and represented officially as recently arrived 'foreign' immigrants, were actually long-term local residents. When the report incorporating these findings was published by the agency concerned, it was promptly banned by the government which had requested it and the agency had the humiliating task of asking all recipients of the report to return it forthwith. Clearly the social anthropologists here had not fulfilled their anticipated, if implicit rather than explicit, role as legitimators.

My own most frustrating personal experience of over-riding political considerations occurred during the early 1980s refugee crisis in Somalia. There had been a long-standing dispute between the Somali Government and the international donor countries on the actual size of the refugee population (a consequence of the 1977–8 Ogaden War). The Somali authorities maintained that there were over one million refugees, while the donors considered that the true figure was less than half that. A compromise 'planning figure' of 700,000 was accepted by the United Nations High Commission for Refugees (UNHCR) and used as a basis for calculating what had become Somalia's most important aid package. The refugee population had, of course, never actually been enumerated. However, in 1985 I was persuaded by the UNHCR Director-General to organize a 're-enumeration' and (very unwisely) agreed to try to do this when I was assured that the Somali Government accepted the project. On this basis, I assembled a small team of demographers and social anthropologists under the aegis of the International African Institute of which I was Director at the time. We proposed to carry out a random sample survey of 10 per cent of camp populations, supplemented by an in-depth anthropological survey of a cross-section of the 40 actual camps. We began with a feasibility study in which we piloted our research methodology. This was based on the concept of 'camp-based population', all those registered as camp refugees, rather than those actually resident in a camp on the day of the survey. With a mainly nomadic and very mobile refugee population, this definition would clearly have favoured a generous count and was fully in accord with UNHCR policy which was sympathetic to the Somali predicament. The Somali authorities well understood this point. However, having completed our feasibility study successfully, and when we were on the point of launching the full project, the Somali Government suddenly announced that it had decided not to ratify the relevant agreement with UNHCR and our research was aborted. As one of the President's advisers explained to me, while the West was prepared to pour money into supporting refugees from Afghanistan without insisting on a refugee census, the Somalis saw no reason why they should have to submit to the 're-enumeration exercise' imposed upon them by UNHCR. And that was that (see Lewis, 1986).

These cases are, of course, by no means unique. Nor is it only in Africa or other developing continents that governments expect social scientists (and other technical 'experts') to legitimate and support their policies. It is easy to think of European parallels (in England and France) which may partly explain why colonial governments rarely actually applied anthropology.

ASSESSING 'SOCIAL SOUNDNESS'

It is evident that the more legitimate it has in practice become for anthropologists to apply their skills in development, the more they are expected to legitimize other interests. It is thus of paramount importance, if professional integrity is to be maintained, that we anthropologists should be clear about what developers expect from us and what we have to offer. At the very least, I would say that there is a useful part to be played here even if it amounts to little more than legitimizing informed common sense. (It is, of course, an interesting commentary on development schemes that they should require professionalized 'common-sense experts', but that is another matter).

It is also the case, I think, that *appropriately qualified* anthropologists can produce significant information and comments on the feasibility and likely implications of particular projects without *necessarily* undertaking extended local field research. This may, however, be required in certain cases since there are always limitations (unless the anthropologist is already a specialist in the area and topics involved) to short-term appraisals made in the course of a few weeks.

Such 'rapid appraisals' by anthropologists (and sociologists) who lack first-hand familiarity with the 'target area' (a significant expression) may yield useful basic socio-demographic data on family organization, household structure, local production units, and patterns of land use, etc. They are inevitably, however, unable to set this in the specific cultural context since socio-cultural studies take much longer and require a working knowledge of the local language.

Where the anthropologist conducting such short-term research is himself already a specialist in the area, the situation is quite different. A case in point, which is also an example of an NGO (non-governmental organization) commissioning research which is both of applied and fundamental significance, is a recent, and very topical, study of indigenous (local-level) peacemaking in northern Somaliland (the 'Somaliland Republic') by the LSE-trained Somali social anthropologist, Dr Ahmed Yusuf Farah. This research, for Action Aid, examines how, with very little external influence or support and in spectacular contrast to the situation in southern Somalia (see Lewis, 1993a and b) the northern traditional lineage elders, have managed to stage a series of successful inter-clan peacemaking conferences. Here, taking my late 1950s analysis (Lewis, 1961 [1982]) of northern Somali lineage organization as his point of departure, Ahmed Yusuf explores how this system functions in the same fashion today, with women as intermediaries, and poets and religious leaders playing their customary role in reconciliation and peace negotiation. In a field study of little more than two months' duration, this 'auto-anthropologist' has been able to document how, despite the wide range of casualties produced by the use of modern automatic weapons, the traditional pattern of compensatory blood-money arrangements, based on contractual agreement (*heer*), is in full operation as well as such old-established procedures as offering women as brides to settle outstanding blood-debts. Apparently linked to demographic and political changes in the way lineages operate when there is effectively no formal state government, he has also found that positions of lineage leadership have multiplied since the 1950s. As well as its immediate practical significance in illuminating peace procedures which cost little (except time) and actually work in Somalia, Ahmed's study provides important new material on the segmentary Somali lineage system in the 1990s (Farah and Lewis, 1993).

There are other aspects of the applied anthropologist's role which require further consideration and discussion. For example, the formalized inclusion of an anthropological component in USAID procedure, which is admired by a number of other agencies which have not yet adopted this practice, could be further improved. It would be easy, for instance, to make the 'social soundness' assessment more thorough and impressive – and more objective – by separating it from the construction of the Project Paper document. This could be vetted by an appropriately qualified social anthropologist who could then deliver as detached and neutral an appraisal as one is regularly expected to make when assessing colleagues' research grant applications. It would be interesting to see how USAID might respond to such a suggestion.

Other issues worthy of discussion concern the advantages and disadvantages of employing locally recruited social anthropologists (and social scientists generally) in development projects where they have local connections. Others involve such broad and complex issues as the freedom to be allowed to discover and publicize 'true facts' which a government may wish to ignore or conceal. In France, academics are state-employed civil servants and, as I know from my own experience, can be subjected to direct political pressure on controversial issues. In Britain, academics are not civil servants, and while they might like to earn the same high salaries as these officials, they cherish their (increasingly eroded) freedom from direct state control.

Academic independence raises wide and complex issues which anthropologists can hardly expect to be greatly influenced by their opinions. However, as sources of research funds in Europe increasingly emphasize the importance of 'relevant' applied work, and as opportunities for development anthropology proliferate, it behoves us as a profession to seek to act responsibly, and to appeal for this freedom to carry out the objective research which is necessary to discover the real dimensions of the 'human problem' in given situations.

As far as professional integrity is concerned, perhaps the least academic anthropologists can do in their respective countries is to seek to develop procedures which discourage inappropriately qualified people from being employed in development work and also to establish appropriate codes of professional practice. In this connection, the formation in England of the 'Group for Anthropology in Policy and Practice' was an encouraging development. GAPP – which was later incorporated under the umbrella of Anthropology in Action – aimed to increase the frequency and quality of anthropology's involvement in policy-making and implementation; to encourage the profession to provide appropriate training; and to foster 'the highest possible standards of professional competence and ethics'.

As I see it, there is still however an important need for independent monitoring of professional standards in the implementation of GAPP's principles. It is important to continue to safeguard the objectivity of assessments of social soundness, and to encourage development agencies to adopt procedures which ensure this. It is one thing for anthropologists to 'legitimate' the cultures they study by immortalizing them in the ethnographic record, and quite another to casually legitimate 'developments' which may be far from beneficial.[8] Here one way forward may be through the kind of collaboration between national and expatriate anthropologists, linked by a common professional network, as pioneered by the Association Euro-africaine pour l'Anthropoplogie du changement social et du développement (APAD).[9]

NOTES

1   For a useful overview of the general situation in Europe in the early 1990s
    see *Development Anthropology Network*, 10, 1, Spring 1992.
2   For my own, not necessarily typical, experience in the British Somaliland
    Protectorate, see 'Confessions of a "Government" anthropologist' in P.
    Loizos (ed.) *Anthropological Forum*, 4, 2 (1977) (revised version in I.M.
    Lewis, 1994).
3   As, for example, in the notorious 'Project Camelot'.
4   See e.g. Gluckman (1975); J. Sharp, *Rain*, 36 (1980), pp.4–5.
5   Author of *An African Survey* (revised edition 1957), and a former Deputy
    Viceroy of India, Hailey was a powerful exponent of the practical
    significance of applied anthropology.
6   *Adult Education and Development*, September, 1976.
7   Later, British Council scholarships were applied to continue this scheme.
    For a fuller discussion of the involvement of anthropologists in development
    projects in the light of American experience, see Hoben (1982). See also
    Firth (1981: 193–201).
8   The British Association of Social Anthropologists of the Commonwealth's
    Ethical Guidelines for Good Practice (1987) has surprisingly little to say on
    these issues in the context of applied anthropology.
9   Based at the Ecole des Hautes Etudes, Centre de la Vielle Charité,
    Marseille, France, and founded in 1991, this organization publishes a
    regular information bulletin.

REFERENCES

Asad, T. (ed.) (1973) *Anthropology and the Colonial Encounter*, London:
    Ithaca.
Brokensha, D. (ed.) (1992) *Development Anthropology Network*, 10, 1.
Brown, R. (1973) 'Anthropology and colonial rule: Godfrey Wilson and the
    Rhodes-Livingstone Institute', in Asad, 1973.
—— (1979) 'Passages in the life of a white anthropologist: Max Gluckman in
    northern Rhodesia', *Journal of African History*.
Farah, A.Y. with I.M. Lewis (1993) *Somalia: The Roots of Reconciliation.
    Peace-making Endeavours of Contemporary Lineage Leaders: A Survey of
    Grassroots Peace Conferences in Somaliland*, London: Actionaid.
Firth, R. (1981) 'Engagement and detachment: reflections on applying social
    anthropology to social affairs', *Human Organisation*, 40, 3.
Gluckman, M. (1975) 'Anthropology and apartheid' in M. Fortes and
    S. Patterson (eds) *Studies in African Social Anthropology*, London:
    Academic.
Hailey, M. (1957) *An African Survey*, Oxford: OUP.
Hoben, A. (1982) 'Anthropologists and development', *Annual Review of
    Anthropology*, 11.
Hymes, D. (ed.) (1973) *Reinventing Anthropology*, New York: Vintage.
Lewis, I.M. (1961) *A Pastoral Democracy: Pastoralism and Politics among*

the Northern Somali of the Horn of Africa, Oxford: OUP (revised edition, Holmes & Meier, 1982).

—— (1977) 'Confessions of a government anthropologist' in P. Loizos (ed.) *Anthropological Forum*, 4, 2, (revised version in Lewis, 1994).

—— (1985) *Social Anthropology in Perspective*, Cambridge: CUP.

—— (1993a) 'Misunderstanding the Somali crisis', *Anthropology Today*, 9, 4 (August).

—— (1993b) 'Making History in Somalia: Humanitarian Intervention in a stateless society', Centre for Global Governance (LSE). Discussion Paper No.6.

—— (1994) *Blood and Bone: The Call of Kinship in Somali Society*, New Jersey: Red Sea Press.

Lewis, I.M. (ed.) (1986) *Blueprint for a Socio-Demographic Survey and Re-enumeration of the Refugee Camp Population in the Somali Democratic Republic*, Geneva: UNHCR.

Vidyarthi, L.P. (1980) 'The rise of social anthropology in India (1774–1972)' in K. David (ed.) *The New Wind: Changing Identities in South Asia*, The Hague: Mouton.

CHAPTER 5

Learning from AIDS:
The Future of Anthropology
Ronald Frankenberg

THE ARGUMENT SUMMARIZED

In most parts of the world, people who feel ill at ease with their bodies, after consulting friends and relatives, visit a doctor or other professional healer, seeking from a recognized expert both an explanation and advice as how best to proceed. When they have been given what they seek, they once more enter into discussion with themselves and with others who, unlike the experts perhaps, know them in health as well as in sickness. Then, in whole or in part, they may reject either explanation or cure or both. Practitioners of biomedicine call this *non-compliance*, an almost abusive term which implies at least ignorance and often also irresponsibility, irrationality and moral blameworthiness. Patients explain it in terms of medical insensitivity and lack of understanding of the problems of 'real' life.

As a result of the emergence of a pattern of bodily symptoms which came to be known as AIDS/HIV, afflicting many people at the same time and therefore described as epidemic, professionally trained healers consulted professionally trained students of culture. An at least three-cornered set of interactions ensued between persons with AIDS/HIV, social scientists and doctors of different viewpoints and disciplines. (Moralists, power brokers, nation-states and international organizations were also involved. For a brilliant but concise analysis of the impact of an epidemic and its generation of diverse explanations and actions see Nichter, 1987.)

As in the case of the patient–healer dyad, misunderstanding and accusations of bad faith sometimes ensued: from persons with AIDS (PWA's) and the seropositive against doctors and anthropologists; from doctors against their patients and those whom they thought they had enlisted to help them help others; and from anthropologists who considered themselves as being helpful to members and potential members of both the other categories but who thought they were misunderstood. This situation was and is complicated in many ways, not least by the fact that some persons may occupy simultaneously two or even all three of the social positions mentioned (see Bolton, 1992; Farmer, 1990; 1992).

This paper has a simple central theme which is that the practitioner of anthropology needs to be educated with a rather different emphasis to that usually considered necessary for the 'expert' biomedical practitioner. It may be that the doctors' 'expert' knowledge of diseases, viruses and vaccines are *directly* applicable to a new situation. Possibly s/he comes with a set of either ready made *answers* or the framework for them, although this is, of course, a not uncontroversial statement. The research-grant-awarding policy of the British Medical Research Council is however based on this presumed scenario. On the other hand, my 'expert' knowledge of Welsh culture in the 1950s, of Zambian culture in the 1960s or of Italian culture in the 1970s and of British and other academic cultures during all these decades is not *directly* relevant to understanding, and certainly not to explaining, social and cultural perceptions in an epidemic in 1990s San Francisco, New York, Uganda, Haiti or Bangkok. However, what may be relevant are the *questions* I have learned to ask and the concepts by which they are framed.

To develop this argument I first briefly address one of the questions which emerges sharply for anthropologists out of the controversies mentioned: namely, who has the right to speak at all. I reject the view that only those most directly involved in a situation can usefully comment on it.

The reason why anthropologists have sought, and been sought after, to become involved at all has been because of their perceived concern with culture. However, not only have non- anthropologists very diverse views about what culture is, but there is also disagreement amongst anthropologists. I suggest this is related to the historically changing culture of anthropology itself. Anthropologists, like other social groups, tend to assume that what they do is natural: cultural activities are confined to others. More recently they have been driven by experience to diversify and elaborate the way culture is perceived. This leads me to recall one of the classical disputes in British anthropology (between Gluckman and followers of Malinowski) about how relationships between different and perhaps opposing cultures could most usefully be analysed. The choice is between seeing the situation either as contact between discrete entities (the latter's view) or as involved in an increasingly integrated but conflictual and asymmetrically power-laden unity.

I suggest that this has continuing resonance and that the triad, anthropologist–administrator–subject is mirrored by the relationship anthropologist–doctor–'patient'. With this in mind I explore in more detail differences and similarities between some of the cultural patterns of professional medicine and those of anthropological approaches. Just as in the earlier argument, the fact that one actor may embody more than one cultural experience complexifies rather than invalidates the argument. There is particular poignancy in the internal self-analysis and struggle which may be involved. (See for example Monks and Frankenberg, 1994, on clinically trained sufferers from multiple sclerosis and Narayan's 1993 discussion based on fieldwork in her father's native village in India.) I argue that the differences in questions posed between anthropology and medicine in general arise directly from the urgent and time-limited pragmatic concerns of biomedicine as against the more usual 'need to understand' allegedly timeless modes of anthropology. Finally I present some of the experience of anthropologists in working directly in the AIDS/HIV field to illustrate not only the difficulties which they underwent in working with agenda set for them but how unexpectedly successful (from an orthodox biomedical point of view) they were, when they were able to set their own. I relate this to the political questions involved not only in the choice of an audience of the first instance, usually fellow professionals, but also more widely. The only effective strategy I suggest is to take sides and to present material in such a way that it enables the people on the sides chosen to act for themselves, to choose *their* own agenda, rather than to enable and empower those who, however well meaning, want to act on or for them.

INTRODUCTION – CULTURE IN AND OF ANTHROPOLOGY

Contrary to present fashionable belief, anthropology always did begin at home in the implicit study of its own national and disciplinary culture. Anthropology constituted and continues to constitute itself as a multicultural society. There is first a pluralism of national intellectual traditions (not, of course, innocent of differential class and gender perceptions and misperceptions): German, Italian, Eastern European and French, for example. There is even a sense at times that the bases of Anglo-Saxon anthropology are merely treasonable translations of selectively (mis?)understood French philosophical speculation. Finally, African, Asian, Australian and bilingually Canadian matured offshoots add further complications to a complex cultural picture. Contrary to the unstated mythical assumptions of the dominance of the fieldwork model over the subject, some of its most influential figures did little or none, and most interchange of ideas amongst the denizens of anthropology is, as in most cultural congeries, intracultural.

As in the cultures of other societies, some traits and practices are adaptive for individuals and groups and others disruptive to the point of destruction. Which traits are which in this regard is graphically revealed in crises of action and interaction. Johannes Fabian, a Dutch stranger within the anglophone gates, in his *Time and the Other* (1983) gave advance notice of such a developing crisis inside the discipline. Clifford (1988) and Marcus and Fischer (1986) issued what they saw as the final warning seen reflexively and individualistically from within; and Said (1979) anticipated and reinforced it from without. The embodiment came in the gay and lesbian slogan, itself born of frustration with the anthropological response to AIDS/HIV, 'These natives can speak for themselves': a slogan which can no longer be either ignored or left out of context. It is well on the way to achievement by women, at least in the industrial countries. It is now echoed by the physically disadvantaged and by the homeless. It was foreshadowed and is asserted with vigour by the marginalized inhabitants of the formerly colonized, and still increasingly indebted, periphery whose crystallized cultural past was rendered static by imprisonment in Western museums and libraries and whose economic future is similarly confined in the vaults of Western banks. They can indeed all speak, but in what circumstances and to whom? Will such voices remain muted amongst the many (including some anthropologists) who are not silent, who speak but are nevertheless not heard (Ardener, 1989a, 1989b; Hardman, 1973)? And what part, if any, might be played by anthropologists who see themselves as interpreters, guardians and advocates of the culture of the other?

THE PROBLEM OF AIDS/HIV – CULTURE AS AN APPLIED CONCEPT

I shall first define by contrast with medical approaches my view of the nature of the anthropological enterprise as encompassed by and within the concept of culture. I also explore the consequences for the future of anthropology and for the concept of culture of its encounter with HIV/AIDS.

When HIV/AIDS was initially identified as a syndrome (but not under this name) in the United States, it was represented as a disease rooted in only partially disguised metaphor: a 'sickness' in social relations; a cultural cancer in the behaviour of the internal (homosexual, heroin-using, hookers, haemophiliacs) or external (Haitian, Hispanic, African) other. Anthropologists did not have to gatecrash this particular clinical and epidemiological party: as 'experts' on culture they were invited in. The brief that they were given was, in the main, to advise on how culture needed to be understood as a necessary prerequisite to changing it, and thus preventing self-infection. They were asked to help prevent, in the words of the British Princess Royal, 'mankind scoring own goals against itself'. Some anthropologists suggested a search for cultural factors which might modify the speed and seriousness of progression of those already infected to the manifestations of the AIDS syndrome. Others sought cultural change or affirmation to enhance the quality of life or remove obstacles to living 'Positively'. These were, at first, applauded, but later regarded as impertinently superfluous by HIV-infected persons. Epidemiologists, laboratory scientists and clinicians within the rapidly growing, medically based, AIDS industry regarded such approaches as either irrelevant or contaminated by association with alternative therapies.

This is not the first time that anthropologists have been invited to contribute to policy decisions. Nor is it the first time that they have been ascribed the role of consultants on the culture of the afflicted, but allegedly ill-informed and certainly silenced, other. In the case of AIDS/HIV, it is the association with the symbolism of 'sinful' sex and untimely death which now gives the epidemic the power to precipitate intellectual crisis and self-questioning, in general, as well as in anthropology.

The potential use of anthropology in helping to order White control of Amerindians in the US or to impose indirect rule in British-colonized Africa was more often unexploited or, at most, itself indirect (but see Asad, 1973). In Britain it existed mainly as one strand, but a relatively minor one, in the training of administrators. The feared influence was even perhaps the other way. When the Association of Social Anthropologists of the Commonwealth was founded as a more exclusive forum than the Royal Anthropological Institute, it was primarily to protect British structural functionalism against US cultural anthropology. It was also intended to exclude the colonial and ex-colonial officials who frequented the former (Max Gluckman, 1950, and John A. Barnes, 1993, personal communications). Nevertheless, the rhetorical principles of indirect rule did require sufficient understanding of local political culture to identify who were the leaders to whom power was to be partially transferred (and who could most effectively recruit labour and collect taxes). And if the so-called principles of 'paramountcy of native interests' and of 'tolerance of native custom', if not abhorrent to universal (i.e. British Victorian) morality, were even to appear to be put into practice, anthropology might again have been useful.

Lately, in countries with migrant workers or settled ethnic minorities, anthropologists have been recruited as teachers on courses for trainee social workers and nurses. They are asked to explain through exposition of cultural practices what *they*, the 'alien' other are really like; to give scientific validation to socially constructed stereotype. Even in India, China and the Russian Empire, anthropologists inherited the role of explaining the culture of 'tribal and aboriginal' peoples to the national majorities. Anthropologists have not usually been encouraged in these contexts to explore the culture of political administration, social work or health provision to see what obstacles it might put in the way of persons unfamiliar with it. Although more recently still, some anthropologically trained insiders to such groups, or others with consciousness raised by the latter or by black and feminist writings, have sought to influence professionals to ask themselves how they can change to relate to a client who, while remaining an individual, has nevertheless a class, educational or ethnic formation different from their own.

All these cumulative experiences, topped by the trauma of partial failure or success in responding to AIDS, have created a crisis of confidence in the key concept of culture itself. Some have suggested that even at this late stage it should be abandoned altogether by the discipline. As an alternative, since it is easier to imagine texts than societies in thing-like terms, some suggest it could be relegated, or transferred along with themselves, to 'cultural studies'. The problem is, of course, that multicultural anthropology has developed, unsurprisingly, many diverse concepts of culture since Boas and Tylor in the nineteenth and early twentieth centuries. Perhaps the most common, in practice if not in definition, is that culture is a thing (realty rather than reality) which is possessed by a group. To the nationalist, and to some well-meaning liberals, it is always a good thing and it can only be fully understood by its owners. To the epidemiologist, the specialist in agricultural development, the 'rational' medical administrator or business consultant, it is always a bad thing; a synonym for mindless conservatism standing in the way of progress and the prevention of disease. A second view sees culture as a framework of choices available to persons at a particular place and time. This has the possible implication of each society having as many cultures as there are social groups (but how are the boundaries of the groups to be defined?) and that within each social group there are as many cultures as there are persons. A third approach, seeking to overcome the problems of the second, is to see culture as an evanescent process which is continually negotiated between persons and within and between groups. Once more a problem of boundaries and continuities in space and time is evoked. There are familiar, if partial, solutions to these like Victor Turner's (Turner & Turner, 1978) view of the dissolution of continuity in the liminal periods of *communitas* at the centres of recurrent crises. These he contrasts to the repetitive reproductions of relatively crisis-free societal flow. Yet another set of solutions is provided by Douglas's cultural theory (1973) where situational change changes the meanings of hierarchical classifications and group memberships and loosens the structure of accepted temporal and spatial norms. More recent approaches to cultural analysis move either outward from the specific society to its embeddedness in historical period and geographical space (Burke, 1987) – its conjuncture; or inward to its embodiment in the incarnate selves of its subjects (Schweder and Levine, 1984, Schweder, 1991). Paradoxically these two directions merge in those anthropologists like Bloch and Bourdieu, Taussig and Toren who, sharing a heritage of phenomenology derived from Hegel, Marx and Benjamin or from Merleau-Ponty, see culture as the living process of the embodiment and re-present-ation of past experience.

THE ANSWERS ARE QUESTIONS: VOICES ECHOING FROM THE PAST

In this section I argue that the enduring *answers* produced by anthropology are more usefully seen as ways of formulating *questions*. There are two sets of reasons why this may be so. The main one can be illustrated by looking at the difference of approach of anthropology and clinical medicine.

Before doing this is useful to look briefly at a dispute between Gluckman and Malinowski's followers about 'Culture Contact in Africa' (Gluckman, 1963; Malinowski 1946) which serves as an object lesson in similar problems. This was an Oedipal clash since Gluckman's analysis of Malinowski's inconsistencies was based on the argument that the latter wanted at once to refute and destroy the divine kingship of his mentor and intellectual father, James Frazer, and to reject his own intellectual offspring: Evans-Pritchard, Fortes, Schapera and Mair. The substantive argument was, however, about discrete perceptions of three separate cultural realities existing side by side, which Malinowski formulates in terms of three basic columns in a table:

White influence, interests and intentions	Processes of culture contact and change	Surviving forms of tradition

Table 5.1

Gluckman used Malinowski's notes to show how these might be applied to African warfare:

European conquest and political control	The new political system as affected by loss of military sovereignty of the African tribe or monarchy and resultant changes in African organization	African Resistance and political submission in tribal memory and reaction

Table 5.2

Malinowski's difficulty was to keep the cultural realities separate as entities and yet still to demonstrate and to analyse their interactions. He tried to achieve this by positing their interaction through institutions. There cannot be conflict within cultural realities because by definition they are functional systems. There cannot be conflict between them because they are separate. Gluckman suggests that this led Malinowski to a theory of social change and applied anthropology very close to the advocacy of separate development, a consensual view in anglophone colonial Africa long before the Afrikaner concept of apartheid, its extreme version, was specifically formulated and adopted as official South African policy (see Gluckman, 1963, pp.217–20).

Gluckman and others found their solution to this impasse by seeing Africans, whites and administrators as interacting persons each using in daily praxis a complex interaction of cultural realities which, while diverse in origin and sometimes separately appropriate to particular situations, are no longer discrete or separable in time or place. Gluckman's (1958 [1940]) *Analysis of a Social Situation in Modern Zululand* is a case study of how this might be done. The sets of examples relating to AIDS below illustrate the continuing reality of these contrasting approaches.

The aims of clinical medicine are to diagnose the causes of the disturbance of bodily function by assimilating it, if possible, to similar episodes with the same combination of symptoms described as a specific disease. The latter can already be well known or, as in the case of HIV/AIDS, 'invented' from a new combination of partially pre-existing symptoms. The disease is described or invented specifically in order to advance understanding of these causes and their effects so as to hasten and to facilitate the disappearance from the affected person of the disease entity. Practitioners may well say 'we think, that is to say we know, that the cause of this is usually . . . ': a statement intended to be interpreted by the patient as 'the causes are, the cure is'. The implication is that if the patient complies with advice or submits to procedure s/he will more or less rapidly become an ex-patient. This pragmatic approach necessitates, if not Occam's Razor, at least his scalpel. What has to be sought is the simplest explanation that will effectively facilitate cure. From this viewpoint, medicine may or may not require to see the patient whole, or indeed, except in the most literal sense, to see the patient at all.

Quantitative probabilities may be enough: the qualitative niceties of social and cultural background may be both redundant and causes of unnecessarily postponing action. The clinical interviewer is not usually interested in, for example, who else is in the room, the mood or feelings of the interviewee or whether s/he would give the same answers or history in a different situation. The patient's notes, the clinical report, the published paper in the *British Medical Journal* or *New England Journal* are expected to be decisive and definitive; the best available current knowledge refuting earlier statements and conclusions. The range of facts taken into account have been for practical and utilitarian purposes limited. Reality is there, but selected reality, – the effectiveness of drugs, the lessons of experimental procedures – not 'all human life'. The clinician and the clinical scientist think in numbers, perforce, because that has been culturally defined for them as the acceptable mode of action-legitimation. As Kleinman (1988, pp.22–3) has argued for psychiatric epidemiology, they are caught in the contradiction of the traditional clinical recognition of the idiosyncratic individual and the epidemiological disregard of the statistically atypical. For the same reasons they are constrained to seek the single linear cause, isolable within the parameters of 'natural' pathology, real episodic disease

Table 5.3

Biomedicine	Social Anthropology
In general outlook:	
Pragmatic – aims towards action	Analytic – aims towards understanding
Complexity if essential for action	Complexity always necessary for holistic view
Diseases as limited episodes	Illness as flow of events
Linear causation by major cause	Overdetermination by multiple factors
Socio-cultural factors secondary	Socio-cultural factors primary
In investigations:	
Formal questions posed	Questions are formal, informal or emerge in process
Focus on the case	Focus on relational context
Publications required to be:	
Definitive and refutational	Consistent but enhancing
Aims at:	
Limited reflection of reality	Totality
Investigator:	
Distanced	Involved
Quantitative analysis required	Quantitative analysis if necessary
Atypical cases disregarded	Atypical cases crucial
Centres on:	
Disease as first focus	*Illness as first focus*
taken for granted, real, body-situated, lesions	Unbounded in time and space socially constructed through situated praxis and then *Sickness* socially, economically and politically determined → *Disease* as social construct
Elicits accounts within its own framework	Tries to be accepting of subjects' discursive frameworks
Ends by providing answers to questions posed at outset	Ends by devising questions to answers from outset
↓	↓
Uncreative but right !	**Creative but wrong ?**

situated in the (somatic, i.e. segmented) body as a lesion (Armstrong, 1987). Multicausality and pluralism of explanation are not necessarily unrecognized but they do have to be ignored in the interests of the pragmatic political economy of cure. Physicians do not merely listen to, but elicit from, the patient a history, an account, within the already learned and taken-for-granted discourse of biomedicine and which provides answers to questions set at the outset of their enquiries.

Anthropologists, by contrast, veer in the opposite direction. Starting with a set of answers emically posed to them by the persons whom they observe and in whose life they seek to participate (in so far as they are able to transcend their own subjective biases and the concerns imposed by the discipline itself), they end by devising new questions. Academic interpretive anthropology, at least, is aimed at the understanding of social process which may or may not turn out to influence the operation of simple causes on the linear outcome of events. They cannot *a priori* assume any action to to be irrelevant, and have therefore to involve themselves in their subjects' experience in a way not only not required of the clinician but also often actually forbidden as either inethical or leading to loss of objectivity. Anthropologists, then, may count and calculate differentiating or differential attributes but, in contrast to clinicians, may never need to tabulate quantifiable answers to questions formally posed to their subjects. If successful they may contribute to knowledges of process through time rather than to a set of instantaneous actions. The outcome of their work is not necessarily expected to be definitive in its individual own right. It must be consistent with earlier work in the field but it may be at once contradictory, enhancing, and transcending without having, like clinical conclusions, totally to replace its predecessors. Nor can there be, as there is (and has to be) in medicine, a simple and recognized hierarchy of decision-makers in which registrars, for example, can only hold the trump card in the absence of consultants. To the looser orthodoxies of anthropologists, pluralisms are unthreatening not least because, imperialist although they may have appeared and still appear to be, they do not directly inscribe their conclusions upon the bodies of their informants.

The discursive practices of clinical science and medical anthropology can thus be seen as a refraction of the similar difference between the past practicalities of political action in colonial territories and the teasing out of tribal law beloved of political anthropology in the 1940s and 1950s. When some anthropologists, like Evans-Pritchard (1949) encountering Italian oppression in Cyrenaica or Gluckman and the Rhodes-Livingstone Fellows vigorously opposing Central African Federation (Epstein, 1992), sought to radicalize themselves, they sought to find ways at worst of advocacy for, at best of co-operation with, their erstwhile subjects of study.

A new liberal applied anthropology of sickness in general and AIDS in particular had to seek similar bridging concepts; but with whom? It thought to find it in a symbiotic relationship with an intercalary discipline like epidemiology which shares some of its values with anthropology and others with more orthodox clinical medicine. If not love at first sight, there was at least a tentative mutual attraction. Epidemiology (see Frankenberg, 1993), in the United Kingdom and most of Europe, unlike in the US, operates from within clinical medicine. It is however a greater challenge to it than, for example, homoeopathy or acupuncture. The last two, in whatever other ways they pose a radical challenge to orthodoxy, remain focused on the individual, unlike epidemiology. Social epidemiology is, as its name implies, just that. It focuses on social rather than individual characteristics, it seeks causes of disorder that remain in the social environment and that are either not or not yet internal to the isolated body. Furthermore it is based on a supposedly (although not always convincingly) morally neutral concept of risk (see Douglas and Wildavsky, 1983; Douglas, 1986) which is discovered by identifying a category of people most likely to be affected by a symptom or syndrome. These are characterized as a risk 'group' (as it will emerge, a dangerous misnomer) and the relevant attributes or behaviours of its members are in turn identified as risk factors. Epidemiology's myth of origin (shared incidentally with medical geography) is The Broad Street Pump. This tells how folk hero John Snow (cited and discussed in Morris, 1976: 206–12) 'linked his prestige as an influential London surgeon to the analytic power of descriptive statistics' (Morris, 1976: 207) and in the Soho cholera outbreak of 1854 (Donaldson and Donaldson, 1983: 115–16) mapped the distribution of deaths by household and found that the frequency fell off with the distance between the household and the eponymous pump. He then sought out what such households had in common and discovered as he expected that they drew their water supplies from it. He clinched the argument by discovering that the distant households visited people in the nearby dwellings and collected their water from there and by a controlled trial using the products of two different water companies. He caused the pump to be closed down and cholera in that neighbourhood ceased. Like his successors, having established the external cause he needed but failed, despite conciliatory language, to satisfy his clinical and commercial critics of the method of transmission into the body. Snow was amongst those who devised standard epidemiological practice as based on *socio-cultural investigation, external to the body* followed ideally by the theorization of a problem, collection and classification of cases, identification of a category or categories of persons at risk, identification of risk factors, *transitional –* demonstration of method of transmission into body, *internal/bionatural* – demonstration of pathological processes.

In the case of AIDS/HIV, epidemiology went quickly through its normal cultural course, little changed since Snow's day. It named five categories as being at risk, the coyly humoral concept of exchange of body fluids (to cover blood transfusion, sexual intercourse and intravenous injection) was invented as a description of the common transmissive risk factor, and the aetiological processes of virus infection and immunological damage were eventually described. At this point, however, they decided that they had a problem of group culture and therefore called in the experts on culture, the anthropologists. The combination of flattery and a vaguely defined, but apparently shared, boundary concept (Star, 1988) is a powerful instrument of intellectual seduction. There was a mutual recognition of possible alliance on the principle that those (respectively within medicine on the one hand and social science on the other) who are not against are for us. This over-rode the more cautious view that uncritically to accept others' definition of the situation is to concur with it. Thus developed an unfortunate complex set of paradoxes that good ethnographies might have disastrous sequelae and bad ones less disastrous ones. Still more galling, it eventually emerged that excellent ethnography with beneficial political outcomes at one place and time might be disastrously misused in different circumstances and at different periods occurring a few months later or a few miles away.

One example of this can be given in hypothetical terms, and illustrates not only this point but the pitfalls of liberal multiculturalism, a truly repressive tolerance of repression itself. British and American governmental and non-governmental agencies and international agencies, including the World Health Organization, pride themselves on filling needs identified mainly by the societies whom they set out to help. In the past, ironically, anthropologists often assumed a false homogeneity of class and gender. They reported hegemonic views without questioning consensus (Frankenberg, 1979). Similarly in work on AIDS/HIV, as in liberal multiculturalism, it is often the views of an elite that are counted as local views (Frankenberg, 1992; Patton, 1990). Thus it has not been uncommon in the current crisis for elites in aid-receiving countries themselves to define the source of HIV infection as being other (just as happened in earlier world epidemics). A favourite source of blame, because they are there, usually female and politically weak, and can be represented as morally so, are foreign prostitutes. A metropolitan government can be persuaded to send anthropologists to study them, and since their access is confined to them, to confirm (without of course technically verifying) the convenient hypothesis. The better and more ingenious the ethnography, the more self-fulfilling the prophetic research. A variation on this is reported by Day (1988, and personal communication, 1993; Day *et al.*, 1988) nearer (my!) home. She found that, at one point of time and in one specific place, prostitute women in London were unlikely because of their use of condoms to give or receive HIV from johns (clients). Her findings at this point countered the stereotype and helped to avert attribution of blame, but were later generalized by an argument for cutting preventive, welfare and clinical services to prostitute women whenever and wherever. A cultural approach then is always contextual and involves conflict and interaction of cultures including those of readers and interpreters.

There are, however, also pitfalls surrounding contextualization. Glick Schiller (1992) is a scholar who contextualizes with care and rigour but even her findings may be muted, as she points out, by being refracted through the spectacles of biomedicine not as science but as agent of US hegemonic ideology. In her article, which she was only able to publish after she was no longer employed on the project, and thus no longer subject to medical censorship, she writes that when bioethicists invited her and her anthropological colleagues to report on their findings, they knew, as good diagnosticians always do, what questions they wanted answering and how to ignore answers which they saw as irrelevant. They demanded to be told about communitarian values in ethnic communities and, when told about the effects of gender and power differentials and economic disadvantage within and between communities and individuals, failed to hear it. Their warm thanks were for what they had learned about what they thought of as being cultural factors.

Culture was also seen as synecdoche, part for the whole, in the other experiences she reports. Her account of black family life was interpreted in terms of cultural matricentrality rather than in terms of the economic necessity which both creates and, at least in micro terms, is created and reinforced by it. Her third example concerns the expectation that she should create a uniform cultural whole, a unified and manageable other, out of disparate, but in the broad sense language-sharing, parts: Hispanicity. The general approach to the problems of different Hispanic groups in the epidemic, e.g. those of Puerto Rican, Haitian, Cuban, Mexican and other Central and South American origin has been to lump them together. Similarly the vast continent and diverse peoples and economies of Africa are often grouped together in the discourse of 'African AIDS'.

Kane (Kane and Mason, 1992) had an even more difficult task. The semantic and clinical confusion created by the 'concept' of risk group not only led to the assumption that there was a discoverable entity, the culture of intravenous drug-users, but that there would also be a culture of the non-drug-injecting, non-HIV-positive spouses or sex partners of drug-injecting, HIV-infected persons. A brief experience of the fact that such people in the city might be bankers or bench-sleepers or of any other occupation or of none; Spanish, English, Chinese, Vietnamese, Russian, French, German or other language, speakers; of various skin colour, of nearly any age; Hindu, Buddhist, Jewish, Christian or Muslim or of any other religion, convinced Kane of the futility of the general task and her employers of her incompetence as an anthropologist, and they eventually parted company (but see Kane 1991: p.1049).

THE CULTURE OF LOCALITY: RESURGENT BUT TRANSCENDED

Faced with a crisis, some anthropologists sought to cooperate, directly or indirectly, rather than merging, with epidemiologists by doing what they always had done. They studied a locality, a culture situated in a bounded place at a particular time. Most of these, encouraged by the new-found clinical interest of medical colleagues and health promoters, returned to the study of sexual cultures and behaviours virtually abandoned since Malinowski. They were now respectably and legitimately able to do what they had always wanted to do and could never afford for lack of funding and fear of stigmatization and future unemployment. These activities have produced a lively and well-crafted literature, although their contribution either to the welfare of persons with AIDS or to anthropological theory has recently been severely and perhaps justly questioned (Bolton, 1992 and 1993; Herdt, 1987, 1992; Parker, 1991, 1992). Furthermore, sometimes, the sharpness and relevance of their analyses have been weakened because they have dealt with the activities of male homosexuals where power relations based on age and wealth are not always as obvious as are those in heterosexual relationships based on gender.

I turn to those who have focused, but with new critical awareness, on problems traditional to the established theoretical concerns of the discipline. One such study is by Douglas and Calvez (1990) based on Calvez's fieldwork in Brittany (1989). In this they develop Douglas's (Douglas and Wildavsky, 1983; Douglas, 1986) concern with personal risk-taking as a culturally rather than a psychologically determined attribute. A fixed, but abstract (see Bellaby, 1990) view of the nature of culture, as expressed in her well-known axes of grid and group, is related to changing cultural realities in an hypothetical 'city'. This is then used to interpret and to predict possible attitudes, beliefs and actions of different social groups as their interacting cultural positions change in response to their respective perceptions of the epidemic. Douglas's ideas about the body, risk and the boundaries of both body as person and body social are beneficially related to each other to generate hypotheses about reactions hopefully generalizable to other 'cities' in similar situations. For example, the core of the city closes its ranks and reaffirms its boundaries, both territorial and corporeal. It strengthens its reliance on its police for the former and its orthodox doctors for the latter. Once disapproved but tolerated deviants, whether eccentric citizens or alternative practitioners, are required to close ranks or are excluded from participation. 'Strangers within the gates' who cannot comply, like homosexuals, outsiders or drug-users, are constrained to form and then to stay within their own boundaries. From the point of view of the latter groups and especially homosexual men 'rejection meets rejection' and in Douglas and Calvez's view, in conservative and hierarchical Brittany, in contrast to solidary and egalitarian gay San Francisco, this leads some within the community to religious or other fatalism and thence to risk-taking in defiance of death. This attitude and behaviour reinforces and creates a dialectic of despair for the oppressed and infected, and callous discriminatory indifference by the respectable core. 'The conscience of the central community is not essentially compassionate to all the citizenry' (Douglas and Calvez, 1990: p.463). The alternative but essentially similar reactions of 'Eat drink and be merry, for tomorrow you may die' and 'Prepare with fasting and prayer to meet your doom' have frequently been reported in epidemics. Douglas seeks to analyse them in terms of a predictive theory of culture rather than as merely haphazard personal choices.

Barnett and Blaikie (1992) have returned to a view of culture and anthropology associated with the publications of the Rhodes Livingstone Institute, in which agriculture was seen to be as earthily and realistically essential as was symbolic culture represented in art, sexual and mortuary practices. They studied what they called upstream vulnerability to infection and downstream vulnerability to socio-economic disadvantage in an area of Uganda where people were most likely to be infected with HIV by heterosexual intercourse and supported themselves through cultivation of their own food. This led them not only to a recognition that the impact of the epidemic varied amongst the indirectly involved as well as in afflicted and affected families and over time, but also on different aspects of culture, including sexual behaviour. They demonstrate the local and general relevance of anthropological study not just to prevention, but also to coping and living with the disease. They are also conscious of its relevance to the ways in which government and world organizations formulate and execute policy (cf. Robertson, 1984). As a result of the last, their voices have been muted, and they have been excluded and marginalized at conferences and in published collections.Their critique of the mainstream of the epidemiological–anthropological alliance makes them seem by definition irrelevant to policy in the real world. Significantly their work is now funded by the Food and Agricultural Organization rather than by health institutions, for whom they have fallen into the residual category of 'intersectoral'.

THE ANTHROPOLOGIST AS SHAMAN

A very different attempt to see culture as process and as experience through time is the work of Paul Farmer in Haiti (1990; 1992). Barnett and Blaikie are in the tradition of relatively pragmatic (even Fabian) British political *economy* and economic anthropology. While they regret anthropology's failure to find ways to collaborate either with outside disciplines like mathematical epidemiology or between warring schools within the discipline, they do use theory but at some times more explicitly than at others (1992, p.8). By contrast, Farmer's theoretical analysis uses an historically based, *political* economic approach to modify the concepts of a phenomenologically informed, clinically derived, American theoretical medical anthropology. In his own words, (cf. Marcus and Fisher's, 1986) he 'attempts to constitute an interpretive anthropology of affliction based on complementary ethnographic, historical, epidemiologic and political-economic analyses' (1992, p.13). Even without the impact of AIDS he would have probably have reacted to his experience as engaged clinician to, and anthropological chronicler of, the Haitian village of Do Kay in the same way. However, the epidemic dramatically demonstrates both the power and the necessity of such an approach (as similar kinds of suffering have in analogous ways for Scheper-Hughes in north-east Brazil, 1992, and for Taussig, 1987, in Colombia). What Farmer and similar writers do is to bring to processual life concepts like semantic network, explanatory model and therapy management group. Paradoxically, he does this by focusing locally, not merely on the village or even the family or group of intimates, but also right down to the body praxis of a single person. However, he situates their cultural experience in a way that is territorially and temporally unbounded. This is 'anthropology as shamanism' in Taussig's (1987) analysis of that phenomenon. The songs of Taussig's Shaman focus the minds of her patients on the simultaneous co-presence of the Putumayo historical past in all its nonlinear representations from the seventeenth century to the present day and in its territorial spread from Spain to the Andes (even linked in his reader's minds through Casement with Congo and Ireland). So Farmer shows that to understand the cultural praxis surrounding the life and death of Dieudonné Gracia (the village's third person to develop AIDS (1992, pp.95–109)) we have to recognize culture as a set of processes limited neither in time nor in place. There were significant events related to it which lasted seconds and others which have endured over centuries. Still other events have every temporal duration in between – minutes, days, months and years. As far as place is concerned, events at the UN in New York the day before, or politics there a century ago, and events in seventeenth-century slave-trading Africa, the contemporary Center for Disease Control in Atlanta, Georgia, the National Institute for Health, Bethesda, and WHO, Geneva, Switzerland, may – through mechanisms of politics, economics, or racist values, or competition between the cultures of clinical and public health medicine – be exercising, even determining, influences on life and death in Do Kay. Nor is it necessarily the closest elements in time or space that had the greatest effect.

While the main audience for both these last two studies may still be anthropological colleagues and the policy-makers and professionalized curers they hope to influence, they appear in my view, to different rationalities. The first seeks to influence through the liberal logic of the administrator; it poses creative possible questions but it also seeks to suggest pragmatic and possible policy answers. The second operates through the grounded praxis of mutual participation; Taussig (1987, pp.460–2) calls it 'dialogic'. It identifies and understands questions in the minds of the subjects but leaves the possibility of answers for cooperative solution in various relevant places (including Washington and Geneva but centrally focused on Haiti and Do Kay). Future and current practical and intellectual problems and answers to them are formulated in and by ever-changing circumstances and continuing conversation. In Fabian's term, it asserts the necessity not only of empathy but of continued co-evality (sharing and participating in daily life in experienced shared time), of real participation. Brooke Schoepf's action research with women in Zaire (1992 and reference list therein) and the best of the sexual behaviour studies in Brazil (Parker, 1991, 1992), Glasgow (McKeganey and Barnard, 1992) and elsewhere share this quality. The time and resource limitations on most anthropologists, and the lack of theoretical imagination of a few, means that such achievement remains mere aspiration for the majority.

CONCLUSION – ADVANCE WITH CULTURE OR RETREAT FROM IT?

In one sense cultural anthropology has been too successful. 'Culture' in its roughly anthropological meaning, as opposed to that of Goering or the *Times Literary Supplement* or the *New York Review of Books*, has become part of the common currency of intellectual analysis. Perhaps, however, caviare has become cod's roe in its transfer to the general. Thus Leo Chavez (personal communication, San Antonio, 1993) as a student of his own Spanish-speaking culture finds that others wrongly appreciate his work as being about the supposed lack of scientific knowledge, the enthusiasm of his subjects for folklore and quaint beliefs like fatalism and God's will. In a similar way I have found that management consultants in the British National Health Service use culture to mean any belief or principle which stands in the way of changes which their government clients wish them to make. These 'irrational' habits they see as shared by all nurses, some doctors and most patients and as being embedded in the way things are done which they want to change.

The effect of work on AIDS seems to have had a schismogenetic (Bateson, 1980 [1958]) effect on anthropologists' use of their core concept of culture. On the one hand, to please those who have appealed to them for help, they have intensified, without even noticing it, their tendency to reify culture, to see it as a thing to be possessed. People who want to act *on* others (and especially those who want to help others to act on others), however noble their intentions, behave in this way.

People who want to act *with* others, on the other hand, have perforce to emphasize the importance of recognizing individually and categorically determined differences in the continuous process of culture creation, use and change.

The culture(s) of anthropology itself imprison(s) the anthropologist in a language which may frustrate if recognition is not given to the creative tension within multicultural cultural patterns. This is as true of the triangle health professional–anthropologist–person with AIDS as it was in the classic triangle in the Gluckman–Malinowski dispute: administrator–anthropologist–African subject. Epidemiologists share the social experience of academic milieux with anthropologists; they may therefore have a similar gaze. The subjects of anthropological study and the objects of would-be behaviour-changers may have had similar experience. The anthropologist's appeal and the appeal to the anthropologist may be based on at first misperceived shared assumptions which unthinking practice has made real. Two such are that events are instantaneous or independent of time, and mind/body dualism. The avoidance of these may lie in the development (in Csordas's (1990) words) of 'embodiment as a paradigm for anthropology' with its recognition that the anthropologist like her/his subject embodies diverse cultural experiences and that the analysis of experience involves both internal and external dialogics (see Haraway, 1988 and 1989: 6–8; Lata Mani, 1990).

However, embodiment in this sense is not just the somatic content, often adequate to biomedical practice, for example, the description of sexual acts independent of meaning experienced or social context in a broad sense. Nor is it the corporeal reality of mere biological conceptions of the body as ecologically situated subsystem. It has to be seen as body incarnate, lived and ongoing cultural practice of the situated person in space and time: remembered, actual and anticipated. The anthropologist's role is to walk and talk with, not just about, such persons. Taking sides is not a new experience for the field anthropologist or for the applied anthropologist. Narayan (1993: 679) recalls Maquet discussing the issue in relation fo the decolonization of Africa as long ago as 1964, and it is, of course, near the surface of the Gluckman critique of Malinowski originally published in 1947. Serious consideration of which side to be on has become less rare but, in the complexities and rapid changes of situations like the AIDS/HIV epidemic, has also become more difficult. Many voices are perhaps the right replacement for forked tongues. The anthropologist has thus to provide clear and forceful argument and overtly revealed viewpoints rather than seek to mimic the increasingly uncertain certainties and prescriptions of medical colleagues.

© Ronald Frankenberg 1995

REFERENCES

Ardener, Edwin (1989a) [1972] 'Belief and the problem of women' in Edwin Ardener, *The Voice of Prophecy and Other Essays*, ed. Malcolm Chapman, Oxford: Basil Blackwell, 1989.

—— (1989b) [1975] 'The 'problem' revisited' in Edwin Ardener *The Voice of Prophecy and Other Essays*, ed. Malcolm Chapman, Oxford: Basil Blackwell, 1989.

Armstrong, David (1987) 'Theoretical tensions in biopsychosocial medicine', *Social Science and Medicine*, 25, 11, pp.1213–18.

Asad, Talal (ed.) (1973) *Anthropology and the Colonial Encounter*, London: Ithaca.

Barnett, Tony and Blaikie, Piers (1992) *AIDS in Africa: Its Present and Future Impact*, London: Belhaven.

Bateson, Gregory (1980) [1958] *Naven*, 2nd edn, London: Wildwood House.

Bellaby, Paul (1990) 'To risk or not to risk? Uses and limitations of Mary Douglas on risk-acceptability for understanding health and safety at work and road accidents', *Sociological Review*, 38, 3, pp.465–83.

Bolton, Ralph (1992) 'Mapping terra incognita: sex research for AIDS prevention – An urgent agenda for the 1990s' in G. Herdt and S. Lindenbaum (eds) *The Time of AIDS: Social Analysis, Theory and Method*, London: Sage, 1992.

—— (1993) 'Rethinking anthropology: the study of AIDS', paper presented at conference on 'AIDS and Anthropology', Free University of Amsterdam, 25 July 1992.

Burke, Peter (1987) *The Historical Anthropology of Early Modern Italy*, Cambridge: Cambridge University Press.

Calvez, Marcel (1989) *Composer avec un Danger: Approche des réponses sociales à l'infection au VIH et au SIDA*, Rennes: IRTS de Bretagne.

Clammer, David (ed.) (1979) *The New Economic Anthropology*, London: Macmillan.

Clifford, James (1988) *The Predicament of Culture;: Twentieth Century Ethnography, Literature and Art*, Cambridge, Mass.: Harvard University Press.

Clifford, James and Marcus, George (eds) (1986) *Writing Culture*, Berkeley: University of California Press.

Csordas, Thomas J. (1990) 'Embodiment as a paradigm for anthropology', *Ethos*, 18, pp. 5–47.

Day, Sophie (1988) 'Prostitute women and AIDS: anthropology', *AIDS*, 2, pp.421–8.

Day, Sophie, Ward, H. and Harris, J.R.W. (1988) 'Prostitute women and public health', *British Medical Journal*, 297, p.1585.

Donaldson, RJ. and Donaldson, L.J. (1983) *Essential Community Medicine*, Lancaster, UK: MTP.

Douglas, Mary (1973) *Natural Symbols: Explorations in Cosmology*, 2nd edn, London: Barrie and Jenkins.

—— (1986) *Risk Acceptability According to the Social Sciences*, London: Routledge & Kegan Paul.

Douglas, Mary and Calvez, Marcel (1990), 'The self as risk taker: a cultural theory of contagion in relation to AIDS', *Sociological Review*, 38, 3, pp.445–64.

Douglas, Mary and Wildavsky, Aaron (1983) *Risk and Culture*, Berkeley: University of California Press.

Epstein, A.L. (1992) *Scenes from African Urban Life: Collected Copperbelt Essays*, Edinburgh: Edinburgh University Press.

Evans-Pritchard, E.E. (1949) *The Sanusi of Cyrenaica*, Oxford: Clarendon.

Fabian, Johannes (1983) *Time and the Other: How Anthropology Makes its Object*, New York: Columbia University Press.

Farmer, Paul (1990) 'Sending sickness: sorcery, politics and changing concepts of AIDS in rural Haiti', *Medical Anthropology Quarterly*, (n.s.) 4, 1, pp.6-27.

—— (1992) *AIDS and Accusation: Haiti and the Geography of Blame*, Berkeley: University of California Press.

Frankenberg, Ronald (1979) 'Economic anthropology or political economy: the Barotse social formation' in David Clammer (ed.) *The New Economic Anthropology*, London: Macmillan.

—— (1988) 'AIDS and anthropology', *Anthropology Today*, 4, 2, pp.13–15.

—— (1992) 'What identity's at risk? AIDS, Anthropology and culture', *Anthropology in Action*, London: British Association for Social Anthropology in Policy and Practice.

—— (1993) 'Risk: anthropological and epidemiological narratives of prevention', in S. Lindenbaum and M. Lock (eds) (1993) *Knowledge, Power and Practice in Medicine and Everyday Life*, Berkeley: University of California Press.

Gluckman, Max (1958) [1940] *Analysis of a Social Situation in Modern Zululand*, Rhodes Livingstone Paper 28, Manchester: Manchester University Press.

—— (1963) *Order and Rebellion in Tribal Africa: Collected Essays with an Autobiographical Introduction*, London: Cohen & West.

Haraway, Donna (1988) 'Situated knowledges: the science question in feminism and the privilege of partial perspective', *Feminist Studies*, 14 pp.575–99 (reprinted in Haraway, 1991, pp.183–202).

—— (1989) *Primate Visions*, London: Routledge.

—— (1991) *Simians, Cyborgs, and Women: The Reinvention of Nature*, London: Free Association.

Hardman, Charlotte (1973) 'Can there be an anthropology of children?' *Journal of the Anthropology Society of Oxford*, 4, pp.85–99.
Herdt, Gilbert (1987) 'AIDS and anthropology', *Anthropology Today*, 3, 1–3.
—— (1992) 'Introduction' in Herdt and Lindenbaum (1992).
Herdt, Gilbert and Lindenbaum, Shirley (eds) (1992) *The Time of AIDS: Social Analysis, Theory and Method*, London: Sage.
Kane, Stephanie (1991) 'HIV, heroin and heterosexual relations', *Social Science and Medicine*, 32, 9, pp.1037–50.
Kane, Stephanie and Mason, Theresa (1992) '"IV drug users" and "sex partners": the limits of ethnographic categories and the epidemiology of risk' in Herdt and Lindenbaum (1992).
Kleinman, Arthur (1988) *Rethinking Psychiatry: From Cultural Category to Personal Experience*, New Tork: Free Press.
Lindenbaum, Shirley and Lock, Margaret (eds) (1993) *Knowledge, Power and Practice in Medicine and Everyday Life*, Berkeley: University of California Press.
McKeganey, Neil and Barnard, Marina (1992) *AIDS, Drugs and Sexual Risk: Lives in the Balance*, Buckingham: Open University Press.
Malinowski, Bronislaw (1946) *The Dynamics of Culture Change: An Enquiry into Race Relations in Africa*, (ed. Phyllis Kaberry, New Haven: Yale University Press.
Mani, Lata (1990) 'Multiple mediations: feminist scholarship in the age of multinational reception', *Feminist Review*, 35: 24–41.
Maquet, Jacques (1964) 'Objectivity in anthropology', *Current Anthropology*, 5: 47–55.
Marcus, George and Fischer, Michael (1986) *Anthropology as Cultural Critique: An Experimental Moment in the Human Sciences*, Chicago: University of Chicago Press.
Monks, Judith and Frankenberg, Ronald (1994) 'Being ill and being me: self, body and time in MS narratives' in Benedicte Ingstad and Susan Reynolds White (eds) *The Anthropology of Disability*, Berkeley: University of California Press.
Morris, R.J. (1976) *Cholera 1832*, London: Croom Helm.
Narayan, Kirin (1993) 'How native is a "Native" anthropologist?', *American Anthropologist*, 95, 3, pp.671–86.
Nichter, Mark (1987) 'Kyasanur forest disease: an ethnography of a disease of development', *Medical Anthropology Quarterly* (n.s.) 1, 4, pp.406–23.
Parker, Richard (1991) *Bodies, Pleasures, and Patterns: Sexual Culture in Contemporary Brazil*, Boston: Beacon.
—— (1992) 'Sexual diversity, cultural analysis and AIDS education in Brazil' in G. Herdt and S. Lindenbaum (eds) *The Time of AIDS: Social Analysis, Theory and Method*, London: Sage.
Patton, Cindy (1990) *Inventing AIDS*, New York and London: Routledge.
Robertson, A.F. (1984) *People and the State: An Anthropology of Planned Development*, Cambridge: Cambridge University Press.

Said, Edward (1979) *Orientalism*, New York: Vintage.

Scheper-Hughes, Nancy (1992) *Death Without Weeping: The Violence of Everyday Life in Brazil*, Berkeley: University of California Press.

Schiller, Nancy Glick (1992) 'What's wrong with this picture? The hegemonic construction of culture in AIDS research in the United States', *Medical Anthropology Quarterly*, (n.s.) 6, 3, pp.237–54.

Schoepf, Brooke Grundfest (1992) 'Women at risk: case studies from Zaire' in G. Herdt and S. Lindenbaum (eds) *The Time of AIDS: Social Analysis, Theory and Method*, London: Sage, 1992.

Schweder, Richard A. (1991) *Thinking Through Cultures: Expeditions in Cultural Psychology*, Cambridge, Mass: Harvard University Press.

Schweder, Richard A. and R.A. Levine (eds) (1984) *Culture Theory: Essays on Mind, Self and Emotion*, Cambridge and New York: Cambridge University Press.

Star, Susan Leigh (1988) 'The structure of ill-structured solutions: boundary objects and heterogeneous distributed problem solving' in Les Gasser and Michael Huhns (eds) *Distributed Artificial Intelligence*, 2, Menlo Park: Morgan Kauffman.

Taussig, Michael (1987) *Shamanism, Colonialism and the Wild Man: A Study in Terror and Healing*, London and Chicago: Chicago University Press.

Treichler, Paula (1992) 'AIDS, HIV and the cultural construction of reality' in G. Herdt and S. Lindenbaum (eds) *The Time of AIDS: Social Analysis, Theory and Method*, London: Sage, 1992.

Turner, Victor and Turner, Edith (1978) *Image and Pilgrimage in Christian Culture*, Oxford: Basil Blackwell.

CHAPTER 6

Feminist Anthropologies
and Questions of Masculinity
Andrea Cornwall and Nancy Lindisfarne

Malinowski, one of the 'founding fathers' of social anthropology, described the discipline as 'the study of man embracing woman' (cited in Moore, 1988: 1). When taken at face value, Malinowski's observation is particularly apposite. Ethnographic writing has always featured female actors, but until the late 1960s, women most often featured in anthropological work solely as subjects who were literally embraced by men: as wives, mothers and daughters, rather than individuals in their own right. The impact of the women's liberation movement and feminist theory on anthropology led to a reappraisal both of the ways in which women had been represented and, more widely, of the Western biases of anthropological research (Caplan, 1988). Since the 1970s, the male bias within the discipline has been constantly challenged and new areas for enquiry have been carved out which extend beyond the confines of anthropology.

While the insights of female and feminist anthropologists have had a broader impact on women's studies and gender studies, within anthropology itself the study of gender has tended to remain a marginal interest. Few inroads have been made into core teaching. Classes have consisted mainly of women students. Shapiro's observation, made in the late 1970s, continues in many ways to hold true: 'Much of the recent cross-cultural research is not only about women, but by women and in some sense for women' (Shapiro, 1979: 269).

Over the last few years, however, there has been a surge of interest in the study of men and masculinity. We are told that on both sides of the Atlantic men are starting to respond to the challenges of feminism, and the spotlight has turned to the heterosexual male. These responses to feminism not only attempt to 'unwrap masculinity' (Chapman and Rutherford, 1988), but also to reassert male prerogatives (Faludi, 1992): perhaps, as Brittan suggests, 'what has changed is not male power as such, but its form, the presentation and the packaging' (1989: 2). As Canaan and Griffin (1990) have suggested, much recent writing in men's studies seems to be part of the male backlash, while other explicitly sociological or anthropological contributions to the genre tend to be anachronistic and uncritically to reproduce earlier, and now defunct, debates in gender studies. One aim of our paper is to suggest how current feminist anthropologies can unsettle such male bias theoretically and practically.

Anthropological studies depend on finding ways of learning how others see the world. Three basic steps are intrinsic to this process. The first is to try and dismantle the conventional categories which dominate thinking on a particular subject. Thus anthropologists would ask themselves what they mean by their use of the terms 'man' or 'woman'. Or they may start with a notion such as 'masculinity' on which everyone seems to agree. By looking in detail at everyday usage and the different ways in which the same people talk of masculinity at different times, great variation soon becomes apparent. The second step is comparative. By examining the difficulties of translating particular meanings of masculinity from one social setting to another, anthropologists challenge the existence of any apparently straightforward universal category and raise questions about the social contexts in which gender categories are used. The third step occurs when anthropologists draw on the insights of ethnographic studies to examine their own preconceptions. Through ethnography, we can ask to what extent the familiar oppositions – male/female, man/woman and masculinity/femininity – are everywhere belied by a much more complex social reality.

Much of this complexity hinges on the way people understand the relation between gender and power, and an important impetus in gender studies is to describe and theorize this relationship. In this respect, our focus on masculinity is deliberate (see Cornwall and Lindisfarne, 1994). Though it is obvious that not all men are equally powerful, in the West being male is often associated with the power to dominate others. As anthropologists we want to investigate this association. Just how accurately does it describe people's everyday social lives? How are ideas of power connected with maleness? Or, conversely, what attributes of maleness are seen as empowering? What happens, for instance, when a man perceives himself as weaker than others? How does he define his masculinity? Is he perhaps no longer seen to be a 'real' man? Once comparative studies expose a diversity of meanings of masculinity, the idea of 'being a man' can no longer be treated as fixed or universal and the cultural premises which associate men with power can be seen as mystifications which benefit some people while disadvantaging most others. Politically, it takes us beyond the 'falsely universalizing perspective of the dominant' (Flax, 1990: 49); theoretically, it obliges us to attend to the *relation* between gendering and power.

This chapter outlines some of the formative debates in the anthropology of gender as a background to some of the intellectual and political issues raised by feminist and postmodernist theory. The feminist critique in anthropology was a seismic event, for it threw into question the whole basis upon which knowledge is constructed. It revealed just how partial, political and gendered are representations of the social world, undermining anthropology's claim to scientific objectivity. Obviously, this had, and continues to have, enormous relevance for the future of the discipline. Some have argued that postmodernist theories have a similar capacity to undermine conventional ways of thinking. However, as this chapter tries to show, 'relevance' also requires an explicit and committed political agenda, and this is one area where postmodernism and feminism often differ. Recent work has moved away from viewing gender as fixed differences to an exploration of the *processes* through which gender differences are created in different settings. Exciting new approaches range from treating gender not as inherent in persons, but as a performance (cf. Kessler and McKenna, 1978; Butler, 1990), while Strathern, whose contribution in *The Gender of the Gift* (1988) we examine in some detail, considers how gender difference construes difference more widely in social life. Our aim is to suggest an approach that responds to the problems posed by the use of Western gender categories *and* addresses people's experiences of inequality. In this respect, our positions as gendered participants in current debates about masculinity are significant. We seek to disrupt the premises which underlie much recent writing on and by men, whether it belongs to the canon of men's studies (cf. Brod, 1987; Kimmel, 1987) or is the work of anthropologists, such as that of Gilmore (1990). In so doing, we offer a perspective for viewing gendered identities which seeks to undermine dominant chauvinisms on which gender, class, race and other hierarchies depend.

FROM THE ANTHROPOLOGY OF WOMEN TO THE ANTHROPOLOGY OF GENDER

With the emergence of the women's movement and its central tenet 'the personal is the political', feminist scholars sought to explore the nature of female experience and to define a female Self, a category 'woman' in which all women could, with suitably raised consciousnesses, find a common cause: a means of tackling their oppression by 'patriarchy' and men (Janeway, 1971; Firestone, 1971; Millett, 1972). During the same period, in the late 1960s and early 1970s, an anthropology of women also began (cf. Ardener, 1985). An initial focus was to analyse descriptions of women in the anthropological literature. Several sources of male bias were identified. It became apparent that male and female anthropologists both had incorporated Eurocentric ideas of male dominance into their fieldwork, with a consequent emphasis on the beliefs and activities of the men within the communities under study. As with the early women's movement in general, the 'problem' for the anthropology of women was to put women back into the picture. The aim was to ask questions and describe the world from a woman's viewpoint and, in the case of applied anthropology, to find strategies whereby women could articulate and remedy their subordinate position *vis-à-vis* men (cf. Rogers, 1980). The categories 'women' and 'men' were not only uncritically accepted as universals, but were definitionally necessary to the new area of study.

This first wave of 'feminist anthropology' provided the impetus for a wider range of detailed ethnographies whose focus was women. Many of these uncritically used comparative notions such as 'women's status', 'role' or 'position' *vis-à-vis* men to document hitherto undescribed lives. Other more challenging works asked basic questions about the relationships between women and men (cf. Goodale, 1971; Strathern, 1972; Singer, 1973; Weiner, 1976). The analytical notions that perhaps had the greatest influence on the character of early women's studies in anthropology were closely related to other contemporary theoretical interests in psychoanalysis, structuralism and Marxist or Weberian social theory. Two influential volumes, by Rosaldo and Lamphere (1974) and Reiter (1975), introduced five key papers – by Ortner, Rosaldo, Sacks, Chodorow and Rubin – which set the scene for an anthropology of gender. The arguments put forward by these five writers continue to reverberate today and, in men's studies, they are often reproduced uncritically in spite of the two theoretically lively decades which have intervened.

Initially, Western dichotomies, such as nature–culture, emotion–reason, passive–active, were borrowed to ask questions about the political implications of the further dualism, women–men, to which they are intimately related. Ortner's (1974) analysis, a direct extension of Lévi-Straussian structuralism, investigated the asymmetry of the nature–culture dichotomy and drew attention to the relation between male dominance and the realm of 'culture'. Rosaldo (1974) discussed another dichotomy, that between the public and the private/domestic domains. She argued informal political processes can remain invisible in accounts that examine the public or formal sites of resource allocation and emphasized that *all* social arenas should be investigated for their political entailments.

By the end of the 1970s, however, the conceptual difficulties in generalizing from Western dichotomies were well known. Though trenchant feminist anthropological critiques of nature–culture (see MacCormack and Strathern, 1980) and public/private (cf. Rosaldo, 1980; Harris, 1981) appeared at this time, these dualisms are still often employed in the field of men's studies (see e.g. Seidler, 1987, 1991). For instance, there are now many accounts which conflate 'the domestic' with men's involvement in parenting (see e.g. Kimmel, 1987), reversing but reinstating the public–private dichotomy. So, for example, Brod criticizes studies of parenting for not examining how men's public roles effect their private fathering activities (1987: 42), but his emphasis hides other considerations. As Segal puts it, men have been allowed to 'retain power in the public sphere while having access to the satisfactions (often without the frustrations) of family life' (1990: 1, cf. 46–9).

Sacks' (1974) return to Engels marked another important trajectory in the development of anthropologies of women. But again, as anthropologists became more sensitive to ethnographic variations in gender relations, the theoretical tools that they had been using became increasingly problematic. The gender-blindness of mainstream social theory, notably Marxism, soon became apparent, raising questions about analyses purporting to explain male dominance in terms of prestige structures (cf. Ortner and Whitehead, 1981) or in materialist terms as production and reproduction (Ramazanoglu, 1989). However, as we shall see below, the same kind of gender-blindness in postmodernism continues to perpetuate male bias theoretically and in career terms.

Chodorow's (1974) neo-Freudian work on the origins of female subordination also depended on set of universalized premises about mothering and the psychological disposition of women as carers and men as controllers. While her work drew attention to the ways in which gender differences are created relationally, her approach was widely criticized within anthropology for its reductionism and Eurocentrism (cf. Fraser and Nicholson, 1990). Nonetheless, Chodorow's work has gained considerable currency in the popular literature and she has the distinction of being cited as one of the major feminist sources in men's studies in the USA (Brod, 1987: 13; and cf. Seidler (1987)), while the anthropologists Herdt (1981, 1984), Brandes (1981) and Gilmore (1990) all adopt neo-Freudian approaches to explain the development of masculine identities.

Finally. Rubin's (1975) work anticipated many of the later debates within feminism and anthropology and was, in many senses, well before its time. Rubin launched a devastating critique of both structuralism and psychoanalysis, demonstrating their congruence as 'in one sense the most sophisticated ideologies of sexism around' (1975: 200). Focusing on what she termed the 'sex-gender system', Rubin attempted to dislodge the 'naturalized' biological notions embedded in Western discourses on sexual difference and brought the term 'gender' into contemporary use, arguing that:

> gender is a socially imposed division of the sexes [which transforms] males and females into 'men' and 'women', each an incomplete half which can only find wholeness when united with each other . . . from the standpoint of nature, men and women are closer to each other than either to it or to anything else. . . . The idea that women and men are two mutually exclusive categories must arise out of something other than a nonexistent 'natural' opposition. Far from this being an expression of natural differences, exclusive gender identity is the suppression of natural similarities (1975: 80).

However, in spite of Rubin's cogent observations, during the following decade a conceptual separation between 'sex', as biological *essence*, and 'gender', as a social *construct*, came to dominate the field of gender studies. It was argued that while 'sex' is 'natural', 'gender' is always produced and defined socially.

At much the same time the debate within feminist politics shifted to concern two competing positions, broadly framed by the politics of equality and the politics of difference. On the one hand, feminists argued that if gender was socially constructed, then there was nothing inherent about being female and no reason why women should not both act to change representations of themselves or assume 'male' roles and statuses. On the other hand, others argued that the experience of being female and male was fundamentally different. This essential difference, they argued, is replicated in all historical and cultural formations, albeit in apparently different ways. These two perspectives gained the labels of 'constructionist' and 'essentialist', respectively. Both approaches tend to collapse the terms of debate into the generalized categories 'women' and 'men'. This often leaves unexplored *intra*-gender difference and questions of agency and oppression: such as the 'patriarchal bargains' women can strike with men to the disadvantage of other women (cf. Kandiyoti, 1988).

Many of the more important recent anthropological studies of gender are constructionist in their emphasis (cf. Caplan: 1987), while feminists, gay scholars and others have also contributed to the burgeoning cross-cultural literature. Much of this work draws on Foucault (e.g. 1979) to describe the ways in which people are gendered male or female within culturally and historically specific discourses (cf. Plummer, 1981). Yet, with the exception of Strathern (1987), few writers have paused to challenge the necessity or salience of gender dichotomies, let alone the presupposition of a 'sex-gender system' or the notion of gender itself.

POSTMODERNISM AND GENDER: CONTEMPORARY CHALLENGES

By exposing the partial perspective of every commentator, postmodernist writing unseats both the certainties of feminism as a political project and the notional objectivity, and authority, of the anthropological observer. It has the effect of making all explanation relative. Everything becomes a matter of perspective, and perspectives change with scale and context (Strathern, 1992). Thus, theories that rely on notions such as 'culture', 'class', 'race' and 'gender' become problematic because they depend on ascribing essences or essential attributes to members of the categories they create. Oppositions like 'men' and 'women' are such essentialist categories, while assertions of gender difference tie us to particular political positions (di Stefano, 1990).

A further unsettling thrust of the postmodernist challenge has been to dismantle the certainties on which Western social theory has rested. Notions of 'truth', 'reason' and indeed 'philosophy' (Rorty, 1980), have been shown to be products of a particular phase in Western thought. Lyotard, a principal commentator on what he terms the *Postmodern Condition* (1984), describes large-scale theories which purport to provide general explanations of social relations as 'grand narratives of legitimation'. Such theories, he argues, purport to generate 'truths' about the human condition, but in fact fail to embrace the complexity of local conditions and 'local stories'.

As Fraser (1989) points out, feminism as a political project has rested and continues in many ways to depend on such 'grand narratives' to theorize women's oppression. Abandoning the larger perspective for localized 'stories' both defuses the potential for women to work together and denies the possibility for larger-scale social policy or transformation. Deconstruction of categories such as 'woman' and the decentering of the subject raise further difficulties: if there is no such thing as 'women', how can they be oppressed? And, if the notion of 'rights' is, as has been argued, a regulative fiction of the West based on the concept of the individual, then shouting about 'women's rights' no longer has a meaning. If everything is relative and there are no grounds on which to base any meta-accounts, moral judgements and ethical positions are completely undermined: anything goes and there is no basis on which contesting versions can be compared or judged as 'right' or 'wrong'. Feminist critiques of social theory become irrelevant as social theory itself becomes meaningless.

As di Stefano, following Hartsock (1987) has asked: why is it now when women, and other silenced populations, are beginning to consolidate their theoretical and political positions that this assault on legitimacy is launched (1990: 75)? And why is it that accounts of postmodernism and post-structuralism are so over-ridingly male (Hodge, 1989)? A further irony is that many of the male anthropologists and who have engaged with postmodernism have dismissed or ignored the work of feminist philosophers and anthropologists (cf. Clifford and Marcus, 1986: 20–1; Mascia-Lees *et al.*, 1989; Abu-Lughod, 1991). And it is ominous that, in much of the men's studies literature, the category 'men' continues to be treated in an essentialist manner. In appropriating the personal (which this literature has done), there has been a tendency to forget the political and ignore the vested interest many men have in resisting change (see, for example, Bly's popular book *Iron John* (1991) which seems to resonate with the fashionable angst of the 'new man', while simultaneously celebrating a version of macho masculinity). As Canaan and Griffin make clear, the issues at stake in the development of men's studies as a discipline go beyond the question of theory to address those of academic privilege. They contend that men's studies may be 'part of the problem rather than part of the solution' (1990: 214). In short, it seems that it is feminist scholars, more than others, who have challenged the political impasse of postmodernism and wrestled with its implications for ethnography and for everyday politics. Perforce this has occurred because the postmodern critique echoes recent challenges within feminism.

Earlier feminism had a very singular and exclusive focus on the oppression of women by men. As with anthropology, early feminist writings were criticized for replicating racist and colonial discourses (cf. Mohanty *et al.*, 1991). The white, middle-class, voices which were raised in protest claimed to speak for 'everywoman'. This effectively silenced marginal and/or dissenting voices, denying the range of identities based on sexuality, race, class or ethnicity and the experience of other forms of oppression (cf. hooks, 1982). Thus, writers like Amadiume (1989) argued that the concern of white western feminists with 'liberating' their 'sisters' in Africa often involved imposing their values on situations they failed to understand.

Clearly, there was a need within feminist theory to find ways in which these multiple identifications and identities could be explored. If feminism as a political project was to remain tenable, the many different struggles of women in other arenas needed to be articulated. In the move to recognize the multiplicity of differences that exist between women, de Laurentis (1986) argues that the singular notion of 'feminism' needs to be replaced by an understanding that we need to talk of multiple, situated 'feminisms' which can, on occasion, be drawn on strategically (cf. Ross, 1989). How this might be done is suggested by Laclau and Mouffe's (1985) reworking of the Gramscian notion of hegemony. They argue that categories overlap as people's interests intersect and diverge: that a web of articulations is created between different interests for different purposes that neither compromise nor preclude interests or identities in other arenas.

This approach is similar to that of Mackey. She synthesizes arguments for a 'politics of location' (see 1991: 11; cf. Mohanty, 1992: 90, n. I; Probyn, 1990), arguing that however we construe our starting point, whether in conceptual or other identity terms, it involves asking anthropological questions about ourselves. And, in answering such questions, we find that we are all located in many different, and fluid, political arenas and that no single construction of identity can ever capture the manifold political interactions in which each of us is engaged. These political encounters occur all the time. The point is to become acutely aware of them and to situate oneself in terms of 'where we are coming from' and the political dimensions of *each interaction*. In short, what Mackey has called a 'revised politics of location' adopts a theoretical position which integrates a postmodern understanding of multiply constituted and ever-changing identities with the outlines of a methodology for situating a contingent political voice.

Such positions are empowering because they automatically include both the personal and political, making it possible to take a radical stance on questions of gendering without losing sight of the experience of inequality, Thus, following Foucault, it is possible to argue that the very notions of 'men' and 'women', as one of many oppressive binaries, are regulative ideals that produce inequalities. Using ideas about 'women's oppression' in political contests, for example, merely reinforces the problem. Rather, change can only come about when the notion of gender difference is transcended. Butler takes this position, arguing that,

> Gender ought not to be construed as a stable identity or locus of agency from which various acts follow; rather, gender is an identity tenuously constituted in time, instituted in an exterior space through stylised repetition of acts (1990: 40).

An important example of such a fluid approach to gendered identity is found in recent feminist work on embodiment.

As we suggested above, there is a paradox at the heart of the constructionist approach to sex and gender: while the social construction of gender categories is carefully described in terms of particularities, the very notion of 'gender categories' presupposes an incontrovertible gender dichotomy, which in turn rests on notions of essential biological difference. In effect, this is simply a reinstatement of the untenable nature–culture dichotomy in a different form. Cultural and historical specificity is overlaid onto presumed biological universals: male and female bodies.

While earlier theorists such as Chodorow (1974; Stoller, 1976) posited universal experiences of the body and of processes of forming gender identity, more recently feminist philosophers influenced principally by feminist appropriations of Lacan (Gatens, 1983; Grosz, 1987; Braidotti, 1991) have sought to transcend the polarized constructionist–essentialist debate to construct a radical and non-essentialist politics of difference.

Feminist theorists of difference have convincingly argued there is no such thing as an unmarked body: 'anatomy' is necessarily as cultural as 'gender'. As Gatens (1983) suggests, the alleged neutrality of the body denies the active subjectivity of the person inhabiting a body, which is always already culturally and historically *sexed*. She goes on to observe that the fact that the male body and the female body have different social significances cannot fail to have an effect on consciousness of self.

However, embodiment of difference consists in a *contingent* rather than necessary, or indeed essential, relation between sex and gender. Thus, the experience of maleness in a male body, or femaleness in a female body, is qualitatively different than that of maleness in a female body, or femaleness in a male body. All of these possibilities are realized in many nuanced ways in contemporary Western culture: the heterosexual macho man – perhaps, the Essex man – is seen to differ from his macho gay man counterpart, the muscle queen (see Forrest, below), the seven-stone weakling, an 'old woman', or an Amazon. So too, does the bimbo differ from the blue-stocking, 'butch' and 'femme' lesbians (Wieringa, 1989) or a male lesbian (Zita, 1992). And, by emphasizing different gendered attributes, individuals may participate in various of these identities simultaneously or sequentially.

The contingency of gender-markers is particularly useful for exploring the complexities of gendering. Contingent markers are non-exclusive and are linked to other ideas in a probabilistic rather than determinate way. So, for instance, baldness or aggressive behaviour are often seen as masculine attributes, but both may also be associated in quite different ways with attributions of age, health and personality which are not necessarily gendered at all. McElhinny (1994), writing of police women in the US, shows how in some situations work identities may take priority over gender in defining personhood. Thus, the police women describe themselves as learning 'to be hard' and 'unemotional' as part of 'doing their job'. To explain why impassivity is seen as an aspect of the masculinity of police men, but transforms women into police professionals, McElhinny shows that masculinity is contingently associated with emotional distance. This allows female police officers to interpret behaviour that is normally and frequently understood as masculine (such as a lack of emotionality or physical violence) as occupational.

Recent work has drawn attention not only to the historical variability of pervasive notions of the body, but also the extent to which they vary within similar social settings; it has also pointed to the political entailments of such representations. Consider but two examples which examine the relation between self-presentations of gendered identity and sexual orientations. Forrest (1994) writes of the emergence of a particular accentuated form of masculinity among gay men who chose to present themselves in terms of body images, sporting activities and clothing, which in earlier stereotypes were associated only with straight men. In effect this 'butch-shift' has dislodged the association between macho masculinity and heterosexual men. Cornwall (1994), by contrast, describes the multifaceted identities of the *travestis* prostitutes of Brazil, possessors of penises who dress in women's clothing and use hormones and silicone implants to feminize their breasts and hips. *Travestis* have both a 'male' and a 'female' body depending on which parts of the body are considered significant in determining 'sex' at any particular moment. Though *travestis* are possessors of penises, as Cornwall shows, there is only a contingent link between the penis and maleness. That is, they can be 'women' or 'men' according to the setting and the activities in which they take part.

THEORISING GENDER AND POWER

As we have mentioned above, the need to find some basis for making moral judgements about experiences of inequality and oppression has become the key postmodetnist problem for feminist anthropologists and others. As Mackey has put it, difference 'is not simply difference as distinction, but rather . . . difference is infused with hierarchies of power' (1991: 2). Gendered differences, when viewed from a historical or cross-cultural perspective, often appear stable or to repeat themselves as variations on a single theme. However, cultural forms are never replicated exactly and an essentialized male–female dichotomy cannot account for the ways in which people are gendered in different places at different times.

If notions of gender difference (and, indeed, the notion of gender itself) are contingent and situational, we need to consider how notions of difference are defined and redefined in interactions in different arenas within the same cultural setting. This raises questions such as: How do individuals present and negotiate a gendered identity? How and why are particular images and behaviours given gender labels? Who benefits from such labelling? And how do such labels change before different audiences and in different settings?

For instance, masculinity and femininity have often been portrayed as polarized opposites which only change in relation to each other. Thus, Kimmel, writing from within the genre of men's studies, informs us: 'Masculinity and femininity are relational constructs. . . . One cannot understand the social construction of either masculinity or femininity without reference to the others' (1987: 12). Behind this popular idea lurks a number of questionable assumptions. Among them is the idea that 'masculine' and 'feminine' qualities cannot be ascribed to a single individual at the same time, yet, as we have seen, such is certainly the case with *travestis*, but it is equally so when an army recruit is schooled in aggression by being called 'a woman'. Indeed, Kimmel's proposition suggests that there is only one vantage point from which gendered identities can be judged. This would ignore both the ambiguities and contradictions involved in gendering human beings and the multiple perspectives from which this is done.

However, attending to the relational character of 'male' and 'female' does raise various intriguing questions. One of these, which has not been that well explored in anthropology, concerns the relation between constructions of personhood and gendered difference. So one might consider the comparative implications of Rousseau's observation that, 'the male is only a male at certain times, the female is a female all her life' (quoted in Seidler, 1987: 88). Or, as in present British constructions, how does a strong woman emasculate a man? And what does he become – a baby, a big woman's blouse, a wimp or a poofter?

It also focuses attention on the ways in which the hierarchical relation between men and women is used to reproduce differences *within* the categories 'men' and 'women' and in other hierarchical discourses on 'class' and 'race'. Thus, the effects of colonialism have often been described in gendered terms. Those who are ruled are sometimes feminized and portrayed as 'of inferior vigour' in relation to the dominant masculinities asserted by the colonizers (cf. Stoler, 1991). Yet as Back's study of youth cultures in London suggests (1994), while racial inferiority may sometimes be expressed in terms of the exaggeration of an animal-like sexuality, fashions or music which convey such an attribute can also be appropriated by others to signal their own hypermasculinity. And, most importantly, a focus on the rhetorical relation between male and female does encourage us to consider where, how and by whom boundaries between 'men' and 'women' are imposed. And this leads us to issues of power and the power effects of gender attributions and to the gendering of power itself.

Carrigan, Connell and Lee (1985) illustrate the ways in which certain notions of what it takes to 'be a man' – what they term 'hegemonic masculinity' – are presented as authoritative versions, used to determine the standards against which other masculinities are defined in ways that marginalize not only women but also some men. They write,

Hegemonic masculinity is . . . a question of how particular groups of men inhabit positions of power and wealth and how they legitimate and reproduce the social relationships that generate their dominance. . . . An immediate consequence of this is that the culturally exalted form of masculinity, the hegemonic model, so to speak, may only correspond to the actual characters of a small number of men. Yet very large numbers of men are complicit in sustaining the hegemonic model (1987: 92).

Nowhere is there only one version of masculinity or femininity operating within any single cultural setting. Rather, in different contexts, different hegemonic versions are imposed by emphasizing certain physical or behavioural attributes and ignoring others. And at the same time, a range of alternative, subordinate, variants exist. Consider, for instance, Kanitkar's (1994) discussion of the 'ripping yarns' of the British Empire which introduced boys to an idealized, hegemonic masculinity associated with white racism, muscular Christianity and imperial power. While idioms of childhood defined the relation between the schoolboys and adult British men, these same idioms also defined the far greater subordination of adult 'native' men – 'boys' – whom the British boys saw as their inferiors and had no hesitation in dominating (cf. Shire, 1994).

By dislocating any single notion of what it is to be a man or a woman, it becames apparent that particular versions emerge in tandem with particular perceptions of equality or inequality. Relations of power are an aspect of every encounter.

In social theory and everyday usage, power has been treated as if it were both an abstraction located in concepts, beliefs and ideologies 'out there' and also a substantive property that can be won, exchanged or lost. Such mystifications of power encourage a focus on institutions, formal relations between the powerful and the weak and on men, whether as members of dominant groups or as dominant individuals in a social hierarchy. Conventional perspectives on power are male-biased, riven with functionalist circularities and unable to account for social change (Davis *et al.*, 1991). Power is often implicitly masculinized. An association between 'men' and 'power' is made to seem natural (as in the comment 'men are [naturally!] more aggressive than women'). Feminists talk of 'sexism','male bias' and 'male dominance' in describing and sometimes implicitly endorsing such an association. Such associations are also made in figures of speech, such as metaphor and metonymy. What is a 'real' man? And, why so often are 'real' men so often associated with images or instruments of power: Popeye's spinach, fast cars, military hardware?

Masculinized power is consistently associated with those who have control over resources, in whose interest it remains to propagate their use. This means that even where hierarchies are created through the deployment of notions of the inferiority of others by virtue of their 'gender', 'class' or 'race', men *and* women who are pre-eminent may be included in particular gendered constructions of power that simultaneously disempower both male and female subordinates. Thus, in Britain one elite masculine style relies on the stiff upper lip, yet it is a style to which the Queen subscribes and enacts on occasions such as the ritual Trooping of the Colour. Images, attributions and metaphors of masculinized power are so pervasive that they are frequently used to signify power in settings in which they have little or nothing to do with men at all. Emily Martin's work on biological idioms – on 'active' sperm and 'passive' egg in conception (1992a) and the masculinized killer T cells and the feminized macrophages of HIV virology (1992b) – provides two stunning examples of how ideas of masculinized power insinuate themselves into supposedly objective research.

To understand the culturally specific ways in which people experience autonomy and efficacy, it is essential to find an analytical frame which can account for the ways power is reified, naturalized and gendered in different settings. In this respect, Foucault's approach is valuable. Power is treated by Foucault as an elusive aspect of all social transactions whose existence depends on a 'multiplicity of points of resistance' (1979: 95). Though Foucault has been rightly criticized for not adequately considering the extent to which control is exercised in particular settings, how it constrains those who are controlled, how metaphors of control are gendered and above all, how they change (Turner, 1985), his theoretical insights can be refined and used to disrupt hegemonic associations of men with power. Thus, as Martin points out, one of the important ethnographic projects in recent years: has been the 'detection of resistances': quoting Abu-Lughod, she notes that we should 'look for and consider nontrivial all sorts of resistance, but instead of taking these as signs of human freedom we will use them strategically to tell us more about forms of power and how people are caught up in them' (Abu-Lughod cited in Martin, 1992b: 410). Such a perspective offers a means of exploring gendered resistance and is directly applicable to both ethnographic studies of masculinity and the ethnography of anthropology.

PROBLEMATIZING 'GENDER'. STUDYING INEQUALITY.

Strathern, drawing on the insights offered by the postmodernist critique of Western dualisms and ways of reasoning, provides a challenge to conventional thinking about gender that takes up some of these problems. In *The Gender of the Gift* (1988), she reformulates the notion of 'gender' as an open-ended category of 'family resemblances' (cf. Wittgenstein, 1963). Strathern notes that identifications as 'male' or 'female' as unitary states only emerge in particular circumstances. She argues that regarding 'gender' as constituted in terms of these unitary states precludes asking more interesting questions:

> Taken simply to be 'about' men and women, such categorizations have often appeared tautologous. Indeed, their inventive possibilities cannot be appreciated until attention is paid to the way in which relationships are construed through them (1988: xi).

Gender constructs, she contends, cannot be reduced to the affairs of men and women and gender ideologies are less reflections of reality than systems for producing differences and inequalities: 'Idealised masculinity is not necessarily just about men; it is not necessarily just about relations between the sexes either' (1988: 65). While it seems that the use of sexual imagery is common to human beings everywhere, neither the character of such images, nor their extension as metaphorical labels for a range of social experience, are determined universals.

Rather than assuming differences, Strathern's approach leads to the exploration of how people assert their own representations of biology, of sociality and of the 'natures' of people, and whether and where this is in terms of a gendered difference at all. In short, Strathern encourages us to ask: how do people think of difference and which differences make a difference, to whom and in which settings? As she suggests, these things cannot be assumed *a priori*:

> It remains a matter of ethnographic verification whether or not 'being a man' or 'being a woman' occupies an organising – representational, systematising – place in the classification of behaviour . . . [and] what the differentiation – the opposition and exclusion – may be about (1988: 65).

By emphasizing local understandings of gendered essences and the parts of people (scents, tastes, touch, thoughts, emotions; substances such as breastmilk and semen; psychic and material conditions – such as those bound up in notions of female virginity, cf. Lindisfarne, 1994) that may be transformed through interaction, Strathern addresses questions about the production of gendered difference. Using the descriptive notion of 'impingement', she considers the effects people have on each other and demonstrates how social life consists of a constant, alternating movement from one state to another. From this position, she addresses the wider question of how people, through oppositions and inclusions, 'deploy gender differences as constitutive of other differences' (1988: 68), such as those that are implicit in discourses about 'ethnicity' or 'race'.

As Overing (1986) and others suggest, Westerners find it virtually impossible not to regard the sexes in a permanent relation of asymmetry. This, combined with perceptions of coercion and collective action, creates a potent image of domination. Strathern cautions that the use of sexual imagery must always be located within the political economy that produces it. Thus, assumptions of difference or symmetry are never simple: an overt ideology of inequality between the sexes will necessarily conceal the combination of their labours. Yet the opposite can also hold true: from images of gender equality, concepts of inequality can also be fashioned (1988: 143).

Strathern overcomes the problems inherent in the use af the categories 'men' and 'women' by using the notion of 'replication' to talk about the collective character of relationships among men or among women. She argues that even in single-sex activities, there are no permanent sexual identities or relations of domination. Rather, these are necessarily constructed with reference to others who are represented as different or/and dominant. Equally, agents do not create asymmetry, but enact it by adopting relative and momentary positions (1988: 333–4).

If, as Strathern argues, male dependence on a female 'other' is a 'precondition for acts of male excess' (1988: 336), much more needs to be said about the rhetoric of such excesses, their incidence and the compliance or resistance of women and other men who are forced into subordinate positions. The task remains to link Strathern's explanation of embodied interactions with processes of negotiation and contested interpretations of power.

CONCLUSIONS

The relativism of postmodern thinking, which precludes the possibility of a centred position from which to make moral judgements can be as apolitical as early feminism was politically extreme in its ideas of male domination. The contemporary problem for anthropologists and others who seek to understand the complexity of people's everyday lives is to discover a convincing theoretical basis for addressing the relation between the two positions.

In one sense, this is easy because the contrast between the two positions has been overdrawn, not least because their respective proponents have often themselves seemed disembodied and their social backgrounds and political interests ignored. Initially, two important steps must be made: first, to be alert to the fact that theoretical positions are *always* enunciated by individuals with particular social identities and material interests and, secondly, to be willing to engage with the political implications of this fact.

The relevance of feminist anthropology to the modern world is implicit in the earlier questions we raised about postmodernist theory and male bias. Such is the case with Foucault's theory of power: the conventional Western associations of men with power is in fact naturalized in most of his work and neither the gendered attributes of power, nor the implications of representations of sexual difference, are explored in any detail (cf. Hartsock, 1990). Equally important is the relation between adopting a particular theoretical perspective and the academic/personal advantages which follow. Thus, it is notable that many men writing in the genre of men's studies continue to reproduce dualistic analyses of the kind which feminist anthropologists and others have now discredited. It is surely not accidental that such analyses both reify the essentialist category 'men' and reinstate male privilege through the unquestioned language and behaviour of masculinized power.

Three further steps are needed to link a feminist politics of location with anthropology (cf. Lindisfarne-Tapper, 1991). First, it is important to accept the postmodern challenge and relinquish any remaining pretext to objectivity and its attendant, and static, essentialisms.

Secondly, if the distinguishing feature of anthropological method is participant-observation, then this must play an *explicit* part in the formation of a political voice. Through the process of fieldwork itself, gendered political identities from 'home' are relocated through interaction in the field. And after such engagement the process of gendered politicization continues. We contend that by attending to this process, individual anthropologists can describe the intersection of their past positions as gendered political agents, their gendered learning and socialization in new social arenas and the ways they reposition themselves in later academic and other debates.

The most problematic third step is producing knowledge about others. If anthropologists dare to speak personally, and thus automatically to speak for others whose points of view they have in part assimilated, it is crucial to ask, who will listen and why? A critical understanding of the relation between the anthropologist's shifting gendered political identity and those of the audience is essential.

We suggest that people's everyday experiences of inequality can be located politically without reintroducing ideas of essentialized 'men' and 'women' or even gendered 'whole' persons (cf. Strathern, 1988; Ouroussoff, 1993). Rather, individuals embody many different subjectivities. And, though hegemonic discourses may suppress, they never totally censor other expressive possibilities. Thus, for example, by focusing on the subordinate variants of hegemonic masculinities, such as the masculinities of male children *vis-à-vis* adults, or of the native 'boy' *vis-à-vis* colonial employers, or that associated with the private soldier *vis-à-vis* the masculine styles valorized among men of the officer class, we can investigate the ways power is gendered. By doing this we necessarily challenge – from our own experiences and those of others whose subject positions we partially understand and share – the authority of dominant social formations. Contrary to current commonplaces, we argue that a postmodernist position cannot exclude moral judgements.

REFERENCES

Abu-Lughod, L. (1991) 'Can there be a feminist ethnography?', *Women and Performance*, 5, 1: 7–27.
Amadiume, Ifi (1989) *Male Daughters and Female Husbands*, London: Zed.
Ardener, S. (1985) 'The social anthropology of women and feminist anthropology', *Anthropology Today*, 5: 24–6.
Back, L. (1994) 'Rituals of masculinity: race and gender in south London' in A. Cornwall and N. Lindisfarne (eds) *Dislocating Masculinity: Comparative Ethnographies*, London: Routledge.
Bly, R. (1991) *Iron John: A Book About Men*, London: Element.
Braidotti. L. (1991) *Patterns of Dissonance*, London: Verso.
Brandes, S. (1981) 'Like wounded stags: male sexual ideology in an Andulusian town' in S. Ortner and H. Whitehead (eds) *Sexual Meanings*, Cambridge: Cambridge University Press.
Brittan, Arthur (1989) *Masculinity and Power*, Oxford: Blackwell.
Brod, Harry (ed.) (1987) *The Making of Masculinities: New Men's Studies*, Winchester, MA.: Allen & Unwin.

Butler, Judith (1990) *Gender Trouble*, New York: Routledge.
Canaan, J and Griffin, C. (1990) 'The new men's studies; part of the problem or part of the solution?', in J. Hearn and D. Dorgan (eds) *Men, Masculinities and Social Theory*, London: Unwin Hyman.
Caplan, Pat (ed.) (1987) *The Social Construction of Sexuality*, London: Routledge.
—— (1988) 'Engendering knowledge: the politics of ethnography', *Anthropology Today*, 4/5, 6: 8–12, 14–17.
Carrigan, Tim, Connell, Bob and Lee, John (1985) 'Towards a new sociology of masculinity', *Theory and Society*, 14, 5: 551–603; also in Harry Brod (ed.) *The Making of Masculinities: New Men's Studies*, Winchester, MA: Allen & Unwin, 1987.
Chapman, R. and Rutherford, J. (1988) (eds) *Male Order: Unwrapping Masculinity* London: Lawrence & Wishart.
Chodorow, N. (1974) 'Family structure and feminine personality' in M. Rosaldo and L. Lamphere (eds) *Women, Culture and Society*, Stanford, CA: Stanford University Press.
Clifford, J. and Marcus, G. (eds) (1986) *Writing Culture*, Berkeley: University of California Press.
Cornwall, A. (1994) 'Gendered identiies and gender ambiguity among *travestis* in Salvador, Brazil' in A. Cornwall and N. Lindisfarne (eds) (1994).
Cornwall, A. and Lindisfarne, N. (1994) (eds) *Dislocating Masculinity: Comparative Ethnographies*, London: Routledge.
Davis, K., Leijenaar, M. and Oldersma, J. (1991) *The Gender of Power*, London: Sage.
De Lauretis, Teresa (ed.) (1986) 'Feminist studies/critical studies: issues, terms and contexts' in *Feminist Studies/Critical Studies*, Bloomington: University of Indiana Press.
Di Stepano, C. (1990) 'Dilemmas of difference: feminism, modernity and postmodernism' in L. Nicholson (ed.) *Feminism/Postmodernism*, New York and London: Routledge.
Faludi, Susan (1992) *Backlash: The Undeclared War against Women*, London: Chatto.
Firestone, Shulamith (1971) *The Dialectic of Sex*, London: Paladin.
Flax, J. (1990) 'Postmodernism and gender relations in feminist theory' in L. Nicholson (ed.) *Feminism/Postmodernism*, New York and London: Routledge.
Forrest, D. (1994) 'We're here, we're queer and we're not going shopping: changing gay male identities in contemporary Britain' in A. Cornwall and N. Lindisfarne (eds) *Dislocating Masculinity: Comparative Ethnographies*, London: Routledge.
Foucault, Michel (1979) *History of Sexuality, Part One*, Harmondsworth: Penguin.
Fraser, Nancy (1989) *Unruly Practices: Power, Discourse and Gender in Contemporary Social Theory*, Oxford: Polity.

—— and Nicholson, L. (1990) 'Social criticism without philosophy: an encounter between feminism and postmodernism' in L. Nicholson (ed.) *Feminism/Postmodernism*, New York and London: Routledge.

Gatens, Moira (1983) 'A critique of the sex/gender distinction' in J. Allen and P. Patton (eds) *Beyond Marx? Interventions after Marx*, Sydney: Intervention.

Gilmore, David (1990) *Manhood in the Making: Cultural Concepts of Masculinity* New Haven and London: Yale University Press.

Goodale, J. (1971) *Tiwi Wives*, Seattle: University of Washington Press.

Grosz, E. (1987) 'Notes towards a corporeal feminism' in J. Allen and E. Grosz (eds) *Feminism and the Body*, special issue of *Australian Feminist Studies*, 5: 1–16.

Harris, Olivia (1981) 'Households as natural units' in Kate Young, Carol Wolkowitz and Roslyn McCullagh (eds) *Of Marriage and the Market*, London: CSE.

Hartsock, Nancy (1987) 'Rethinking modernism: minority vs. majority theories', *Cultural Critique*, 7: 187–206.

—— (1990) 'Foucault of power: a theory for women?' in L. Nicholson (ed.) *Feminism/Postmodernism*, New York and London: Routledge.

Herdt, G. (1981) *Guardians of the Flutes: Idioms of Masculinity*, New York: McGraw-Hill.

—— (1984) *Ritualized Homosexuality in Melanesia*, Berkeley: University of California Press.

Hodge, J. (1989) 'Feminism and post-modernism: misleading divisions imposed by the opposition between modernism and post-modernism' in A. Benjamin(ed.) *The Problems of Modernity*, London: Routledge.

hooks, b. (1982) *Ain't I a Woman? Black Women and Feminism*, London: Pluto.

Janeway, Elizabeth (1971) *Woman's Estate*, Harmondsworth: Penguin.

Kandiyoti, Deniz (1988) 'Bargaining with patriarchy', *Gender and Society*, 2, 3: 274–90.

Kanitkar, H. (1994) '"Real true boys": moulding the cadets of imperialism' in A. Cornwall and N. Lindisfarne (eds) *Dislocating Masculinity: Comparative Ethnographies*, London: Routledge.

Kessler, Susan J. and McKenna, Wendy (1978) *Gender: An Ethnomethodological Approach*, New York: John Wiley.

Kimmel, Michael (1987) *Changing Men: New Directions in Research on Men and Masculinity*, California: Sage.

Laclau, Ernesto, and Mouffe, Chantal (1985) *Hegemony and Socialist Strategy*, London: Pluto.

Lindisfarne, N. (1994) 'Variant masculinities, variant virginities: Rethinking 'honour and shame' in A. Cornwall and N. Lindisfarne (eds) *Dislocating Masculinity: Comparative Ethnographies*, London: Routledge.

Lindisfarne-Tapper, N. (1991) 'Local contexts and political voices', *Anthropology of Action*, 10: 6–8.

Lyotard, Jean-François (1984) *The Postmodern Condition: A Report on Knowledge*, Manchester: Manchester University Press.

MacCormack, C. and Strathern, M. (eds) (1980) *Nature, Culture and Gender*, Cambridge: Cambridge University Press.

McElhinny, B. (1994) 'An economy of affect: objectivity, masculinity and the gendering of police work' in A. Cornwall and N. Lindisfarne (eds) *Dislocating Masculinity: Comparative Ethnographies*, London: Routledge.

Mackey, Eva (1991) 'Revisioning "home"work: feminism and the politics of voice and representation', unpublished MA term paper, University of Sussex.

Martin, Emily (1992a) 'Body narratives, body boundaries' in L. Grossberg, C. Nelson and P. Treichler (eds) *Cultural Studies*, New York and London: Routledge.

—— (1992b) 'The end of the body?', *American Ethnologist*, 19, 1: 121–40.

Mascia-Lees, F., Sharpe, P. and Ballerino Cohen, C. (1989) 'The postmodernist turn in anthropology: cautions from a feminist perspective', *Signs: Journal of Women in Culture and Society*, 215, 1: 7–33.

—— (1992) 'Feminist encounters: locating the politics of experience' in M. Barrett and A. Phillips (eds) *Destabilizing Theory: Contemporary Feminist Debates*, Cambridge: Polity.

Millett, Kate (1972) *Sexual Politics*, London: Abacus.

Mohanty, Chandra Talpade (1987) 'Feminist encounters: locating the politics of experience', *Copyright*, 1: 'Fin de Siecle 2000', 30–44.

Mohanty, Chandra Talpade, Ann Russo and Lourdes Torres (eds) (1991) *Third World Women and the Politics of Feminism*, Bloomington: Indiana University Press.

Moore, Henrietta (1988) *Feminism and Anthropology*, London: Polity.

Nicholson, Linda (ed.) (1990) *Feminism/Postmodernism*, New York and London: Routledge.

Ortner, Sherry (1974) 'Is female to male as nature is to culture?' in M. Rosaldo and L. Lamphere (eds) *Women, Culture and Society*, Stanford, CA: Stanford University Press.

Ortner, Sherry and Whitehead, Harriet (eds) (1981) *Sexual Meanings*, Cambridge; Cambridge University Press.

Ouroussoff, A. (1993) 'Illusions of rationality: false premisses of the liberal tradition', *Man*, 28, 2: 281–99.

Overing, J. (1986) 'Men control women? The "Catch 22" in the analysis of gender', *International Journal of Moral and Social Studies*, 1, 2: 135–56.

Plummer, Ken (ed.) (1981) *The Making of the Modern Homosexual*, London: Hutchinson/Gay Men's Press.

Probyn, E. (1990) 'Travels in the postmodern: making sense of the local' in L. Nicholson (ed.) *Feminism/Postmodernism*, New York and London: Routledge.

Ramazanoglu, C. (1989) *Feminism and the Contradictions of Oppression*, London: Routledge.

Reiter, Rayna (ed.) (1976) *Toward an Anthropology of Women*, New York: Monthly Review Press.

Rogers, Barbara (1980) *The Domestication of Women*, London: Tavistock.

Rorty, Richard (1980) *Philosophy and the Mirror of Nature*, Princeton: Princeton University Press.

Rosaldo, Michell (1974) 'Women, culture and society: a theoretical overview' in M. Rosaldo and L. Lamphere (eds) *Women, Culture and Society*, Stanford, CA: Stanford University Press.

—— (1980) 'The use and abuse of anthropology: reflections of feminism and cross-cultural understanding', *Signs: Journal of Women in Culture and Society*, 5, 3: 389–417.

Rosaldo, Michelle, and Lamphere, Louise (eds) (1974) *Women, Culture and Society*, Stanford, CA: Stanford University Press.

Ross, Andrew (ed.) (1989) *Universal Abandon?*, Edinburgh: Edinburgh University Press.

Rubin, Gayle (1975) 'The traffic in women; Notes on the "political economy" of sex' in Rayna Reiter (ed.) *Toward and Anthropology of Women*, New York: Monthly Review Press.

Sacks, Karen (1974) 'Engels revisited: women, the organization of production, and private property' in M. Rosaldo and L. Lampher (eds) *Women, Culture and Society*, Stanford, CA:, Stanford University Press. Also in R. Reiter (ed.) *Toward an Anthropology of Women*, New York: Monthly Review Press, 1975.

Segal, L. (1990) *Slow Motion: Changing Masculinities*, Changing Men, London: Virago.

Seidler, V. (1987) 'Reason, desire and male sexuality' in P. Caplan (ed.) *The Social Construction of Sexuality*, London: Routledge.

—— (1991) *Recreating Sexual Politics*, London: Routledge.

Shapiro, Judith (1979) 'Cross-cultural perspectives on sexual differentiation' in H. A. Kachadourain (ed.) *Human Sexuality: Comparative and Development Perspectives*, Berkeley: University of California Press.

Shire, C. (1994) 'Men don't go to the moon: language, space and masculinities in Zimbabwe' in A. Cornwall and N. Lindisfarne (eds) *Dislocating Masculinity: Comparative Ethnographies*, London: Routledge.

Singer, A. (1973) 'Marriage payments and the exchange of people', *Man*, 8, 1: 80–92.

Stoler, A. (1991) 'Carnal Knowledge and imperial power; gender, race and morality in colonial Asia' in M. di Leonardo (ed.) *Gender at the Crossroads of Knowledge; Feminist Anthropology in the Postmodern Era*, Berkeley: University of California Press.

Stoller, Robert (1976) *Sex and Gender*, London: Hogarth.

Strathern, Marilyn (1972) *Women in Between: Female Roles in a Male World: Mount Hagen, New Guinea*, London: Seminar.

—— (1987) 'An awkward relationship: the case of feminism and anthropology', *Signs*, 12, 2: 276–92.

—— (1988) *The Gender of the Gift*, Berkeley: University of California Press.

—— (1992) *Partial Connections*, London: Rowman & Littlefield.

Turner, Bryan (1985) 'The practices of rationality: Michael Foucault, medical history and sociological theory' in R. Fardon (ed.) *Power and Knowledge*, Edinburgh; Scottish Academic Press.

Weiner, A. (1976) *Women of Value, Men of Renown*, Austin: University of Texas Press.

Wieringa, Saskia (1989) 'An anthropological critique of constructionalism: berdaches and butches' in D. Altman (ed.) *Homosexuality, which Homosexuality? Essays from the International Scientific Conference on Lesbian and Gay Studies*, London: Gay Men's Press.

Wittgenstein, L. (1963) *Philosophical Investigations*, Oxford: Basil Blackwell.

Zita, J. (1992) 'Male lesbians and the postmodernist body', *Hypatia*, 7, 4: 106–27.

CHAPTER 7

Tourism, Modernity and Nostalgia
Nelson H.H. Graburn

The contemporary world presents many problems and opportunities for anthropologists. Gone are the days when anthropology was the natural science of so-called primitive peoples, or even the comparative study of small-scale societies. The typical subject-matter of anthropological monographs, the functionally intact small-scale non-Western society, no longer exists – if indeed it ever did. We can be certain that the classic structural-functional analyses which attempted to find and explain equilibrium in small-scale socio-cultural and ecological systems would bc inadequate today, and probably also were during the colonial period when most classical anthropological monographs were written.[2]

The subject-matter of anthropology broadly conceived is 'difference', the study and understanding of 'otherness' in its various forms, socio-psychological, socio-cultural and temporal (as in history and archaeology) . The classical anthropological model of difference was evolutionary, the assumption that those peoples apparently more different from the observer – who was usually middle-aged, white, male – were temporally different in that they or their societies represented earlier stages in the grand, directional sweep of human history.

Though major anthropological figures such as Franz Boas (1896) and Bronislaw Malinowski (1922) rejected the evolutionary model, they and Radcliffe-Brown (1923) continued the tradition that the observer was urban, white, male and the observed were darker and from less metropolitan societies. Though these approaches gave way to French structuralist (Levi-Strauss, 1949), symbolic and processual (Turner, 1969) and even Marxist (White, 1949) forms of anthropology, the often implicit geographical and simple-to-complex evolutionary framework of difference remained.

As so often has happened, anthropology has had to catch up with the events of the world, following after journalists and novelists. Anthropologists, more so perhaps than members of other disciplines, have often remained wedded to their paradigm even after it was out of date. The colonial world of the sixteenth to nineteenth centuries sped up the creation of the world system (Wallerstein, 1974; Wolf, 1982) which included metropolitan (and academic) centres and more rural, exploited (and ethnographically described) peripheries. Flow between the metropoles and peripheries was not just outwards, but included an exchange, and centripetal flow of the elites – with the partial exception of the slave trade – from the peripheries to the centres; elites such as Ghandi, Ho Chi Minh or Kenyetta, who later became the leaders of the decolonizing movements of the twentieth century.

Since the Second World War and the formal end of most external colonialisms, even larger movements have taken place, often between those areas formerly linked by the bonds of colonialism. Paradoxically, this transnational exchange is one of tourists flowing 'North-to-South' on vacation (Turner and Ash, 1975) and immigrants, legal and illegal, migrating in the opposite direction in search of work (Buck-Morss, 1987; Carter, in press).

Some have said that the former subjects of anthropology have come from everywhere to meet them on their home ground, and others have pointed out that tourists, like anthropologists, are scouring the whole world trying to explain 'difference' in their own particular ways (MacCannell, 1976). The very different world, created by advanced capitalist enterprises and liberal political institutions that surrounds us now has been called postmodern (Jameson, 1985) as well as post-colonial, though we are still not sure that we can equate the two (Appiah, 1991).

This postmodern, post-colonial world again presents a paradox. It is said to be characterized by increasing 'diversity, fragmentation and differentiation, in place of the homogeneity and standardization that were once the hallmarks of modernism and mass society' (Ahmed and Shore, this volume) – meaning that the old metropoles are now full of ethnic diversity, mixtures, blending and contrasting 'traditions', and competing value systems. On the other hand, from a touristic point of view, the world is fast homogenizing (see also below), since the *same kinds* of mixtures, blends and incongruities can be found almost anywhere, channelled by the same sorts of techno-bureaucratic institutions (Freidman, 1990; Hannerz, 1987).

The other set of characteristics of postmodernity, that of superficial identities, replication and the collapse of history, results both from the technical revolutions – first the photographic (Benjamin, 1968), then electronic – and from the impulse of advanced capitalism to promote endless consumerism by the proliferation of minor product differentiations. These characteristics have a profound effect on tourism in bringing to the fore people's philosophical concerns about authenticity, an authenticity which appears to be receding as fast as it is approached, as well as about commercial concerns to 'invent traditions' and to promote nostalgia.

Anthropologists are also having problems with the authenticity of their 'truths'. They increasingly find themselves taken for 'mere' tourists (Bruner, 1989; Errington and Gewertz, 1991) if not more sinister characters. If anthropologists cannot find their 'subject' (or is it their 'object'?) in geographically and cultural distinct packages – or if they find bits of them everywhere – how can they carry out their research? Anthropological accounts are their own particular kind of 'construction of reality' (Berger and Luckman, 1966), obviously but one more form of replication of culture (Marcus and Fischer, 1986). And recently anthropologists have questioned the very existence of any original 'thing' like culture (Wagner, 1975). In a world of repeated replications and multiple co-existing truths, are the results of anthropological research any different from (or better than) journalism, or tourists' accounts? And, lastly, the descendants of the former anthropological subject peoples are no longer spatially apart or culturally confined: they may be academics in the metropolis too. Why therefore would they need the children of ex-colonials to describe and analyse their societies? Who if anyone has the authority to speak for anyone any more (Marcus and Fischer, 1986), or even to grant them 'agency'?

Luckily, 'authority' is not the only reason why anyone might want to listen to or read the works of anthropologists. Our works can be entertaining as well as informative. Our findings can strike empathetic and aesthetic as well as didactic cords. If anthropologists are open to the models and voices ('world views' in old parlance) of other commentators and other cultures, they – like novelists involved in participant observations (Mukherjee, 1989) – stand in a particularly advantaged position to elaborate on the contemporary world.

Anthropology has always been cross-cultural and is now transnational. Anthropologists are conducting quests of understanding of 'Otherness' which both parallel and compete with the lay quests of tourists and travelers (MacCannell, 1976; Van den Abeele, 1980). Anthropologists have been immersed in colonial and post-colonial situations and have specialized in the examination of ethnicity, reconstructed or otherwise (cf. Graburn, 1980). As annual tourist and transnational flows approach 500 million a year, anthropologists are both part of, and commentators on, these phenomena.

In this short paper, I shall examine contemporary phenomena, such as tourism, for their ability to throw light on the nature of macro-cultural processes. I have focused on a set of phenomena including nostalgia, authenticity and hyper-reality, all of which have been said to be major components of motivation for contemporary tourists and all of which are central to intellectual debates on tourism and modernity.[3]

THE MEASURE OF TRAVEL AND TOURISM

The growth of the tourism and travel industry in the West and in Asia since the 1950s has paralleled the growth in personal freedom and economic affluence as well as lowering of international barriers and thawing of international relations. But overseas tourism is also a measure of inequalities of wealth – between the touring and the host peoples. Contemporary tourism is taking place within the setting of political and natural disasters driving migrants in the opposite direction.

The size of the demographic and economic flows are staggering. Since 1960 the number of known international visitor arrivals (for all purposes, but over 80 per cent are tourists) has grown from under 70,000,000 annually to over 500,000,000 in 1993.[4] The expenditures of these travelers has risen from $6,900,000,000 in 1960 to $334,000,000,000 in 1993 (in constant 1992 dollars). The World Tourism Organization expects that international travel will continue to grow to over 750.000,000 people spending $720,000,000,000 by the year 2,000 AD (Edgell, 1993); the number of international travellers is expected to surpass 1 billion (1,000,000,000) people a year before the year 2010.

Nearly twenty years ago the American futurologist Herman Kahn (1976) predicted that by the end of this century tourism would be one of the largest international industries in the world; it appears that he was correct. Already the international tourism and travel industry is four times as large as the international arms trade and twice as large as the trade in petroleum products. Though comparative figures are difficult to find, by 1990 tourism expenditure in the United States, including both domestic and overseas, was nearly twice as large as expenditure an all forms of education and was only surpassed by the health and medical services industry. If we are to add expenditures on world domestic tourism to international tourism, we already have an industry with expenditures of over $2,000,000,000,000 a year which is clearly the largest in the world.

This brief historical examination of travel and tourism shows the interplay between the social structural forces of tradition and change in their dialectic relation to the opportunities and constraints of technological innovations.

Hunting and gathering peoples were impelled to travel for seasonal sustenance, but also chose to for social gatherings and information exchange. As mankind settled into villages and towns with the spread of agriculture, people were increasingly controlled by centralized governments. The ability to travel, and indeed to continue to hunt, was often reserved for the more powerful members of the society. During the past two millenia, peaceful means of travel were usually confined to pilgrimages, especially in the great civilizations of India, China, Japan and Europe. In Tokugawa Japan, *shomin* [commoners] were only allowed to leave home for religious or health reasons, so the great shrines and temples and *onsen* [hot spring areas] became the foci of regular mass travel, as were places like Canterbury, Lourdes and Rome for the ordinary people of Europe.

The origins of modern tourism in Europe have been traced to the Grand Tour which started in the late fifteenth century after the Age of Discovery had brought a new affluence (Trease, 1967). The Grand Tour of Continental Europe was undertaken by young British aristocrats accompanied by their tutor-advisers. This regular activity broke with the previously religious sanctioned pilgrimage-travel of the medieval period, and reflected the growing secularization of elite society, with its interests in scholarship, natural history and science, and learning foreign languages and manners.

This was a very elite form of tourism, with the practical goal of educating each new generation of men for leadership by making political alliances with the leading wise men and nobles of other countries. Similar experiences were also found among the upper strata of China and Japan, where Confucius said 'To travel 10,000 *li* is worth reading 10,000 books.'

Later, peace and the growth of prosperity through trade brought an expansion of the Grand Tour to the upper middle classes of increasingly bourgeois Europe. The tour exchanged its political goals for educational purposes; tutor-advisers became more like guides, as serious learning gave way to sightseeing (Adler 1989). But change of another kind was brought about by the Industrial Revolution of the late eighteenth century and the spread of railways and steamships in the nineteenth.

While the affluent classes stayed with their horses and their stage-coaches in the 1840s, Thomas Cook, a Methodist minister, arranged for the poor people of the polluted and gin-soaked new industrial cities of northern England to visit the countryside and the mountain areas on day-long excursions using the newly invented steam trains (Brendon, 1991). Soon he expanded these trips to overnight stays in more distant places like Wales and Scotland, and even helped members of the newly formed labour unions take excursions to such wonders as the Great Exhibition ('Crystal Palace') in London in 1851. Though it is true that Thomas Cook soon went on to see the great possibilities of modern commercial tourism – he invented travellers' cheques, hotel and railway class systems and tickets, package tours and so on – the original motivation for travel was a moral and political one: the alienation of the industrial revolution was inverting the relative moral value of the cities and the countryside. One might also add that Cook was empowering the poor to emulate the ability of the more prestigious class to leave their home environment.

The success of Thomas Cook and other travel companies in the nineteenth century, brought the expansion of touristic travel (*a*) to all parts of the world, (*b*) by people all of the middle classes within society and (*c*) more and more nationalities. There was a spreading democratization of travel, paralleling the democratization of education and politics in much of the world. A common theme of modern travel and much else in the modern capitalist world is 'freedom': freedom of movement, freedom of education, freedom of speech, and freedom of market choice. In the religion-bound feudal world, remnants of which still remain in Asia and the Middle East, one does not find these kinds of freedom.

The twentieth century has seen two major qualitative changes in the evolution of tourism. The first was the advent of the personal car and the subsequent system of roads, motels, gas stations, vans and even mobile homes which started in the United States but has now spread throughout the advanced industrial world. Automobile use increased the choices of travellers in two major ways: firstly, they could choose where and when to travel, not following the routes and schedule of the omnibuses, trains and ships; this led to the touristic penetration of the furthest corners of the land, leaving few people or landscapes untouched by modernity. Secondly, it allowed people to travel in small groups, families or even alone, *without* having to go along with the groups and crowds characteristic of the culture of pre-modern travel. Of course, the increase in numbers of cars brought more crowds, leading to more road-building and commercialization, changing the very nature of the destinations where people sought recreation.

The second major change was the advent of the jet age, inaugurated by the British Overseas Airways Corporation (BOAC) with the de Havilland Comet in the 1950s, followed by the Boeing 707 and the DC-8. This mass form of transportation permitted the extension of modern patterns of group travel to almost anywhere in the world. But it remained group travel, and the recreational goals of 'fun in the sun' or touring famous historical and natural sites remained more like the nineteenth century, less exploratory than tourism by car.

Japanese tourism, both domestic and overseas, is now among the fastest growing in the world, reflecting Japan's technological advancement and economic power. Whether its history of tourism, now paralleling but lagging behind that of the West, reflects a convergence of civilizations is a major question for some social scientists. Like other forms of tourism in Asia but unlike the West, the essential structure of most contemporary Japanese tourism stems directly from a secularization of the millenia-old religious pilgrimage system, with *sendatsu* [priest/leader] and *dantai* [pilgrimage/company group] now replaced by the *annainin* or *gaido* [tourist guide] and *guruupu* [packaged group].

It is the dialectic interplay between the technological aspects of travel and the socio-cultural side that makes the topic so fascinating. These changes have brought a huge growth of tourism all over the world, and in turn a new set of politico-economic and moral concerns about socio-cultural, economic and environmental impacts (Smith, 1989) which remain very important to us now and in the foreseeable future.

THE CREATION OF NEW DESTINATIONS

Under the pressure of an ever-greater proportion of the growing world population wanting to travel, not only must new regulations be imposed to protect fragile destinations, but new attractions are constantly found or constructed. Not only is the demand growing but advanced capitalism stimulates consumption by the proliferation of saleable products, in this case the production of experience. But the ability to produce destinations to fit different tastes depends on their character.

Ordinary 'fun in the sun', *bronzer-idiot* beach tourism (Thurot and

Thurot, 1983) is the most easily duplicated. Transnational companies and wealthy local elites in the Third World make available for international tourists their most beautiful sites (and too often their youth), in the never-ending effort to promote 'development', to earn foreign exchange and to create new employment. The competition between destinations keeps prices down, but there will always remain a relative shortage of unique natural and historical heritage sites.

Ironically in the dynamic capitalist countries of the world, where tourism is booming and new attractions are created all the time, it is 'old' attractions that are growing fastest of all. Everywhere historical events are being memorialized, old buildings are renewed or even rebuilt, and museums are opening to house collectibles as never before (Lowenthal, 1985). These sites are chosen, refurbished, and put on the map. They must be preserved and promoted, and they are the targets of almost over-whelming numbers of visitors. Japan, of course, is replete with both impressive heritage sites and great natural features which have been 'culturalized' as targets of pilgrimage and tourism (Graburn, 1983b). Japan was one of the first nations to list and classify its national treasures, an example followed by others.

Both natural wonders and historical heritage sites are now recognized and listed by the United Nations as 'world heritage' sites for all mankind, not just for the people of the nations where they are situated. This assumes international tourism is a permanent phenomenon and spreads the homogenizing preservationist ideal throught the world. But there is a great difference between natural and cultural/heritage attractions. While both can be conserved, we have shown above that it is possible to create the latter, man-made, attractions where none existed before.

One may ask how this is possible, and we can answer that everything that is ordinary and new – houses, clothes, cars, furniture, art, photos – soon gets to be old, remarkable, quaint, collectible, and worth preserving if you keep it long enough. Marshall MacLuhan once said 'All obsolete technology becomes art'; and Michael Thompson's book *Rubbish Theory* (1979) explains how used and discarded objects regain value in the hands of the right classes.

One of the key forces imbuing power to tourist attractions is nostalgia, the sentimental longing for feelings and things of the past. Though one cannot return to the past, recreations of the past through buildings, re-enactments and evocations of the past, through taste, smell, feel, music and atmosphere are keys to the success of many new tourist attractions. It is possible, of course, to reveal or even to create some new features of natural scenery though it takes considerable effort – like damming rivers or reclaiming marshland – which then become tourist attractions; but the creation of heritage is a growth industry into the future.

Whose nostalgia?

The manufacture of heritage responds to one of the most powerful of all modern tropes of attraction: nostalgia. Nostalgia, originally meant the pain of homesickness and was first diagnosed in the seventeenth century as a fatal disease (Davis, 1979). It has now come to mean the anguish occasioned by *temporal displacement*, the loss of something past, presumably once familiar, or something which is a symbol or affective marker of that past.

One may ask whether nostalgia is a singular phenomenon, whether it is special to conditions of modernity or postmodernity, or whether it is part of the human condition. It is certainly a driving force in many forms of tourism, whether nature- or history based, and of course is particularly subject to commercial and political manipulation. Tourism is undoubtably related to alienation, but this 'wish for the past' can be purely personal, class or group-based or all embracing.

It has been suggested that nostalgia can be a personal effort to slow down one's life cycle, to return to an earlier stage or to counter rapid change, with the individual fear that one is getting obsolete. Such people might take a holiday in a place whether they were brought up, try to undertake more youthful activities such as cycling or surfing, or even engage in a second honeymoon. In Japan the major railway company has put out a series of advertisements for *sirubamun* [silver moon] holidays – combining the 'silver' of old age with the possibility of a honeymoon.

Social position can also stir up specific kinds of nostalgia. One might splurge on holiday or try to emulate a higher class lifestyle, if one's family once enjoyed such a background (one could of course be social climbing too!). A special version of this is what Rosaldo (1989) called 'imperialist nostalgia', a kind of regret that people of the Western world have for the destruction they have wrought on other ways of life through colonization, or on nature through industrial exploitation. A lot of Third World and eco-tourism is based on these impulses. A special case of this is exemplified in one form of Japanese tourism to Indonesia (Matsuda, 1989). The tourists emulate the former colonial lifestyle, positioning themselves with the West in general and white colonizers in particular and, at the same time, they identify with the Indonesians as 'we Asians' *vis-à-vis* white tourists from Australia and Europe.

Then there is the question whether nostalgia is a particular characteristic of the present historical era, with its loss of faith in science, progress or even humanity itself. Obviously regret of the passing of time is the *sine qua non* of nostalgia, and should be found in all societies conscious of history. Even in the tenth-century novel *Genji Monogatari*, about the Heian Japanese court, the young Prince Genji was bemoaning the lack of men like his ancestors.

But MacCannell (1976) among others has put forward powerful arguments that much tourism is based on alienation from today's urban fast-paced present, that there is a longing for the alledgedly simpler life of nature, of rural areas and people, and of history. This nostalgia is a search for more 'authentic' experiences for people seeking connectedness and community, imagining it is found in 'simpler, gentler' lifestyles. This has led to the museumification of primary and manufacturing cultures, with a twist that for an urban people, authenticity is to be found in rural cultures or *non*-service forms of work. This may turn out to be a kind of 'imperialist nostalgia' over the pace of socio-technical change, and it might be found in any historical period of fast change. The converse might be found in science fiction, when alienation from the present drives one to imagine a better future!

In addition to opening up natural areas for recreation, and the discovery, framing and advertising of new 'heritage' sites, entirely 'artificial' theme parks are the most popular form of new destination. For instance, the total number of paying visitors to the Disney Empire (in California, Florida, Japan and France) is now over 55 million a year, greater than the annual intake of foreign tourists of any country in the world except for France. After museums and cultural centres, theme parks and other 'artificial' amusements are the most numerous new and most profitable of tourist attractions.

However, the long-held distinction between theme parks and amusement parks on the one hand and museums and cultural centres on the other – between the popular and the authoritative – is blurring fast. Major new museums, such as the new National Museum of Civilization in Ottawa, Canada, are less sure of full governmental subsidy, and are therefore conscious of having to compete for the tourist income. So they are modelling themselves after successful theme parks. Conversely, parks like Disney World contain museum-like representations of exciting and famous places from all over the world. Just as the major international world's fairs of the nineteenth century always included the 'serious' exhibitions, and the amusement-park-like Midway with its rides and its freak-shows (Benedict, 1983), modern museums are studying how to make themselves more fun-like and attractive so that they can make money out of the visiting public.

MODERNITY, POSTMODERNITY AND THE CULTURE OF TRAVEL

Post-industrial societies are those in which the major industrial production is not of objects but information, service and experience. Just as we have previously considered the historical changes between premodern and medieval travel to the modernity at the time of the industrial revolution, we can now see a change from the modern tourist to the postmodern.

During 'late modernity' – since the Second World War – the middle-class people of the Western industrialized world (and recently Japan) have developed a sub-culture of tourism as they travel all over the world (MacCannell, 1976). Some of course have been interested only in relaxation or 'getting away from it all', but most are interested in specific attractions outside of their home area. Modern tourists travel the world looking for confirmation of the nature of the world as they have been taught about it – in school, through the mass media, or by word of mouth. This is particularly obvious in Japan where in most elementary school texts and in books, cartoons, travel books, brochures and offsite and on-site maps the socially approved site is represented iconically. Tourism then consists of relating the icon to the sight while ignoring the rest, and taking the *kinen shashin* [photo of record] of one's group in front of the sight.

Much of modern tourism is about authenticity and 'otherness' – learning about other places and peoples, other foods and languages, and about other times – in tourism to museums and old places – and other geographies by looking at nature and the environment. Modern tourists expect the world 'out there' to confirm their beliefs about the way it should be. If it is different from their expectations they may be worried that it is not 'authentic'.

Many people in the modern world are concerned about the proliferation of copies and reproductions, especially since the invention of rapid printing, photography (Benjamin, 1968), plastics and the modern electronic media; many modern urban people believe that much of the world in which they live is no longer really authentic. A strong trend within the underlying philosophy of modernity is that 'authenticity' lies somewhere outside of everyday modern urban life: in the countryside or in nature, or in the lives of more 'natural' peoples of the countryside, or equally that authenticity is a quality of the past and of history that has somehow been lost in modern life (MacCannell, 1976). We can easily see these attitudes among people who enjoy natural foods or want natural childbirth, wear ethnic clothing, or collect old or natural objects to display at home.

Unfortunately for modern tourists, the entrepreneurs who make the arrangements for mass tourism know these values and often manufacture authenticity. In theme parks such as the Polynesian Cultural Center in Hawaii, Ancient City in Bangkok or Momoyama Castle near Kyoto and at many other historical destinations, tourists are presented with reproductions of the originals. Old attractions may be copied, and new ones created (and validated through history or nature); many tourists know this and are disappointed that they have spent their money and have travelled to find things 'out there' no more real than at home or on television. Thus they often search for 'reality' by looking further than the attractions offered them, looking for some 'back stage' where 'real reality' lies. They may again be disappointed or they may be able to boast of serendipitous meetings with the local people, finding real bargains in local markets, or spotting wild species unexpectedly!

Whose authenticity?

Frow (1991) has pursued the question raised by MacCannell (1976) about the nature of the authenticity sought by tourists. Obviously, authenticity, like tradition itself (Horner, 1990) is not a cross-cultural absolute, out there to be found, but it is culturally constructed by whoever benefits from making such judgements. In this case it is the academic authorities who have set themselves up as the arbiters of the worth or futility of the tourists' search. They almost sound like museum curators pronouncing on the authenticity of some newly found art object, revelling in their exposés. They label the stories behind the cultural productions where the tourists seek truth as 'myths'. Some, like MacCannell, infer that there is or was an original 'something' but that tourists are doomed to fail. Others such as Baudrillard (1915) assert that all representations are simulacra, i.e. facsimiles, images of images.

From their outsiders' position they are right, but their position is very essentialist and rigid. Following Hobsbawm and Ranger (1983), we have had a spate of 'invention of tradition' literature in which the omniscient analysist exposes as fake claims to truth on behalf of lesser beings; one controversial recent case is the claim by Hanson (1989) that many traditions and origin myths revered by the present day Maori were in fact erroneously invented by nineteenth-century *pakeha* scholars. However, Cohen (1988) has already demonstrated that under certain conditions, authenticity is flexible, negotiable and possibly multivocalic.

'Give me one firm spot on which to stand and I will move the world', said Archimedes. Sometimes even the cleverest of cultural critics come to admit the plurality of constructed truths. Handler and Saxon (1988: 245) consider an 'authenticity of experience', the phenomenological fleeting gut feeling that actors in 'living history' re-enactments claim is authentic; the authors then take ten pages of philosophical argument to state that the actor could not possibly feel authentically the same as the historical personage they are *acting*!

There are other examples of this 'authenticity of experience', especially in musical and dance performances. Voodoo dance performers in Haiti go into trance even in tourist hotel lounges. Even under 'late Communism', professional Cuban rumba dancers get equally carried away in spite of the commercial politicized conditions of their current performances (Daniel, 1995). In both these cases the performers and co-ethnic audience members were carried away by the same experiential states of consciousness – in front of the tourist audience – as in their prior community-based versions of their performance. One man's 'myth' can be another man's reality. One could imagine the scene in the Port au Prince Hilton: the mass tourists thinking that they are watching a 'real' Voodoo performance, the post-tourists (Urry, 1990: 100, see below) [and some of our authorities] laughing at the fakery and commercialization of the show, and the dancers in trance knowing that they have communicated with their Yoruba Orisshas! Perhaps their experience is one of hyper-reality.

The possibility of this kind of disappointment is not so common yet with most Japanese tourists: they do not expect so much, they are more concerned with the comfort and social life of the tour, nor do they usually question what they see as much as MacCannell's typical Western tourist. But, it is obvious that many Japanese are increasingly alienated from their crowded urban environments. They make efforts to leave it and find their recreation in the more 'natural' countryside – at golf courses, fishing or *onsen* – or in socially satisfying smaller communities that resemble the ideologically nostalgic *furusato* (Graburn, 1995). This is the modern culture of travel.

In the West, the modern culture of travel is changing from the modern to the postmodern (Urry, 1990). In the urban centres of the contemporary world, the seriousness of modernity and the addiction to authenticity is waning. Many younger educated people know that tourist circuits are full of reproductions and staged authenticity, that the people they meet may be 'acting' for them, and that souvenirs may not actually come from the place where they are sold. Rather than struggling to find authenticity and searching for reality backstage, they prefer to enjoy the experience as it is. Indeed, they may enjoy a feeling of superiority over those who are still seriously concerned with the authentic vs. the reproduction (Thurot and Thurot, 1983). This playful, even cynical, attitude is part of the postmodern culture of travel. These people have been called 'post-tourists' characteristic of the post-modernism era. Their lack of concern for authenticity is not to be mistaken for ignorance; it is quite deliberate, a kind of irreverence and mocking of traditional values perhaps akin to the younger *shinjinrui* [new-human-beings] generation in Japan.

HOMOGENIZATION AND HYPER-REALITY

Equally critical is the pervasive trend towards modernization that tourism brings with it. This is not necessarily good or bad, but tourists often travel to places because they are different – exotic, ethnic, foreign, more natural or even 'primitive' – and if these differences are diminished, the destinations thereby lose some of their attraction. It is paradoxical that the very changes that make for an efficient and growing tourist industry – infrastructure, mechanized transportation, electronic communications, large hotel complexes, and so on – are the very visible things which appear to homogenize the world. In many ways the airlines, buses, hotels, and even restaurants and cuisine of places as far apart as Seoul, Sydney, Bombay or Bremen now resemble each other more than they differ. Why should one want to go to the expense of travel if remaining distinctions are erased?

The maintenance of obvious difference – in architecture and dress, cuisine and colour schemes, language (or at least accent) and music, even secular and festivals – can be artfully contrived to satisfy tourists, but modernization is a more subtle and pervasive phenom-enon. The very success of the tourist industry brings with it a way of life – work schedules, pay rates and promotions, literacy and electronic skills, bureaucracy and attitudes – which are imported along with the tourists (Lanfant and Graburn, 1992). At the same time, a successful tourist industry can bring affluence to the local people, especially to formerly poor workers and farmers, so that they too can purchase the desired goods of the middle-class world, dwellings and cars, as well as habits of education, vacation and even the opportunity to travel already enjoyed by the tourists themselves.

Would anyone want to deny them these benefits? Homogenization, the Western-originated middle-class life plan is very seductive and is emulated all over the world. As ordinary people become more and more similar – of course we still have a long way to go before eliminating all difference – other features emerge as the core attractions of tourism. These are nature and history.

The wonderful and different natural landscapes of the world and the living species that inhabit them are major tourist attractions already. Most countries have already attempted to ensure their preservation through a network of national and state parks, seashores, forests, and so on. Some countries even go so far as to calculate the economic worth of maintaining these landscapes for tourism – such as wild animal parks in East Africa – as against other possible uses such as farming or industrialization. Similarly, many of the world's landscapes are already farmed but constitute attractive landscapes for tourists, such as the terraced ricefields of Japan or Indonesia, and the rolling farmlands of England or Italy. Though politico-economic rationales may dictate other more productive uses for these lands, they are never-ending attractions for foreign and domestic tourists alike.

Whose hyper-reality?

Our period of history is increasingly one of imitation and reproduction, sometimes so that the copies are 'better than' the originals, a situation that has been called hyper-reality (Eco, 1986). Thus Tokyo Disneyland is thought by many Japanese to be better than the original in Orange Country, California, and many of the old farmhouses in rural 'folk villages' and eco-museums like Yu-no-kuni-no-Mori, Kanazawa Prefecture, are probably cleaner and in better shape than the originals ever were. It was on his journalistic high speed tour around North America that Eco introduced the concept of hyper-reality. MacCannell (1994) has refined the notion:

When the reconstructed traditional object is fetishized to the point where it is intended to be better than the original, the result is 'hyperreality'. In hyperreality, acceptance of tradition is in the mode of total and perfect control; that is, reincorporation of the traditional on the condition that it assumes the form of a perfected version of itself.

Here MacCannell, following Eco, makes the same assumptions that Frow (1991) pointed out in his earlier work, i.e. that there *is* some original tradition somewhere, that is (or was) authentic, and that the unlucky modern tourist is only presented with a manipulated version of it.

Of course Eco, like Baudrillard in his *America* (1990), found hyper-realism in America, as that was what he was looking for:

> The theme of our trip is the Absolute Fake; and therefore we are only interested in absolutely fake cities . . . Disneyland and Disneyworld are obviously the chief examples . . . [but] the United States is filled with cities that imitate a city . . . some are reasonably authentic . . . but more interesting are those born from nothing, out of pure imitative determination. (Eco, 1986: 40)

While not denying the existence or even the usefulness of the term 'hyper-reality' for North America, one might call to Eco's attention the sacred representations erected by his Catholic Church (or by the Buddhist Church in Japan and China) over the past millenia. One would find differing insider and outsider views about the reality and authenticity of the 'originals'. The glorious marble or gilded statues, the paintings and stained glass windows are of course all simulacra, and undoubtably bigger and better than the 'original'. Both the Buddhist and Catholic Churches qualify for MacCannell's statement that 'the acceptance of tradition is in the mode of total and perfect control'.

Contemporary technology and the urge and ability to make copies is leading towards a homogenization of the world. Not only is life in different societies getting more similar, but regional differences within nations are being smoothed out too. Already certain aspects of different national cultures are very similar, such as airlines, airports, major hotels, automobiles and trucks, gas stations, supermarkets, fast foods and beer; and increasingly street furniture, heating and lighting systems, toilets, everyday clothing, middle-class houses and apartments, and so on.

Attempts are made to maintain national and cultural differences in many other aspects of life, such as foods, festivals, bathing systems, bedding, architectural details. These objects of cultural difference have also 'migrated' so that they are available in most metropolitan areas of the world (MacCannell, 1992, 1993). For instance one can get Japanese and Thai food in America and Europe and one can get Chinese food anywhere in the world. Aspects of Japanese architectural and gardening design have been incorporated into Western buildings and gardens, and skyscrapers and flower gardens are common in Japan and China. *Shoji, zori, futons, and sake* are becoming popular in the West, just as air conditioning, glass windows, athletic shoes, wine and beds are found nearly everywhere in Japan. One could extend this list to many items and lifestyles from many parts of the world.

Though some major differential features such as language and scenery have not disappeared, attempts to narrow differences are being made: more and more signs in Japan are in *romaji* (Roman orthography) and more people in Japan, and especially in Europe and China, speak English; also more geographical areas in Japan are comparing themselves to foreign places, such as 'the Japan Rhine', the 'Japan Alps', or Takarazuka 'Tivoli'.

The changes of the past 25 years are so enormous that if the pace keeps up, in another 25 years socio-cultural differences will be further reduced and much of what travellers find in any one place will already be familiar to them. Even major geographical and architectural features will be reproduced or at least familiar to most people. Some people have recently asked the question (MacCannell, 1993), if much of the world is becoming homogenized, increasingly resembling other parts, why would anyone want to travel any more? I would answer by stating that first of all, there are still many societies, sites, natural features and climates that 'do not travel well', i.e. that cannot be reproduced satisfactorily. Secondly, much of the homogenization and familiarity of which we are well aware, *instead of preventing people from travelling, makes it easier for them to overcome cultural and linguistic barriers.* For instance now that fast foods, cafeterias, hotels and so on are common in Japan, it makes it easier for Japanese people to travel to the West with some self-confidence that they will get along easily. The similarities between Europe and North America are even closer making it easy for tourists to travel in both directions.

As metropolitan institutions are spread all over the world, mainly for the convenience of tourism and transnational business, it *also* makes it easier for peoples of those areas, the Third World, to travel and adapt to living in the metropoles. Thus there is a vast movement of both peoples and their goods and ways of living from the metropoles to the peripheries and in towards the metropolitan centres. Anthropologists are both participants and observers in this movement.

NOTES
1   The author would like to thank the editors of this volume and Peter Phipps, Nancy Frey Breuner and Sandra Cate of the University of California, Berkeley, for their comments on an earlier draft of this paper. The ideas expressed herein remain, however, the responsibility of the author.
2   The clearest exception to the theoretical and political blindness of much of British socio-cultural anthropology is Nadel's *Black Byzantium* (1942).
3   Examples are drawn mainly from the author's research particularly in Japan and among the Canadian Inuit (Graburn 1969, 1976, 1983b, 1987, 1995).
4   These figures cannot be taken as perfectly accurate because of the different definitions and strategies taken in counting travellers, and because the unrecorded flows of those who bypass the official points of entry. However, the relative size and rate of increase are what is important.

REFERENCES
Adler, Judith (1989) 'The origins of sightseeing', *Annals of Tourism Research*, 16: 7–29.
Appiah, Kwame (1991) 'Is the post- in postmodernism the post- in postcolonial?' *Critical Enquiry*, 17, 2: 336–57.
Baudrillard, Jean (1975) *Mirror of Production*, trans. by Mark Poster, Saint Louis: Telos.
—— (1990) *America*, London: Verso.
Benedict, Burton (1983) *The Anthropology of World's Fairs*, Berkeley, CA: Scolar.
Benjamin, Walter (1968) 'The work of art in the age of mechanical reproduction' in Walter Benjamin (ed.) *Illuminations*, New York: Harcourt, Brace & World.
Berger, Peter L. and Luckman, Thomas (1966) *The Social Construction of Reality: A Treatise in the Sociology of Knowledge*, Garden City, NY: Doubleday.
Brendon, Piers (1991) *Thomas Cook: 150 Years of Popular Tourism*, London: Secker & Warburg.
Bruner, Edward (1989) 'Of cannibals, tourists and ethnographers', *Cultural Anthropology*, 4, 4: 438–45.
Buck-Morss, Susan (1987) 'Semiotic boundaries and the politics of meaning: modernity on tour – a village in transition' in Marcus G. Raskin and Herbert J. Bernstein (eds) *New Ways of Knowing: The Sciences, Society and Reconstructive Knowledge*, New York: Rowman Littlefield.
Carter, Donald (in press) *Invisible Cities: Touba Turin, Senegalese Transnational Immigrants in Northern Italy*, Minneapolis: University of Minnesota Press.

Cohen, Erik (1988) 'Authenticity and commoditization in tourism', *Annals of Tourism Research*, 15: 371–86.

Daniel, Yvonne (1995) *Rumba, Dance and Social Change in Contemporary Cuba*, Bloomington IN: Indiana University Press.

Davis, Fred (1979) *Yearning for Yesteryear: A Sociology of Nostalgia*, New York: Free Press.

Eco, Umberto (1986) *Travels in Hyperreality*, New York: Harvester/Harcourt Brace Jovanovich.

Edgell, David L. (1993) *World Tourism at the Millenium*, Washington DC: US Travel and Tourism Administration.

Errington, Fredrick, and Gewertz, Deborah (1989) 'Tourism and anthropology in a post-modern world', *Oceania*, 60: 37–54.

Evans-Pritchard, Edward E. (1940) *The Nuer: The Modes of Livelihood of a Nilotic People* Oxford: Oxford University Press.

Friedman, Jonathan (1990) 'Being in the world: globalization and localization' in Mike Featherstone (ed.) *Global Culture: Nationalism, Globablisation and Modernity*, London: Sage.

Frow, John (1991) 'Tourism and the semiotics of nostalgia', *October*, 57: 123–51.

Graburn, Nelson H.H. (1969) *Eskimos Without Igloos: The Social and Economic Development of Salluit*, Boston: Little, Brown.

—— (1976) (ed.) *Ethnic and Tourist Arts: Cultural Expressions from the Fourth World*, Berkeley: University of California Press.

—— (1977) 'Tourism: the sacred journey' in Valene Smith (ed.) *Hosts and Guests: The Anthropology of Tourism*, Philadelphia: University of Pennsylvania Press.

—— (1980) 'Teaching the anthropology of tourism', *International Social Science Journal*, 32, 1: 56–68.

—— (1983a) (ed.) 'The anthropology of tourism', special issue of *Annals of Tourism Research*, 10, 1.

—— (1983b) *To Pray, Pay and Play: The Cultural Structure of Japanese Domestic Tourism*, Aix-en-Provence: Centres des Hautes Etudes Touristiques.

—— (1987) 'Material symbols in Japanese domestic tourism' in Dan Ingersoll and Gordon Bronitsky (eds) *Mirror and Metaphor: Material and Social Constructions of Reality*, Lanham, MD: University Press of America.

—— (1995) 'The past and the present in Japan: nostalgia and neo-traditionalism in contemporary Japanese domestic tourism' in Richard Butler and Douglas Pierce (eds) *Change in Tourism: Peoples, Places and Processes*, London: Routledge.

Handler, Richard, and William Saxon (1988) 'Dyssimulation: reflexivity, narrative, and the quest for authenticity in living history', *Cultural Anthropology*, 3, 3: 242–60.

Hannerz, Ulf (1987) 'The world in creolization', *Africa*, 57: 546–59.

Hanson, Allan (1989) 'The making of the Maori: culture invention and its logic', *American Anthropologist*, 91, 4: 890–902.

Hobsbawn, Eric, and Ranger, Terence (eds) (1983) *The Invention of Tradition*, Cambridge: Cambridge University Press.

Horner, Alice E. (1990) *The Assumption of Tradition: Creating, Collecting and Conserving Cultural Artefacts in the Cameroon Grassfields*, Berkeley: PhD Dissertation in Anthropology.

Jameson, Fredrick (1985) 'Postmodernism and consumer society' in Hal Foster (ed.) *Postmodern Culture*, London: Pluto.

Kahn, Herman, William Brown and Leon Martell (1976) *The Next 200 Years*, New York: William Morrow.

Lanfant, Marie-Françoise and Graburn, Nelson (1992) 'International tourism reconsidered: the principle of the alternative' in Valene Smith and William Eadington (eds) *Tourism Alternatives* Philadelphia: University of Pennsylvania Press.

Lévi-Strauss, Claude (1949) *Les structures élémentaires de la parenté*, Paris: Plon.

Lowenthal, David (1985) *The Past as a Foreign Country*, Cambridge: Cambridge University Press.

MacCannell, Dean (1976) *The Tourist: A New Theory of the Leisure Class*, New York: Schocken (2nd edn 1989).

—— (1992) *Empty Meeting Grounds: The Tourist Papers*, London: Routledge.

—— (1993) 'The new tourist' paper presented at the symposium on 'New dimensions in tourism studies', National Museum of Ethnology, Osaka, Japan, 1–3 July.

—— (1994) 'Misplaced tradition' in Jean Pierre Jardel (ed.) *Le Tourisme International entre Tradition et Modernité: Actes du Colloque International, Nice, 1992*, Paris: URESTI-CNRS et WG5 de l'Association Internationale de Sociologie de Prospective du Tourisme, Nice.

Malinowski, Bronislaw (1922) *Argonauts of the Western Pacific*, London: Hodder & Stoughton.

Marcus, George E. and Fischer, Michael M.J. (eds) (1986) *Anthropology and Cultural Critique: An Experimental Moment in the Human Sciences*, Chicago: University of Chicago Press.

Matsuda, Misa (1989) *Japanese Tourists and Indonesia: Images of Self and Other in the Age of Kokusaida*, Canberra: Australian National University, MA Thesis in Asian Studies.

Moeran, Brian (1983) 'The language of Japanese tourism', *Annals of Tourism Research*, 10, 1: 93–108.

Mukherjee, Bharati (1989) *Jasmine*, New York: Grove Weidenfeld.

Nadel, Siegfried (1942) *Black Byzantium: The Kingdom of Nupe in Nigeria*, London: Oxford University Press.

Radcliffe-Brown, Alfred R. (1923) 'Ethnology and social anthropology', *South African Journal for the Advancement of Science*, 20: 124–47.

Rosaldo, Renato (1989) 'Imperialist nostalgia', *Representations*, 26: 197–22.

Smith, Valene (ed.) (1989) *Hosts and Guests: The Anthropology of Tourism*, Philadelphia: University of Pennsylvania Press (1st edn 1977).

Thompson, Michael (1979) *Rubbish Theory: The Creation and Destruction of Value*, Oxford: Oxford University Press.

Thurot, Jean-Maurice, and Thurot, Gaetane (1983) 'The ideology of class and tourism: facing the discourse of advertizing', *Annals of Tourism Research*, 10, 1: 173–89.

Trease, G. (1967) *The Grand Tour*, London: Heinemann.

Turner, Louis and Ash, John (1975) *The Golden Hordes: Tourism and the Pleasure Periphery*, London: Constable.

Turner, Victor (1969) *The Ritual Process*, Ithaca NY: Cornell University Press.

Urry, John (1990) *The Tourist Gaze: Leisure and Travel in Contemporary Societies*, London: Sage.

Van den Abeele, G. (1980) 'Sightseers: the tourist as the theorist', *Diacritics*, 10: 3–14.

Wagner, Roy (1975) *The Invention of Culture*, Englewood Cliffs, NJ: Prentice-Hall.

Wallerstein, Immanuel (1974) *The Modern World System*, New York: Academic.

White, Leslie (1949) *The Science of Culture: A Study of Man and Civilization*, New York: Farrar & Straus.

Wolf, Eric (1982) *Europe and the People without History*, Berkeley: University of California Press.

CHAPTER 8

Prospects for Tourism Study
in Anthropology
Dennison Nash

Tourism has become an obviously important social fact in today's world. Driven by increasing productivity, advances in social welfare and improving transportation, it now is on the verge of being the world's largest industry, with important connections in the Third World in which many anthropologists have done their work. There, it has become an important developmental tool. Any human subject of such magnitude cries out for anthropological analysis. But despite substantial growth since the pathbreaking article about tourism in a Mexican village by the anthropologist Theron Nuñez (1963) - enough growth to permit recent critical overviews by Crick (1989) and (for neighbouring sociology) Cohen (1984) – the interest of anthropologists in this field still would not seem to match its scientific and practical relevance. One can still count the number of anthropologically oriented scholars with a serious interest in tourism on the fingers of one's hands.

Of course, it takes time for a new field of study to become established, but there seems to be more to it than that. Those of us who came aboard early have speculated about the delay; and because we have close ties with colleagues in neighbouring disciplines, we know that we are not alone in this. Speaking for the state of tourism study in political science, Matthews and Richter (1991: 122) say, 'For years, scholarly research on tourism was seen as "frivolous" and not appropriate for mature scholars.' In anthropology, where field research is almost a sacred rite, the charge of frivolity in far-away places may still discourage some potential recruits. Even so, we now have enough work on tourism by anthropologically oriented scholars to form some notion of general trends, to subject them to critical analysis, and on the basis of all this, attempt some projections into the future.

AN ANTHROPOLOGICAL APPROACH TO TOURISM

These days, there are so many different anthropologies that it might seem presumptuous to speak of anthropology as a whole. Nevertheless, it still seems that there have been common understandings about approach to subject-matter that have prevailed over time. First, there has been the tendency to see human social action as part of a larger picture which includes a culture or society, its setting and its history. Second is the tendency to view subject-matter in a transcultural context that can include all of humanity. Third is the tendency to consider social action to have a component of meaning that must be got at and communicated. It has been customary to get at that meaning during a field trip. Social anthropology often is identified with fieldwork, particularly among non-Western peoples, though this is not necessarily so these days. Finally, unlike some of my colleagues, I consider anthropology to be a generalizing and explanatory science which is capable of finding out what humans are like and why they are as they are.[1]

The all-encompassing view of tourism that follows grows out of this anthropological approach. It takes the tourist to be the principal actor in a tourism drama that can have many parts. True, tourists come in different forms, and true, as Crick (1989) points out, there is disagreement about what a tourist is, but if one pays attention to scientific and anthropological criteria, the definition of a tourist as a leisured traveller is inviting. Since leisure, which, according to Dumazedier (1968), involves freedom from 'fundamental' or 'primary' cultural obligations such as work, and travel appear to exist in all societies, cross-cultural comparisons of tourisms are possible.[2] For furthering anthropological and other social scientific work, I think it preferable to make the study of tourism an adjunct of leisure studies rather than of travel or migration, as Cohen (1974) would have it.

The tourist is only one of the actors in the tourism drama whose actions must be understood and explained. Hosts of various kinds, travel specialists, and those who are touched by any of these also participate in a *touristic process*, which Nash (1981: 464) points out, can be seen as

> originating with the generation of tourists and tourisms in some
> society or sub-society, continuing as the tourists travel to other places
> where they encounter hosts with a different culture, and ending as the
> give-and-take of this encounter affects the tourists, those who serve
> them, and the various societies and sub-societies involved.

In addition, this process can take the form of a *touristic system* 'which, itself, could be embedded in some broader social context'. Continuing the dramatic analogy, one or another actor in this system or process may become the 'star' of the drama, depending on the theoretical problem which organizes a research project.

So far, most anthropological studies of tourism have been carried out from one of three perspectives.[3] These perspectives, which certainly do not exhaust possible ways of looking at the subject can provide a basis for future research on tourism, They view tourism as (1) development or acculturation, (2) a personal transition, (3) a kind of superstructure. The first of these has been of greatest importance in anthropological research; the last, though potentially of great significance, is, so far, barely recognizable. In this essay, I will review the work that has been carried on from the different perspectives, assess it for its anthropological value, and suggest what kind of foundation it provides for the future.

TOURISM AS DEVELOPMENT OR ACCULTURATION

In anthropology, as Nuñez (1977, 1989) and others have pointed out, an interest in tourism arose out of a concern for development or acculturation that has preoccupied anthropologists ever since the enormous impact of Western cultures on non-Western peoples began to be recognized. The emphasis on Western–non-Western culture contact continues today (often framed in a context of colonialism or imperialism) with many authors (e.g. Crick, 1989) seeming to assume that the only tourism worthy of anthropological consideration involves the intrusion of Western tourism into non-Western, less-developed societies, an unjustifiable assumption considering that this kind of touristic contact is only a small part of the total.

Early work by anthropologists often began as a spin-off from other research on acculturation or development. Typically, researchers would find that tourism had to be dealt with because it was implicated in socio-cultural change. Nuñez (1977: 207) says that 'since the beginning . . . the study of tourism by anthropologists has been marked by serendipity'. This continues, but Lett (1989: 275), who writes the epilogue to Nuñez's posthumously published revision in Smith's revised edition of *Hosts and Guests* (1989), notes a new trend, which is that 'anthropologists have lately, purposefully turned their attention to the study of tourism'.

Anthropologists studying native peoples in the context of (neo-)-colonialism or imperialism have, characteristically, tended to take a negative view of the changes going on among these people. Very few, if any, have thought that, without significant intervention, host peoples will ultimately benefit from Western contact, a position that countered early enthusiasm for tourism as a developmental tool (see Jafari, 1990). From studies of tourism development by anthropologists and some other social scientists, one learns a good deal about the negative consequences of touristic input. Jurdao's (1990) impressive study of Mijas (Costa del Sol) is an example. According to this economist-anthropologist, who is a local resident, the development of residential tourism in Mijas and beyond has resulted in depletion of the underground water supply, displacement of indigenous peoples, domination and exploitation from the outside, conflict between new residents and locals, and disproportionate benefits to outsiders and elite hosts.

On the other hand, a few early researchers, like McKean (1976) in Bali, and Cohen (1979a) in Thailand, found tourism to be a benign and possibly beneficial agent of change. Those attending a seminar convened by the World Bank (de Kadt, 1979) took a more cautious view, that is, that tourism could have a range of consequences from good to bad for the hosts, but that proper intervention could emphasize the good. The seminar concluded with a set of policy recommendations for promoting benefits to host peoples (de Kadt, 1979: 339–47). Applied analyses such as that for the Pacific rim by Pye and Lin (1983) have followed in the same vein.

The notion that tourism is either good or bad still informs a good deal of anthropological work on tourism, and tendencies to either dismiss it or make snap judgements about it still prevail. There are, however, some indications that a more dispassionate, analytic attitude is emerging in anthropological studies. For example, in his revised article for the second edition of *Hosts and Guests* (Smith (ed.), 1989), Davydd Greenwood (1989: 181–5) sees that the outrage he earlier had felt about tourism-induced changes in a Basque festival prevented him from exploring the full extent of those changes. Another indication of the advance of a more scientific attitude in tourism studies may be found in the deliberation of the International Academy for the Study of Tourism in their Zakopane seminar (Nash and Butler, 1990; Smith and Eadington, 1992). In this seminar of social scientists, including anthropologists, the participants recognized the term 'alternative tourism' to be a morally-tinged, ideological reaction to apparent depredations of mainstream, Western tourism in the Third World. (A subsequent meeting convened by the World Tourism Organization in Algeria arrived at a similar conclusion.) The participants in the Zakopane seminar decided that there was not a single 'alternative' (i.e. 'good') tourism, but many forms of tourism, each of which might be more or less sustainable. They proposed that the phrase 'alternative forms of tourism' be used instead in order to get on with the scientific task of analysing fully the variety of forms of tourism development and their consequences, a general position that Jafari (1990) would characterize as the Knowledge-Based Platform in which scientific considerations prevail.

In studies of tourism development, the aim has been to show that tourism has been responsible for changes in a host society and its setting. The usual method has been to suggest an association between some kind of touristic input with changes at the host end of the touristic process: say, the depletion of the underground water supply. But because there are often other inputting agencies (e.g. industrialization), such a procedure can establish a causal linkage only if necessary controls are in place. Since this has rarely been so, anthropologists' statements about the role of tourism development in a host society have to be considered with caution.

But there are signs of increasing sophistication in this regard. In the first edition of Valene Smith's *Hosts and Guests* (177), the authors of the case-studies of tourism development confined themselves pretty much to touristic input. In the revised edition (1989), there is a gratifying increase among them in recognizing extra-touristic factors as possible sources of change. In the revision of her article on tourism development among Alaskan Eskimos (1989: 75–7), Smith herself argues that tourism is not a major agent of change among the Eskimos. Rather, it has been the development of extractive industries, the contest between the United States and Russia, and US governmental policies on welfare that have been largely responsible. Still, until appropriate experimental procedures involving the manipulation of sites or of data are adopted, this has to be taken only as an informed hypothesis.

Dann, Nash and Pearce (1988) point out that mature scientific research is marked by high methodological sophistication, which they discuss in terms of procedures for conceptualization, operationalization, measurement, data gathering and data analysis. They do not give the 'various ethnographic approaches typically favored by many anthropologists, historians, and political scientists' very high marks for methodological rigour (Dann, Nash and Pearce, 1988: 4). Though there seems to have been some improvement of the conceptual front among anthropologists studying tourism, it remains to be seen whether such sophistication will spread to the other methodological operations including distinctive anthropological preoccupations such as giving the points of view of 'others' being studied their due and putting everything into context.[4]

Dann, Nash and Pearce (1988: 4–5) further argue that in mature scientific research there is an interaction of theoretical awareness with methodological sophistication. On the acculturation or development front, there is not a great deal of theoretical progress to report in anthropologically oriented studies. The Social Science Research Council Summer Seminar that proposed research on acculturation defined acculturation as 'culture change that is initiated by conjunction of two or more cultural systems' (SSRC Seminar, 1954: 474). Culture change, therefore, is seen here to result from factors external to the cultural system, as, for example, tourism. Research was to consider all elements of this process: the cultural systems involved in the contact, the contact situation and social relations that followed, and the resulting processes of change in the cultures.

In practice, anthropologists have tended to focus on acculturation involving more-developed Western peoples and less-developed natives, which has assumed the form of a dominant–subordinate relationship. Though some promising work has been done on the contact situation, as in Aspelin's (1978) analysis of a Brazilian case of indirect tourism, the various articles on tourism and ethnicity in a special issue of the *Annals of Tourism Research* edited by Van den Berghe and Keyes (1984), and MacCannell's (1992) analysis of the 'empty meeting grounds' in which tourists from the Western world and their non-Western hosts meet in postmodern emptiness, anthropologists have been mostly concerned with tourism-induced changes in host cultures. From their research, we know a good deal more about the elements and processes involved, but theoretical syntheses have mostly been lacking. For example, the SSRC Seminar took it for granted that the cultures involved in an acculturation situation were integrated wholes, but the implications of this view have hardly been realized in studies that focus on the consequences of touristic input for hosts. Economists, with notions such as the much-discussed ripple effect, have done better.

Some signs of a theoretical awakening in this specific area of tourism research may be noticed in the incorporation of Marxist-inspired critiques of rosy capitalist scenarios into research on development (see e.g. Gunder Frank, 1972). The argument of neo-Marxist dependency theorists, that reliance on outside capital leads to dependence, economic leakage, structural inequalities and resentment by hosts, has been examined by political scientists (see Erisman, 1983; Francisco, 1983), but so far it has served as little more than a heuristic or orienting device (see e.g. Schlechten, 1988, discussed below) in anthropological studies. Undoubtedly, this theoretical perspective will continue to be useful in the future, but the sophisticated scientists should know that neither it nor contending economically based theories (neo-classical, structuralist) have, according to de Kadt (1992: 48), so far given 'satisfactory overall explanations of development or of its "absence"'. Certainly, as Adams (1992) found out for Sherpa tourism, it is important for the anthropologist to recognize that a belief in the sweeping power of touristic metropoles over non-Western development may sometimes be overdone. Concerning the staying power of this particular host culture, she (Adams, 1992: 534) says, 'Despite nearly 40 years of involvement in tourism and its heavy demands for wage labor, Nepalese Sherpas have found ways to reconstitute traditional productive relations in their new economy.'

Finally, there is the problem, discussed more extensively below, of the considerable contemporary tourism that does not touch less-developed host cultures and therefore does not fit the acculturation or development paradigm that has guided anthropological work to date. Eventually, anthropologists will have to consider the kind of theory that is applicable for analysing tourism between developed countries such as Germany and France, tourist migration from rural areas to cities, and other forms of tourism not found in their usual choice of subject-matter. Douglas Pearce's (1992) suggestion of the manifold ways for conceptualizing tourism development could help in this.

In summary, if the criteria for a mature science used by Dann, Nash and Pearce are applied, anthropological research on tourism's impact on hosts cannot be given high marks. For the most part, it is neither high in methodological sophistication nor theoretical awareness. But we have come to know more about developmental processes in which tourism is involved, especially on the host side, and the sometimes far-ranging acculturation contexts in which they take place.

To conclude this section, consider a recent study which I take to be something of a high water mark in research on tourism development by anthropologists. In *Tourism balnéaire ou tourisme rural integré?: Deux modeles de développement sénégalais*, Marguerite Schlechten (1988) compares the nature and consequences of two forms of tourism development in Senegal. One of these is mainstream, Western-style tourism on the beach, which involves large numbers of tourists in fairly isolated enclaves; the other, which is an example of the alternative form of tourism development suggested for the Tourism for Discovery project by Christian Saglio (1979) (a project currently suspended because of the secessionist struggle in the area), involves small, traditional camps which are fully integrated into village life. The two forms differ in scale, in style, and in the degree to which local people have been involved in the development and operation of the tourist projects. Schlechten wants to find out which of these forms benefit local people the most.

The author prepared herself by a thorough study of relevant literature and carried out fieldwork, during which she was able to observe development as it was actually taking place. She interviewed officials, tourists and their hosts, and appears to have been a diligent participant observer. Procedures used in the field were standardized and non-standardized. Quantitative measures were rarely employed.

Schlechten sees tourism development in Senegal occurring in a neo-colonial context, the over-riding characteristic of which is dependency on Europe. Non-touristic forms of development such as urbanization and industrialization, which are occurring simultaneously, are considered, and though her somewhat impressionistic way of making assessments prevents her from indicating the exact contribution of each to changes in the host communities, she is able to suggest whether they work in the same or different directions. For example, tourism in the beach resorts and urbanization are both seen to promote disintegration of extended kin groupings through migration, and the demonstration effect of tourists in both forms tends to reinforce the effects of Western-oriented mass media, schooling, etc.

From this brief digest, one can see that Marguerite Schlechten's study is theoretically informed, although one might question what appears to be an uncritical acceptance of dependency theory. Her research shows considerable methodological sophistication in that it combines the prescribed (for anthropologists) intimate involvement with subjects with a research design that enables her to begin to distinguish the consequences not only of two different forms of tourism development, but of other forms of development as well. That her conclusions about the benefits of the Senegalese alternative to mainstream tourism are somewhat ambiguous is probably the result not only of the lack of quantitative measures, but also the magnitude of her research problem. More studies of this kind are certainly needed.

TOURISM AS A PERSONAL TRANSITION

It will be recalled that the study of acculturation involves tracing the consequences of culture contact for the various peoples involved. As mentioned above, those anthropologists who have followed in this tradition have stressed the consequences of Western contact for non-Western peoples. What about the consequences for the tourists? Anthropological work on this problem has tended to concentrate on the experiential dimension and to follow the model for transition rites developed by Victor Turner (1969) in a research tradition that goes back to Arnold Van Gennep (1960[1908]). The general idea is that tourists, like pilgrims or initiates, pass through three stages: (1) *Separation*, in which a person is separated from their ordinary social group. (2) *Liminality*, in which a person enters a subjective world where the structured certainties of ordinary life dissolve into an undifferentiated state that can have a sacred aura and involve feelings of 'communitas' with associates. (3) *Reintegration*, in which the person passes back into the structured day-to-day life of his social group.

A number of anthropologists have found liminality in tourists' experiences, as for example Lett (1983) among charter yacht tourists in the Caribbean. Graburn (1983) and Jafari (1987) have referred to a kind of inversion that takes place during the liminal period of the touristic odyssey; and Graburn (1983: 11) has gone so far as to suggest that this inversion fulfils a need for alternation or re-creation in people's lives.

The basic idea underlying the concept of liminality is that the experience of significant change (in this case, through travel) tends to destructure or open up the individuals subjective world. This can happen, but a not-uncommon reaction to this is a kind of shock, which excites anxiety and defenses that include a psychological closing up (see D. Nash, 1970: 123–68; 1991). Not all sojourners are shocked though, and Furnham (1984: 54) points out the limited applicability of the concept of culture shock to tourists' reactions.

Indeed, there appear to be quite a variety of long- and short-term reactions to the experiences that tourists encounter, and a number of them appear not to be comprehended by even a broadened and deepened conception of liminas. Philip Pearce (1982: 85–93) refers to studies which indicate an impressive variety of long- and short-term effects of touring. The desirable model for such research is the experimental method of difference in which the psychological changes of tourists are compared with those of non-tourists. Needless to say, the entire acculturation situation, which is the central feature of the touristic, process, ought to be considered in explaining tourist reactions. So far, this context has been conspicuously missing in research derived from the theory of transition ritual.

In the Turner paradigm, *liminas* is often associated with *communitas*, which would seem to open up another fruitful line of tourism research. Tour groups can sometimes dominate tourists' lives and regulate encounters with hosts. An important research question, which certainly has its applied side, concerns the solidarity or morale of such groups. Geva and Goldman (1991), for example, found group morale to be rated high in importance and satisfaction by people in Israeli-guided tours to Europe and the United States; and the tour guide was rated higher still – a finding for which we were prepared by a special issue of the *Annals of Tourism Research* on tour guides (Cohen, 1985).

To conclude, the notion of tourism as a personal transition would seem to have limited promise for comprehending tourist experiences and reactions. One way to further realize its potential would be to take Turner's notion of the experiential destructuring that occurs in liminas to point to the issue of particular cultures' hold over people (internalization) during culture contact or change. Those psychological studies, reported by Pearce, which have investigated traits like ethnocentrism or authoritarianism would contribute to such a programme. As suggested above, the issue must always be addressed in the framework of some specific acculturative context in which all relevant actors are included.

TOURISM AS SUPERSTRUCTURE

In his 1981 paper, Dennison Nash (1981: 465), pointed out that 'the tourist generating situation is fertile ground for anthropological investigations; but it is difficult to find significant research in this area.' Crick (1989: 326) says essentially the same thing. By concentrating on destination areas, anthropologists are missing a potentially productive line of research at the tourist-generating end of the touristic process. Here, by thinking of tourism as a kind of dependent superstructure, they could integrate their work with long-standing issues of social scientific interest, that is, how different elements of socio-cultural systems relate to each other and the manner in which a society maintains itself and changes.

The habit of looking at the activities of a society in terms of base or infrastructure and superstructure is most closely linked with Marxist materialist analysis. Thus, Godelier (1980: 3–4), taking a broad materialist point of view, sees infrastructure, which consists of a society's productive arrangements, exercising a determinative role 'in the last instance' on other social activities. A good case can be made for the applicability of this view to tourism in general, though more specific base or infrastructural elements would be proposed for different forms. In the discussion which follows I will broaden the Marxist conception to include all of these elements. It also should be kept in mind that, as far as the tourist-generating situation is concerned, tourism is not without social influence. It is just that, in the long run, it is more determined than determining.[5]

The idea that a society tends to generate the kind of tourists or tourisms that are consonant with its nature, however conceived, has been suggested by Krippendorff (1986: 518), who sees tourism as 'the result, and at the same time, one of the components of the industrial social system', and the Thurots (1983) who, following Baudrillard (1975), work through advertising in viewing tourism as an aspect of a society of consumption. It also has appeared in the form of a dispute between Dean MacCannell (1976), who thinks tourism fulfils a need for authenticity that is lacking in the everyday life of modern society, and Daneil Boorstin (1964), who sees in modern tourists' pursuit of pseudo-events an extension of what they have been accustomed to at home. Though the specific positions of these and other authors taking this approach can be criticized (see, e.g. Cohen, 1988; Nash and Smith, 1991), the essential argument that the character of tourists and tourisms reflect the nature of some tourist-generating situation looks promising.

An anthropological interest in this question was affirmed by Nelson Graburn and his associates in a special issue of the *Annals of Tourism Research* devoted to the anthropology of tourism (Graburn (ed.), 1983). In his introduction to this issue, Graburn (1983: 19) says that 'one must explain in general terms why specific tourist modes are attached to particular social groups at the historical period when they are found'. He suggests several explanatory variables that account for a society's touristic style. Whatever the explanatory power of these or other variables, Graburn's reference to what can be called the infrastructure or base in tourist-generating situations is theoretically important.

One article in the Graburn issue by Patricia Albers and William James (1983), provides an interesting example of the applicability of the notion of tourism as superstructure. These authors see the picture postcards of American Indians as reflecting and reinforcing the increasingly stereotyped image of the American Indian held by white Americans (see also Albers and James, 1988). Some additional steps in this line of research are taken by Gwen Reimer (1990), who studies the role of Canadian tour operators in defining and marketing vacation dreams, John Urry (1990), in his analysis of heritage tourism as a reflection of postmodern conditions, and Dennis Hardy (1990), who, in a study of English lower-class holidaymaking, acknowledges the effect of social class on vacation styles, but insists on the importance of creative human agency in working out particular alternatives. Finally, consider the various kinds of tourists and tourisms suggested by various authors (see, e.g. Cohen, 1979b), all of which could qualify as superstructural alternatives.

To illustrate how the interconnections between touristic superstructure and infrastructure or base might be worked out, consider again the suggestion by Albers and James that romantic, stereotyped images of American Indians on picture postcards and other touristic literature responded to the interests of white Americans who were experiencing the increasing problems of an urban, industrial-commercial existence. The call of the wild, in which the American Indian played an important part, was heard from the early days of the American republic (see Hallowell, 1957), but it became particularly compelling with the disappearance of the frontier at the end of the nineteenth century. Then, according to Roderick Nash (1967: 231), 'enough doubts had arisen about the beneficence of civilization's achievements to make possible a widespread popular enthusiasm for the uncivilized'. Nature came to be conceived as a retreat, refuge or balance for the urban, industrial or commercial way of life. The various depictions of the American Indian in the postcards analysed by Albers and James, therefore, may be thought of as manifestations of an ideology that was increasingly enthusiastic about the primitive.

As a number of authors (see e.g. Heiman, 1989) have argued, this romantic ideology worked to shore up the urban, industrial or capitalist society of which it was a part by offering an opportunity for social rejuvenation. Thus, the touristic alternative suggested by the literature, can be seen as *one* 'rejuvenating' response to the 'business' side of American society.

This romantic ideology may then be thought of as being variously interpreted by potential tourists, each having their own set of motivations. As Graham Dann (1981) has pointed out, such motivations, however conceived, may be thought of as 'push' factors that here respond to the 'pull' of Indian territory that, according to Albers and

James (1988: 151–2), was given a 'picturesque, exotic, and enchanted character' in touristic media productions.

How are such predispositions transformed into decisions to travel and choice of particular destinations? Mansfield (1992) and Crompton (1992) work through the psychological side of this, particularly in regard to destination choice; and Jones and his associates (1983), following a line taken early on by Boyer (1972), demonstrate how important situational constraints can be for understanding travel decisions.

Thus, in this little overview (which is only one of a number that could be offered), connections have been made from airy theoretical issues having to do with the nature of society itself through a number of analytical levels to one of much significance for market researchers and their clients. It shows how fertile the research ground is for basic or applied anthropology in the tourist-generating situation.

Finally, a natural extension of this line of research would consider the consequences of touristic superstructures for the tourist-generating situations that produce them, as well as relevant host situations, which follows the theoretical view that superstructures are not only reactive, but also active. Marta Weigl's (1989) suggestion that the development of the American south-west into a kind of giant Disneyworld by, among other agencies, the Fred Harvey Company and the Santa Fe Railroad, is a natural outgrowth into the host situation of the line of research undertaken by Albers and James.

BROADENING HORIZONS

Most anthropological work on tourism has been guided by an acculturation or development paradigm that emphasizes the impact of developed Western metropoles on lesser developed, non-Western host societies. Perhaps this is as much a reflection of the constitutional disposition of most present-day anthropologists to side with the 'little peoples' of the world in their struggles over domination as of a tendency to follow a path of research for which funding is available. That anthropologists still remain stuck on this orientation is indicated by Crick (1989: 324) who says, '[a]n essentially imperialist imagery is evident in much of the recent language social scientists use about international tourism.' The same concentration on recipient cultures in the Third World remains in the case studies in both editions of Valene Smith's influential *Hosts and Guests* (1977 and 1989). anthropologists doing these studies may recognize that they are dealing with only one aspect of tourism, but their disclaimers, which appear from time to time, are not enough. They should know that a good part of touristic input world-wide occurs in other acculturation situations including quite a number in which the host society has a good deal of control over what transpires. So, unless the concept is redefined and more carefully applied, the notion of tourism as a form of imperialism may be at times inapplicable.

There are other problems. Some tourists do not travel internationally, but only domestically. In 1970, for example, most French vacationers did not go abroad (see Boyer, 1972: 40, 58). Moreover, to confine tourists and tourism to the contemporary Western world, as many social scientists seem bent on doing, would seem to be unjustifiable given the existence of obviously touristic practices in other places and times. Finally, it is important to remember that the issue of tourism's impact is only one of the questions about tourism that anthropologists can attend to.

Can anthropologists studying tourism go beyond the reigning views of the subject towards the fulfilment of the classical anthropological charge to study human behaviour wherever it occurs? First, consider the matter of domestic versus international tourism. The anthropological stress on international tourism is illustrated by Crick's review article (1989). Nevertheless, there have been notable studies in the domestic sphere too, as, for example, in the special issue on domestic tourism of the *Annals of Tourism Research* edited by Smith and Wanhill (1986). A review of these studies suggests that the two forms of tourism may be compared and used for making generalizations.

Anthropologists' awareness of the transcultural range of the subject-matter also is increasing. Using the definition of tourist as leisured traveller, D. Nash (1979) was able to identify tourists and tourisms in societies at all levels of social complexity. It is gratifying to note, there-fore, an accumulation of anthropologically oriented work, including that by a small but growing number of non-Western scholars, on the subject in an increasing variety of societies not only in the contemporary world, but also in the past. For example, we are becoming more enlightened about tourism in rapidly disappearing centrally planned economies (see e.g. Allcock and Przeclawski, 1990) and about tourism in the past of Western (see e.g. Towner, 1985) and non-Western societies (see e.g. Singh, 1989). To put all of this information together anthropologically requires the routine use of transcultural conceptual schemes such as the one used here.

So, too, do the varieties of tourism that became the principal talking point of the Zakopane seminar (Nash and Butler, 1990; Smith and

Eadington, 1992). We have been aware that tourists come in various forms since tourism began to be studied. Thus, Smith, in her introduction to *Hosts and Guests* (1977, 1989), speaks of seven kinds of tourists (explorers, elite, mass, etc.). Cohen (1979b) suggests five modes of touristic experience. Yiannakis and Gibson (1992) identify at least 13 tourist roles. The exact number of tourists or tourisms is unimportant. It will be more or less depending on the subject-matter, the point of view taken, and the level of abstraction. What is important is that anthropologists understand that tourism comes in many forms and that there be some scheme for comparing them.

TOURISM STUDY IN ANTHROPOLOGY

Though there has been growth in the anthropological study of tourism, the field is far from being integrated into the anthropological mainstream.[6] What of the legitimacy of the field of tourism research for anthropologists and other social scientists? Even though progress has been made, I do not feel that the scepticism about tourism study in anthropology has disappeared. Whatever the reason for this, it is unfortunate. here is a new field ripe for the application of theories and offering many possibilities for cross-fertilization. For example, consider the problem of the relationship between tourism and industrial development in the former Yugoslavia that has been investigated by the English sociologist, John Allcock (1989). To what extent do general principles of industrial development, formulated by Raymond Aron (1967), apply to tourism in host societies? Only the most parochial anthropologist would not be stimulated by the light which Allcock's study throws on this question.

Integration is, of course, a two-way street. No matter how easy it is to blame the establishment, anthropologists studying tourism will have to show greater scientific maturity and demonstrate the applicability of central anthropological concerns to their subject. So far, they have not done very well in this. Davydd Greenwood's comment about his early attitude towards tourism-induced changes in the *alarde* ritual among the Basques is illustrative. In reflecting on what was in fact his earlier rush to judgement, Greenwood (1989: 185) points out that anthropologists now ought to know better. They should occupy a vantage point that 'requires linking the study of tourism to the broadest theoretical issues in the discipline'. An example of a move in this direction is the new curriculum of the Roehampton Institute (UK) for the postgraduate degree in the sociology and anthropology of tourism (see Selwyn,

1990), which, among other things, relates questions of tourism research to anthropological theory.

On the establishment side, the subject of tourism now seems to be linked to a growing concern of anthropologists with themselves and their procedures, including issues of validity and authority. This self-reflexive trend, which became evident several decades ago, has had the consequence, according to Clifford (1986: 22), of 'dislodging the ground from which persons securely represent others'. As a result, ethnographers and their point of view have been subjected to increasing scrutiny; and the old question of whether anthropology is an interpretivist art or a science (see e.g. Hollingshead, 1991; Dann, Nash and Pearce, 1988) is once more debated. In the process of questioning themselves and their procedures, more anthropologists seem willing to take the tourist seriously.

Is it possible that the tourist may have a point of view that is as authoritative as that of the ethnographer? Clifford (1990: 55) points to the similarities between ethnographers and travel writers, and Redfoot (1984: 299–301) even thinks of the anthropologist as a kind of tourist. The issue of ethnographic authority, which was raised in tourism studies by Dean MacCannell (1976), is addressed by the anthropologists Errington and Gewertz (1989: 37) who point out how visiting tourists made them question the authenticity of their own view of a group of New Guinea natives. These authors ultimately come down on the anthropological side, a position that is not so easy to maintain in the face of what Hill (1992: 814) sees as the assertion of 'new relativizing counter-hegemonic discourses' in and outside of anthropology. Whatever the ultimate answer to the question about the authenticity of the anthropological point of view, the advent of the new pluralism about the observer among anthropologists should further erode whatever scepticism remains about tourists and students of tourism in anthropology. It will be easier, then, to accept the study of tourism on its scientific merits only.

FOR THE FUTURE

Anthropologists have established a foundation for the study of tourism. From this base, where ought they now to be heading? To conclude this essay, let me state some general strictures for the consideration of tourism as an anthropological subject. No specific theory nor methodology will be suggested because the field remains open to a variety of approaches form many disciplines. Needless to say, whatever the particular approach used, it should be theoretically informed and methodologically adequate according to some scientific criterion.

First, assuming that comparisons across cultures are an essential part of the anthropological approach, all concepts and procedures used should be cross-culturally applicable. Thus, the conception of the tourist as a kind of sightseer (see e.g. MacCannell, 1976; Urry, 1990) or of tourism as a specialized activity (see e.g. Dumazedier, 1968), though possibly applicable in industrial or modern societies and those they have touched, leaves out the vast array of pre-industrial societies in which something very much like what we take to be tourism is quite evident (see D. Nash, 1979). Negative reflexes ought to be activated by any notion of tourism that confines it to specific cultures or a limited range of cultures. Forms of analysis also need to be transculturally viable. As Nash and Smith (1991: 22) say, '[i]f cross-cultural comparisons cannot ultimately be made, statements about tourism, its causes and effects cannot further anthropological insights.' The definition of tourist as a leisured traveller and the concepts of touristic process and system, used here, help to foster a transcultural perspective while, at the same time, allowing different varieties of tourism and forms of analysis to have their way.

Second, the laudable openness of anthropologists studying tourism to others' views should continue. As Crick (1989) has pointed out, and as the recent compendium, 'Tourism Social Science', edited by Graburn and Jafari (1991) demonstrates, tourism is a multifaceted phenomenon which can be profitably viewed in a variety of ways. This means that anthropologists should be cosmopolites not only about the practices of tourism, but also the different social sciences that consider them.

Third, as was emphasized by the Zakopane seminar, mentioned above, from whatever point of view it is seen, tourism takes a variety of forms, and it is this variety that will serve as the basis for scientific explanations. Why does one form of tourism differ from another? Here, reference will be made to various aspects of a touristic system that generate and maintain different forms. What are the consequences for hosts, tourists and their societies of different forms of tourism? My view is that the anthropological emphasis on the latter question should be balanced by an equivalent emphasis on the former. Though no single theoretical point of view will be adequate for dealing with either of these questions, I do believe that the broad conception of tourism as a kind of superstructure will prove useful in providing a general orientation to the first question. As for the second, the field would seem to be open, but as far as the contemporary world is concerned, any analysis should begin with the shadow that increasingly international metropoles cast over touristic systems.

Fourth, as has been suggested throughout this essay, basic and applied research on tourism can move along hand in hand. though privately funded research on the subject is rare, public support of investigations of tourism by organizations such as the United Nations, the World Bank, and various national and local governments has been substantial. Applied research of this kind, as Nash and Smith (1991) have argued, can contribute to the basic side. Of course, the usual cautions about 'selling out' apply to both kinds of research. What is needed here and elsewhere by the anthropologist is an acute awareness of self and social position as well as the significant others involved in the research, including not only those others being studied, but also those who may be sponsoring the research. The advance of self-reflexive anthropologies, which involve not only an awareness of oneself and one's social position, abut also of the procedures used for gathering and communicating information, should help in this.

Finally, I would like to follow Crick (1989: 338) and issue another call for more, increasingly adequate research. In anthropology, as this review has shown, the possibilities for the study of tourism have only begun to be realized. Crick stresses that in such research the voice of the other needs to be given its due. Even though there is disagreement about how much sharing there should be between anthropologists and their subjects in the production of texts (see Sanjek, 1990: 406–7), all anthropologists probably would subscribe to this view. But there also should be a sophisticated awareness of the subject of tourism and of the possible ways of conceiving and studying it from an anthropological point of view. As this essay has demonstrated, that awareness is growing among an increasing number of scholars, anthropologists included who do not need to be convinced of the importance of tourism in human affairs. If current trends continue, these scholars will represent a much broader spectrum of humankind and points of view than did the small group of European and North American enthusiasts who began the study of tourism. So much the better.

NOTES

1　The anthropological approach through the years has ranged from the hard-nosed scientific to the soft humanistic. A recent offshoot of the latter has crystallized into what Spiro (1992: 34) has referred to as hermeneutic with a particularistic focus. This line of thought maintains that anthropology cannot be a generalizing science, or even a science, because it is impossible to know 'others' who are radically different not only from the observer, but from each other. Therefore, the pursuit of substantial cross-cultural generalizations is a fruitless quest. Following Spiro (1992: 34–43), I do not believe that the intent to make anthropology a cross-cultural science is misguided. That peoples think differently does not mean that they cannot be understood; nor does it mean that generalizations about human behaviour are impossible.

2   There probably are societies in which something like the Western concept of leisure does not exist, but if leisure activities (including tourism) are taken loosely to refer to those performed in the time left over form the work of the world, a good case can be made for its universality. Of course, as with other universals traditionally investigated by anthropologists such as religion, kinship and economy, it varies in form.

3   My categorization of approaches to tourism by anthropologically oriented scholars overlaps those of Crick (1989) and Cohen (1988), but it is more closely tied to what I take to be the principal concerns of anthropology than either of these.

4   The issues of empathy and of sharedness or control in the production of an ethnographic text, about which anthropologists have different views, is discussed extensively in Sanjek (ed.) (1990); that of putting things in context has always been important in anthropology.

5   The view here is deliberately general. It is that though all aspects of a socio-cultural system play a role in normal human social life, they are not equally important in its reproduction. So, less important superstructural aspects, though capable of acting as well as reacting, are less determinative of the course of social life than are more important infrastructural or base elements. Tourism everywhere would seem to be a kind of superstructure with its ultimate base in the productive system, but specific kinds of tourism have their base in a broad range of socio-cultural elements.

6   Considering the growing specialization of anthropological interests, it might be argued that there is no anthropological mainstream. Though time-honoured notions about anthropology are being challenged and though the area of agreement about what constitutes anthropology may be shrinking, I do believe that there remain common standards for anthropological behaviour. It is these that I am referring to as the anthropological mainstream.

REFERENCES

Adams, V. (1992) 'Tourism and Sherpas, Nepal: reconstruction of reciprocity', *Annals of Tourism Research*, 19: 534–54.

Albers, P. and James, W. (1983) 'Tourism and the changing image of the Great Lakes Indian', *Annals of Tourism Research*, 10: 128–48.

—— (1988) 'Travel photography: a methodological approach', *Annals of Tourism Research*, 15: 134–63.

Allcock, J. (1989) 'Tourism and industrialization: the transformation of

Yugoslav rural society', *Problems of Tourism (Problemy Turystyki)*, 12: 3–24.

Allcock, J. and Przeclawski, K. (eds) (1990) 'Tourism in centrally planned societies', *Annals of Tourism Research*, 17, 1.

Aron, R. (1967) *Eighteen Lectures on Industrial Society*, London: Weidenfeld & Nicholson.

Aspelin, P. (1978) 'Indirect tourism and political economy: the case of the amamaindê of Mato Grosso, Brazil' in *Tourism and Economic Change*, ed. V. Smith, Studies in Third World Societies, 6. Williamsburg, VA: College of William and Mary.

Baudrillard, J. (1975) *The Mirror of Production*, St Louis: Telos.

Boorstin, D. (1964) *The Image: A Guide to Pseudo-Events in America*, New York: Harper & Row.

Boyer, M. (1972) *Le Tourisme*, Paris: Editions du Seuil.

Clifford, J. (1986) 'Introduction: partial truths' in *Writing Culture; The Poetics and Politics of Ethnography*, ed. J. Clifford and G. Marcus, Berkeley: University of California Press.

—— (1990) 'Notes on (field)notes' in *Fieldnotes: The Makings of Anthropology*, ed. R. Sanjek, Ithaca, NY: Cornell University Press.

Cohen E. (1974) 'Who is a tourist? A conceptual clarification', *Sociological Review*, 22: 527–55.

—— (1979a) 'The impact of tourism on the hill-tribes of Northern Thailand', *Internationales Asienforum*, 10: 5–38.

—— (1979b) 'A phenomenology of touristic experiences', *Sociology*, 13: 179–201.

—— (ed.) (1979) 'The sociology of tourism', *Annals of Tourism Research*, 6 (1 and 2).

—— (1984) 'The sociology of tourism: Approaches, issues, and findings', *Annual Review of Sociology*, 10: 373–92.

—— (ed.) (1985) 'Tourist guides: pathfinders, mediators, and animators', *Annals of Tourism Research*, 12, 1.

—— (1988) 'Traditions in the qualitative sociology of tourism', *Annals of Tourism Research*, 15: 29–46.

Crick, M. (1985) 'Tracing the anthropological self: quizzical reflections on fieldwork, tourism, and the Ludic', *Sociological Analysis*, 17: 71–92.

—— (1989) 'Representations of international tourism in the social sciences: sun, sex, sights, savings, and servility', *Annual Review of Anthropology*, 18: 307–33.

Crompton, J. (1992) 'Structure of vacation choice sets', *Annals of Tourism Research*, 19: 420–34.

Dann, G. (1981) 'Tourist motivation: an appraisal', *Annals of Tourism Research*, 8: 187–219.

Dann, G., Nash, D. and Pearce, P. (1988) 'Methodology in tourism research', *Annals of Tourism Research*, 15: 1–28.

De Kadt, E. (ed.) (1979) *Tourism: Passport to Development?* Oxford: Oxford University Press.

—— (1991) 'Making the alternative sustainable: lessons from development for tourism' in *Tourism Alternatives: Perspectives on the Future of Tourism Research*, ed. V. Smith and W. Eadington, Philadelphia: University of Pennsylvania Press.

Dumazedier, J. (1968) 'Leisure', *International Encyclopedia of the Social Sciences*, 9: 248–53.

ECTWT (Ecumenical Coalition on Third World Tourism) (1986) *Third World Peoples and Tourism: Report of the 1986 Conference Proceedings*, Chorakhebua, Bangkok: ECTWT.

Erisman, M. (1983) 'Tourism and cultural dependency in the West Indies', *Annals of Tourism Research*, 10: 337–62.

Errington, F. and Gewertz, D. (1989) 'Tourism and anthropology in a post-modern world', *Oceania*, 60: 37–54.

Francisco, R. (1983) 'The political impact of tourism dependence in Latin America', *Annals of Tourism Research*, 10: 377–94.

Furnham, A. (1984) 'Tourism and culture shock', *Annals of Tourism Research*, 11: 41–58.

Geva, A. and Goldman, A. (1991) 'Satisfaction measurement in guided tours', *Annals of Tourism Research*, 18: 177–85.

Godelier, M. (1980) 'The emergence of Marxism in anthropology in France' in *Soviet and Western Anthropology*, ed. E. Gellner, New York: Columbia University Press.

Graburn, N. (1983) 'The anthropology of tourism', *Annals of Tourism Research*, 10: 9–33.

—— (ed.) (1983) 'The anthropology of tourism', *Annals of Tourism Research*, 10, 1.

Graburn, N. and Jafari, J. (eds) (1991) 'Tourism social science', *Annals of Tourism Research*, 18, 1.

Greenwood, D. (1989) 'Culture by the pound: an anthropological perspective on tourism as cultural commoditization', in *Hosts and Guests: The Anthropology of Tourism*, 2nd edn, ed. V. Smith, Philadelphia: University of Pennsylvania Press.

Gunder Frank, A. (1972) *Lumpen-Bourgeoisie and Lumpen-Development: Dependence, Class and Politics in Latin America*, New York: Monthly Review.

Hallowell, A.I. (1957) 'The impact of the American Indian on American culture', *American Anthropologist*, 59: 201–17.

Hardy, D. (1990) 'Sociocultural dimensions of tourism history', *Annals of Tourism Research*, 17: 541–55.

Heiman, M. (1989) 'Production confronts consumption: landscape perception and social conflict in the Hudson River Valley', *Society and Space*, 7: 165–78.

Hill, J. (1992) 'Contested pasts and the practice of anthropology: overview', *American Anthropologist*, 94: 809–15.

Hollingshead, K. (1991) 'A riposte for anthropology: ellipsian ethnography explained', *Annals of Tourism Research*, 18: 653–8.
Jafari, J. (1987) 'Tourism models: the sociocultural aspects', *Tourism Management*, 8: 151–9.
—— (1990) 'Research and scholarship: the basis of tourism education', *Journal of Tourism Studies*, 1: 33–41.
Jones, P.M., Dix, M.C., Clark, M.I. and Reggie, I.G. (1983) *Understanding Travel Behavior*, Brookfield, VT: Gower.
Jurdao Arrones, F. (199) *España en Venta*, 2nd edn, Madrid: Ediciones Endymion.
Krippendorff, J. (1986) 'Tourism in the system of industrial society', *Annals of Tourism Research*, 13: 517–32.
Lett, J., Jr. (1983) 'Ludic and liminoid aspects of charter yacht tourism in the Caribbean', *Annals of Tourism Research*, 10: 35–56.
Lett, J. (1989) 'Epilogue' in *Hosts and Guests: The Anthropology of Tourism*, 2nd edn, ed. V. Smith, Philadelphia: University of Pennsylvania Press.
MacCannell, D. (1976) *The Tourist: A New Theory of the Leisure Class*, New York: Shocken.
—— (1992) *Empty Meeting Grounds*, New York: Routledge.
Mansfield, Y. (1992) 'From motivation to actual travel', *Annals of Tourism Research*, 19: 399–4419.
Matthews, H. (ed.) (1983) 'Political science and tourism', *Annals of Tourism Research*, 10, 3.
Matthews, H. and Richter, L. (1991) 'Political science and tourism', *Annals of Tourism Research*, 18: 120–35.
McKean, P. (1976) 'Tourism, culture change and culture conservation' in *Ethnic Identity in Modern Southeast Asia*, ed. D. Banks, The Hague: Mouton.
Millman, R. (1988) 'Just pleasure: the churches look at tourism's impacts', *Annals of Tourism Research*, 15: 555–8.
Mitchell, L. (ed.) (1979) 'Geography of tourism', *Annals of Tourism Research*, 6, 3.
Nash, D. (1970) *A Community in Limbo: An Anthropological Study of an American Community Abroad*, Bloomington, IN: Indiana University Press.
—— (1979) *Tourism in Pre-Industrial Societies*, Aix-en-Provence: Centre des Hautes Etudes Touristiaques.
—— (1981) 'Tourism as an anthropological subject', *Current Anthropology*, 22: 461–81.
—— (1991) 'The course of sojourner adaptation', *Human Organization*, 50: 283–6.
Nash, D. and Butler, R. (1990) 'Alternative forms of tourism', *Annals of Tourism Research*, , 17: 302–5.
Nash, D. and Smith, V. (1991) 'Anthropological study of tourism', *Annals of Tourism Research*, 18: 12–25.
Nash, R. (1967) *Wilderness and the American Mind*, New Haven: Yale University Press.

Nuñez, T. (1963) 'Tourism, tradition, and acculturation: *Weekendismo* in a Mexican village', *Southwestern Journal of Anthropology*, 21: 347–52.

—— (1977) 'Touristic studies in anthropological perspective' in *Hosts and Guests: The Anthropology of Tourism*, ed. V. Smith, Philadelphia: University of Pennsylvania Press.

—— (with Epilogue by J. Lett) (1989) 'Touristic studies in anthropological perspective' in *Hosts and Guests: The Anthropology of Tourism*, 2nd edn, ed. V. Smith, Philadelphia: University of Pennsylvania Press.

Pearce, D. (1992) 'Alternative tourism: concepts, classifications and questions' in *Tourism Alternatives: Potentials and Problems in the Development of Tourism*, ed. V. Smith and W. Eadington, Philadelphia: University of Pennsylvania Press.

Pearce, P. (1982) *The Social Psychology of Tourist Behavior*, Oxford: Pergamon.

Pye, E. and Lin, T-B. (1983) *Tourism in Asia: The Economic Impact*, Singapore: Singapore University Press.

Redfoot, D. (1984) 'Touristic authority, touristic angst, and modern reality', *Alternative Sociology*, 7: 291–309.

Riemer, G. (1990) 'Packaging dreams', *Annals of Tourism Research*, 17: 501–12.

Saglio, C. (1979) 'Tourism for discovery: a project in the lower Casamance' in *Tourism: Passport for Development?*, ed. E. de Kadt, Oxford: Oxford University Press.

Sanjek, R. (1990) 'On ethnographic validity' in *Fieldnotes: The Makings of Anthropology*, ed. R. Sanjek, Ithaca, NY: Cornell University Press.

—— (ed.) (1990) *Fieldnotes: The Makings of Anthropology*, Ithaca, N: Cornell University Press.

Schlechten, M. (1988) *Tourisme balnéaire ou tourisme rural integré: Deux modeles de développement sénégalais*, Fribourg: Editions Fribourg Suisse.

Selwyn, T. (1990) 'Postgraduate studies in sociology and anthropology of tourism', *Annals of Tourism Research*, 17: 637–8.

Singh, T. (1989) *The Kulu Valley: Impact of Tourism Development in the Mountain Areas*, New Delhi: Himalayan.

Smith, V. (1989) 'Eskimo tourism: micro models and marginal men' in *Hosts and Guests: The Anthropology of Tourism*, 2nd edn, ed. V. Smith, Philadelphia: University of Pennsylvania Press.

—— (ed.) (1977) 1989) *Hosts and Guests: The Anthropology of Tourism*, 1st and 2nd edns, Philadelphia: University of Pennsylvania Press.

Smith, V. and Wanhill, S. (eds) (1986) 'Domestic tourism', *Annals of Tourism Research*, 13, (3).

Smith, V. and Eadington, W. (eds) (1991) *Tourism Alternatives: Potentials and Problems in the Development of Tourism*, Philadelphia: University of Pennsylvania Press.

Spiro, M. (1992) *Anthropological Other or Burmese Brother?* New Brunswick, NJ: Transaction.

Srisang, K. (1989) 'The ecumenical coalition for Third World Tourism', *Annals of Tourism Research*, 16: 119–21.

SSRC Seminar (1954) 'Acculturation: an exploratory formulation', *American Anthropologist*, 56: 973–1002.

Thurot, J.M. and Thurot, G. (1983) 'The ideology of class and tourism: confronting the discourse of advertising', *Annals of Tourism Research*, 10: 173–89.

Turner, V. (1969) *The Ritual Process*, Chicago: Aldine.

Turner, V. and Turner, E. (1978) *Image and Pilgrimage in Christian Culture*, New York: Columbia University Press.

Urry, J. (1990) *The Tourist Gaze: Leisure and Travel in Contemporary Societies*, London, Newbury Park and New Delhi: Sage.

Van den Berghe, P. and Keyes, C. (eds) (1984) 'Tourism and ethnicity', *Annals of Tourism Research*, 11, 3.

Van Gennep, A. (1960[1908]) *The Rites of Passage*, Chicago: University of Chicago Press.

Weigl, M. (1989) 'From desert to Disneyworld: the Santa Fe Railway and the Fred Harvey company display the Indian Southwest', *Journal of Anthropological Research*, 45, Spring: 115–37.

Yiannakis, A. and Gibson, H. (1992) 'Roles tourists play', *Annals of Tourism Research*, 19: 287–303.

CHAPTER 9

Lost Horizons Regained: Old Age and the Anthropology of Contemporary Society
Haim Hazan

The organization of cultural knowledge in contemporary Western society appropriates old age either as a source for gaining access into unknown realms of experience, such as dying (see e.g. Elias, 1985; Hockey & James, 1993) or as a social problem. In this sense, old age is 'problematized', designated as a deviance, and hence excluded from offering commentary and reflection relevant to the hub of contemporary living. This chapter is set to revise this approach.*

The challenge of studying contemporary living in (so-called) post-modern society is met by current anthropology in a rather erratic and hesitant manner. In part this is due to a basic incongruence in the master codes of these two dramatic personae: postmodernism and anthropology. Glossed over, anthroplogy can be described as based on context-bound principles oriented toward holistic perspective. Anthropology is (still to a large extent) dominated by the modernist quest for form, purpose, design, hierarchy, totalization, significance, authenticity and truth-values; postmodernism, in contrast, consists of antiform, play, chance, anarchy, deconstruction, differance, contingency and irony (for the complete table of adjectives, see Hassan, 1985).

The dilemmas arising from such incompatibility could be subsumed under six problem areas, which I address in detail below. These problems arguably put at stake the validity and, indeed, the future of social anthropology as a corpus of knowledge and knowing relevant to deciphering contemporary existence. None of them are new to anthropology; however, many of their former solutions now seem conspicuously obsolete. Evidently the impetus to perpetuate the survival of the discipline generates a variety of creative mutations designed to offer new ways of interpretations and novel angles of doing ethnographic fieldwork. Such attempts are often guided by the tacit assumption that it is the relations between the anthropologist and his fieldwork which needs to be modified, i.e. become more 'reflective', 'interpretative', 'polyphonic', etc. Rarely has it been suggested that in order to change its theoretical viewpoint, anthropology should seek to change its subject-matter. It is precisely those types of fields which characterize contemporary living in which anthropologists are still, to a large extent, novices. Fields such as in-vitro fertilization, the mass media, advertising and other impersonal, non-reactive contacts, could all serve to ascertain profiles of new anthropological models.

I propose that the study of ageing, considered through a 'post-modernist' perspective, can be accounted as one of these fields. Furthermore, it is my conviction that anthropology – deflected from the attempt to understand old age – could be restored to some of its original concerns and concepts. To pursue this argument two steps must be taken. The first is a brief scanning of the six major anthropological concerns; the second is to present the study of old age as a source for anthropological reflections upon those concerns. Following this introduction, a general purview of anthropology drawn from the author's own study of ageing will be presented. In that sense the structure of the chapter reflects a reversed course of investigation, where the source of anthropological knowledge is placed *after* its conclusions. This inversion is due to the realization that the study of old age has occupied a marginal place in general anthropology and hence most readers are unfamiliar with its scope, interests and contributions. It is, however, this marginality that perhaps enables anthropologists studying old age to claim a unique perspective on the whole discipline, a perspective anchored in the liminal position of the professional 'stranger'.

THE SIX DEMONS OF ANTHROPOLOGY REAWAKENED

In our fragmented society, the traditional anthropological quest for human universals within cultural diversity is rendered increasingly problematic (cf. Carrithers, 1992). Postmodern fragmentation defies the old notion of closed systems and set boundaries for socio-cultural units. Unifying conceptions such as 'tribe', 'nation', 'social systems', 'symbolic order', 'tradition' and 'society' are thus becoming analytically questionable.[1] In the absence of unifying framing devices, the exploration of social commonalities becomes almost implausible. The first dilemma, therefore, is whether it is still possible to look for human universals. Is there some sort of a 'language' of 'deep structures', which could be recognized in the multitude of diverse and incongruent symbolic codes and cultural bricollages – indeed, is it still legitimate to look for such a language?

Here one can find two anthropological traditions, or schools, ensnared in conflict. In opposition to the structuralist project and other universal explanations (see Brown, 1991) stands the anthropological insistence on 'grounded theory' (see Glaser and Strauss, 1967) and 'emergent properties' (Kapferer, 1972). Since anthropology construes the particular field as the only legitimate source of knowledge, a universal language may be prevented from being developed. But here postmodernism raises its head again. The very notion of the anthropological 'field' is being challenged, in postmodernist reality, by both the dissolution of marked social, temporal and spatial boundaries, and the accompanying tendency to relinquish holistic, all-embracing ethnographic descriptions. Instead, cross-sectional and flexible methodologies have been devised to accommodate the condition of social lability and openess. Semiotic analysis, radical pragmatics and theories of use, 'dispersive' structuralism as well as the rise of socio-biology are but a few expressions of this quest. The second problematique, to which I now come, that of losing the illusion of the wholeness, is a direct derivation of that pursuit.

The anthropological rationale for breaking down the holistic principle is the realization that postmodern settings represent neither closed systems nor unilateral processes (see also Strathern, 1992). With this awareness in mind, the anthropologist seeking an ethnographic field has to decide whether to arbitrarily delimit the scope of research or to follow the snowball effect of the enquiry and drift into a free-floating, purposeless study. In fact, the very idea of 'a study' which spells planning, control and comparison, is jeopardized and arguably defied by such a state. This bears far-reaching implications for the plausibility of developing further orthodox research interests such as community,[2] nation-state and even simple interpersonal human interactions, which become non-reactive and impersonal.[3]

The third problem pertains to social change and is governed by the arrow of time. Perspectives on the social construction of time could be analysed in a variety of ways. Universal and holistic perspectives regarding social time are premised on the assumed ability and desire of humans to live in a contrived temporal universe consisting of linear progression interwoven into cyclical phases (Leach, 1971; Zerubavel, 1982, 1985). However, the mechanism striking the fine and unpredictable balance of the two is rarely considered. Contemporary living might disrupt this comfortable dinstinction by interweaving cyclical and linear phases through the non-teleological nature of life in a 'post-historical' era where ideology ceases to inform behaviour and social divisions are deemed to be horizontal and ephemeral rather than hierarchical and perrenial (see Dumont, 1972). The notions of the happening, the Baudrillardian (1983) simulacrum and Giddens' (1991) time–space distancing are all pertinent here. With such blurred lines, time loses its distinct properties as a social structuring device and becomes more diffused and amorphic than ever before. This disjointed temporal world is particularly manifested and reflected in the ways through which contemporary self is constituted, to be further exemplified in the following section.

The fourth anthropological dilemma is to re-examine the nexus between self and society. It was Schutz who first entertained the notion of 'multiple realities' in the life of modern man; an idea which was taken up and developed by many of his exponents (Berger, Berger and Kellner, 1973; Schutz and Luckman, 1973) and reinherited within other conceptual frameworks such as Lifton's (1986) 'doubling' and Ewing's (1990) multiple selves. This growing trend in the behavioural sciences which has found its theroetical underpinnings in social psychology (Shotter and Gergen, 1986), sociology (Grathoff, 1977) and anthropology (Geertz, 1983; Carpenter, 1972) responds to an irresolvable dilemma concerning modern living. This is the dissolution of long-term contextual settings of 'life-term arenas' (Moore, 1978) and their replacement with 'limited term arenas' where commitments, allegiances and memories are short-lived. The phenomenon of the 'homeless mind' thus becomes a prevalent feature of postmodern existence with its moral, symbolic and social far-reaching implications. As opposed to the traditional idea of the Mertonian 'role set', the concept of multiple selves does not presuppose a unifying spinal cord around which those selves are clustered and organized. In its extreme versions it maintains a disparity of unconnected, unrelated entities inhabiting one corporeal being.

The idea of multiple selves challenges both theoretical conventions and methodological assumptions since the knowledge of the 'other' can no longer rely on preconceptions of continuity and integrity of identity. The two dimensions of anthropological enquiry thus seem to be potentially misguided: the anthropos – the other under study, and the logia – the concepts employed to understand and academically tame that object of study. Anthropological constructs and their repercussions are the subject of the fifth dilemma, which stems from the quest for new conceptual constructs befitting the postmodern condition (see also Fabian, 1983).

Claiming scientific authority or even communicative properties necessitates a common language of shared concepts. When such terms are no longer available, anthropology might find itself on a track leading to alternative paradigms, new conceptual frameworks or radically different research methods. It could be argued that all of these possibilities are indeed happening within the limits of current anthropological discourse. However, even though research approaches are reformulated, the paradigm of anthropological knowledge still awaits its change. This presumably is neither a consequence of slack intellectual fervour nor the result of lack of academic input from other disciplines. The root of the failure to replace traditional constructs with suitable alternatives is probably embedded in the problem of anthropological representation in contemporary society, so amply discussed (cf. Pels and Nancel, 1991) and yet so poorly resolved. Postmodern society has largely moved beyond the analytical reach of anthropology, which needs a new conceptual language in order to represent it. It is a society where social structure is no longer an identifiable and hence definable 'structure', social boundaries become boundless, symbolic orders lose their external meanings, collapse into themselves (Sperber, 1975) and turn into 'myths' (Barthes, 1976). Social time is not only multidimensional, reversible and a-synchronized, but also chaotic and quantum-like.

Two options are open to the frustrated ethnographer. The first is the introduction of a new conceptual language capable of handling postmodern reality. Such a choice can account for the welcoming reception given in American anthropological circles to works by French scholars such as Foucault, Lyotard, Bourdieu and especially Baudrillard. However, these writers have not in the main been properly appropriated and incorporated into anthropology. The second option is to question the very basis of reportability between the studied subject and its depiction, the ethnography. This could be epitomized in the much used and abused term, 'othering', which brings me to the sixth dilemma.

It would be superfluous to recount the multitude of recent anthropological debates around the issue of representing the 'other'. The ability of the anthropologist to enter the world of the researchee and to be transformed into one of its inhabitants, is premised on two complementary stipulations bringing this discussion to a closure and returning it to its opening remarks. The first is the assumption that there is some fundamental human common denominator between researcher and researchee, enabling the process of 'othering' to take place. The second is that this common denominator can transcend cultural masks, go beyond social divisions and ignore personal idiosyncracies. The study of ageing will be shown as an acid test for these preconceptions as, indeed, it is for all the other issues hitherto broached.

This short shrift to anthropological substance serves both as a summary of and a preamble to framing the ethnographic study of old age within current anthropological discourse. Our approach states that by suspending or 'bracketing' social commitment and culturally engendered predispositions, the issue of old age can throw into relief some intriguing, otherwise hidden, anthropological cues encoded in that particular study. In that sense, the anthropology of ageing has not been as yet sufficiently credited with significant contributions to the discipline at large. With few notable exceptions (Fontana, 1976; Keith, 1982a; Kertzer and Keith, 1984), that potential has not been recognized or realized. Interestingly enough, though, there are some authors who view elderly people in contemporary society not merely as victims of modernity, urbanization, industrialization and social alienation, but rather as vanguards of postmodern experience (Featherstone and Hepworth, 1991) and as creative pioneers of modern living (Silverman, 1987). In both analyses the elderly are perceived as people who find themselves in the unique position of being at the brink of inclusion and exclusion (see Dowd, 1986), endowed with the necessary distance for engendering self-awareness and social creativity. Such social creativity is contrary to prevailing stereotypes, a quality deriving from the loosening of social constraints and the newly acquired freedom gained in later life.[4] Still its supposed instigator, namely awareness, stems from typical considerations of old age as generating reflexivity and allowing for the development of critical faculties in the form of so-called 'wisdom' (C. Turnball, 1983), 'life review' (Butler, 1970) and 'philosophizing' (Myerhoff, 1978, ch. 2). In short, elderly people could be considered as possessing some of the essential provisions for the making of an anthropologist. Elderly people inevitably experience the anthropological distancing as they undergo such 'splitting processes' separating mind from body (de Beauvoir, 1975), past from present (Hazan, 1980), personal time from social time (Hazan, 1992), core cultural identity from circumstantial guises (Kaufman, 1986) and ultimately inner from outer self (Neugarten, 1972; Hazan, forthcoming). All these prerequisites for reflexive anthropological perspective are the source and the justification for the following review of the six aforementioned dilemmas of understanding contemporary living as highlighted by the study of ageing.

GIVING THE DEMONS A BODY: ANTHROPOLOGICAL LESSONS FROM THE STUDY OF OLD AGE

Universality versus diversity

Having studied the process of debunking the elderly in the United States of their cultural identity, Anderson (1972) coined the term 'deculturation' which spells, alongside its negative meaning, a human condition where the construction of the self ceases to be mainly social and draws on other sources of self-definition. This issue of the old socially stark beings was taken up by some other anthropologists who, besides making the plea that old people are first and foremost people (Keith, 1982b) sought to ascertain the underpinnings of an identity uninformed by social norms. Myerhoff (1978) suggested that the elderly resort to cultural origins conceived of as both meaningful and timeless. Thus their current symbolic invisibility imposed by society could be replaced by identity derived from their mythical heritage. Through 'definitional rituals' a sense of 'oneness' and belonging was firmly established. These rituals, unexpected and unreproducible, are one-time events or "nonce symbols" (Leach, 1976) so characteristic of contemporary culture where symbolic orders are fragmented, labile and ephemeral, sometimes to the extent of filling an extremely short-lived, fleeting phase in one's life. However, Myerhoff's analysis suggests something else which at first glance appears to be diametrically opposite to the former idea. This is the reinstitution of myth as a cultural hub of reorganizing identity. Myth was something to which traditional anthropology attached great importance, but has gradually abandoned since turning to study highly literate societies. Its recent revival in the form of 'master narratives' is hence also echoed in the anthropology of ageing. But this 'echoing' takes a unique nature.

The idea of myth is based on oral traditions of narration. As elderly people are still regarded as (perhaps the last) cultural narrators, the phenomenon of story-telling could have been revived in the study of old people. Furthermore, if Lévi-Strauss's (1967) conception of 'cold societies' i.e. non-cumulative myth-based cultures versus 'hot societies' – i.e. cumulative history-based culture – is to be taken as a principle for classifying human approaches to chronology, then Myerhoff's elderly transformed themselves from the latter mode to the former. In fact, a close study of Myerhoff's presentation and findings would reveal that her researchees were in no position to be on a historical cumulative course. Between satisfying the exigencies of daily existence on the one hand, and the timeless experience of living in a mythical world on the other, there was no linear context of negotiation and progress left for them. It is, therefore, hardly surprising that Myerhoff's deficient description of the organization of the day care centre where she carried out her research – background information about the local community and so forth – is made inherently justified by the perceived dearth of such context in the life of the people under study. In an age where the 'end of ideology' and the 'end of history' become acceptable and much discussed concepts, the members of the Aliyah Center in Venice, California, seem to be, albeit unwittingly, vanguards of a postmodern era. Teleological, unilateral and progress-oriented values cease to inform the equally significant symbolic orders of everyday life.

Evidence that elderly people themselves are aware of the lack of the sense of history, of the process of deculturation they undergo and of their own strife for mythical expression of identity could be adduced from the following case study. It deals with a literary piece entitled 'the disguised egg' which served as a reading material for women students of an adult education program in an Israeli urban renewal setting (see Hazan, 1990b: 128–9). 'The disguised egg', a short children's story, tells the adventures of a change-seeking egg in a constantly frustrating pursuit of a suitable metamorphosis. Having disguised itself as a whole range of similarly shaped objects and being snubbed and rejected by all of them, the disenchanted, yet experienced, egg resigns itself to the fact of its egginess, and eventually hatches to become a chicken.

The women students offered a common interpretation to this story which emphasized the fatalistic acceptance of one's position in life. The individual's fate, they argued, is shaped by constraints beyond his control. Personal efforts to escape this fate may be heroic and unexpected, but in the end of the day also ineffective.

These women were fully conscious of their place in a certain historical course of change: they have changed their social position when immigrating to Israel, then this position was again altered by the impact of Ashkenazi-Orientals relations in their new homeland, and once again it was put under the aegis of change as their neighbourhood became an 'urban renewal area'. All these changes, whether forced upon or voluntarily taken, also implied profound transformations of identity. Yet these women were determined that their 'core identity' could not have been altered. By becoming the vicarious authors of their own life narrative, they authenticated what they deemed to be the essence of their existence which was beyond change and outside circumstances.

The whole and its parts

The case of the 're-educated' elderly women could serve as an apt opening for a discussion of the wholeness of the field. These women were part of a sponsored community, a government perpetrated project of urban renewal. Their 'community' was therefore a socially and politically contrived cultural idiom designed to promote vested interests of various political and social agents. It would seem that only in this sense, namely of social engineering, can the long established, almost taken-for-granted, construct of community be once again made into viable anthropological turf. Urban society with its ever-increasing differentiation and fragmentation provides less and less definable arenas of human action whose social properties conform to the traditional model of community. Interestingly, 'community' as a term is often reserved for those who are thought to be its principal victims – the disabled, children, the mentally sick and the elderly.

Anthropologists who sought to study the life of elderly people within their communities were forced, by the apparent absence of such social units, to wonder about the nature and meaning of interpersonal relationships of those who are supposed to inhabit seemingly extinct communities. It would appear that Townsend's (1957) classic study of the community life of elderly residents in the East End of London in the early 1950s was the last in a series of research projects to demonstrate the place of the old within a locally based extensive social network. After that, anthropologists took issue with that phantom phenomenon by pulling it in various directions, each of which touches upon a mode of living in a postmodern era. There are at least six such modes representing six options of functioning in a society whose flexible boundaries and variegated mechanisms of social control allow for a broad range of enforced or voluntary alternative realities.

Research into urban milieux expectedly shows that a great number of elderly people live alone in single occupancy residence (Sokolovsky, 1990) under harsh conditions of poor housing, poverty and social isolation. Others dwell in hotels either as a form of sheltered accommodation (Teski, 1979) or as an expression of resistance of welfare agencies, thus claiming personal autonomy (Stephens, 1976). Hochschild (1973) found at the heart of the deserted inner city 'an unexpected community' of elderly widows who created their own social support network. The association between age, gender and social commitment could be seen as one of the springboards for the spiralling interest in feminist studies in general[5] and of the growing importance attached to age boundaries as a marker of social stratification in our society (Kertzer and Keith, 1984). They both stem from the realization that community boundaries no longer exist in their traditional form.

The third mode of operating with a 'community' in an age of the 'eclipse of community' is indeed an anthropological gaze into attempts of engineering such communities. The locution 'community creation' which was chosen as the hallmark of emergent groupings of the social life of elderly people within sponsored settings (Keith, 1980) is debatable since the set boundaries of residential home (Keith, 1982a), day care centres and commmunal settlements for the old, are all definitional markers of organizational contexts rather than terms of social interaction. Thus the discovery of 'we-feeling' (Keith, 1982a) and cultural innovation in age-homogenous sponsored 'communities' are contingent upon the setting rather than on its incumbents. Francis (1984) found that in a comparative study of two communities of elderly people, the one set within a highly organized framework – a day care centre – displayed much more vitality and close-knit interactions than the one that was not. A glance at the spread of social contexts composing contemporary living would show that a great number of these are of the same social form. Places of work, schools, clubs, leisure facilities, recreational arrangements, etc., are all pre-organized settings, and all-too-often settings of high degree of normative control.

The fourth mode seems a logical extension of the third. In their quest for community, anthropologists of old age discovered that many elderly people are integrated within a web of meanings and their symbols without being dependent on interpersonal contacts. This becomes necessary as persons are deemed to move further in the life course. Face-to-face relationships, traditionally regarded in anthropology as the cornerstone of human behaviour, hence become irrelevant. Unruh (1983) maintains that the elderly's 'invisible lives', i.e. their non-interactional universe of meaning, is constructed without the incorporation of reactive social agents. Such lives are constructed from lifelong interests, hobbies, mass-media images and cultural prototypes.

The sixth mode brings us back to the first issue of myth and stark humanity. This is what Myerhoff (1978) describes as 'oneness', Keith as 'we-feeling', Kaufman (1986) as 'cultural themes' and Hazan (1980) as 'limbo state'. Despite the inherent vagueness, not to say obscuricism, of all these terms, they presumably allude to Turner's (1969) concept of 'communitas'. This is a state prevalent in the liminal phase of rites of passage where the novices enter a stage of being 'human raw material', stripped of all social and cultural insignia and put into a twilight zone of obliteration of role differences, status and hierarchical order. Widely discussed and little understood, such transitional states are not confined to simple societies but are highly prevalent in a variety of social situations and contexts in contemporary Western living (see Turner, 1969). An overview of the extensive literature on age-homogenous communities would easily reveal that many properties of this human condition are typical of the life in those settings. Myerhoff's already discussed study is but one example of the striking similarities between the state of being old in our society and the experience of liminality. In terms of the pursuit of 'community' this must be regarded as the pole of the 'commune' in a continuum whose opposite pole is the formal hierarchical organization. The apparent analogy, however, is far from being isomorphic since in the case of the elderly in a secular society an impasse rather than transition frames that state. One could safely expand this observation to be applicable to many other social situations of mass togetherness with no sense of salvation or millenial promise.[6]

Time Restructured
The notion of myth, the state of communitas, the social impasse and the decontextualized world that the elderly can be said to inhabit, all converge to form a unique temporality. In Western society, the connection between the old person's universe of meaning and his or her ability to control it is disrupted. On the one hand, the aged are seen as being at a social standstill; on the other, the changes occurring in their lives are extraordinarily rapid and sharp. As a possible result of this conflict, the aged person may engage in constant and continual repetition of habitual behaviors over days and years, re-enacting the past, maintaining and refuelling a former identity and, at the same time, denying access to change or decline. During old age, many people develop a tendency to convert linear life trajectories into circular elements infused with a sense of existential continuity, resistant to change.

In my study of 'The Limbo People' (Hazan, 1980) I described the construction of such a temporal universe within a day-care centre for elderly Jewish residents of the East End of London. At the time of the study, their lives were marked by rapidly accelerating processes of deterioration. As first-generation descendants of East European immigrant Jews, these people were subject to poverty, illiteracy, and social alienation, both from their better-off Jewish peers, and from the non-Jewish working-class residents of the East End, who regarded them as an economic threat. Many of the younger generation had migrated to other, better parts of London, leaving the ageing population suffering from a lack of community life, lowered standards of living, and social isolation.

The centre members constructed various methods to 'arrest' the flow of time and to encapsulate it within a present-bound 'structure-in-itself'. Various excuses were made to dismiss the possibility of transferral into old-age homes or geriatric wards. When death occurred it was ignored. Members often renounced their own families and, instead, referred to one another as 'brothers' and 'sisters'. When talking about the distant past, members often implied that, unlike the current outside world, their early relationships had been predominated by mutual aid and community care. Inside the Centre, neither 'favors' nor 'rewards' had any place. The giving of care constituted the criterion for esteem and the right to give and receive help was unconditional.

The importance of this moral code to the perspective on time rests in the structure of its practices rather than in its content. In the Center, the unconditional acts of giving and taking were independent of each other – no act instituted any future indebtedness on the part of donor or recipient. Hence, the establishment of a present-bound society was made possible. This liminal framework, which could be termed 'limbo time', together with the suppression of creativity and denial of personal achievement, generated an environment immuned to change.

It is almost called for to compare that temporal structuring to the experience of marginal groups such as sects, communes, inmates in total institutions, and to situations of 'liminoid' character (Turner, 1969) such as mass demonstrations, festivals and carnivals. Another comparison was made by Laslett (1989) who, using my concept of 'limbo time', drew an analogy between the existential state of the aged and that of a growing sector of the population in the Western world – the unemployed.

Self and Society
Anthropologists of old age in Western society, following Erikson (1982), cultivated the view that elderly people strive for integration of the self in order to reach a meaningful conclusion to their lives.

The concepts of 'life's career' (Myerhoff and Simic, 1978) and 'The Ageless Self' (Kaufman, 1986) were developed to signify the idea and the conviction of the personal and cultural continuity sought and constructed by the elderly.

This assumption could be challenged on a few fronts including the validity of its psychological premises, its preconceptual view of identity formations and its socio-cultural theoretical undepinnings. If, as postmodernist sociologists assert, the self inhabits multiple realities and the mind is 'homeless' and compartmentalized, then precluding old age from that general typification of modern life would be yet another form of discrimination and ageism.

Let us give an empirical body to this perspective on the ageing self by connecting it to the use of language by the elderly. Scant attention has been paid in anthropological literature to the voice of the elderly. Too often was it masked by the advocating voice of the anthropologist, who lamented the 'invisibility' of the elderly but in fact generated their 'inaudibility'. The following case study reports on a group of English elderly who commented upon their world through a set of three unrelated 'languages', or rather three modes of articulation stemming from different frames of reference to reality.

This group was gathered in the University for The Third Age in Cambridge, where a selected number of participants, noted for their intellectual abilities and rhetorical skills, formed a discussion group whose task was to experiment various pathways to ageing. Verbal communication among members of this group included three modes of relating to themselves and to the world. The first mode was a frame of reference common to both old and non-old, articulated through a metaphorical language. This was, for example, the language with which that group wrote its research report on *The Image of the Elderly on TV*, (Lambert, Laslett and Claym 1984) which presented the results of a television monitoring survey carried out by members of the University of the Third Age. In this survey, members freely used academical jargon with reference to the stereotypes, images and roles conferred upon the elderly as depicted in TV programs.

The second frame of reference was pragmatically oriented, designed to obtain optimal gains and resources from the environment in order to enhance daily comforts and encounter hardship. It was contextual in nature, referring through local codes to situations well known to the aged members and the professionals from whom they demanded support. The third mode was altogether different. Rather than serving relationships with the non-aged, it abandoned any conception of time, place and circumstances and strove to uncover what the elderly of the U3A called 'first principles'. Those essential components of human existence were deemed to lie beyond culture and to surpass any social divisions. They were presented as immutable, omnipotent as well as ubiquitous. The members who discussed this third frame of reference identified three main components in it. The first was the genetic code determining physionomy, and remain, except for mutations, unaffected by the environment. The second is the corpus of myths which despite different cultural variations and versions stays unaltered in its innermost thematic structure. The third is a bond of mutual commitment that unites human beings regardless of origin, class or creed.

These three modes of articulating respective realities – metaphorical, contextual and essential – were not interlinked by or subsumed under a metalanguage capable of interweaving them into one form of articulation.

This strict separation, which rendered experience divisible, reflects three divergent realities each of which sustains a different construction of the self. The first distinguishes between object and subject, and is concerned with the social identity, the 'me'. It seeks to map out the possibilities of such a 'me' by differentiating and contrasting the 'subjective' self from its 'objectified' social stereotypes and cultural reifications. The second frame of reference is radically pragmatic, merging subject and object by contextualizing both. The third attempts to transcend both objective reality of space and time *and* the subject as historically constituted within these contextual coordinates. Its quest is a (Kantian) 'transcendental ego', an *a priori* 'I' seen as an end in itself.

It is interesting to note that the structural properties of contemporary living provide for the development of a corresponding set of mechanisms of personal adjustment and 'self processing'. Theoretically we are at a junction where phenomonological thinking meets structuralist hints and is informed by cues of practical reasoning (Harris, 1980). This conceptual mesh makes the case of the aged into a testing ground for experimenting new constructs and models of understanding how the 'self' is produced and reproduced both by the individual and society at large.

Surrogate Concepts of Analysis
The purpose of the following is to introduce sketchily three novel conceptual models arising from the study of old age. The three are

amenable to replace conventional constructs whose analytic capablities were proven, again by the study of old age, to be defunct. The three are particularly suitable for studying old age and other postmodernist phenomena whose temporal, spatial and causal dimensions collapse. They share an a-contextual quality which makes them applicable to situations of inconsistency, lability and a-temporality.

These three surrogate concepts consist of 'symbolic types', 'limbo time' and 'social worlds' – respectively selected to replace the negative concepts of (1) 'deculturation' and 'rolelessness', (2) 'discontinuity' and 'disengagement' and (3) 'disintegration' and 'anomie'. Let me briefly articulate the analytic properties of each of these surrogate concepts.

Symbolic types (Grathoff, 1977; Handelman, 1990, 1992) are personified reifications of a cultural paradigm. Types such as the Madman, the Clown and the Rogue are autonomous of context, independent of social negotiation, yet carry with them a reality of their own. Hence they arise when social order collapses and interactions become inconsistent. Symbolic typing was studied, in the context of ageing, both as being employed by the aged as a substitute to former abandoned roles and a solution to present devalued statuses (see Raz, 1993) as well as used by the media to label 'old people' as symbolic types.

These symbolic types are one class among the inhabitants of the 'social world', which is a social network in which interactions are made through abstract communicational channels and personal, face-to-face acquaintances are no longer a requisitory for participation. Geographical-territorial parameters, formerly a must in community studies, are here given secondary importance, while the focus on personal face-to-face interactions is replaced by structural rules autonomous of their human performers (see Strauss, 1978, 1982; Hazan, 1990a).

One of the most pertinent structural codes in the social worlds of older people can be, as we saw, the reconstruction of time as cyclical and synchronic. This unique temporal perspective is termed 'limbo time' (Hazan, 1980), and arguably offers opportunities for cultivating new referential scopes and meanings. These three dimensions converge to constitute the following case which presents a cultural interpretation of old age as projected in an ethnography of a relevant media event (Hazan, 1990b). It will be shown how by suspending social time and through the maintenance of a social world centred around charity, society constitutes the old as a symbolic type straddling life and death and belonging to neither.

In 1986, Israeli television and radio dedicated an entire day of nationwide broadcasts to the plight of the elderly in Israel. The highlight of the day was a seven hour television show entitled 'Teletrom for the Old' which, using documentary film, interviews, and appeals by leading public figures and top entertainers, appealed to viewers for monetary contributions to be distributed among various organizations caring for the old.

The construction of the symbolic type of the old generated in the course of the broadcast followed a four-stage developmental sequence during which the image of the old was transformed from that of victim into a social sacrifice. The four stages constituted an interlocked pattern whereby one stage emerged from the previous one and heralded its successor. This connection was engendered by a series of interlinking dilemmas, each of which mediated between stages by suggesting a problem implicit in the former stage to be answered in the subsequent one.

A parallelism between the old as a category and the elderly as the incumbents of such a category was drawn by describing all the aged as '10% of the population who are lonely, vulnerable and destitute'. This collective terminology not only ignored the facts of Israeli society, but also failed to recognize any heterogeneity among those depicted. The general term 'the old' was used to articulate the condition of all old people, as evident in the statement: 'Imagine the old, lonely person living in a cramped flat without furniture and with no conveniences.' The inevitable dependency on society ensuing from such a plight was conveyed and amplified throughout the broadcast. Another aspect of this dependency was the vulnerability to physical assault, with the old person depicted as a defenceless potential victim. The discrediting of the old was underpinned by their portrayal as incapable of self-help and by the assumption that their state as a problem-riddled category is fundamentally insoluble. The dilemma, therefore, posed by such a presentation was why the old constitute a permanently problematic phenomenon.

The 'solution' to this dilemma, presented in the second stage of the broadcast, was the excommunication of the old as implied by the distinction made between the natural and the human. This dichotomy between the old as a product of a natural (i.e. physio-biological) process and the non-old as social entities was expressed by imputing various essential attributes to the elderly. The medicalization of ageing played an important role in projecting an image of the old as conditioned by deterministic objective factors. Thus, reports from geriatric wards and nursing homes were accompanied by interviews with elderly persons being asked questions such as 'When did age first hit you?', the interviewer also implying that nature must despise the old to treat them the way it does.

Deprived of their human guise, the old were presented as the result of inevitable pathological changes, unrelated to any social context and, therefore, not subject to a given moral order or system of accountability. This image of the old – their humanity rendered dubious – served to justify their alienated position in society.

The ambivalence embedded in the ill-defined borderline between the human and the non-human lent itself to be handled in jocular terms whereby the inconsistent and the self-contradictory were transformed into an object of ridicule. The old person was depicted as a hypochondriac, clownish character, the highlight of which was the showing of a group of members of an old-age pensioners' club performing *The Hypochondriac* by Molière. The performance was presented by both actors and presenter as a show of self-derision based on the insignificance of real or feigned disease in the face of incurable old age.

'Othering' and The Other

Any idea of understanding the other must by definition be based on an assumption of separation. The language of separating the old from 'society' receives a variety of manifestations, the best-known of which is the branding of old people as belonging to a category of 'normal' old age or being consigned to its opposite – the pathological. Gubrium (1986) shows how the descriptive practices executed through minutes of meetings and professionally produced documentation generate classifications which divide old people into just 'old timers' or 'Alzheimers'. The grey areas between the two are wide enough to accommodate 'real' cases, thus making the business of accounting and reporting in itself into most effective social instruments of allocating cultural territories and assigning identities. Such descriptive activities constitute a great deal of everyday, bureaucratically controlled experience. In a more subtle fashion but with no less vigour and impact, there are other descriptive procedures that designate people as others by means of indirect, at times latent, textual presentations. Advertisements, newspapers, electronic media and other forms of publicly available impersonal information are the channels through which such assignations are encoded. As anthropologists we are obviously concerned with the ethnographic encoding of 'the other'. Notwithstanding the special characteristics of that genre, it should be viewed within a broader framework of both textual exposure on public display and a form of literacy intended for a few but available to many. Ethnographic accounts of old age are part of a broader corpus of growing academic literature on the subject. It would be enlightening to track down the manner by which the image of the old as 'the other' is projected in such texts.

Such a screening of the jacket design of various academic books related to the subject of old age revealed, perhaps not surprisingly, a distinct narrative sequence of separation and dissolution. Jackets could be characterized as hinting at decay and inevitable deterioration; for example, the elderly couple depicted on the jacket of *Adulthood and Ageing*: not looking at each other, they stand on a flimsy ground of sand and sea engulfing their unseen feet and their visible legs, while at the midst of the drawing, in the area of the couple's genitalia, appears a strong shadow of a seemingly youngish couple holding hands and looking lovingly at each other.

The amorphization of old age is further accentuated in *Old Age in a Changing Society*, where the cover shows a blurred face of an elderly man surrounded by a clock penetrated by a unidirectional arrow leading to nowhere (but death?). Life and death, ageing and society, social and biological death, are prominent aspects in the semiotics of separation.

The ambiguity of encoding the other ought to be regarded within the context of contemporary reality where symbolic boundaries are blurred, human universality is tempered with cultural relativism and the 'global village' is riddled with strifes and bastians of distinct identities. In a sense the dual message of the old as 'one of us' or as the UFO-ic stranger is presumably not peculiar to the cultural treatment of old age nor does it uniquely apply to academic reflections on the subject. It pervades an infinite range of cultural references to the question of 'us' and 'them' and thus touches upon one of the most pressing issues preoccupying anthropological epistemology – the problem of representing the subject.

CONCLUSION: A QUESTION OF REPRESENTATION

Confronted with issues of timelessness, a-contextuality and multiple selves, the student of old age might find it difficult to reflect the authenticity of the researchees while doing justice to anthropological conventions. This problem, however, can serve as an Archimedean point from which some of anthropology's major concerns can be highlighted.

Anthropologists seek to place their subjects within bounds of time, space and meaning, and from that vantage point they attempt to translate the cultural language of the 'field' into the cultural language of the researcher, namely the socio-anthropological community. This dialectical process of double translation vacillating between the two languages (Asad, 1986) is premised on an assumption of one-to-one contact between at least two human agents placed in a defined contextual setting, emitting joint communication which is the basis upon which ethnographic practices are carried out (Crapanzano, 1980). The study of old age, however, suggests that the accomplishment of such rapport is not contingent upon seeing the researchee as a whole person but rather on seeing his parts. That is, the aged person should be represented as a narrator of dispersive and fragmented texts of identity. Furthermore, elderly researchees often do not trust the capacity of their audience to understand their 'stories'. They invest a special effort in finding a common channel of communication audible to the researcher. This means that the act of recording the 'other' becomes, in effect, a procedure of translating a translation, looking at a looking-glass self. One tries, in Geertz's phrase, to locate the spider amidst its webs, only to find himself trying to mend these webs with his fingers.

It is hence the study of texts that inevitably substitutes the study of contexts (Strathern, 1987), and the multiple codes of transla-tion that replace the agonies of holistic participant observation. In this sense the study of old age is well interlocked into the major postmodernist issue concerning all human sciences, namely the question of representation.

Realistic narratives, such as those employed by conventional anthro-pology, are based on the assumption that reality, existing autonomously 'out there', can be loyally depicted by a neutral observer. This classical (and, indeed, 'scientific') notion of 'representation' has been replaced, in the postmodernist perspective, with 'interpretation'. Know-ledge claims were substituted by language games, grand narratives by parody and pastiche, and fragmented reality had to be matched with a new form of fragmented textuality – one of a 'dialogicity' of voices and a multiplicity of perspectives (cf. Atkinson, 1992; Tyler, 1987; Hobart, 1990). Contemporary anthropologists are thus left with the knowledge that the ontological tenacity of their descrip-tive practices of 'culture', 'society', 'persons' and 'self' is being gravely challenged by the apparent (or perhaps simulated?) nature of postmodern reality.

The departure from context, person, relationship, networks and structure poses a very real threat to the endurance of the anthropological project. Studying 'texts of identity' rather than identity, accounts rather than accountability or work rather than 'lives' could mark the end of traditional anthropology by consigning it to the realm of 'modernism' and denying its place in the postmodern agenda. This predicament must be so daunting to some anthropologists that they can be seen to conduct a brave but hopeless battle, defending a cherished tradition, turning a petrified fossil thrown at the shore of the postmodern sea.

The world of the aged as presented in this chapter is capable of restoring some of that lost self-confidence to anthropologists by demonstrating how the study of human beings living in our midst can be understood without the conventional holistic assumptions regarding society and self. Although this paper spoke of anthropology in a rather disdaining and disenchanted manner, anthropology and postmodernism must not be a contradiction in terms. The opposite is true. Anthropology has a responsibility in this postmodern world where all too often 'difference' is pathologized, medicalized, demonized or criminalized – as is the case with the elderly and various other social categories (see a similar critique by Shweder (1993) with regard to 'America's Childhood').

In its attempt to rehumanize the elderly, bring them back to the territories of the living, the anthropology of ageing joins forces with that fragile thing called postmodern humanism. Furthermore, it can provide us with the necessary postmodernist perspective on ageing. Bauman (1992) distinguishes between two symbolic types of 'identity seekers': the postmodernist nomads and the Protestant (modernist) 'pilgrims through life'. The former wander between unconnected places, have no pre-set itinerary, and hence only momentary identities, identities 'for today', until-further-notice identities. The latter have their destination preselected, guide their life according to a 'life project', crystallizing a single core identity throughout this 'path of life'.[7] The former can be said to move further in the 'life span', the latter 'progress' in the 'life course'. Western society, postmodern and all, still considers its elderly according to the second narrative. Ageing is when 'the life cycle is completed' (Erikson, 1959), where the 'ageless self' is revealed (Kaufman, 1986). In contrast, the anthropology of ageing as presented here, and as I would like to see it, regards the elderly as being first and foremost nomads. In this it shares a crucial standpoint with postmodernism.

In a universe of changing paradigms and dismantled contexts, the work on the aged might provide such a laboratory where materials as well as devices are already beyond the petrifying spell of disciplinary convention. Thus it is neither regained tribal wisdom nor pastiche perspectives that the study of the old offers the confused anthropologist grappling with his own wisdom. Rather it is an encounter with a kind of authenticity stemming from being on the verge of culture and context which in many respects is so akin to the kind of lost authenticity so bemoaned and yearned for by contemporary anthropologists.

NOTES

* I am greatly indebted to my colleague A. Raz for his useful contribution to this chapter.

1 The analytic properties of these concepts – generalized, simplistic and coin-ciding with everyday language – were also questioned before postmodernism. See the critical discussion of the notion of tribe by Fried (1975), Hobsbawn (1983), on the 'invention of tradition', and Thornton, (1988) on the elusive concept of 'society'.

2 The notion of 'community' has been subjected to analytical deconstruction in recent years. Stacey (1969) argued against the myth of community studies; Stein (1972) observed the eclipse of community in the US; Anderson (1983) called it 'imagined community' and Cohen (1985) reduced 'community' to its symbolic boundaries; and I myself (Hazan, 1990) deal with it elsewhere as a form of rhetorical production.

3 The concept of the 'social world perspective', developed by Strauss (1978), addresses the condition of non-reactive foci as generators of social action and human communication.

4 The idea of the emancipated elderly could be found in several ethnographic manifestations, most striking of which is the transformation among elderly women from male-dominated religious activities to a female-dominated form of symbolic code (see e.g. Sered, 1992).

5 The scholarly juxtaposition between Hochschild's work on elderly women and her later research on the management of women's emotions (Hochschild, 1983) could testify to that argument.

6 For a discussion of the gerontological narratives of salvation see Manheimer (1990).

7 I would like to advance here a compatible metaphor, taken from the world of computers, for these two types of identity. The first identity discussed, the 'nomadic', is perhaps best imagined as consisting of different, unconnected floppy diskettes which one enters according to one's need; 'when people go to the post office, they act post office', as Jerome Bruner (1986) says in his *Actual Minds*. The second identity, that of the 'pilgrims', can then be regarded as a hard disk, where all data is centralized, interconnected

and kept together. The two identities, then, are but two kinds of software stored on different hardwares. Contemporary imagery being dominated as it is by computers, not holy grails, updating the identity metaphor seemed in order.

REFERENCES

Anderson, B. (1972) 'The process of deculturation – its dynamics among United States aged', *Anthropological Quarterly*, 45:209–16.

——— (1983) *Imagined Communities*, London: Verso.

Asad, T. (1986) 'The concept of cultural translation in British social anthropology' in J. Clifford and G. Marcus (eds) *Writing Culture*, Berkeley: University of California Press.

Atkinson, P. (1992) *Understanding Ethnographic Texts*, London: Sage.

Barthes, R. (1976) *Writing Degree Zero and Elements of Semiology*, trans. Annette Lavers and Colin Smith, Boston: Beacon.

Baudrillard, J. (1983) *Simulations*, New York: Semiotext(e).

Bauman, Z. (1992) *Mortality, Immortality and Other Life Strategies*, Cambridge: Polity.

Berger, P., Berger, B. and Kellner, H. (1973) *The Homeless Mind*, London: Random House/Vintage.

Brown, D.F. (1991) *Human Universals*, New York: McGraw-Hill.

Butler, R.N. (1969) 'Age-ism: another form of bigotry', *The Gerontologist*, 9: 243–6.

——— (1970) 'Looking forward to what? The life review, lackacy and excessive identity vs. change', *American Behavioral Scientist*, 14: 121–8.

Carpenter, E. (1972) *Oh, What a Blow that Phantom Gave Me!* London: Paladin.

Carrithers, M. (1992) *Why Humans Have Cultures: Explaining Anthropology and Social Diversity*, Oxford: Oxford University Press.

Cohen, A.P (1985) *Symbolic Construction of Community*, London: Tavistock.

Clifford, J. (1988) *The Predicament of Culture: Twentieth Century Ethnography, Literature and Art*, Cambridge, MA: Harvard University Press.

Crapanzano, V. (1980) *Tuhami: Portrait of a Moroccan*, Chicago: University of Chicago Press.

De Beauvoir, S. (1975) *The Coming of Age*, New York: Warner.

Dowd, J.J. (1986) 'The old person as a stranger' in V.W. Marshall (ed.) *Later Life: The Social Psychology of Aging*, Beverley Hills: Sage.

Dumont, L. (1972) *Homo Hierarchicus*, Chicago: University of Chicago Press.

Elias, N. (1985) *The Loneliness of the Dying*, Oxford: Basil Blackwell.

Erikson, E. (1959) *Identity and the Life Cycle*, New York: W.W. Norton.

——— (1982) *The Life Cycle Completed*, New York: W.W. Norton.

Ewing, K.P. (1990) 'The illusion of wholeness: culture, self and the experience of inconsistency', *Ethos*, 18: 251–78.

Fabian, J. (1983) *Time and the Other: How Anthropology Makes its Object*, New York: Columbia UP.

Featherstone, M. and Hepworth, M. (1991) 'The mask of ageing and the post-modern life course', in M. Featherstone, M. Hepworth and B. Turner (eds), *The Body: Social Process and Cultural Theory*, London: Sage.

Fontana, A. (1976) *The Last Frontier*, Beverley Hills, CA: Sage.

Francis, D. (1984) *Will You Still Need Me, Will You Still Feed Me, When I'm 84?*, Bloomington: Indiana University Press.

Fried, M. (1975) *The Notion of Tribe*, Menlo Park, CA: Cummings Publishing Company.

Geertz, C. (1983) *Local Knowledge: Further Essays in Interpretative Anthropology*, New York: Basic.

Giddens, A. (1991) *Modernity and Self-Identity: Self and Society in the Late Modern Age*, Cambridge: Polity.

Glaser, B. and Strauss, A. (1967) *The Discovery of Grounded Theory*, Chicago: Aldine.

Grathoff, R. (1977) *The Structure of Social Inconsistencies*, The Hague: Nijhoff.

Gubrium, J.F. (1986) *Oldtimers and Alzheimer's: The Descriptive Organization of Senility*, Greenwich, CT: JAI.

Handelman, D. (1990) *Models and Mirrors*, Cambridge: Cambridge University Press.

—— (1992) 'Symbolic types, the body, and circus', *Semiotica*, 85–3/4: 205–27.

Harris, M. (1980) *Cultural Materialism: The Struggle for a Science of Culture*, New York: Vintage.

Hassan, I. (1985) 'The Culture of Postmodernism', *Theory, Culture and Society*, 2: 119–31.

Hazan, H. (1980) *The Limbo People: A Study of the Constitution of The Time Universe Among The Aged*, London: Routledge & Kegan Paul.

—— (1990a) 'Victim into sacrifice: the construction of the old as a symbolic type', *Journal of Cross-Cultural Gerontology*, 5: 77–84.

—— (1990b) *A Paradoxical Community*, Greenwich, CT: JAI.

—— (1992) *Managing Change in Old Age*, New York: State University of New York Press.

—— (forthcoming) *Old Age: Constructions and Deconstructions*, Cambridge: Cambridge University Press.

Hobart, M. (1990) 'Who do you think you are? The authorized Balinese' in R. Fardon (ed.), *Localising Strategies: Regional Traditions of Ethnographic Writing*, Edinburgh: Scottish Academic Press, and Washington, DC: Smithsonian Institution.

Hobsbawm, E. (1983) 'Introduction: inventing traditions', in E. Hobsbawm and T. Ranger (eds) *The Invention of Tradition*, Cambridge: Cambridge University Press.

Hochschild, A.R. (1973) *The Unexpected Community*, Englewood Cliffs, NJ: Prentice-Hall.

—— (1983) *The Managed Heart*, Berkeley: University of California Press.

Hockey, J. and James, A. (1993) *Growing Up and Growing Old: Ageing and Dependency in the Life Course*, London: Sage.

Kapferer, B. (1972) *Strategy and Interaction in An African Factory*, Manchester: Manchester University Press.

Kaufman, S.R. (1986) *The Ageless Self: Sources of Meaning in Late Life*, Madison: University of Wisconsin Press.

Keith, J. (1980) 'Old age and community creation' in C.L. Fry, (ed.) *Aging in Culture and Society*, New York: J.F. Bergin.

——— (1982a) *Old People – New Lives*, Chicago: University of Chicago Press.

——— (1982b) *Old People as People: Social and Cultural Influences on Aging and Old Age*, Boston and Toronto: Little, Brown.

Kertzer, D. and Keith, J. (Eds) (1984) *Age and Anthropological Theory*, Ithaca: Cornell University Press.

Kimmell, D.C. (1974) *Adulthood and Aging*, New York: John Wiley.

Lambert, J., P. Laslett and H. Clay, (1984) *The Image of the Elderly on TV : Report of the Research Committee Project*, Cambridge: University of the Third Age.

Laslett, P. (1989) *A Fresh Map of Life – The Emergence of the Third Age*, London: Weidenfeld & Nicolson.

Leach, E. (1976) 'Kronos and chronos' in his *Rethinking Anthropology*, London: Athlone.

Lévi-Struass, C. (1967) *The Savage Mind*, Chicago: University of Chicago Press.

Lifton, R. (1986) *The Nazi Doctors*, New York: Basic.

Manheimer, R. (1990) 'The narrative quest in qualitative gerontology', *Journal of Aging Studies*, 3: 253–62.

Moore, S.F. (1978) 'Old age in a life-term social arena: some Chagga of Kilimanjaro in 1974' in B. Myerhoff and A. Simic (eds) *Life's Career - Aging*, Beverley Hills, CA: Sage.

Moore, S., and Myerhoff, B. (eds) (1977) *Secular Ritual*, Assen: Van-Gorcum.

Myerhoff, B. (1978) *Number Our Days*, New York: Dutton.

Myerhoff, B., and Simic, A. (eds) (1978) *Life's Career – Aging: Cultural Variations on Growing Old*, Beverley Hills, CA: Sage.

Neugarten, B.L. (1972) 'Personality and the aging process', reprinted in S.H. Zarit (ed.) *Readings in Aging and Death: Contemporary Perspectives*, New York: Harper and Row.

Pels, P. and Nancel, L. (1991) 'Introduction: critique and the deconstruction of the anthropological authority' in their (eds) *Constructing Knowledge*, Beverley Hills, CA: Sage.

Raz, A. (1993) 'The reinherited self: a case study in the dynamics of a social world' in N.K. Denzin (ed.) *Studies in Symbolic Interaction*, Greenwich, CT: JAI Press.

Schutz, A. and Luckman, T. (1973) *The Structure of the Life World*, Evanston, IL: Northwestern University Press.

Sered, S. (1992) *Women and Religion*, Oxford: Oxford University Press.

Shotter, J. and Gergen, K. (eds) (1986) *Texts of Identity*, London: Sage.

Shweder, R.A. (1993) 'Why do men barbecue? and other postmodern ironies of growing up in the decade of ethnicity', *Daedalus*, 122, 1: 279–307.

Silverman, P. (ed.) (1987) *The Elderly as Modern Pioneers*, Bloomington: Indiana University Press.

Smith-Blau, Z. (1973) *Old Age in a Changing Society*, New York: New Viewpoints.

Sokolovsky, J. (ed.) (1990) *The Cultural Context of Aging: Worldwide Perspectives*, Westport, CT: Bergin & Garvey.

Sperber, D. (1975) *Rethinking Symbolism*, Cambridge: Cambridge University Press.

Stacey, M. (1969) 'The myth of community studies', *British Journal of Sociology*, 20: 134–47.

Stein, M.R. (1972) *The Eclipse of Community* (expanded edition) Princeton: Princeton University Press

Stephens, J. (1976) *Loners, Losers and Lovers: Elderly Tenants in a Slum Hotel*, Seattle: University of Washington Press.

Strathern, M. (1987) 'Out of context: the persuasive fictions of anthropology', *Current Anthropology*, 28, 3, June.

―――― (1992) 'Parts and wholes: refiguring relationships in a post-plural world' in A. Kuper (ed.) *Conceptualizing Society*, London: Routledge.

Strauss, A. (1978) 'A social world perspective' in N.K. Denzin (ed.) *Studies in Symbolic Interaction*, vol. 1, Greenwich CT: JAI.

―――― (1982) 'Social worlds and legitimation processes' in N.K. Denzin (ed.) *Studies in Symbolic Interaction*, vol. 4, Greenwich, CT: JAI.

Teski, M. (1979) *Living Together*, Washington DC: University Press of America.

Thornton, R. (1988) 'The rhetoric of ethnographic holism', *Cultural Anthropology*, 3: 285–303.

Townsend, P. (1957) *The Family Life of Old People: An Inquiry in East London*, London: Routledge & Kegan Paul.

Turnball, J. (1966) *Old and Alone*, London: Routledge & Kegan Paul

Turnball, C. (1983) *The Human Cycle*, London: Jonathan Cape.

Turner, V. (1969) *The Ritual Process – Structure and Anti-Structure*, Chicago: Aldine.

―――― (1977) 'Introduction' in S. Moore and B. Myerhoff (eds) *Secular Ritual*, Assen: Van-Gorcum.

Tyler, S.A. (1987) *The Unspeakable: Discourse, Dialogue, and Rhetoric in the Postmodern World*, Madison: University of Wisconsin Press.

Unruh, D. (1983) *Invisible Life: The Social Worlds of the Aged*, Beverly Hills, CA: Sage.

Zerubavel, E. (1982) *Hidden Rhythms*, Chicago: University of Chicago Press.

―――― (1985) *The Seven Day Circle*, New York: Free Press.

CHAPTER 10

Cultural Imperialism and
the Mediation of Otherness
David Morley and Kevin Robins

The helicopter landed with the body in a metal casket, which revolutionary guards carried on their shoulders a short distance to the grave. But then the crowd surged again, weeping men in bloody headbands, and they scaled the barriers and overran the gravesite.

The voice said, Wailing chanting mourners. It said, Throwing themselves into the hole.

Karen could not imagine who else was watching this. It could not be real if others watched. If other people watched, if millions watched, if these millions matched the number on the Iranian plain, doesn't it mean we share something with the mourners, know an anguish, feel something pass between us, hear the sigh of some historic grief? . . . . If others saw these pictures, why is nothing changed, where are the local crowds, why do we still have names and addresses and car keys?

Don DeLillo

Already by action we maintain a living relationship with a real object; we grasp it, we conceive it. The image neutralises this real relationship, this primary conceiving through action.

Emmanuel Levinas

That two non-anthropologists (one working in the field of media studies, the other in cultural geography) should be invited to contribute to a volume on the future of anthropology is, in itself, a situation worthy of some comment. Clearly we hold no brief for the future of anthropology as a discipline. At the same time, our own work has, in recent years, been influenced by debates within anthropology (particularly, debates concerning questions of ethnography, representation and the relation of the global to the local). Of course, these are issues of concern for scholars working in a range of other disciplines, to whom anthropologists have things to say of considerable import. At the same time, we would suggest that no one discipline (anthropology included) can pretend to the position of exclusive or privileged knowledge. To that extent we would also argue that anthropologists can profitably learn from the current work of scholars in communications and media studies, cultural studies and cultural geography. It is in that interdisciplinary spirit that our enterprise is couched.

Our basic argument is in three parts. Historically, it was the question of media imperialism which principally exercised scholars in this field, focusing on the effects of (mainly) American TV programming on other nations. That issue, we argue, must now be addressed in the broader context of three considerations. Firstly, there is the evidence that imposed 'foreign' programmes do not necessarily have direct effects on the audiences who consume them (but see Morley, [1992: Introduction]) for a critique of recent tendencies in media/cultural studies towards overemphasizing, if not romanticizing, the 'interpretive freedom' of the 'active audience'). Secondly, rather than simply focusing on the issue of the effects of imported content there is the need to address the question of the role of contemporary media in transferring the relationship between physically distinct places. Thirdly, we suggest there is the need to address the effects of the present system of international communications on audiences in the West (rather than the effects of exported Western product on the Rest) in terms of the modes in which 'otherness' is represented in the West.

MEDIA IMPERIALISM

Anthropology has always been concerned with studying the variety of forms of social and cultural organization within human societies, across geographical space. In this context, a major focus of interest within the discipline has been on the impact of the imperial cultures of Europe, ever since the 'Age of Discovery', on the indigenous populations of the 'discovered' territories and on their cultures. Whether this has been discussed in terms of imperialism or of modernization, the underlying issue has been the gradual homogenization of world cultures under the impact of those powerful, foreign invasions.

A number of commentators have agreed that one of the distinguishing characteristics of the present period is the role played both by improved systems of physical transportation and by various forms of symbolic communication in linking the different parts of the world together. It has been observed that the role of geographical distance in human affairs is much diminished (Meyrowitz, 1985), and that 'time-space compression' is constitutive of our supposedly postmodern condition (Jameson, 1985; Harvey, 1989). These might be seen as no more than extrapolations of Marshall McLuhan's well-worn adage about the contribution of communications media to the construction of a 'global village'; however, as many of McLuhan's critics have emphasized, this is no mere technological phenomenon, not least in so far as the media technologies in question have a very particular (Western or Euro-American) point of origin and are controlled by identifiable interests (Walt Disney, News Corporation, Berlusconi, Time Warner, Bertelsmann, etc.), engendering a largely one-way 'conversation', in which the predominant pattern is for the West to speak and the Rest to listen.

All of this clearly points to the need for anthropologists, as much as anyone else, to pay close attention to the role of the media in this process of cultural encounter. How are we to understand the influence of the media? Within media studies, there is a long-standing tradition which has addressed the issue in terms of 'media imperialism'. In the work of, for example, Armand Mattelart *et al.* (1984), Herbert Schiller (1969) and Jeremy Tunstall (1977), there has been considerable analysis of the cultural consequences of the West's long-exercised control over the world's media systems. The flaw in this body of work, however, has been in its reliance on a simplistic 'hypodermic' model of media effects – a model long discredited within the mainstream of media studies, in which it is assumed that media products have direct and necessary cultural 'effects' on those who consume them. (It is perhaps worth noting that, on this particular question, we would take issue with one of the editors of the present volume, in so far as his own discussion of the effects of the 'evil demon' of the Western media seems often to rely on precisely this kind of direct causal model of automatic media effects (Ahmed, 1992a).) This is not to fall prey to any kind of foolish presumption that the media do not exercise profound forms of cultural influence, but it is to insist that the ways in which they have influence over their audiences are rather more complex than any hypodermic model can allow (Morley, 1992), and it is to insist that, in analysing the implication of the media in transcultural encounters, we must adequately deal with that complexity.

We can perhaps best develop the point by reference to the debates which went on throughout the 1980s over the almost global popularity of the American television series *Dallas*. It is perhaps worth recalling that, in Britain, the then Director-General of the BBC, Alistair Milne, chose this programme as the symbol of the dangers facing British television in its future, fully deregulated form. Milne argued that the liberalization of public service broadcasting would produce 'wall-to-wall *Dallas*'. Indeed, by the mid-1980s *Dallas* had become the privileged hate symbol for all those who saw the worldwide popularity of the programme as an indication of the growing threat to the variety of world cultures that was posed by American dominance over the world's media industries.

The problem with this argument, or assertion, is that all the subsequent audience research on the consumption of *Dallas*, in different cultural contexts, far from demonstrating any automatic 'media effects', has tended, rather, to demonstrate that viewers from different cultural backgrounds literally 'read' the programme in quite different ways, depending on their own cultural contexts. Thus, Ien Ang (1985) demonstrates how many Dutch women interpreted the programme ironically, through the grid of their own feminist agendas. Eric Michaels (1988) showed how Australian aboriginals reinterpreted *Dallas* through their particular conceptions of kinship so as to produce quite different readings from those intended by the programme's makers. And, most exhaustively, Tamara Liebes and Elihu Katz (1990) have demonstrated the ways in which viewers from American, Russian, North African and Japanese backgrounds came to see quite different things in the programme and took quite different 'messages' from their encounter with *Dallas*. Against this, Gripsrud (forthcoming) makes the important point that, while these ethnographic findings concerning varieties of reception in different contexts are of considerable interest as counterevidence to any simple-minded theory of 'hypodermic' media effects, we would be foolish to conclude that the continuing world dominance of the Hollywood film and television production base is therefore of no consequence.

Certainly, one should not overestimate the freedom of the media consumer to make whatever he or she likes of the material transmitted. Even if they could, their choice of materials to reinterpret would still be limited to the 'menu' constructed by powerful media organizations. Moreover, such programmes are usually made in such a way as to 'prefer' one reading over another (Hall, 1981) and to invite the viewer to 'take' the message in some particular way, even if such a 'reading' can never be guaranteed. Clearly, we should not respond to the deficiencies in the hypodermic model of media effects by romanticizing the consumption process and cheerfully celebrating the 'active' viewer as a kind of semiotic guerilla, continuously waging war on the structures of textual power (Curran, 1990). We must balance an acceptance that audiences are in certain respects active in their choice, consumption and interpretation of media texts, with a recognition of how that activity is framed and limited, in its different modalities and varieties, by the dynamics of cultural power.

Equally, we should not fall into any technologically determinist argument. Even if media technologies have, historically, been developed and controlled by the powerful countries of the West, they are, nonetheless, always capable of being appropriated and used in other ways than those for which they were intended. Eliut Flores (1988), for example, describes how expatriate Puerto Rican families in New York use video conferencing facilities (designed for business applications) during evenings and weekends, when rates are low, to substitute for an air trip 'home'. Similarly, Stephen Greenblatt (1992) describes certain uses of modern video technology in Bali, in which the technology is in effect incorporated into traditional rituals, to the extent that it is unclear who is assimilating whom, in the process through which the villagers incorporate a sophisticated version of international capitalism's representational machinery into their own patterns of activity. We should resist *a priori* ideological determinism, he argues, and recognize that cultures have 'fantastically powerful assimilative mechanisms . . . that work like enzymes to change the ideological composition of foreign bodies'. In this example, video technology is by no means 'unequivocally and irreversibly the bearer of the capitalist ideology that was the determining condition of [its] . . . creation' (Greenblatt, 1992: 4). In a similar vein, Daniel Miller (1992), one of the few anthropologists who has offered any direct analysis of processes of media consumption, in an analysis of the viewing of the American series *The Young and the Restless* in Trinidad, helpfully offers the concept of 'indigenization' (on the model of digestion, incorporation and assimilation) as a way of understanding how 'local' cultures are continually refashioned out of elements initially produced elsewhere. Criticizing the traditional model in which authentic local cultures are seen as being invaded by 'foreign' and 'corrupting' influences, Miller suggests we should develop an alternative approach in which 'authenticity' is defined *a posteriori*, as a matter of local consequences rather than of local or 'foreign' origins.

So far, we have been concerned principally with debates about the consequences of Western media for other cultures. In addressing this issue, we have kept to the terms of a fairly conventional model of communications, which many authors (for example, Baudrillard, 1988; Harvey, 1989) would argue is, in fact, inadequate to our present situation. In their view, the condition of so-called 'postmodernity' is in fact characterized by a new ordering of experience and the creation of new sense of place, a complex process in which the media play a particularly vital role.

CULTURE, GEOGRAPHY AND MEDIA

The central issue here concerns the effects of modern media in constructing new geographies. Already apparent, in some of the examples we have given, is the fact that the media have consequences for the way we imagine space and place. Doreen Massey (1991) has argued that places themselves should no longer be seen as internally homogeneous, bounded areas, but as 'spaces of interaction' in which local identities are constructed out of resources (both material and symbolic) which may well not be at all local in their origin, but are nonetheless 'authentic' for all that.

In an anthropological context, James Clifford (1992: 100) takes up the same issue, noting that 'villages' inhabited by 'natives' and conceived as bounded sites of residence, which stand as metonyms for a whole culture, have long been the focus of anthropological fieldwork. Against this traditional preoccupation of anthropology, however, he emphasizes that cultures are not 'in' places in any simple sense. The focus on 'rooted', 'authentic' or 'native' culture and experience fails to address 'the wider world of intercultural import–export in which the ethnographic encounter is always already enmeshed.' Clifford supports Arjun Appadurai's contention that 'natives, people confined to and by the places to which they belong, groups unsullied by contact with a larger world, have probably never existed' (Appadurai, 1988: 39). We should work, he argues, not only with a model of 'ex-centric' natives, conceived in their multiple external connections, but with a notion of places as sites of travel encounters as much as sites of residence. Clifford suggests that we should be attentive to 'a culture's farthest range of travel, while *also* looking at its centres; to the ways in which groups negotiate themselves in external as much as internal relations; to the fact that culture is also a site of travel for others and that one group's core is another's periphery.' This is to argue for a multi-locale ethnography of both 'travelling-in-dwelling' and 'dwelling-in-travelling', when it comes to those 'permanently installed in the wanderground between here and there', those facing the question not so much of where they are from, as of where they are between (Clifford, 1992: 107–9).

Eric Wolf (1982:18) makes the fundamental criticism that, on the whole, the 'concept of the autonomous, self-regulating and self-justifying society and culture has trapped anthropology inside the bounds of its own definitions'. His point is that the methodological tail of anthropology's commitment to 'fieldwork' has too much wagged the discipline's theoretical dog, in terms of the basic model of what constitutes a 'society' or a 'culture'. As 'fieldwork' has become a hallmark of anthropological method, heuristic considerations have often been improperly converted into theoretical postulates about society and culture. As Wolf argues, 'limitations of time and energy in the field dictate limitations in the number and locations of possible observations and interviews, demanding concentration of effort on an observable place and on a corpus of specifiable informants' (ibid.: 13–14) – which is then treated relatively unproblematically, as a metonym of the larger 'society' or 'culture' being studied. As far as he is concerned, the problem with the study of the 'living cultures' of specified populations in 'locally delimited habitats' is that the model wrongly presumes an *a priori* closure in its conception of its unit of study. In the context of centuries of imperialism and cross-cultural contact, we would do better to think of human societies as open systems 'inextricably involved with other aggregates, near and far, in weblike, netlike connections' (Alexander Lesser, quoted in Wolf, 1982: 19).

The conventional model of cultural exchange, then, presumes the existence of a pure, internally homogeneous, authentic, indigenous culture which then becomes subverted or corrupted by foreign influences. The reality, however, is that every culture has, in fact, ingested foreign elements from exogenous sources, with the various elements gradually becoming 'naturalized' within it. As Said argues 'the notion that there are geographical spaces with indigenous, radically "different" inhabitants who can be defined on the basis of some religion, culture or racial essence, proper to that geographical space is a highly debatable idea' (quoted in Clifford, 1988: 274). As many authors have noted (for example, Appadurai, 1990; Bhabha, 1987; Hall, 1987), cultural hybridity is, increasingly, the normal state of affairs in the world, and in this context any attempt to defend the integrity of indigenous or authentic cultures easily slips into the conservative defence of a nostalgic vision of the past – what Salman Rushdie (1982) has described as an 'absolutism of the pure'.

Let us consider more carefully how the media are implicated in this transformation of both real and imaginative geographies. At its simplest, the point was well expressed some sixty years ago by the art historian Rudolf Arnheim, who speculated that the principal social consequences of television followed from the fact that it is 'related to the motor car and the aeroplane – as a means of transport for the mind'; as such, it 'renders the object on display independent of its point of origin, making it unnecessary for spectators to flock together in front of an original' (quoted in Rath, 1985: 199). If, in days of old, explorers and anthropologists set off on long journeys into the unknown, to bring us back written accounts of the strange customs of exotic Others in distant places, today we are all ethnographers, to the extent that all kinds of Others are exposed to our gaze (nightly on the regular television news and hourly on CNN) in the form of electronic representation on the television screens in our own living rooms. These days we have only to sit on the couch and press a button to behold the Other or the Exotic.

As early as 1946, Max Read recognized how media technologies can shape our perceptions of social reality:

> The radio not only reports history, it seems to make it. The world seems to originate from the radio. People still see things and events, but they become real only after the radio has reported the event and the newspaper has run a picture of it. The radio apperceives, registers and judges for people. Our souls are immediately connected to the radio and no longer to our own sensory organs. People no longer have an inner history, an inner continuity, the radio today is our history, it validates our existence (quoted in Kaes, 1989: 197).

In a classic article, Donald Horton and Richard Wohl (1956: 215) argued that through the new mass media, remote people are met 'as if they were in the circle of one's peers' in a 'seeming face-to-face relationship', a 'simulacrum of conversational give and take which may be called para-social interaction'. In a recent extension of this perspective, the German psychoanalyst Claus-Dieter Rath (1985: 203) has argued that, increasingly, we all live within a 'television geography'; where what counts is the space of electronic transmission, which often cuts across national borders, as we view television representations of 'planetary affairs which we face privately in our cosy living rooms' (Rath 1989: 88). On occasion, these televisual forms of para-social contact can be celebratory – sometimes literally, as when a recent papal ruling concluded that, for the sick and the ill, who are unable to go to church, the celebration of mass 'live', through television, was valid – though it was not if recorded and time-shifted on video because of the consequent loss of 'immediacy'. At other times, the contact may be intrusive, as was the case with the American television series *Julia*, one of the first to show black people in leading roles on prime-time American television, where the producers received a number of irate letters from white viewers, complaining that, having succeeded in physically keeping blacks out of their neighbourhoods, they did not want to come home and find them invading their living rooms through the television screen (Bodroghkozy, 1992).

On occasion, even trauma can be transmitted through this para-social kind of interaction. In 1990, in response to claims made by relatives of those who died in the televised tragedy at Hillsborough Football Ground, the Liverpool High Court ruled that people who suffer psychological illness after watching live television coverage of tragedies involving close relatives are eligible to claim damages in the same way as those witnessing the events *in situ* (*Guardian*, 1 August 1990). Indeed, the judge pointed out that a television watcher might be even more traumatized, by virtue of the camera's ability to bring into sharp focus events that might not be as clear to an observer of the real event. The point is that television,

> allows us to share the literal time of persons who are elsewhere. It grants us . . . *instantaneous* ubiquity. The telespectator of a lunar landing becomes a vicarious astronaut, exploring the moonscape at the same time . . . as the astronauts themselves. The viewer of a live transmission, in fact, can in some respects see better than those immediately on the scene (Stam, 1983: 24).

In this respect television transforms us into 'armchair imperialists'; through its all-encompassing viewpoint, we become 'audio-visual masters of the world' (ibid.: 25).

This is a situation rife with its own ironies. The *Guardian*'s Southern African correspondent, David Beresford, offers a telling account of the transformed meaning of 'being there' geographically, in relation to news events in the contemporary media environment, on the occasion of his own attempt to report Nelson Mandela's speech on his release from prison in South Africa, in April 1990. For Beresford, being physically 'on the spot', but merely one of hundreds of reporters jostling for position, unfortunately entailed being unable either to see or hear Mr Mandela. Beresford recounts this as an experience of both 'being there and not being there', where being the 'man on the spot' had the perverse effect of making him unable to witness the images and hear the words being clearly relayed, via the well-positioned television cameras, to the global audience-at-home.

In a similar vein, Joshua Meyrowitz has offered a fascinating analysis of the impact of electronic media on social behaviour, in transforming the 'situational geography of human life'. Meyrowitz's concern is for the way in which electronic media have undermined the traditional relationship between physical setting and social situation, to the extent that we are 'no longer "in" places in quite the same way' we once were, or thought we were (1989: 333). The media, he argues, make us 'audiences to performances that happen in other places and give us access to audiences who are not physically present' (Meyrowitz, 1985: 7). His central contention is that these new media redefine notions of social 'position' and 'place', divorcing experience from physical location. Thus, '*Live Aid* was an event that took place nowhere but on television' (1989: 329), the ultimate example of the freeing of communications experience from social and physical constraints. The electronic media have transformed the relative significance of live and mediated encounters, bringing 'information and experience to everyplace from everyplace' as state funerals, wars or space flights become 'dramas that can be played on the stage of almost anyone's living room' (1985: 118).

In this way, the media create new 'communities' across their spaces of transmission, bringing together otherwise disparate groups around the common experience of television, and bringing about a cultural mixing of here and there. Television thereby becomes the basis of common experiences and interactions: 'to watch television is to look into the common experience and to see what others are watching' (ibid.: 145–7). Thus, the millions who watched the assassination of Kennedy 'were in a "place" that is no place at all . . . the millions of Americans who watch television every evening . . . are in a "location" that is not defined by walls, streets or neighbourhoods but by evanescent "experience" . . . more and more, people are living in a national [or international] information-system, rather than in a local town or city' (ibid.: 146). It is in this sense that the electronic media are transforming our sense of locality and relocating us in terms of the 'generalised elsewhere' of distant places and 'non-local' people. As Lidia Curti (1988: 16–17) puts it:

In every country the media pose the problem of the shifting boundaries between the national and the foreign, otherness and sameness, repetition and difference. *Italia TV* shows sharply how different countries mingle and blend on the national screen, in a flow of fictions . . . it highlights how *Dallas* is naturalised in . . . Naples, how California-ness can become part of the imaginary of a Southern Italian housewife, how the proximity of a poor Roman 'bargata' to a petty bourgeois household in Rio, to a mansion in Denver, Colorado is made acceptable and plausible, by its appearing on the same flat screen, in the same household, in close succession.

Through the electronic media we have seen the construction of a new experience of virtual space and place and of virtual community. It is with virtual reality that we now have to come to terms. As Christopher Coker (1992: 197) has suggested, 'the impact of television lies not at the level of opinion and concepts, but "sense ratios" and patterns of perception. A profound structural change in the world has been brought about in human relations in terms of scale, models and habits'.

LIVING IN A MEDIATED WORLD

Anthropologists, as much as anyone else, need to take the contemporary media very seriously indeed, not least for the simple reason that the media now make us all anthropologists in our own living rooms, surveying the world of all those others who are represented to us on the screen. Edward Said (1979: 26) has argued against any comforting notion that technically improved communications media will necessarily improve intercultural relations, claiming that the media have, if anything, increased regressive tendencies. Indeed, he argues, one aspect of the electronic postmodern world is that there has been a reinforcement of the stereotypes by which the Orient is viewed: 'So far as the Orient is concerned, standardisation and cultural stereotyping have intensified the hold of the nineteenth-century academic and imaginative demonology of the "mysterious Orient".' Seeing by way of the media may even be an obstacle to understanding. Paul Hartmann and Charles Husband (1972) long ago offered good evidence that, largely as a result of media images of black people, racism in Britain is strongest in areas where white people have less day-to-day contact with blacks and are thus more dependent on media images for their knowledge (indeed largely as a result of media obsessions with 'numbers' in debates about race, the average white person overestimates the number of black people in Britain by a factor of ten).

We are all largely dependent on the media for our images of non-local people, places and events, and the further the 'event' from our own direct experience, the more we are dependent on media images for the totality of our knowledge. It is at this point that the question of media representations of otherness relates directly to the growing debate within anthropology concerning the ethics of anthropological depictions of the Other. In the light of the contributions of Said (1979), Clifford and Marcus (1986) and Marcus and Fischer (1986), many anthropologists have begun to address the Foucauldian version of the question of representation – as always involving a relation of power, as well as a relation of knowledge, between representer and represented (whether or not the Other concerned is wearing 'exotic' tribal dress). Put crudely, the question is, of course, 'who are we to represent them?' (Rabinow, 1986). As James Clifford (1986: 13) insists, it is the reflexive questions – 'Who speaks? When and where? With or to whom? Under what institutional and historical constraints?' – that are the vital ones. At its strongest, the case is put by authors such as the late Bob Scholte (1987: 35–6), who suggested that anthropology as a whole may simply be 'a way Europeans have invented of talking about their darker brethren or sisters'. 'Ethnography' itself is a word that carries a heavy ideological burden, in so far as, if its denotative meaning can be defined innocently as 'the description of peoples' connotatively the implication is always that the 'peoples' to be described are Others – non-whites, non-Europeans, non-Christians: 'Them' (Fabian, 1990: 758). Trinh Minh-Ha (1989: 73) explores the metaphor of anthropology's attempt to 'grasp the marrow of native life' as itself a cannibalistic rite, arguing that today 'the only possible ethnology is the one which studies the anthropophagous [metaphorically cannibalistic] behaviour of the white man.'

The point of the analogy is that just as, historically, it is Western anthropology that has arrogated to itself the right to represent the 'native', so today, given the largely one-way nature of the flow of international communications, it is the Western media which arrogate to themselves the right to represent all non-Western Others, and thus to provide 'us' with the definitions by which 'we' distinguish ourselves from 'them'. To extend, and complicate, our central metaphor, the television screen on which the Other is represented to (and for) us functions at a number of different levels. If, in one sense, screening means that 'they' are made present to 'us' in representation, it is also the case that the image of 'them' is screened in the different sense of being filtered, with only certain selected images getting through. At the same time, in a psychic sense, the screen is not only the medium through which images are projected for us, but also the screen onto which we project our own fears, fantasies and desires, concerning the Others against whom our identities are defined and constructed. If this is a routine process, at particular moments of crisis, its operations can be highlighted, as basic dilemmas are thrown into dramatic relief, under the glare of the world media spotlight.

The crucial question, then, is 'who are we who are screening them?' The reflexive question is the vital one:

> The viewer experiences events, not at first hand, but through perception. What he perceives will inevitably trigger an individual response to the nature of identity. There is a vital connection between what the world imposes and the mind demands, receives and shapes. Everything seen on the screen says something about ourselves. It challenges us to respond, to relate what we see to what we are. It compels us to validate our own identity (Coker, 1992: 197).

What we have to come to terms with is the power of our technologies of surveillance and the behaviour they make possible. What should concern us is how, through the screen, we devour images of the Other. The screen is implicated in the construction of the fundamental antinomies of 'self-us-good' versus 'other-them-bad'. Kobena Mercer (1990: 69) has referred to the 'sheer difficulty of living with difference', and Paui Hoggett (1992: 352) to the fundamental psychic dilemma in which 'unity without difference' is the only form of unity tolerable to the troubled psyche. We are not suggesting that any of this is new but rather that its significance has not always been fully registered. Tzvetan Todorov's masterly analysis of the representation of the Other by the Spanish, in the process of conquest and colonization of the 'New World', addresses the same fundamental dilemma. On the one hand, the Spaniards can conceive of the Indians as human, and therefore as 'identical' to themselves and having equal rights, in which case they are then ripe for the 'assimilation' of Spanish values; alternatively, they can recognize difference, but that is then immediately translated into the terms of superiority and inferiority, into the belief that the Indians are subhuman, and therefore into a justification for their enslavement. As Todorov puts it 'what is denied is the existence of a human subject truly other, someone capable of being not merely an imperfect state of oneself'; what is at stake is 'the failure to recognise the Indians, and the refusal to admit them as a subject having the same rights as oneself, but different. Columbus discovered America but not the Americans' (Todorov, 1984: 42, 49).

UNDER WESTERN EYES

Nowadays, our 'discoveries' of otherness are made not so often by means of long and perilous sea crossings, as by use of the remote-control device, as we flick between the varieties of exotica on offer on different television channels, in televisual encounters. However, we find many of the same fundamental processes in play; the same compulsion to split Good from Evil in some absolute way, the same inability to tolerate difference without relegating the different to the subhuman or inhuman category of the 'monster'. This we saw very clearly in the media presentation of the Gulf War, when Saddam Hussein was portrayed as representing all the forces of irrational barbarism that must be contained and controlled by the forces of reason and sanity. It was up to Europe and its civilizational offspring, America, to slay the dragon, to vanquish the alien: the UN crusaders had to take on the 'beast of Baghdad' and his 'empire of terror'. Reason, supposedly universal reason, had to be made to prevail. The problem, of course, is that it is all too easy to project all the evil outwards, and then to believe that all is well in our own community. The demonization of the enemy and the accusations against the Evil Other for their criminality and bestiality were related to the desire to purify our own culture and civilization. To see the Evil Other as the embodiment of irrationality is to be certain of our own rational cause and motives. The Western media's symbolic damnation of Saddam-Hitler revealed, then, a great deal about the fears, anxieties and guilt at the heart of Western modernity and rationality.

While we would wish to distinguish our argument clearly from Baudrillard's (1991) contention that the Gulf War could not, and indeed did not, exist, except as a media event (see Norris (1992) for a trenchant critique of Baudrillard's position), we do think it important to attend to the media dimension of such events. This is, not least, because it was as an experience mediated by CNN that most people outside Iraq were put into some kind of relation to, and given some form of knowledge of, the actual events that took place. However, our principal interest here lies in the role of various media in constructing a sense of the reality (or otherwise) of events in one place for people in other places. On a visit to the United States during the Gulf War, Judith Williamson observed: 'It is the unreality of anywhere outside the US, in the eyes of its citizens, which must frighten any foreigner. Like an infant who has yet to learn there are other centres of self, this culture sees others merely as fodder for its dreams and nightmares . . . It isn't that Americans don't *care* (God Knows, they care) but that, for most of them, other lands and other people cannot be imagined as real' (1991: 21). Having earlier criticized 'hypodermic' theories of media effects at the social or cultural levels, we have no intention of reinstating such a theory at the psychic level (see Morley, 1992, ch. 2 for a critique of such tendencies in cultural theory). However, we would argue that, in order to explore adequately the unconscious dynamics in play in the reception of media materials, we do need recourse to concepts derived from a psychoanalytic perspective (cf. Robins, 1993, for an elaboration of this prospective). We turn now to the Western media's 'screening' of the crisis in Bosnia in order to explore briefly some of these issues.

Recently, as a horrific sequel to the Gulf massacre, we have seen another war filling our screen time. This time in Europe itself, television has shown the horrors of concentration camps, massacre, rape and terror. As Branka Magas (1992: 102) puts it, 'the year 1992, scheduled to be a milestone on the road to European unity, has seen Sarajevo and other Bosnian cities slowly bombarded to pieces and their inhabitants starved before the television eyes of the world.' This is a war that is closer to the quick of our own lives here in the west end of Europe. 'The crisis of Bosnia,' as Akbar Ahmed (1992b: 14) says, 'is the crisis of Europe itself' and 'in failing to salvage Bosnia, it is clear that Europe is failing to salvage itself.' This war is closer, dangerously closer, to home.

Writing from Croatia, Slavenka Drakulić movingly describes her own experience of the war: how, from being a distant reality, an external event, it entered into her soul and changed her life. 'All last year', she writes, war was a distant rumour, something one managed to obscure or ignore – something happenning to other people, to people in Knin or Slavonia on the outskirts of the republic, but never to us in the centre, in Zagreb. We were busy with our private lives, with love, careers, a new car. War was threatening us, but not directly, as if we were somehow protected by that flickering TV screen – we might just as well have been in Paris or Budapest (Drakulić, 1993a: 18).

For some time, it was possible to keep the war at a distance, to see it only as 'familiar media images':

> While it still seemed so far away, it had a mythical quality. Everyone knew about its existence, but not many people had seen it and the stories we heard sounded so horrible and exaggerated that it was difficult to believe them. Everyone read reports, listened to the news and looked at the television images but its mythical dimension remained preserved by the distance – the majority of us had no direct experience (Drakulić, 1993b: xiv).

But it was not possible to go on screening out the reality of the conflict: 'for a long time we have seen able to fend off the ghost of war; now it comes back to haunt us, spreading all over the screen of our lives, leaving no space for privacy, for future, for anything but itself' (Drakulić, 1993a: 18). Living in the war zone has meant coming to live with war and coming to be profoundly changed by it.

Outside the war zone, we may still be protected by the flickering screen; the mythical dimension of the war is still preserved through the distancing effect of the screen images. Outside that zone, there is a sense of comfort in the knowledge that the war is not only happening to other people but that it is happening to another 'kind' of people. In Western Europe, the war is often seen as an atavistic affair, being acted out by primitive and tribal populations. Arjun Appadurai (1986: 357–8) describes how, in anthropological theory, places become associated with what he calls 'gatekeeping concepts', that is to say 'concepts that seem to limit anthropological theorising about the place in question, and that define the quintessential and dominant questions of interest in the region. . . . The point is that there is a tendency for places to become showcases for specific issues over time.' This is not, of course, restricted to theoretical anthropology. In the case of the Balkans, what often limits our understanding is the ideologically concealed association of this unfortunate region with the passions of ethnic hatred and primordial violence. Our cherished reason may then recoil, as we witness what, to us, are irrational and incomprehensible acts of savagery. This is a mad place, we are easily tempted to say, and these are mad people, unlike us.

The fear is that the madness might be contagious. 'New tribalism threatens to infect us all', proclaims a recent article in the *Guardian* (Hutton, 1993). 'In the place of evil empires', as Paula Franklin Lytle (1992: 304) observes, 'are resurgent nationalisms, and the terms used to describe them are images of infection and disease'. The point about this kind of imagery is that it interprets events in the former Yugoslavia as pathological and as the consequence of some kind of catastrophic natural force. The Balkans are then seen 'as a body infected by nationalism, rather than as a war possibly amenable to any form of mediation or intervention' (ibid.: 316). The vital metaphor can then excuse Western inaction or ineffectiveness. More than this, it can come to legitimate a policy of disengagement and withdrawal: 'In the absence of an effective vaccine, the alternative response to viral contagion is quarantine' (ibid.: 306). We must be screened from the infecting body.

The television screen may well be one key mechanism through which this distancing has been achieved. An issue of *Newsweek* (17 August 1992: 8) drew attention to the 'shocking images' of ethnic cleansing: 'Now the grim results are finally showing up on television screens and the front pages of newspapers. Pictures sear the conscience of the world'. And yet, it goes on, 'the response of the outside world so far – a lot of hand-wringing and a few relief supplies for one besieged city, Sarajevo – looks pathetically inadequate.' The television images do not necessarily involve us in the plight of those distant others: what they may rather do is to bring us voyeuristically, and perhaps even cognitively, closer, whilst maintaining an emotional distance and detachment. The screen is then a separation, a shield, a protection.

In considering what he calls 'the postmodern call of the other reaching towards us from the mediatised image', Richard Kearney (1988: 387–8) poses the crucial question: 'Are not those of us who witness such images (as well as those who record and transmit them through the communications network) obliged to respond not just to surface reflections on a screen but to the call of human beings they communicate?' Most of us know what we would want to answer individually. We are also aware of what our collective response has ended up being. How are we to explain the uses of the screen that seem to preclude moral response and engagement?

At one level, of course, we can see it in terms of a mutation in television journalism which is associated with an increasing 'analytical paralysis' in its account of the world (Ferro, 1993). As Ignacio Ramonet (1991: 18) argues, television has become a medium in which 'it is the force of the image that prevails': 'the objective is not to make us understand a situation, but to make us take part in an event.' Or again, according to Paolo Carpignano and his colleagues (1990: 36) we have seen the demise of journalistic authority and the creation of a state of affairs in which 'information has created a world rich in events but devoid of shared experience.'

But it is more than just the transformation in media technologies and journalistic techniques that is at issue. There is something more fundamental at work in the process of screen mediation, something that is more than a technological matter. The journalistic organization of the 'world as a show' responds to individual and collective psychological demands. In this respect, it can also be said that 'the media are used by the unconscious mind as an auxiliary system (the screen), which stabilises and takes care of the personal and direct relationships which are too painful and lie between dream and reality' (Dufour and Dufour-Gompers, 1985: 320). In looking at the television screen, the watcher can say to himself or herself:

> I see that these anxieties, hatreds, killings and destructions are not me . . . I can see that these hungers for power and these continual confrontations are not me . . . I see that these inhibited, distorted sexual appetites are not me . . . in a word, all this craziness is not me (ibid.: 321).

The television screen can be seen as functioning, then, in terms of psychic defence and screening. The psychoanalyst Isabel Menzies (1960: 117) described how social organizations can come to function as mechanisms of defence against anxiety. 'The social defence system', she suggested, 'represents the institutionalisation of very primitive psychic defence mechanisms, a main characteristic of which is that they facilitate the evasion of anxiety, but contribute little to its true modification and reduction.' What we need to take account of is how the imaginary institution of television can become just such a collective mechanism of defence.

What needs to be understood, as much as what is actually going on in the Balkans, is what is going on in the TV audience, watching the war from a safe distance. We are invited by the nature of the

TV coverage, to take up the position of the 'armchair anthropologist', gazing at the 'Other', on the screen, in the living-room. One must recognize that in so far as this war is 'viewed' as something (mythical) happening to 'Other' people, this can make its viewers insensitive to their own psychic investments in the material viewed. Anthropologists (and media scholars) must be attentive, then, not only to the ethics of everyday depictions, but also to the psychic investments made in such depictions. If the western audience is tempted to organize its collective fantasies around the idea of 'the Balkans as the Other of the West', in the process, this can easily serve to obscure how, 'far from being the Other of Europe, ex-Yugoslavia was rather Europe itself in its Otherness, the screen onto which Europe projected its own repressed reverse' (Žižek, 1992).

In all of this, the relation of the 'mediated' and the 'real' is a complex one. It could certainly be argued that the airlift of wounded children from Sarajevo in August 1993 was a real event almost entirely shaped by the media. The strategy seemed mainly designed to boost the standing of the Western powers in their own voters' eyes, by virtue of the good publicity generated through the consequent photo-opportunities for politicians to pose with 'rescued' children. However, when it became clear that strictly medical priorities would mean that the first plane-load of evacuees would contain not only sick children, but also some severely wounded adults, the British popular media were outraged, running headlines complaining of Muslim duplicity in 'tricking' the Western charities and doctors. The presence of wounded Muslim adults among the evacuees was certainly taken to represent a kind of 'pollution' of the Western crusade on behalf of innocent children. It seems that wounded Muslim children are predominantly seen as children, and thus deserving of help, whereas wounded adults are predominantly seen as Muslims, and thus represent 'matter out of place' on a Western crusade. The cynicism of the British Government in the whole episode, its attempt to exploit this tragic situation for political publicity, was perhaps best summed up in the words of a UN representative, Sylvana Foa, (*Guardian*, 14 August 1993): 'Does that mean Britain only wants to help children? Maybe it only wants children under six, or blond children, or blue-eyed children?' Our own analysis would lead us to believe that her question, even if rhetorical, is nonetheless pertinent for that.

'What can happen next, is this the end of the horror?' asks Slavenka Drakulić (1993b: xiii) in a letter to her publisher in London. 'No, I am afraid that we will have to live with this war for years. But you too will have to live with it, and it will change you, not immediately, but over time.' For the moment, we are still watching the flickering screen. For the moment, we still have names and addresses and car keys. Meanwhile, in Sarajevo, it is reported (*Guardian*, 26 August 1993) that the price of an almost new Volkswagen Golf has fallen to around $150, as few people can get hold of the petrol they need to run a car.

REFERENCES

Ahmed, A. (1992a) *Postmodernism and Islam*, London: Routledge.

—— (1992b) 'Palestine Revisited', *New Statesman and Society*, 20 November: 14.

Ang, I. (1985) *Watching Dallas*, London: Methuen.

Appadurai, A. (1986) 'Theory in anthropology: center and periphery', *Comparative Studies in Society and History*, 28, 2: 356–61.

—— (1988) 'Putting hierarchy in its place', *Cultural Anthropology*, 1: 36–49.

—— (1990) 'Disjuncture and difference in the global cultural economy' in M. Featherstone (ed.) *Global Culture*, London: Sage.

Baudrillard, J. (1988) *Selected Writings*, Cambridge: Polity.

—— (1991) *La Guerre du Golfe n'a pas eu Lieu*, Paris: Editions Galilée.

Bhabha, H. (1987) 'Interrogating identity' in L. Appignanesi (ed.) *Postmodernism and the Question of Identity*, London: Institute of Contemporary Arts.

Bodroghkozy, A. (1992) 'Is this what you mean by color TV?' in L. Spigel and D. Mann (eds) *Private Screenings*, Minneapolis: University of Minnesota Press.

Carpignano, P. et al. (1990) 'Chatter in the age of electronic reproduction: talk television and the "public mind"', *Social Text*, 25/26: 33–55.

Clifford, J. (1986) 'Introduction: partial truths' in J. Clifford and G. Marcus *Writing Culture*, Berkeley: University of California Press.

—— (1988) *The Predicament of Culture*, Cambridge, MA: Harvard University Press.

—— (1992) 'Travelling cultures' in L. Grossberg *et al.* (eds) *Cultural Studies*, London: Routledge.

Clifford, J. and Marcus, G. (eds) (1986) *Writing Culture*, Berkeley: University of California Press.

Coker, C. (1992) 'Post-modernity and the end of the Cold War: has war been disinvented?', *Review of International Studies*, 18, 3: 189–98.

Curran, J. (1990) 'The "new revisionism" in mass communications research', *European Journal of Communication*, 5, 2–3: 135–64.

Curti, L. (1988) 'Imported utopias', unpublished paper, Istituto Orientale, Naples.

Drakulić, S. (1993a) *Balkan Express: Fragments from the Other Side of War*, London: Hutchinson.

—— (1993b) *How We Survived Communism and Even Laughed*, London: Vintage.

Dufour, Y.R. and Dufour-Gompers, N. (1985) 'Journalists, anxiety and media as an intra-psychic screen', *Israel Journal of Psychiatry and Related Sciences*, 22, 4: 315–24.

Fabian, J. (1990) 'Presence and representation: the other and anthropological writing', *Critical Inquiry*, 16: 753–72.

Ferro, M. (1993) 'Médias et intelligence du monde', *Le Monde Diplomatique*, January: 32.

Flores, E. (1988) 'Mass media and the cultural identity of the Puerto Rican people', paper presented to the conference of the International Association for Mass Communications Research, Barcelona.

Greenblatt, S. (1992) *Marvellous Possessions*, Oxford: Oxford University Press.

Gripsrud, J. (*forthcoming*) *Dynasty: Dollars, Dreams and Dilemmas*, London: Routledge.

Hall, S. (1981) 'Encoding/decoding in TV discourse' in S. Hall *et al.* (eds), *Culture, Media. Language*, London: Hutchinson.

—— (1987) 'Minimal selves' in L. Appignanesi (ed.) *Postmodernism and the Question of Identity*, London: Institute of Contemporary Arts.

Hartmann, C. and Husband, P. (1972) 'Race and the British media' in D. McQuail (ed.) *The Sociology of Mass Communication*, Harmondsworth: Penguin.

Harvey, D. (1989) *The Condition of Postmodernity*, Oxford: Basil Blackwell.

Hoggett. P. (1992) 'A place for experience: a psychoanalytical perspective on boundary, identity and culture', *Environment and Planning D: Society and Space*, 10, 3: 345–56.

Horton, D. and Wohl, R.R. (1956) 'Mass communication and para-social inter-action: observations on intimacy at a distance', *Psychiatry*, 19: 215–29.

Hutton, W. (1993) 'New tribalism threatens to infect us all', *Guardian*, 1 February.

Jameson, F. (1985) 'Postmodernism and consumer society' in H. Foster (ed.) *Postmodern Culture*, London: Pluto.

Kaes, A. (1989) *From Hitler to Heimat*, Cambridge, MA: Harvard University Press.

Kearney, R. (1988) *The Wake of Imagination*, London: Hutchinson.

Liebes, T. and Katz, E. (1990) *The Export of Meaning: Cross-Cultural Readings of Dallas*, Oxford: Oxford University Press.

Lytle, P.F. (1992) 'US policy toward the demise of Yugoslavia: the "virus of nationalism"', *East European Politics and Societies*, 6, 3: 303–18.

Magas, B. (1992) 'The destruction of Bosnia-Herzegovina', *New Left Review*, 196: 102–12.

Marcus, G. and Fischer, M. (1986) *Anthropology as Cultural Critique*, Chicago:

University of Chicago Press.

Massey, D. (1991) 'A global sense of place', *Marxism Today*, June: 24–9.

Mattelart, A. *et al.* (1984) *International Image Markets*, London: Comedia.

Menzies, I.E.P. (1960) 'A case study in the functioning of social systems as a defence against anxiety', *Human Relations*, 13, 2: 95–121.

Mercer, K, (1990) 'Welcome to the jungle' in J. Rutherford (ed.) *Identity: Community, Culture, Difference*, London: Lawrence & Wishart.

Meyrowitz, J. (1985) *No Sense of Place*, Oxford: Oxford University Press.

—— (1989) 'The generalised elsewhere', *Critical Studies in Mass Communication*, 6, 3: 326–34.

Michaels, E. (1988) 'Hollywood iconography: a Warlpiri reading' in P. Drummond and R. Paterson (eds) *Television and its Audience*, London: British Film Institute.

Minh-Ha, Trinh T. (1989) *Woman, Native, Other*, Bloomington: Indiana University Press.

Miller, D. (1992) '*The Young and the Restless* in Trinidad: a case of the local and the global in mass consumption' in R. Silverstone and E. Hirsch (eds) *Consuming Technologies*, London: Routledge.

Morley, D. (1992) *Television, Audiences and Cultural Studies*, London: Routledge.

Norris, C. (1992) *Uncritical Theory*, London : Lawrence & Wishart.

Rabinow, P. (1986) 'Representations are social facts' in J. Clifford and G. Marcus (eds) *Writing Culture*, Berkeley: University of California Press.

Ramonet, I. (1991) 'L'ère du soupçon', *Le Monde Diplomatique*, May: 11, 18.

Rath, C.-D. (1985) 'The invisible network: television as an institution in everyday life' in P. Drummond and R. Paterson (eds) *Television in Transition*, London: British Film Institute.

—— (1989) 'Live television and its audiences' in E. Seiter *et al.* (eds) *Remote Control*, London: Routledge.

Robins, K. (1993) 'The war, the screen, the crazy dog and poor mankind', *Media, Culture and Society*, 15, 2: 321–7.

Rushdie, S. (1982) 'Imaginary homelands', *London Review of Books*, October: 18–19.

Said, E. (1979) *Orientalism*, Harmondsworth: Penguin.

Schiller, H.I. (1969) *Mass Communications and American Empire*, New York: Beacon (second edition, updated, San Francisco: Westview, 1993).

Scholte, R. (1987) 'The literary turn in contemporary anthropology', *Critique of Anthropology*, 7, 1: 33–47.

Stam, R, (1983) 'Television news and its spectator' in E. Kaplan (ed.) *Regarding Television*, vol. 2, New York: American Film Institute.

Todorov, T. (1984) *The Conquest of America: the Question of the Other*, New York: Harper & Row.

Tunstall, J. (1977) *The Media are American*, London: Constable.

Williamson, J. (1991) 'Mad bad Saddam', *Guardian*, 31 January.

Wolf, E. (1982) *Europe and the People Without History*, Berkeley: University of California Press.
Žižek, S. (1992) 'Ethnic dance macabre', *Guardian*, 28 August.

CHAPTER 11

After Emotion: Ethnic Cleansing in the Former Yugoslavia, and Beyond
Stjepan G. Meštrović

One would expect that anthropologists and other analysts of culture would have much to offer in the way of theory, research, and social commentary to help one make sense of the dizzying course of events in post-communist Eastern Europe and the former Soviet Union that culminated in the cruel war in the former Yugoslavia. Yet anthropologists, sociologists, postmodernists and other students of culture have been mostly silent on the new wave of genocide in Europe, and elsewhere. Instead, intellectuals such as Francis Fukuyama (1992), the philosopher who worked for the US State Department, have usurped the philosophically informed approach to cultural studies that was the staple of early anthropological theory and research, dating back to Alexis de Tocqueville and David Emile Durkheim (as interpreted by Bellah *et al.* (1985), Riesman (1950) and others). Whereas Tocqueville and Durkheim focused on emotionally-loaded 'habits of the heart' and 'collective representations', respectively, as the fundamental unit of analysis in cultural studies (Meštrović, 1992a), Fukuyama and his disciples claim that the 'end of history' has occurred. The end of history is supposed to signal the end of emotional phenomena such as ethnic identity, nationalism, and tradition. The recent genocidal violence in the world should have silenced Fukuyama and his disciples, as argued by Daniel Patrick Moynihan (1994) but it has not. Postmodernists have pursued a similar 'end of history' approach (see Rosenau, 1992) by predicting tolerance, globalism, and other benign phenomena that are supposed to follow from a rebellion against the modernist, so-called grand narratives derived from the Enlightenment (Lyotard, 1984)

The difference in cultural studies (including but not limited to anthropology) between the previous *fin de siècle* and our *fin de siècle* (Meštrović, 1992b) helps to explain why so many cultural analysts were caught off guard recently, not only by the fall of Communism but by the fission, fragmentation and other phenomena related to Balkanization since then (Meštrović, 1991). Social scientists, cultural analysts, and laypersons alike are using either positivistic assumptions (that social forces are universally valid, and that all peoples are motivated by enlightened, rational self-interest, as argued recently by Seidman and Wagner, 1991) or anti-cultural assumptions (the end of history, postmodernism, the end of nationalism, discussed in Meštrović, Letica and Goreta, 1993) to apprehend events that surprised them by their unpredictability and irrationalism.

. One might hope that a return to qualitative or ethnographic studies in formerly communist nations might yield useful data to offset this anti-cultural trend. But the postmodernist discourse has changed even the ethnographic tradition by accusing it of Eurocentrism, an arrogant attitude toward natives, and above all, the impossibility of truly grasping the objectivity of data (Atkinson, 1990, Geertz, 1973, 1988). Jean Baudrillard (1986) has openly declared the end of culture in his postmodernist vision of the world, and if that were true, it should signal the end of anthropology, the end of sociology, and the end of other social sciences that were concerned with culture.

It is clear that, despite the many endgames that are being invoked in intellectual discourse recently, history, culture, tradition, and nation – among other emotionally laden phenomena – are staging a dramatic comeback. What we are witnessing in the former Soviet Union, Eastern Europe, the Balkans, as well as much of the Islamic world is an explosion of what Arthur Schopenhauer (1965[1818]) referred to as 'the heart' (as opposed to the Kantian focus on 'the mind'). In direct contradiction to the modernist predictions of Hegel and Marx as well as the positivists and defenders of Enlightenment-based liberalism, nationalism as a powerful force motivating persons has become more, not less, important as the twentieth century draws to a close. In fact, I would claim that nationalism has emerged as the most significant cultural force in the present *fin de siècle*. Religion has reasserted itself throughout the world, including the West (witness the anti-abortion campaign in the United States). Barbaric tendencies towards revenge based on historical grievances and the destruction of others for the sake of spite – not even a 'rational' goal or purpose – have emerged as powerful indicators that hyper-rational social theories cannot explain events captured by the post-Holocaust genocide in the Balkans.

In this essay, I will attempt to introduce a new anthropological and sociological concept, post-emotionalism, and will use the current

Balkan War as a vehicle for a much larger discussion that involves postmodernism, the Balkanization of the West (Meštrović, 1994), and the inadequacy of current hyper-rational approaches that involve more than the current perceptions of this war. If the Gulf War has been called the postmodern war (Baudrillard 1991), it is helpful to think of the current Balkan War as a watershed event that might be called the first post-emotional war. The text that follows should be read as a preliminary attempt at delineating this new concept as an alternative to postmodernism, so that the reader should expect to find all the inconsistencies and rough edges that typically accompany new ideas. This essay is an invitation to discussion and further development, not the final word. But for this discussion to proceed, a number of related issues must be examined first.

EUROCENTRISM

Nowadays, whenever one discusses the current Balkan War, one is subjected immediately to the accusation of engaging in Eurocentrism. It is often said that the Belgrade-sponsored genocide in the Balkans pales in comparison with the genocide in Rwanda and Burundi or other historical as well as current sites of genocide. United Nations Secretary-General, Boutros Boutros-Ghali, referred to this Balkan War as a 'rich man's war' when compared with Somalia (*New York Times*, 16 October 1993:a7). But in fact, this Balkan War has entered living-rooms all over the world because it is covered through the miracle of the television medium. No longer is this European, Balkan War just in the Balkans. It is, in fact, everywhere, due to the television screen, so that the Balkans are everywhere too.

One finds Francis Fukuyama and others claiming that this is America's century, and after the fall of communism, America has reached the end of history. Paradoxically, if it is true that America and American ideas of democracy and capitalism have taken over the world to some extent, then 'their' problems (the 'they' are people in the Balkans, Africa, and all others who have not reached this utopian state of the end of history) become 'our' problem. For this reason, too, 'their' Balkanization becomes 'our' Balkanization.

Those who use the sociological and anthropological imaginations will find ethnic and religious violence dominated by media images in the West, from the Los Angeles riots to the murder of doctors who perform abortions. Those who look will find Balkanization and barbarism in the so-called 'civilized' West (Meštrović, 1993). Thus, where I live, teach and work in Texas, at Texas A&M, the campus is overwhelmingly white, while twenty minutes down the road in Prairie View A&M one finds an almost completely African American faculty and students. There is apartheid in the United States, but most people don't want to call it that. There is 'white flight', a sociological phenomenon in which white people live in suburbs, and have allowed the inner cities to remain almost completely ethnic. One needs to perceive the ethnic turmoil in the Balkans as a reflector of a kind of Balkanization of the West. For example, consider that collective guilt is not only used by the Serbs as a rationalization for their persecution of Muslims and Croats (*Washington Post*, 19 June 1994:A12). My university students in the United States engage in serious discussions during class in which they allege collective guilt of white persons for slavery committed against African-Americans; of the collective guilt of men for past patriarchal oppression of women; and so on for wrongs committed in the past against Hispanics, Native Americans, and others. All of these examples suggest that Bosnia is about more than Bosnia, which is precisely why it has mesmerized the popular consciousness.

Another reason why this Balkan War is not just Eurocentric is that it involves Muslim interests (Ahmed, 1993a). At Friday prayer services all over the Islamic world, the faithful are being told that Bosnia is the last straw in the arrogant West's effort to wipe out Islam (Ahmed, 1993b). Furthermore, it is not clear whether this Balkan War is being fought over 'there' in the present or in the past. Huge chunks of European and other history as well are being invoked (Ahmed, 1994). For example, the suspected war criminal, Radovan Karadžić, is constantly and shamelessly telling the West that he's doing them a favour by persecuting the Muslims (*New York Times*, 14 July 1994:A5). Karadžić invokes the Crusades, as if the Crusades were a good thing, and not an exercise in genocide. The Serbs hark back to the Battle of Kosovo in 1389, which is sort of Alamo for them. They lost their turf over 600 years ago, and in many ways the ethnic cleansing directed against Bosnian Muslims is revenge for that event.

Another set of very emotional events that are often brought up by Serbian propagandists are the atrocities committed by Ante Pavelić and his Croatian Ustasha regime in the Second World War (*Washington Times*, 20 June 1994:A10). But the Serbs never mention the Nazi Quisling regime that was in place in Serbia during that war (Cohen, 1992, 1994). This misuse of emotional history evokes Holocaust memories, and all these phenomena – past and present, East and

West, Christianity and the fate of Semitic peoples – become intertwined and it becomes truly very difficult to determine whether this war is being fought in the present, or in the past (Miles, 1994) . Yet another reason why this Balkan War is something that involves all peoples who live outside the Balkans is that compared to the Holocaust, and compared to other sites of genocide, everyone on the planet knows about this one in the Balkans. The excuse given for the Holocaust is 'we didn't know'. There is no excuse this time around. Massive coverage has been given to this situation in Bosnia, more than Rwanda, Cambodia, or any other.

It is true that there are over 30 wars going on as of this writing, and that many of them involve genocide. Yet it is cynical to conclude that, simply because so much media attention has been given to this Balkan War, there is something Eurocentric in this concern. The more important points seem to be that so much attention has been given to it and yet it goes on unabated, despite the massive media coverage; that the charge of Eurocentrism is an abnegation of Europe's responsibility in stopping genocide on its continent and in its former colonies; and that, in fact, most of the developing world is modelling itself on Europe and the United States.

Instead of confronting Europe's role in post-communist changes, the West has become a postmodern voyeur. The information highway that Vice President Al Gore has talked about has made us all, in a sense, accomplices to genocide that occurs in the postmodern world. In the wake of Walter Benjamin's (1968) and Georg Simmel's (1991[1900]) theories of abstractionism, it is useful to invent a new term for the sort of revisionism that television coverage of genocide allows, a revisionism that involves the repackaging of quasi-historical emotional vestiges from the past. We are used to thinking that Holocaust revisionism, or other revisionism, involves a distortion of the past, but in fact we have here revisionism going on in real time and in the present. As Belgrade-sponsored genocidal aggression goes on in the Balkans, it is rationalized immediately, and distorted, into euphemisms such as tribalism, civil war, 'ethnic cleansing' and other phenomena. For example, the United Nations told us a few months ago Sarajevo was not under siege even though, by all acceptable standards of judging factual reality, the Serbian stranglehold of Sarajevo is nothing but a siege (Diždarević, 1994).

A new theoretical framework is needed to grasp the significance of this phenomenon, peculiar to the postmodern age (Tester, 1992) for understanding where the world is going. Ethnic violence, ethnic conflicts, and ethnic cleansing, unfortunately, are proving to be increasingly important in the forthcoming era. In this essay I will propose a new term, 'post-emotionalism', to capture some of the dimensions of this phenomenon. I use post-emotional rather than postmodern largely because postmodernists have reduced the world to a *text*. A text is something that consists of cerebral images, so that any discussion of the world as text merely perpetuates modernist prejudices, and does not constitute a genuine rebellion against modernity. Postmodernists fail to factor in the many emotions that are being invoked in the post-communist world, and the Balkans in particular, as well as the rest of the world. Yet these are dead emotions. They are emotions that are being displaced from the past (for example, 1389, the Ustasha episode, or in Rwanda, the Belgian colonial era) and are being manipulated by various media and governments.

FROM DURKHEIM TO THE BALKANS

Before proceeding further, it is helpful to analyse briefly this author's 'place' and interest in issues of this sort. Given my aims and premises in pursuing this line of enquiry, it would be disingenuous to characterize my approach as purely 'disinterested' according to some fictitious standard of how scientists operate. Prior to the outbreak of this war, I was concerned mainly with the sociology of David Emile Durkheim. It is interesting that he has been passed down to anthropologists and sociologists as Emile Durkheim – the Jewish first name, David, has been dropped. And he has come down to us as a French sociologist. Sociologists almost never mention that he was Jewish, that his family fled persecution in Germany, that he lived as a minority member (German Jew) in France, and that he was descended from eight generation of rabbis, a veritable dynasty, which is a rather important fact that no doubt influenced his later declaration that sociology is the 'science of morality' (for a rare exception, see Alpert (1993[1939]). Durkheim did not follow his father's footsteps in becoming a rabbi, but he did preserve his father's moralism (see Meštrović, 1988). In general, just as Western intellectuals have tried to put a cerebral, mental image on this Balkan War as tribalism that need not concern those who bask in the lands where the end of history took hold, the theoretical tools that might be used to understand it, including the sociology of Durkheim, have been almost completely denatured of the moral import of Durkheim's sociology. Durkheim's passionate social theory has been transformed into a sterile and cerebral functionalism. Durkheim was concerned with *emotions*, particularly the emotions that hold societies together as well as the ones that tear it apart (see Meštrović, 1993). Thus, I would suggest one more reason why Westerners are having a hard time grasping what in fact has gone wrong in the Balkans, namely, that they have been engaging in a kind of post-emotionalism even in sociological theory. I think that when we examine Durkheim's sociology and anthropology, and focus on his concerns, such as the central distinction between the sacred and the profane, the difference between individual and collective responsibility, among other dualisms invoked by Durkheim, we note that these did not fit in very well with French culture at the time. Durkheim's concerns did and do fit well with Durkheim's Jewish minority background, however.

I have a friend, Rabbi Peter Tarlow, who exclaimed, when I explained Durkheim's terminology to him, 'Stjepan, this sounds like the Separation Prayer I pray every Saturday.' He explained that Jews thank God every Saturday for the separation of night and day and other dualisms up to and including the sacred and the profane. And he asked me how did Durkheim define the sacred, and I answered, that which is separated from the rest and treated with all respect. And he said that this definition does not come from French positivism but from Jewish tradition.

Durkheim wrote extensively on how societies move from tradition to modernity. Part of this process involves moving away from notions of collective guilt and collective responsibility to notions of individual guilt and responsibility (Durkheim 1933[1893]). Durkheim insisted that a crucial aspect of modern societies is that guilt should be an individual matter. At the same time, because he saw that these and other phenomena are inseparable and involve an inexorable dualism, he also argued that modernists will never completely outgrow collective consciousness. There will always be a part of modernist collective consciousness that will act traditionally and emotionally. So the individualism peculiar to modernity never supersedes the collectivity of traditionalism. In short, individualism, for Durkheim, is itself a collective phenomenon.

Western anthropologists and sociologists rarely acknowledge that, in his lifetime, Durkheim had to deal with anti-Semitism, and in particular the Dreyfus Affair. Captain Dreyfus, a Jew, was wrongly imprisoned during the 1890s for allegedly passing war secrets to the Germans. This event ripped apart French intellectual society from the previous *fin de siècle* (Weber, 1987), yet even today many French citizens refuse to admit that Dreyfus was wrongly accused and imprisoned precisely because he was a Jew. It is equally noteworthy that contemporary

French society refuses to discuss openly the anti-Semitism that was part of the Vichy collaborationist government. Even when French President Francois Mitterrand admitted recently that he worked for Vichy, he added quickly that he was not aware of anti-Semitism during Vichy, and was not personally an anti-Semite (Péan 1994). Given this long record of denying anti-Semitism in French society, it is significant that Durkheim had married a Dreyfus, related to the famous Dreyfus, and that he was passionately involved in the Dreyfus Affair, was on the Jewish committee for war orphans in the First World War, and participated in other Jewish affairs,[1] but almost all treatises on Durkheim gloss over his Jewish heritage. And this despite the loud rhetoric of alleged sensitivity to multiculturalism and minority issues in the West!

One has to remember that about a hundred years ago, Jews were very split about the guilt or innocence of Dreyfus. Half of them thought he was guilty; the other half either thought he was innocent or embarrassed at the fact that he was bringing out the issue of Jewishness. Most Frenchmen at the time thought that anti-Semitism was a thing of the past, that Jews were assimilated into French society, and that things were moving forward. Yet one of Durkheim's most memorable lines is the observation that when Dreyfus was found guilty, French people were out singing and dancing in the streets. He said this was a time of great sorrow. In an essay entitled 'Individualism and the Intellectuals', Durkheim (1975[1898]) demanded French justice for Dreyfus, that he be treated as a French citizen and get justice under French law and, in fact, not be treated as Jewish. Like so many other minority members, Durkheim had to write in code, but it is clear that Durkheim was insisting that Dreyfus be judged according to widely accepted standards of *individual* responsibility, not the implicit *collective guilt* that many Frenchmen attributed to Jews *vis-à-vis* Dreyfus.

The reason that I make this connection is so that this discussion does not become completely abstract. One has to consider the writer, who in this case is Croatian-American. Much like Durkheim had his Dreyfus Affair, I became interested in this post-Holocaust instance of genocide because, in a sense, Croatian and Muslim 'collective guilt' is being implied much like the alleged 'collective guilt' of Jews was being projected onto Dreyfus a century ago. It may be worth noting that my ancestors on my father's side were Bosnian Muslims who converted to Christianity many centuries ago, while the ancestors on my mother's side are Croatian. Durkheim had to become involved about a century ago much as I feel I must get involved in the issues surrounding the current Balkan War. One might object almost immediately: 'Now, wait a minute, Dreyfus was innocent.' Again, I want to emphasize that this is evident only in retrospect. At the time, many if not most people assumed that Dreyfus was guilty, and in a burst of anti-Semitism, generalized from his alleged guilt to the alleged guilt of the entire Jewish people. And that's what made the Dreyfus Affair such a watershed event of the previous *fin de siècle*.

Thus, the juxtaposition of Dreyfus and Balkan Affairs leads to the question: Is it just to allow an entire people to be over-run by genocidal aggression based on alleged collective guilt from the past (specifically, the Battle of Kosovo in 1389 for the Muslims and the Ustasha episode for the Croats)? The modern answer is an immediate, 'No.' As children of the Enlightenment, we cannot imagine that a Croatian baby born in the 1990s should have its limbs blown off by Serbian grenades based on something that ancestral members of the baby's ethnic group might have done in the Second World War. The crippling of a Bosnian Muslim baby in the 1990s for what happened in 1389 seems even more insane. There is something monstrous about such a doctrine. On the other hand, the fact is that this argument is being made and being said in very high places,[2] that Croats deserve what they are getting, based on the crimes of the Ustasha in the Second World War, and that the Muslims are invading Europe again. These collective beliefs are an aspect of traditional collective consciousness that Durkheim was concerned with, and they do not seem to be dissipating despite modernism. It is a very difficult issue to deal with on a purely cerebral level because it does in fact involve emotion. And for that reason, it is not taken seriously by anthropologists and other contemporary students of culture who have been trained to eschew emotion.

Thus, one finds that Radovan Karadžić is frequently quoted in the western media, and refers to Mr Yakushi Akashi, the UN representative to the Balkans, as his friend. Mr Akashi refers to Mr Karadžić as a 'man of peace'. The UN is perceived by the Muslims and Croats as working on the side of the Serbs. The United Nations Protection Force or UNPROFOR is nicknamed by the Croats and Muslims as SERBOFOR because Serbia's victims see that wherever UNPROFOR troops are posted, Serbs get to hold on to their conquests and the status quo is maintained (*The Times*, 7 July 1994:A7). And they see the United Nations as handing them over to the enemy (*New York Times*, 6 July 1994:A3).

The Bosnian Muslims have 'won' this war symbolically as pure victims, at least on a conscious level. In fact, if one examines critically what the UN is doing from a Bosnian perspective, it allows Bosnian babies to be blown up by Serbian grenades, brings bandages afterwards, but it will not intervene in a way that will prevent the slaughter from occurring in the first place. All Western fact-gathering organizations, from the United States State Department to Helsinki Watch have concluded that the Belgrade regime is committing genocidal aggression. Nevertheless, the UN charter against genocide is not being invoked. What has to happen is that the West must deal with this Balkan tragedy in relation to the *emotions* of the present. And for that to happen, social scientists must become involved in theory and research pertaining to genocide in ways reminiscent of Durkheim's involvement in the Dreyfus Affair.

A POST-EMOTIONAL WORLD

My encounters with anthropologists, sociologists and other social scientists concerning the current Balkan War reveal that most of them reflect the opinions and prejudices of Western governments, media and the masses in their assessments of current genocide. Holocaust studies continue in Western universities without cultural analysts making the connection to the fact that despite the refrain, 'Never Again', genocide is occurring in Europe, again. The fact that the current Balkan War has been reduced to an emotional metaphor (an instance of tribalism), and has received tremendous media coverage, while genocide in Cambodia, Angola, Rwanda and elsewhere in the world has not received such coverage, does more than point to an implicit *Eurocentrism* in the media which is of concern to those engaged in the postmodernism discourse. The perceived Eurocentrism might be explained with reference to a *post-emotional* albeit unconscious assumption that Europe is 'superior' to other continents *vis-à-vis* civilization, and therefore genocide should not be occurring in Europe in the 1990s, even if it is. Thus, the resolution of the cognitive dissonance caused by this set of facts is to deny the genocide that is occurring and reduce it to the fictitious process called tribalism. But, more importantly, the alleged Eurocentrism might also be a variation of a more blatant European prejudice in the sense that the allegedly 'tribal' Balkans are being equated with 'tribal' Africa in the Euro-American collective consciousness. The term 'tribalism' seems to be the most frequently used term by Western journalists seeking to describe the current Balkan War as well as the genocidal wars in Africa and Asia.

It seems that post-emotionalism holds more explanatory power than the now fashionable concept of postmodernism. My argument is that postmodernism refers to that broad intellectual movement that centres on nostalgia, the blurring of the distinction between fiction and reality, and other anti-modern tendencies, But the phenomena described above are more than nostalgia; rather, they involve the transference of 'dead emotions' from the past into the living present. Instead of the circulation of fictions described by Baudrillard, it is more accurate to point to the co-existence of reality with emotionally charged 'fictions', or what might be termed circulating emotions; e.g. Helsinki Watch reports condemning Serbian aggression alongside sympathy for Serb fears of the Muslims and Croats. Thus, there appears to be a need to move beyond the parameters of postmodernism in anthropology and cultural studies.

Most newsworthy events pertaining to this Balkan War hark back in a post-emotional manner to the past. Thus, the best-selling diary by 13-year-old Zlatka Filipović (translated into 22 languages), which describes the hell of living during the Serbian siege of Sarajevo, has been compared to Anne Frank's diary:

> In a world numbed by television images of daily atrocities in Sarajevo, in a Western Europe racked by guilt over its failure to halt the 21 month old conflict in Bosnia, the voice of an innocent child still carries special weight. Her publisher has predictably proclaimed Miss Filipovic to be the Bosnian War's version of Anne Frank (*New York Times*, 6 January 1994.A1).

Compare this reaction with the fact that Diždarević's *Sarajevo: A War Journal* also received publicity, but not as much as this new Anne Frank's book. Such widespread, collective displacement of emotions deserves analysis.

Let us return to Jean Baudrillard – frequently cited as the foremost postmodernist writer – and his observations that the Gulf War and Vietnam Wars did not happen, that these and other postmodern wars are just fictions played out on the television screen. It is not enough to dismiss cruel genocidal wars of the present as fictions, because, after all, *real* people continue to suffer and die in contemporary wars. The postmodern discourse, broadly speaking, fails to address this obvious point. Thus, the more interesting question becomes: Why is it that the world's postmodern audience treats war – current as well as past – *as if* they were fictions, but fictions charged with emotionalism borrowed from the past? Thus, the current Balkan War becomes, for the Americans, a 'Vietnam Quagmire', for the Serbs, revenge against 'the Turks' for 1389 and a quest for *Greater Serbia*; for the French and British, a revival of *German expansionism*; for the Russians, another instance of the West picking on their 'little Slavic brothers', the Serbs. What is surprising is that these quasi-historical arguments are printed in a matter-of-fact fashion in Western newspapers despite all the loud rhetoric concerning the end of history.

How does one distinguish fiction from reality when it comes to the conceptualization of the current Balkan War? How has its 'reality' been transformed into various metaphors, euphemisms, and fictions? Are these euphemisms really just 'circulating fictions' as argued by Baudrillard, or do they make a kind of sense? Some of these metaphors, euphemisms and fictions (all of which are emotionally laden) will be addressed briefly – for the sake of illustratlon – including the following *neo-Orwellian* characterizations of the current Balkan War/Wars:

- the Bosnian Muslims as the new Palestinians
- the Bosnian Muslims as Native Americans on reservations or 'safe havens'
- 'safe havens' over-run by Serbs
- making 'peace' in war zones merely by sending in unarmed 'peacekeepers'
- the social construction of 'humanitarian aid': sending the Bosnians war-rations left over from the Gulf War and other specific foods, but not cigarettes (which they request), and not psychiatric help for their rape victims, etc.
- 'peace negotiations' versus terms of surrender
- 'all sides are equally guilty'
- Germany is largely responsible for the current Balkan War because of its 'premature recognition' of the sovereignties of Slovenia and Croatia
- the West is not 'involved', despite the weapons embargo imposed by the West on Serbia's victims
- 'tribes' in Europe
- the cultural imperialism discussed by Edward Said: 'we' are 'civilized' and 'they' are 'barbaric'
- this Balkan War is like a natural disaster that requires bureaucratic (UN) assistance, but there is no question of putting an end to the suffering once and for all

- ethnic division as a problem in mathematics, proposed by the European Community. That is, the EC told the 'warring parties' to divide Bosnia into certain percentages of Croats (17 per cent), Muslims (30 per cent) and Serbs (53 per cent). But what about mixed marriages and mixed parents? What about the millions of people who do not fit this neat, mathematical formula?
- Former Secretary of State Lawrence Eagleburger's statement that the conflict will end when all the parties exhaust themselves. A wrestling match? A brawl?

and so on.

Given that the above characterizations read like a laundry list of class projects from a course on Marketing 101, yet are apparently treated very seriously by the culture industry, one arrives at the following crucial issue: *Are we living in an age in which emotionalism and marketing have merged in a distinctive neo-Orwellian form?* More precisely, the centrepiece of our alternative explanation is the concept of *post-emotionalism*. We point to a common pattern in all these euphemisms and metaphors: in an ideal type rational social universe that ran according to principles derived from the Enlightenment, a finding of genocide by respected fact-finding organizations demands action by the world community to stop the genocide. This principle is enshrined in the UN Charter. Instead of reacting in this way to the situation at hand, Western politicians, diplomats, media and laypersons react on the basis of *past* events that obfuscate the present. A significant aspect of this reaction is that it does involve emotion, only the emotion is displaced, Hence, Baudrillard and others are wrong to claim that there is no pity in the dawning postmodern world, no compassion among postmodern mass societies. On the contrary, plenty of emotion is shown in the postmodern 1990s, and the term 'compassion fatigue' is used, but the emotion always involves history, and fails to address the situation at hand, from Rwanda to Bosnia.

For example, German Nazism is invoked from the Second World War to 'explain' Serbian fears of Croats, as an allegedly pro-Nazi 'genocidal people'. *Yet the Nazi collaboration of the rest of Europe is NOT invoked; the horrors committed by Communists are left out of the discourse completely; and no effort is made to contrast contemporary Germany with the prevalent image of Germany – left over from the Second World War – as an 'expansionist' power* (see Cohen, 1992; Finkielkraut, 1992; Vukovic, 1991). In this regard, it is important to raise the question: *What are the economical and ideological reasons for selective political memory?*

Similarly, the Bosnians are not like the Palestinians, because Bosnia is a duly recognized nation-state, and Mr Izetbegović does not offer a programme like Mr Arafat's. Yet, the contemporary crisis of the Bosnian nation-state is muffled in the incorrect transference to the long-standing, deeply emotional, yet completely different, problem of Israeli–Palestinian relations.

Humanitarian aid bespeaks a nostalgic image that the West has of itself as a generous culture. Yet, humanitarian aid is nomally offered to victims of natural disasters, such as floods and hurricanes, not during an active and ongoing war of genocide. Moreover, nations and peoples on the margins of the West do not see the West as generous or compassionate. A recent example might be the general hostility shown by Russians to the cruel economic 'shock therapy' being imposed upon them by the West in the name of Western humanitarian ideals.

UN 'peacekeeping' harks back to the mission of the UN during the Cold War to engage itself quickly in hot spots so that the former Soviet Union and US would not go to war. But clearly, sending in unarmed 'peacekeepers' in the middle of a genocidal war fails to address the demands of the present situation.

These and other examples seem to point to a new and distinctive Orwellian *double-speak* that has been perfected by the culture industry according to the rules of Marketing 101 with the aim of post-emotional displacement.

To understand the concept of post-emotionalism, one might invoke (1) Georg Simmel's *Philosophy of Money* (1991[1900]); (2) a new reading of Durkheim's *anomie* as a post-emotional state of weariness, exasperation, and emotional fatigue as opposed to the widespread mis-understanding of anomie as normlessness (Meštrović, 1988: 154–76); (3) David Riesman's other-directedness (from *The Lonely Crowd*, 1950); and (4) theorists of the Frankfurt school, who point in the direction in which we are heading: What is often referred to as postmodern society is more easily grasped as a post-emotional society. It is possible to draw from aspects of the postmodern discourse to help clarify these dimensions: the widespread return of *nostalgia* on a mass scale; kitsch and pastiche; the widespread use of *sentimentality* in the media, etc. Only, unlike the postmodernists, we do not hold that these developments are random nor necessarily liberating nor necessarily conducive to tolerance.

In a sense, what is called postmodernism seems to confound the action, 'I feel', with the action, 'I think'. But this tendency is not adequately treated by writers engaged in the postmodernist discourse. Modernists have depicted a reified, bounded and fixed world of bloodless categories; postmodernists seem to imply an abstract world of rootless fictions devoid of emotions; while post-emotionalism implies a concrete world of rooted fictions saturated with emotions that are *displaced*, misplaced, and manipulated by the culture industry. Durkheim's notion of 'collective effervescence' (1965[1912]) serves as an excellent basis for this elaboration. Durkheim argued that there exist times of rapid social change in which collective representations seem to explode as if they had been contained under tremendous pressure, and then suddenly released. The key difference between Durkheim's and the postmodernists' versions of 'fictions' is that, for Durkheim, these representations can be traced to a cultural point of origin and involve *emotion*. They seem haphazard and misplaced only because of the tremendous release of pressure. The end of communism constitutes such a 'release of pressure', and it has given rise to representations that have been repressed up to now, pertaining to the Holocaust, the Yugoslav civil war in the midst of the Second World War, the Vietnam syndrome, the quest for a Greater Serbia. But far from these centres of representationalism colliding into one another spontaneously, they are manipulated by *modernist* centres of the culture industry emanating from Belgrade, London, Paris, and Washington, among others.

This analysis leads to the following question: Is there a difference between the TV cartoon show Beavis and Butt-Head and the evening news? Some intellectuals engaged in the postmodern discourse seek to find deconstructive insight in Beavis and Butt-Head, and would therefore find modernist meaning in both this programme and the evening news. But in an anomic world of post-emotional excess, 'real' blood and 'real' killing becomes a cartoon. Killing seems funny,[3] and killing occurs without context even when, and perhaps precisely because it is so graphic and detailed. Post-emotional violence is depicted contrary to Aristotle's dictum that to be tragic, violence must occur off stage, and the characters in a tragedy must be developed contextually. Postmodern, post-emotional violence occurs 'on stage' (on screen) in a matter of seconds flat, and out of context. Hence, it can never evoke anything more than some post-emotional echo of a previous event. For example, this might explain why large groups of young people were asked to leave the theatre for laughing uncontrollably during the presentation of *Schindler's List* in San Francisco (*Houston Chronicle*, 17 January 1994:4).

If this Balkan War is the penultimate post-emotional war, then President Clinton might be termed the post-emotional President: the coverage given to his notorious love affair: his famous. 'I feel your pain' line; his inability (as indicated by polls) to lead, etc. For example, opinion-makers on both sides of the political spectrum in the USA have labelled Mr Clinton's recent NATO Summit and 'Partnership for Peace' as all smoke and no substance. (More surprisingly, the post-summit opinion polls show that President Clinton's public approval ratings *increased* in the USA.) President Franklin Roosevelt also referred to a 'Partnership for Peace', and it was equally insubstantial. Mr Clinton 'fits' the post-emotional times in which he lives (in a Durkheimian sense) in that he 'plays' on the old emotional images of the 1960s, of John F. Kennedy (with whom he has been compared frequently), and, in general, on the needs of the aging Baby Boomers who are looking back at their collective youth in the 1960s with considerable nostalgia,[4] and transferring some of that emotional energy onto the present.

One could argue that despite all this soothing talk from President Clinton, he and other Western leaders (primarily British and French) have kept the victims of the Balkan slaughter outgunned and unable to defend themselves. One could argue that these leaders pretend to condemn 'ethnic cleansing' but propose to keep the 'peace' between a gulag of disarmed Muslim ghettos and the armed ethnic cleansers themselves. The post-emotionalism concept enables one to *expose* the emotional and other discrepancies in how the West arrived at this point, pushing ethnic partition and division when its own cultural principles point to pluralism.

We review the situation: From 1991 to 1994, the President of Serbia, Slobodan Milošević, used the Yugoslav People's Army directly to arm the suspected war criminal, Radovan Karadžić, and directly to help seize and cleanse one-third of Croatia, and then 70 per cent of Bosnia. He succeeded by convincing the West that the Serbian minority in Croatia was right to fear the Croats as an allegedly 'genocidal people' because of the atrocities committed by the Second World War Ustashe. To repeat, the Serbian line makes skilful use of the emotionally charged and traditional phenomenon of collective guilt, which runs contrary to principles derived from the Enlightenment, principles which hold only individuals responsible for crimes. But the more important point, for the purposes of the present discussion, is that this *post-emotional* argument worked on the West. And another important point is that collective guilt is an integral aspect of Euro-Christian culture even though it is denied, and despite the smokescreen of the Enlightenment. Euro-American politicians routinely punish whole peoples for the actions of a few: witness the trade sanctions against Iraq and Haiti, the British bombing of Dresden, the weapons embargo against Israel in 1947, etc. Very few sociological and anthropological treatises have explored this ambiguity in the West regarding collective guilt (the Durkheimian disciple Paul Fauconnet's *La Responsabilité*, published in 1920, comes to mind).

Thus, ordinary people are led to believe that the peoples of the former Yugoslavia have succumbed to 'tribal' hatred, and that the West should not get involved. This is an interesting, seemingly postmodern mixing of metaphors, Nazism and primitive tribes. Yet the West *is* involved. Instead of standing up for a pluralistic society, which is a key Western ideal and especially a key component of American civil religion, it is the West that is promoting a quasi-apartheid system of ethnic partition in Bosnia-Herzegovina. And the West is doing this ostensibly on the basis of an *post-emotional* humanitarianism. It is ironic that the Bosnian government is trying to stand up for pluralism derived from an Islamic tradition dating back to the Ottoman Empire, whereas President Clinton seems to be supporting the ethnic partition proposed by Lord Owen and the Europeans that is the central component of the so-called peace plan that has been on the table in Geneva. President Clinton rebuffed President Izetbegović's plea for military help, and instructed him to cut the best deal that he can with those who seek to dismember his country along ethnic lines.

Instead of standing up for the Western principle of national and territorial sovereignty with regard to both Croatia and Bosnia-Herzegovina, the West is trying to rationalize away its diplomatic recognition of these countries. For example, Secretary of State Warren Christopher, and others, blame Germany for contributing to this Balkan War allegedly because Germany urged the rest of the West toward a 'premature' recognition of these nations. In fact, Slovenia and Croatia were not granted diplomatic recognition until January of 1992 and the current war in the former Yugoslavia began in June of 1991. More specifically, diplomatic recognition came after Serbia blatantly violated dozens of cease-fires. Moreover, diplomatic recognition was coupled to the maintenance – established at Serbia's request – of a weapons embargo that benefited Serbia and hurt Serbia's victims.

Even after the international community recognized the sovereignties of Croatia and Bosnia-Herzegovina, it continued to deprive these nations of their inviolable right to self-defence, as set forth in Article 51 of the UN Charter. Certain emotionally charged aspects of Western political culture seem to be violated here, most notably the principle of 'fair play'. It is important to observe that the United States and other democracies can act relative to the inherent right to self-defence without permission or even endorsement by the UN Secretary-General. The UN Charter acknowledges the right of individual and collective self-defence as inherent. That is, this right existed before there was a Charter or a UN. Yet, the rationalization for withholding weapons from Serbia's victims that has been made by Western heads of state has been that more weapons would only prolong the 'fighting'. Again, this explanation can be characterized as emotional, even compassionate (albeit paternalistic), but *post-emotional* in that it fails to address the slaughter – as it is called by Bosnian Muslims – occurring in the present.

We need to guard against reifying the West here according to the ideals it sometimes espouses. We use these ideals in order to expose the inconsistency of Western actions relative to its *post-emotional* rhetoric of concern and sympathy. But the real intent is to deconstruct this rhetoric, and expose the Western penchant for ethnic partition, collective guilt, and acquiescence to genocide that is so very evident from a glance at European history.

If it is true that the Gulf War was a memorable major war fought under the 'illusion' (in the postmodern) sense of the West standing up to aggression, then the current Balkan War is a watershed event in that it is a 'major' war (symbolically) in the sense of the West appeasing aggression under the guise of humanitarian and compassionate concern. Even here, the concept of *post-emotionalism* adds a new dimension to discourses of this sort. For example, the Gulf War is frequently characterized as a 'war for oil', or as an example of anti-Muslim racism, or even as a war for President Bush's manliness. I would add, in the present context, that for the United States it was a war for overcoming the emotional wounds of the Vietnam War: a 'neat and tidy' war which America led and won in order to show the world that its humiliating defeat in Vietnam was not the last word. (One should add that the quick and smaller wars in Grenada and Panama lend themselves to a similar interpretation.) But this *post-emotional* complex has now blocked intelligent responses to Belgrade-sponsored aggression, and is causing new problems on the world's political scene: would-be dictators and extremist parties in the former Soviet Union are watching eagerly as the West fails to live up to its ideals. The West is fantasizing that Boris Yeltsin will succeed in a post-Cold War, Disneyworld process of magical, instant democratization and 'free-market reform' even though it is giving the green light to anti-democratic forces. On the threshold of the next century – a time that promises to be one of ethnic and religious violence dominated by propaganda images on the television screen – the West has apparently learned little from a bloody twentieth century. Is all this leading to a major European War for the third time in this century?

CONCLUSIONS

The keystone of my analysis is the new concept, post-emotionalism. I use this concept to capture the confusion, hypocrisies, hysteria, nostalgia, ironies, paradoxes and other emotional excesses that surround Western politics toward the post-communist Balkans as well as the inability of Western cultural analysts and intellectuals to make the Balkan War intelligible to the masses. Post-emotionalism holds greater explanatory power than postmodernism, because postmodernism holds that one should revel or feel comfortable in the face of the ironies, inconsistencies, and contradictions such as the ones that we have uncovered (Bauman, 1992). But we hold that genocide and crimes against humanity are neither an occasion for revelry nor situations that make one feel comfortable. Thus, like the postmodernists, we debunk, demystify, and criticize the explanations given by the media and governments involved. Unlike the postmodernists, we go beyond their argument that social life consists of a mental text that consists of circulating fictions that are not supposed to make sense to include the emotions. And we point out that the postmodern goal of tolerance is not being achieved: extreme intolerance seems to be the rule, not the exception, in the post-communist world, as the world heads for the end of the century.

Far from being an instance of Eurocentrism, the current Balkan War seems to be a watershed event in our *fin de siècle* that involves Islamic, European and American cultural interests. It seems to be foreshadowing ethnic violence that has already increased, and will probably increase in the coming century: Rwanda, Angola, the southern fringes of the former Soviet Union, and so on. If critical theory was largely a response to the horrors of modernism exemplified by Stalin and Hitler; if postmodernism was largely a foreshadowing of the collapse of the modernist system in communism and a reaction to the last stages of modernist capitalism; I propose that post-emotionalism ought to be regarded as a new theoretical construct to capture the fission, Balkanization, ethnic violence and other highly *emotional* phenomena of the late 1990s.

NOTES

1 Information relayed to me by Durkheim' s grandson, Etienne Halphen.
2 As relayed to me by the US Ambassador to Croatia, Peter Galbraith, in 1993, for example, and the correspondent for the *New York Times*, Chuck Sudetic, during extensive conversations in 1992 as part of my Fulbright-sponsored research in Croatia.
3 Consider the episode of the programme *TV Nation* broadcast on NBC in the United States on 16 August 1994. The show's host parodied 'shuttle diplomacy' between Croats and Serbs by having their respective ambassadors sing a love song from the children's TV programme, *Barney* (Barney is a loveable dinosaur who promotes postmodern tolerance). The host had the Serbian Ambassador to the US cut a Pizza according to ethnic divisions in the former Yugoslavia and even fix his Yugo automobile. In sum, this NBC programme made genocide an object of satiric humour, which constitutes sadism, in the sense that sadism involves pleasure at the expense of someone else's suffering.
4 Consider the re-enactment of the Woodstock concert in August 1994.

REFERENCES

Ahmed, Akbar (1993a) *Living Islam*, London: BBC Books.
—— (1993b) 'Bosnia: new metaphor in the "new world order"' *Impact International*, 12 (March): 24–7.
—— (1994) 'Mutiny in the mosque', *Guardian*, 10 March: 24.
Alpert, Harry (1993)[1939] *Emile Durkheim and His Sociology*, London: Gregg Revivals.
Atkinson, Paul (1990) *The Ethnographic Imagination: Textual Construction of Reality*, London: Routledge.
Baudrillard, Jean (1986) *America*, London: Verso.
—— (1991) 'The reality Gulf', *Guardian*, 11 January: 25.
Bauman, Zygmunt (1992) *Intimations of Postmodernity*, London: Routledge.
Bellah, Robert HN., Madsen, Robert, Swidler, Anne, Sullivan, William and Tipton, Stephen (1985) *Habits of the Heart*, Berkeley: University of California Press.
Benjamin, Walter (1968) 'The work of art in the age of mechanical reproduction' in *Illuminations*, ed. Hannah Arendt, New York: Harcourt, Brace & World.
Cohen, Philip J. (1992) 'History misappropriated', *Midstream*, 38, 8: 18–21.
—— (1994) 'Ending the war and securing peace in former Yugoslavia', *Pace International Law Review*, 6, 1: 19–40.
Dizdarevic, Zlatko (1994) 'What kind of peace is this?' *New York Times Magazine*, 9 April: 9.
Durkheim, Emile (1933)[1893] *The Division of Labor in Society*, New York: Free Press.

—— (1975)[1898] 'Individualism and the intellectuals' in *Durkheim on Religion*, ed. W.S.T. Pickering, London: Routledge & Kegan Paul.

—— (1965)[1912] *The Elementary Forms of the Religious Life*, New York: Free Press.

Fauconnet, Paul (1920) *La Responsabilité*, Paris: Felix Alcan.

Finkielkraut, Alain (1992) *Comment peut-on être Croate?* Paris: Gallimard.

Fukuyama, Francis (1992) *The End of History and the Last Man*, New York: Free Press.

Geertz, Clifford (1973) *The Interpretation of Cultures*, New York: Basic.

—— (1988) *Works and Lives: The Anthropologist as Author*, Stanford: Stanford University Press.

Lyotard, Jean-Francois *The Postmodern Condition*, Minneapolis: University of Minnesota Press.

Meštrović, Stjepan G. (1988) *Emile Durkheim and the Reformation of Sociology*, Totowa, NJ: Rowman & Littlefield.

—— (1991) 'Why East Europe's upheavals caught social scientists off guard', *The Chronicle of Higher Education*, 25 September: A56.

—— (1992a) *Durkheim and Postmodern Culture*, Hawthorne, NY: Aldine de Gruyter.

—— (1992b) *The Coming Fin de Siècle*, London: Routledge.

—— (1993) *The Barbarian Temperament*, London: Routledge.

—— (1994) *The Balkanization of the West*, London: Routledge.

Meštrović, Stjepan G., Slaven Letica and Miroslav Goreta (1993) *Habits of the Balkan Heart*, College Station, TX: Texas A&M University Press.

Miles, Jack, (1994) 'Auschwitz and Sarajevo', *Tikkun* (March/April): 17–21.

Moynihan, Daniel P (1994) *Pandaemonium*, New York: Oxford University Press.

Péan, Pierre (1994) *Une jeunesse française*, Paris: Fayard.

Riesman, David (1950) *The Lonely Crowd*, New Haven: Yale University Press.

Rosenau, Pauline (1992) *Post-Modernism and the Social Sciences*, Princeton: Princeton University Press.

Schopenhauer, Arthur (1965)[1818] *The World as Will and Representation*, New York: Dover Press.

Seidman, Steven and Wagner, David (1991) *Postmodernism and Social Theory*, Oxford: Basil Blackwell.

Simmel, Georg (1991)[1900] *The Philosophy of Money*, London: Routledge.

Tester, Keith (1992) *The Life and Times of Post-Modernity*, London: Routledge.

Vuković, Tomislav (1991) *The Mosaic of Betrayal*, Zagreb: St Cyril & Methodious Press.

Weber, Eugen, (1987) *France, Fin de Siècle*, Cambridge: Harvard University Press.

CHAPTER 12

Epilogue
Notes on the Future of Anthropology
Anthony Giddens

Let me start with a list: Malinowski, Radcliffe-Brown, Fortes, Evans-Pritchard, Leach, Firth, Mead, Benedict, Lévi-Strauss. What an extraordinary diversity of talent and accomplishment there is in this array of names! Others could of course be added to anthropology's hall of fame over the period from the 1930s to the early 1970s. But one couldn't think of more than one or two individuals of comparable prominence in the younger generation, even given the fact that intellectual reputations take a good deal of time to establish. Should we (or at least those of us who don't have teaching jobs which depend upon the continuance of the subject) simply declare an end to anthropology, along with all those other endings which are so freely spoken about today? For nearly all of the societies and cultures which were once the specialised 'field of study' of anthropology have now disappeared or become altered almost beyond recognition.

Let's add a second list: old age, tourism, heritage, masculinity, Aids, cultural imperialism. These are in fact the contents of this book. But a critical critic might say that they don't seem to have much to do with anthropology; nor is it obvious that the prime anthropological research method, fieldwork carried out over the long term in the local community, has any particular relevance to them.

Anthropology today faces two sets of problems. First, there are those which it shares with the other social sciences. Together with the other social science disciplines, anthropology has felt the impact of postmodernism, the apparent collapse of foundationalism in epistemology, and the rise of a much more reflexively organized intellectual culture. Newspapers, magazines and TV deal in much the same sources and ideas now as do academic authors, but reach audiences of millions rather than a few hundreds or thousands.

In addition, however, anthropology has its own distinct litany of problems, wearyingly familiar to anyone working in the subject. Here the question plainly isn't only the disappearance of the exotic, the far-away places which were once so inaccessible. Anthropologists used to deal with individuals and groups who by and large didn't answer back. The anthropologist would go off to some distant corner of the world, carry out the obligatory fieldwork, and some while after return to write the whole thing up in the form of a monograph. The book would become lodged in a number of university libraries, most of them in Western countries, to be safely ignored save for a few specialists within the anthropological profession. In a world of developed reflexivity, this sort of situation rarely applies. Those who are the subjects of anthropological treatises are likely to read them, react to them and perhaps use them in local and even global political battles. Moreover, anthropology is widely seen as tainted by its association not just with the West, but specifically with colonialism. No doubt the connections between anthropology and colonialism were complex. One could hardly say, as some of the cruder attacks upon anthropology have maintained, that anthropologists were the complicit agents of colonial expansion and administration. Particularly where it turned against evolutionism, and the idea of the 'primitive', anthropology became in some part the defender of non-modern cultures in the face of the Western onslaught. Yet obviously anthropology did draw much of its sustenance from the colonial relation.

None of the contributors in fact wants to see an end to anthropology, these difficulties notwithstanding. This is hardly surprising, given that most or all get their livelihood from the active teaching and practice of the subject. They would not want to bite too badly the hand that feeds them. But what justification actually is there for a continuing role for anthropology, and if there is indeed such justification what shape might the discipline henceforth assume – where would its distinctiveness lie?

There are various ways in which the autonomy of anthropology has in the past usually been understood. The specifity of anthropology might be seen in substantive, methodological or theoretical terms, or some sort of mixture of these. Substantively, the distinctiveness of anthropology, particularly in relation to sociology, was normally thought of as bound up with its concern with the non-modern. Sociology, by contrast, concerns itself with the nature and impact of modernity. Today, however, as many of the contributors to the book note, modernity is everywhere. Sociologists might see their province as primarily that of the First World while anthropologists concentrate upon the Third World.

Yet as globalization develops apace, divisions between First and Third World societies crumble; and in any case the Third World is the creation of modernity rather than simply standing outside it. To persist with a substantive definition of anthropology as about non-modern societies and cultures would mean turning the subject into a version of museum studies. The anthropologist would be a sort of curator of an historical museum of humanity's past.

On a methodological level, the distinctiveness of anthropology has sometimes been supposed to lie in its devotion to intensive fieldwork – that is, to ethnography. Yet an argument could be made that intensive fieldwork was developed in sociology before anthropology. It is in any case a form of research method which is used across the social sciences rather than distinguishing any one of them. The mystique of fieldwork in anthropology was closely bound up with the idea of anthropology investigates the exotic; for the more alien a group or community appears, the more an immersion in its practices and customs is necessary to understand them. But with the dissolution of the exotic, the claim that what is distinctive about anthropology is its method is not a particularly convincing one.

That leaves theory. Like all academic subjects, anthropology has its own theoretical traditions. Sociologists and anthropologists might both lay claim to Durkheim, for example, but otherwise the intellectual ancestries to which they look tend to diverge. How much continuing intellectual mileage is there in the traditions of theory that have dominated anthropology? The answer would seem to be only a limited amount. Evolutionary anthropology quite rightly finds few supporters in the present day. Versions of anthropological theory coming from later periods, including structural functionalism and American cultural anthropology, are commonly recognized to have marked limitations. Each tended to picture the theoretical object of anthropology as the self-contained local community. Neither developed sophisticated conceptions of power, ideology or cultural domination.

A discipline which deals with an evaporating subject-matter, staking claim to a method which it shares with the rest of the social sciences anyway, and deficient in its core theoretical traditions – these things do not exactly add up to defensible identity for anthropology today. Yet things are by no means as bleak for anthropology as such an assessment seems to suggest. We cannot just turn from anthropology towards sociology, because orthodox sociological traditions have as much difficulty in grasping the changes now transforming local and global social orders as do those coming from anthropology. Partly because of the differences in their areas of substantive concentration, anthropologists quite often have addressed questions which have passed sociology by; and some of these questions have now returned to full prominence in the current period. They include, for example, the resurgence of ethnicity, the seeming revival of 'tribalism' in some form or another, and the continuing importance of religion and ritual – among other issues. Anthropologists and sociologists in large part now concentrate upon common areas of interest – the list of topics contained in this book could appear in any sociology text. In discussing them, however, anthropologists and sociologists tend to draw upon at least partly different literatures; and the insights which can be brought to bear from contexts of anthropological thought might often prove more valuable than those coming from sociology. A refusal to declare an end to anthropology, therefore, doesn't simply reflect the inertia inherent in an established academic enterprise. Anthropology does have a past which has to some degree to be lived down, but that past contains ideas that either remain as important as they ever were, or have actually become more significant today.

The problem of relevance crops up quite a lot in this book. If anthropology is not a dead enterprise how might it make its mark again, intellectually and practically? Could one hope for a renewal of that wonderful fund of creativity represented by the list of authors mentioned at the beginning?

I do not see that anthropology in this respect is in a different position from the other social sciences. A number of issues must be faced. Should anthropology remodel itself in relation to the fall of epistemology and the arrival of postmodernism? How does, or should, the academic discourse of anthropology relate to other forms of knowledge-production in a world of heightened reflexivity? What implications do answers to these first two questions have for the practical connotations of anthropology?

Of some things we can be fairly sure. A new flowering of anthropological theory and research will not come about from succumbing to postmodernism, or from a prolonged preoccupation with the theory of knowledge. A newspaper article on contemporary social thought once gave the following definition of postmodernism: 'Post-modernism: this word is meaningless: use it often.' The irony was apt. It is in fact a word we might do well to forget altogether, while acknowledging that some who have used it have directed our attention to important social changes and intellectual dilemmas. In my opinion much of what passes for postmodernism suffers from its association with another 'post' – post-structuralism. Post-structuralism in the majority of its versions, I think, has a defective theory of meaning, and therefore of representation, which can be traced right back to the origins of structuralist linguistics in Saussure. Meaning is understood in relation to the play of signifiers, not – as it should be – in the context of practical experience. Although I shall not elaborate the argument here, it seems to me that those who speak of a crisis of representation in anthropology, or who see anthropological work merely as a species of creative fiction, are the victims of such a false theory of meaning.

This point is closely connected to issues in epistemology. One should not confuse what Ulrich Beck has called 'reflexive modernisation' – an intensifying of social reflexivity – with the collapse of defensible knowledge-claims. Reflexivity is a social or institutional phenomenon; it does not, or should not, refer to the particular position of the anthropological observer. A reflexive universe of social action, simply put, is one where nobody is outside. Everyone, more or less throughout the world, has to filter and react to many sources of incoming information about their life circumstances. Such information is not simply part of the 'external world'; in their reactions to, and usages of, information social agents construct, reconstruct and deconstruct the action environments which such information sought to describe or interpret in the first place.

In a reflexive world we are all knowledge-producers and the phenomena of tribal groups making videos about their communities, or television journalists making sophisticated programmes drawing upon the same sorts of intellectual resources as academics do when they write their books, become commonplace. Can the professional academic compete in such circumstances? Is there, indeed, any role for the intellectual at all where the intellectual is at most one 'expert' among many others? Academics and other intellectuals will have to get used to the fact that their claims and findings are likely to be routinely interrogated by those outside the groves of academe. They can no longer act as high priests – the generous dispensers of arcane knowledge to a generally ignorant populace. These things, however, do not destroy the usefulness of the academic. The usual differences between academic specialists and lay people continue to obtain. Academic professionals normally engage with a subject-matter in a more thoroughgoing and catholic fashion; and the researches and theoretical innovations of the social sciences are necessary resources upon which wider forms of public reflection draw.

The practical connotations of anthropology are likely to depend more upon a rekindling of the anthropological imagination than upon a narrowing-down of the subject to limited social policy issues. I don't think this necessarily means that anthropology has to be an 'uncomfortable discipline'. Anthropology must be ready to contest unjust systems of domination, along the way seeking to decide what 'injustice' actually is, and be prepared to bring potentially controversial issues to light. Yet there is a limit to the unmasking of power and there are problems and issues over which it is important to seek to build a collective, even global, consensus. Pre-established forms of anthropological enterprise, including the classic intensive study of the local social arena, may often be of practical importance. Numerous instances exist, in both the developed and less developed countries, where policies undertaken with the best of intentions have rebounded, or proved destructive, because they were based upon mistaken or inadequate knowledge of the groups to whom they were targeted. Anthropology today, nevertheless, must be deployed above all to get to grips with the extraordinary changes now transforming all our lives. What has practical relevance in anthropology depends not just, or even primarily, in finding 'technological' solutions to discrete problems, but rather in forging new perspectives, new ways of looking at things. Anthropology should contribute to the collective effort that the social sciences as a whole need to make to confront a social world which has changed almost out of recognition in a few short years. Perhaps then there will emerge a new generation of anthropological thinkers on a par with the old?

Index

Abeles, M., 28, 41
Abu-Lughod, L., 141, 148, 152
acculturation, 36, 181–8, 191
Adams, V., 185, 197
Adler, J., 162–3, 175
Afghanistan, 104–5
Africa, 55–6, 75–6, 95, 100–5, 121, 129; Eurocentrism and post-emotionalism, 253, 260; feminism, 142; HIV/AIDS, 112, 114, 117, 124, 126–7; media and cultural imperialism, 231, 236; tourism, 172
African Political Systems, 50–1
Afrikaaners, 95, 117
ageing, 28, 37–8, 74, 80–1, 203–23, 272
Ahmed, A., 14, 23, 29, 41, 254, 270; media imperialism, 230, 242; and Donnan, H., 13, 41; and Shore, C., 12–40, 159
aid, for the elderly, 217–18; as media event, 237; mutual, 214; overseas, 26, 34–5, 94–107, 237, 244
AIDS/HIV, 19, 35–6, 110–30, 272
Akashi, Y., 259
Akbar, M.J., 22
Akeroyd, A., 70, 90
Alaska, 183
Albers, P. and James, W., 189–91, 197
Algeria, 182
Aliyah Center, 210
Allcock, J., 193, 197–8; and Przeclawski, K., 192, 198
Allende, Isabel, 23

Alpert, H., 256, 270
Althusser, 18
Amadiume, I., 142, 152
American Anthropological Association, 22
Amerindians, 114, 189–90, 241
amusement parks, 167–8, 172, 191
Anderson, B., 21, 41, 209, 224
Ang, I., 231, 247
Angola, 260, 269
Anthropology in Action, 22, 28, 71-2, 80
Anthropology and Nursing Association (ANA), 71
Anthropology Today, 22
Anthropology Training and Education (ATE) group, 71
apartheid, 39, 95, 254, 267
Appadurai, A., 233–4, 243, 247
Appiah, K., 169, 175
applied anthropology, 26, 34–5, 66–73, 88, 94–107; legitimacy of, 99–105; sickness and AIDS, 121; tourism, 182, 196
Apthorpe, R., 81, 90
architecture, 14, 171, 173–4
Ardener, E., 113, 130
Ardener, S., 137, 152
Armstrong, D., 118–20, 130
Arnheim, Rudolf, 235
Aron, R., 193, 198
Asad, T., 15, 18, 41, 76, 94, 108; indirect rule, 114, 130; languages of field and researcher, 221, 224; policy or programme community, 79, 90

Ascherson, Neil, 22
Asia, 56, 112, 161, 163, 182, 260;
    Central, 28–9; South-East, 75; *see
    also* China; India; Japan
Aspelin, P., 184, 198
Association Euro-africaine pour
    l'Anthropologie du changement
    social et du developpement
    (APAD), 107
Association of Social
    Anthropologists (ASA),
    67–72, 89–90
Association of Social
    Anthropologists of the
    Commonwealth, 114
Atkinson, P., 221, 224, 252, 270
Austen, Jane, 21–2
Australia, 21, 112, 167, 231
authenticity, 98, 160, 168–70,
    203, 233

Back, L., 146, 152
Bagehot, Walter, 22
Bali, 232
Balkan War, 23, 25–6, 242–4,
    252–70
Balkanization, 39, 251–4, 269–70
Bangladesh, 56
Barley, N., 27, 41
Barnes, J.A., 114
Barnett, T. and Blaikie, P.,
    125–6, 130
Barthes, R., 14, 41, 207, 224
Basques, the, 193
Bastide, R., 83, 90
Bateson, G., 128, 130
Baudrillard, J., 169, 173, 175, 232–3,
    252–3; new conceptual language,
    207, 224; postmodern wars as
    media events, 241, 247, 261–3,
    270; social constructions of time,
    205–6, 224; tourism and society
    of consumption, 189, 198
Bauman, Z., 269, 270
Beck, U., 13, 41, 276
Belgium, 95, 256
Bellaby, P., 125, 130
Benedict, B., 16, 18, 168, 175, 272

Benjamin, W., 116, 159–60, 168,
    175, 255, 270
Benthall, J., 23, 41
Beresford, D., 236–7
Berger, P. and Luckman, T.,
    160, 175
Berger, B. and Kellner, H., 206, 224
Bhabha, H., 234, 247
biomedicine, 36, 110–12, 119–24,
    129
Bloch, M, 18, 41, 116
Bly, R., 141, 152
Boas, F., 16, 17, 49, 115, 158
Bodroghkozy, A., 236, 247
Boissevain, J., 13, 16, 41
Bolivia, 77
Bolton, R., 111, 124, 130
Boorstin, D., 189, 198
Bosnia, 22–6, 38–9, 242, 254–68
Bourdieu, 116, 207
Boutros-Ghali, Boutros, 253
Boyer, M., 191–2, 198
Bradbury, Malcolm, 12
Braidotti, L., 143, 152
Brandes, S., 139, 152
Brazil, 20, 127–8
Britain *see* UK
Britan, G.M. and Cohen, R., 78, 90
British Association for Anthropology
    in Policy and Practice
    (BASAPP), 71–2
British Medical Anthropology
    Society (BMAS), 71
British Medical Journal, 118
British Medical Research Council,
    111
British National Health Service, 128
British Overseas Airways
    Corporation (BOAC), 164
British Overseas Development
    Administration (ODA), 94
Brittan, A., 134–5, 152
Brod, H., 136, 139, 152
Brown, D.F., 205, 224
Brown, R., 95, 108
Bruner, E., 160, 175
Buck-Morss, S., 159, 175
bureaucracy, 33, 36, 58–9, 80–1,

171, 262
Burke, P., 116, 130
Burma, 18
Burton, Capt R., 17–18
Burundi, 253
Bush, President George, 268
Butler, J., 136, 143, 153
Butler, R.N., 208, 224

Cairo, 56
Cambodia, 255, 260
Campbell, Beatrix, 22
Canaan, J. and Griffin, C., 135,
    141, 153
Canada, 21, 85, 112, 167, 174
Cannell, F., 28, 41
capitalism, 12, 21, 36–7, 75, 77,
    160, 269; and Balkanization, 253;
    tourism, 159–60, 163, 165
Caplan, P., 134, 140, 153
care, community, 80–6, 212–14
Caribbean, 187
carnivals, 214
Carpenter, E., 206, 224
Carpignano, P. *et al*, 245, 247
Carrigan, T., Connell, B. and Lee, J.,
    146, 153
Carrithers, M., 204, 224
Carter, D., 159, 175
Centers for Disease Control, 127
Central African Federation, 121
Chapman, R. and Rutherford, J.,
    134, 153
Chavez, Leo, 128
children, child abuse, 28;
    development and government
    policy, 78–9; of ex-colonials,
    160; media and aid, 246
China, 115, 162, 174
Chodorow, N., 137–9, 143, 153
Chomsky, N., 13, 42
Christopher, Warren, 267
citizenship, 25
class, 13, 26, 112; feminism and
    masculinity, 142, 148; tourism,
    162–3, 168, 172–3; used and
    discarded objects, 165
Clifford, J., 54–5, 113, 130, 194,

198, 239, 247; multi-locale
    ethnography, 233–4, 247; and
    Marcus, G., 46–7, 61–3, 130,
    141, 153, 239, 247
Clifford, M. and Marcus, G., 15, 42
Clinton, President William, 266–7
Coggins, Ross, 97–8
Cohen, A., 80, 83, 90
Cohen, E., 179–80, 182, 188–9, 193,
    198, 254, 263
Coker, C., 240, 247
Cold War, 18, 30, 264
Collins, J., 80, 88
colonialism, 21, 52, 74–5, 85,
    105; applied anthropology,
    94–6; classical anthropology,
    18; decolonization, 129, 159;
    HIV/AIDS, 113; otherness,
    240–1; post-emotionalism, 256;
    tourism, 159–61, 166–7, 181–2
commercialism, 33, 163
communism, 95, 170, 251–3,
    263–5, 269
community, care in the, 80–6, 214;
    study of a, 73–86
Congo, 77
consumerism, 160, 189
Cook, Thomas, 163
Cornwall, A. and Lindisfarne, N., 15,
    27, 37, 134–52, 153
council policies, 35, 80–1
Crapanzano, V., 32, 42, 221, 224
creativity, 53–4, 58
Crick, M., 179–81, 188, 191,
    195–6, 198
crime, 26
Critique of Anthropology, 22
Croats/Croatia, 21, 242, 254, 258–68
Crompton, J., 191, 198
Csordas, T.J., 129, 130
Cuba, 124, 170
culture, 75, 79–80, 83–6, 105;
    areas and specialization, 100;
    colonisers and the colonised,
    15–16; cultural imperialism,
    228–47, 232, 272; fall of
    communism and Balkanization,
    251–3, 264–70; feminism and

masculinity, 137–40, 143–4;
HIV/AIDS studies, 35–6,
110–30; management, 32; new
identities and postmodernity,
13–14; and old age, 204, 207–10,
215–21, 223; present challenges,
21–3, 27–30, 35–40; scientific
ethnography, 58, 79–80; tourism,
36–7, 158–64, 170–4, 181–6
Curran, J., 231–2, 247
current affairs, 25–7
Current Anthropology, 22, 75
Curti, L., 237–8, 247
Cyrenaica, 120

Dalley, G., 80, 84, 90
Daniel, Y., 170, 176
Dann, G., 190–1, 198; Nash, D. and
Pearce, P., 183–5, 194, 198
Darwin, Charles, 49
Davis, F., 166, 176
Davis, K. *et al*, 147, 153
Day, S., 123, 130; *et al*, 123, 130
de Beauvoir, Simone, 56, 208, 224
de Kadt, E., 182, 185, 198–9
de Laurentis, T., 142, 153
De Waal, A., 23, 42
DeLillo, D., 228
democracy, 78–9, 163, 253, 268–9;
scientific, 51
description, 65
development, 79, 94–107; and
tourism, 182, 191
di Stefano, C., 140–1, 153
Dickens, Charles, 21–2
Dilley, R., 32, 42
Disappearing World (Granada
Television), 27
disasters, 25, 69, 236, 264
distancing, 38–9, 65–6, 73–8;
and masculinity, 144; and old
age, 208
diversity v. universality, 209–11
Dizdarevic, Z., 255, 270
Do Kay, 127–8
Donaldson, R.J. and Donaldson, L.J.,
121, 131
Donnan, H. and MacFarlane, G.,

28, 30, 42, 69, 72, 90; studying
up/down policies, 78–9, 83
Douglas, M., 116, 121, 131; and
Calvez, M., 125, 131; and
Wildavsky, A., 121, 125, 131
Dowd, J.J., 208, 224
Drakulic, S., 242–3, 247, 248
Dreyfus Affair, 257–60
drug-users, 113–14, 124–5
Dufour, Y.R. and Dufour-Gompers,
N., 245, 248
Dumazedier, J., 180, 195, 199
Dumont, L., 206, 224
Duncan, E., 22, 42
Durkheim, E., 50–1, 256–8, 265,
270–1, 274

Eagleburger, Lawrence, 263
East Africa, 172
East Timor, 25–6
Eco, U., 172, 173, 176
ecology, 32, 129, 158
Economic and Social Research
Council (ESRC), 70
education, 19, 26, 162–3, 163, 186
Edwards, J. *et al*, 28, 42
elderly *see* old age
Elias, N., 203, 224
Elliott, B. and McCrone, D., 87, 90
empowerment, 79–82; tourist
attractions, 165
Engels, F., 138
Ennew, J., 28, 42
environmental issues, 32, 101, 158,
164, 168
epidemiology, 115, 121–6,
129
epistemology, 15, 220, 276
Erikson, E., 214, 222, 224
Erisman, M., 185, 199
Errington, F. and Gewertz, D., 160,
176, 194, 199
ethics, 32–3, 35, 98–100; depictions
of the Other, 239; studying down
and distancing, 73–8; *see also*
moral issues
ethnicity, 13, 21–2, 28–33; ethnic
cleansing, 22, 244, 251–70;

feminism and masculinity, 142;
HIV/AIDS, 115; tourism, 159
ethnography, 15–22, 98, 158–9,
207, 252, 274; definition of, 239;
feminism and masculinity, 134–5,
148–9; media imperialism, 231;
multi-locale, 85, 233–4; and
old age studies, 108, 205, 220;
policy and practice in Britain,
35; scientific, 16, 34, 46–61; and
travel writing, 194
Ethnography of the North of England
(1988 conference), 69
Eurocentrism, 252–6, 260, 269
Europe, 112, 162, 167, 188, 214,
263; cultural imperialism, 229,
241–3; epidemiology, 121;
homogenization, 174; immigrants,
214; post emotionalism, 260;
tourism, 174; *see also* under name
of country, eg: France
European Community (EC), 263
Evans-Pritchard, E.E., 17–18, 42,
50–1, 76, 116, 272; political
issues, 120–1, 131
evolution, 49, 158, 274
Ewing, K.P., 206, 224
exhibitions, 167–8
"expert", the, 96–100

Fabian, J., 113, 126, 128, 131,
206–7, 224; otherness, 239, 248
Fairclough, N., 82, 90
Faludi, S., 134, 153
family, 26, 29, 33, 78, 105; and
homosexuality, 85–6; and
tourism, 164
famine, 25, 33
Fanner, P., 126
Farah, A.Y., 106; and Lewis, I.M.,
106, 108
Farmer, P., 111, 126, 131
Fauconnet, Paul, 267
Featherstone, M. and Hepworth, M.,
208, 225, 327
feminism, 15, 37, 77, 85, 134–52;
media imperialism, 231; scientific
ethnography, 47, 55–6

Ferro, M., 245, 248
festivals, 171, 182, 214
fieldwork, 19–21, 46–7, 50–2, 58,
94, 234, 274; changes of subject
matter, 203–4; and current
affairs, 25–6; fidelity of foreign
fieldworkers, 98; HIV/AIDS,
112–13; and tourism, 180
Filipovic, Zlatka, 261
Finkielkraut, A., 263, 271
Firestone, S., 137, 153
Firth, R., 18, 35, 65–7, 73, 86, 90,
108, 272
Fischer, M., 28, 42
Flax, J., 136, 153
Flores, E., 232, 248
Foa, S., 246
Fontana, A., 208, 225
Food and Agricultural Organization
(FAO), 35, 94, 126
Forrest, D., 144, 153
Forster, E.M., 21–2
Fortes, M., 18, 50, 116, 272; and
Evans-Pritchard, E.E., 63, 76, 90
Foucault, M., 14, 37, 42, 87, 90, 239;
and gender, 140, 143, 148, 153;
new conceptual language, 207
Fox, R., 12, 16, 17, 20, 42, 76, 91
France, 21, 55, 125, 167, 185, 192
Francis, D., 212, 225
Francisco, R., 185, 199
Frankenberg, R., 19, 27, 31, 35–6,
110–30, 122, 131
Fraser, N., 140–1, 153; and
Nicholson, L., 138, 154
Frazer, J., 17, 116
Freidman, J., 159, 176
Freudianism, 14–15, 138
Frow, J., 169, 176
Fukuyama, F., 29, 253, 257
Furnham, A., 187, 199

G-7, 13
Gardner, K., 56, 63
Gatens, M., 143, 154
Gedicks, A., 77, 91
Geertz, C., 24, 29, 42, 54, 57,
63; objectivity of data, 252,

271; researcher/researchee communication, 221, 225; self and society, 206, 225
Gellner, E., 23, 29, 42
gender, 13, 28, 33, 37, 69, 134–52; HIV/AIDS research, 112–13
General Agreement on Tariffs and Trade (GATT), 13
genocide, 252–5, 260–6
Germany, 185, 256–7, 263, 267
Geva, A. and Goldman, A., 188, 199
Giddens, A., 14, 28, 39, 40, 42; time-space distancing, 206, 225
Gilmore, D., 136, 139, 154
Glaser, B. and Strauss, A., 205, 225
globalization, 12–14, 33, 47, 273–4
Gluckman, Max, 57, 63, 95, 108, 120–1; critique of Malinowski, 111, 114–17, 129, 131
Godelier, M., 18, 188, 199
Goodale, J., 137, 154
Goody, J., 57, 63
Gordon, C., 87, 91
Gore, Vice President Al, 255
Gough, K., 75, 91
government policies, 26, 28, 33, 35, 73–88; "Care in the Community", 80–6; hidden hierarchies, 78; US welfare, 183; written, 81
governmentality, 87 8
Graburn, N., 36–7, 39, 158–75, 187, 189, 199; and Jafari, J., 195, 199
Grand Tour, 162–3
Grathoff, R., 206, 217, 225
Great Britain *see* UK
Greenblatt, S., 232, 248
Greenwood, D., 182, 193
Greer, Germaine, 22
Grillo, R., 67, 69–70, 72, 75, 89
Grimshaw, A., 56, 63; and Hart, K., 16, 27, 34, 39, 63
Gripsrud, J., 231, 248
Grosz, E., 143, 154
Group for Anthropology in Policy and Practice (GAPP), 68–9
Gubrium, J.F., 219, 225
guilt, collective/individual, 39, 257–8, 261, 266–7

Gulf War, 25–6, 38–9, 241–2, 253, 261–2, 268
Gunder, F.A., 184, 199

haemophilia, 113–14
Hailey, Lord Malcolm, 95–6
Haimendorf, 18
Haiti, 113, 126, 128, 267
Hall, S., 13, 42, 231, 234, 248; and Jacques, M., 12, 42–3
Handelman, D., 217, 225
Handler, R., 23, 43; and Saxon, W., 170, 176
Hann, C., 28, 43
Hannerz, U., 159, 176
Hanson, A., 169–70, 177
Haraway, D., 129, 131
Harding, S., 77, 91
Hardman, C., 113, 132
Hardy, D., 190, 199
Haringey Council, London, 85
Harris, M., 216, 225
Harris, O., 138, 154
Hartman, P. and Husband, C., 238, 248
Hartsock, N., 141, 154
Harvey, D., 13, 36–7, 230, 233, 248
Hassan, I., 203, 225
Hazan, H., 37–8, 203–23
health care, 69, 78, 80–1, 101
Hebdige, D., 13, 43
Hegel, G.W.F., 116, 252
Heiman, M., 190, 199
Help the Aged, 94
Helsinki Watch, 260–1
Herdt, G., 124, 132, 139, 154
heritage, 28, 37, 39, 165, 272
High Modernity, 14
highways, 30-1
Hill, J., 194, 199
Hispanics, 113–14, 124, 254
history, 12–13, 37, 49, 58–60; of anthropology, 17–18; commercialization, 37; ethnic cleansing, 254–5; feminism and masculinity, 139–40, 143; local, 22; media imperialism,

229; tourism and travel, 159–64, 168–9, 172, 189
HIV/AIDS, 19, 35–6, 110–30, 148
Hobart, M., 221, 225
Hobsbawm, E., 13, 225; and Ranger, T., 169, 177
Hochschild, A.R., 211–12, 225
Hockey, J. and James, A., 203, 226
Hodge, J., 141, 154
Hoggett, P., 240, 248
Hollingshead, K., 194, 200
Holocaust, the, 254–5
homelessness, 19, 33, 113, 215
homogenization, 12, 171–4
homosexuality, 19, 36, 85, 112–13, 125, 144–5
Horton, D. and Wohl, R., 235, 248
host societies, 183, 185, 191
housing, 78, 101–2, 121, 173, 211
Huizer, G., 77, 91
Human Organisation, 28
"Human Problem" expert, 96–100
Hunt, J., 17
Hutton, W., 244, 248
Hymes, D., 16, 17, 18, 43, 94–5, 108
hyper-reality, 170, 172–5

identity, 13, 159, 219, 222; gender, 142–4, 149; mythical expression, 210; in old age, 210–11, 216
Ignatieff, Michael, 22
immigrants, 21, 56, 103–4, 115, 214; Puerto Ricans in New York, 232; *see also* refugees
imperialism, 52, 58, 75–6, 77, 137, 181–2; cultural, 228–47, 272; new age of, 13; nostalgia, 166
India, 18, 22, 56, 95, 115, 162
Indonesia, 166
industrialization, 14, 33, 49, 163, 172, 183
information technology, 13, 14, 20, 69; 1987 conference, 69
institutions, 31–2, 35, 66; academic, 16, 31–2; European Union, 28; financial, 69; government policies, 13, 80–2, 87

International Livestock Centre for Africa (ILCA), 94
International Monetary Fund (IMF), 13
International Union of Anthropological and Ethnographic Sciences (IUAES), 71
Iraq, 25–6, 241–2, 267
Irish, 21
Israel, 210, 217–28, 264, 267

Jackson, A., 27, 43
Jafari, J., 183, 187, 200
Jamaicans, 21
James, W., 74, 76, 91
Jameson, F., 43, 46–7, 177, 230, 248
Janeway, E., 137, 154
Japan, 162–7, 170, 172, 174, 231
Jencks, C., 14, 43
Jews, 21, 213–14, 254–8
journalism, 21–5, 26, 160, 236–47
Jurado, A., 183, 200

Kaes, A., 235, 248
Kahn, H., 161, 177
Kandiyoti, D., 140, 154
Kane, S. and Mason, T., 124, 132
Kanitkar, H., 147, 154
Kant, I., 216, 252
Kapferer, B., 205, 226
Karadzic, Radovan, 254, 259
Karp, I., 15, 43
Kaufman, S.R., 208, 212–3, 222, 226
Kayapo Indians, 20
Kearney, R., 244, 248
Keat, R. and Abercrombie, N., 31, 43
Keith, J., 208–9, 212, 226
Kennedy, President John F., 237, 266
Kenya, 55-6, 100
Kertzer, D. and Keith, J., 208, 212, 226
Kessler, S.J. and McKenna, W., 136, 154
Kimmel, M., 136, 138, 145–6, 155
kinship, 33, 48, 83, 186, 231
Kleinman, A., 118–9, 132
Krippendorff, J., 189, 200

Kroeber, 18
Kroker, A. and Cook, D., 14, 43
Kurds, 21, 22

La Fontaine, J., 28, 43
Laclau, E. and Mouffe, C., 142, 154
Lamb, C., 22, 43
Lambert, J., Laslett, P. and Clay, H.,
   215, 226
Lanfant, M-F. and Graburn, N.,
   171–2, 177
language, 22, 25, 124, 162, 171, 174;
   biological idioms, 148; of deep
   structures, 204–5; feminism and
   masculinity, 147–8; knowledge
   of local, 105; and old age, 215,
   219–21; and scientific authority,
   207; tourism and imperialist
   imagery, 191
Laslett, P., 214, 226
Late Modern Age, 14
Leach, E., 18, 23, 34, 60, 67, 272;
   nonce symbols, 209, 226; social
   time, 205, 226
Lesser, A., 234
Lett, J., 181, 200
Lett Jr, J., 187, 200
Levi-Strauss, C., 158, 177, 209,
   226, 272
Levinas, E., 228
Lewis, I.M., 31, 94–107, 109
liberalism, 14, 87, 122–3, 252
liberation anthology, 77
Liebes, T. and Katz, E., 231, 248
Lienhardt, G., 17, 43
Lifton, R., 206, 226
liminality, 187, 214
Lindisfarne-Tapper, N., 151, 154
lineage systems, 51, 106
literature, 21–5, 220; children's
   diaries, 261; scientific
   ethnography, 47, 50–7;
   tourism and travel, 36, 158,
   169–70, 194
Llobera, J., 25, 43
Lloyd, P., 71, 80, 82, 91
local history, 22
Loizas, P., 74, 91

London School of Economics
   (LSE), 101
Lyotard, J-F., 140, 155, 207,
   257, 271
Lytle, P.F., 244, 248

MacCannell, D., 159–60, 167–9,
   172–7, 184, 189, 194–5, 200
MacCormack, C. and Strathern, M.,
   138, 155
McCourt-Perring, C., 81, 92
McElhinny, B., 144, 155
McKean, P., 182, 200
McKeganey, N. and Barnard, M.,
   128, 132
Mackey, E., 85, 89, 91, 142,
   145, 155
McLennan, J.F., 17
MacLuhan, M., 165
Magas, B., 242, 248
Maine, Sir Henry, 17
Mair, L., 72, 91, 116
Malinowski, B., 16–19, 23, 30,
   49–59, 91–4, 132, 272; feminism
   and masculinity, 134; and
   Gluckman controversy, 111,
   114–17, 129, 131; and pure and
   applied anthropology, 65–7, 72;
   rejection of evolutionary model,
   158, 177; studying down and
   distancing, 75–6
Mandela, President Nelson (S.
   Africa), 236
Mani, L., 129, 132
Mansfield, Y., 191, 200
Maoris, 170
Maquet, J., 129, 132
Marakwet, the, 56
Marcus, G., 77, 92; and Fischer, M.,
   14, 43, 113, 126, 132, 160, 177;
   representation and otherness,
   239, 248–9
Marcus, J., 76, 78, 79, 92
market orientation, 32
Marquez, Gabriel Garcia, 23
Marsden, D. and Oakley, P., 80, 92
Marsh Arabs, 25–6
Martin, E., 148, 155

Marxism, 14–15, 18, 116, 137–8, 184–5, 252
Mascarenhas-Keyes, S., 70, 92
Mascia-Lees, F. *et al*, 141, 155
masculinity, 28, 134–52, 272
mass demonstrations, 214
Mass Observation, 87
Massey, D., 233, 249
Matsuda, M., 166, 177
Mattelart, A. *et al*, 230, 249
Matthews, H. and Richter, L., 179, 200
Mead, M., 16, 18, 23, 30, 272
media, 20, 22–3, 26–7, 168, 229–41, 272; and the elderly, 215, 217–19; and former Yugoslavia, 256, 259, 263–4; media imperialism, 229–33; media orientated identity, 13, 186; psychological distancing, 38, 39
medical anthropology, 110–30
Meethan, K., 81, 84, 92
Melanesia, 18
Menzies, I.E.P., 245, 249
Mercer, K., 240, 249
Merleau-Ponty, 116
Mestrovic, S.G., 27–9, 39, 251–76; Letica, S. and Goreta, M., 252, 271
Mexico, 124, 179
Meyrowitz, J., 230, 237, 249
Michaels, E., 231, 249
Middle East, 163
Mies, M., 77, 92
Miles, J., 255, 271
Miliband, R., 87, 92
military strategy, 31
Miller, D., 232, 249
Millett, K., 137, 155
Milne, Alistair, 230–1
Milosevic, President S., 266
Milton, K., 28, 43
Minh-Ha, T. T., 239, 249
mining communities, 77
Mintz, S., 18, 77, 92
Mitterand, President Francois, 258
modernity, 158–75, 273–4; *see also* postmodernity

Mohanty, C.T., 142, 155; *et al*, 142, 155
Moliere, 219
Monks, J. and Frakenberg, R., 112, 132
Moore, H., 55–6, 64, 89, 155
Moore, S.F., 206, 226
moral issues, 110, 114–15, 150–2, 164, 206; mediatised images, 244; *see also* ethics
Morgan, H., 17, 50–1
Morley, D., 230, 242, 249; and Robbins, K., 20, 27–8, 38–9, 228–47
Morris, R.J., 121, 132
Moynihan, D.P., 257, 271
Mukherjee, B., 160, 177
multiculturalism, 20–1, 85
museums, 20, 85, 167–8, 172
Muslims, 254, 258–61, 266, 268
Myerhoff, B., 208–10, 212, 226; and Simic, A., 215, 226
myths, 9, 22, 94, 243; and the elderly, 207, 209–10, 213; epidemiology and myth of origin, 121; travel and erroneous invention of, 169–70; war and the media, 246

Nader, L., 16–17, 24, 30, 33, 43, 78–9, 92
Narayan, K., 112, 129, 132
Nas, R., 190
Nash, D., 36, 77, 179–96, 200; and Butler, R., 192–3, 200; and Smith, V., 189, 195–6, 200
National Institute for Health, 127
National Museum of Civilization, 167
national parks, 172
nationalism, 21, 28, 58, 75, 252
nationality, 13, 21
NATO, 266
nature, 137–8, 168, 172, 233
Nazism, 254, 263
Nepal, 185
Neugarten, B.L., 208, 226
New Guinea, 194

newspapers, 39, 275
Norris, C., 241, 249
Northern Ireland, 72, 127
nostalgia, 158–75, 165–8, 264, 266
Nuer, the, 51
Nunez, T., 179, 181

objectivity, 19, 27, 34, 74–5, 88,
    136; scientific ethnography, 46,
    51–3, 55–6
O'Kane, Maggie, 22, 23
old age, 28, 37–8, 74, 80–1,
    203–23, 272
Organizations (1990 and 1991
    conferences), 69
Ortner, S., 137–8, 155; and
    Whitehead, H., 138, 155
Orwell, George, 21, 262–3
otherness, 38–9, 113, 158,
    207–8, 219–20, 238–40; male
    dependence on female, 150;
    tourism, 168
Ouroussoff, A., 152, 155
Overing, J., 150, 155
overseas aid, 26, 34–5, 94–107,
    237, 244
Overseas Development Agency, 35
Owen, Lord David, 267
Oxfam, 35, 94

Pacific rim, 182
Pakistan, 22
Palestine, 21, 264
parents, single mothers, 26
Parker, R., 124, 132
participatory anthropology, 77
Participatory Development (1992
    conference), 69
Patton, C., 123, 132
Pavelic, Ante, 254
Pean, P., 258, 271
Pearce, D., 185, 201
Pearce, P., 187, 201
Pels, P. and Nancel, L., 207, 226
pilgrimages, 162
Plummer, K., 140, 155
policies, British Medical Research
    Council, 111; *see also* council
    policies; government policies

political correctness, 19
political discourse, 84
political scientists, 26
Pollier, N. and Roseberry, W., 15, 44
Pollitt, C., 88, 92
post-emotionalism, 39, 252–6, 260–9
post-structuralism, 141, 276
postmodernity, 12–15, 29, 32–40,
    79, 98, 275–6; and feminism,
    136, 138, 140–5, 152; former
    Yugoslavia, 252–3, 256–7, 261,
    265; and old age, 203–7, 215; and
    tourism, 159–60, 170–1
Priestley, J.B., 21
primitive societies, 19, 47–8, 50,
    51–2, 57, 158, 273
Princess Royal, British, 114
Probyn, E., 142, 155
project identification documents
    (PIDs), 102
project papers (PPs), 102
prostitution, 35, 113–14, 123;
    travestis, 144–5
psychiatric epidemiology, 118–19
psychoanalysis, 137, 139, 245
pure anthropology, 26, 35, 66–73,
    88, 196
Pye, E. and Lin, T-B., 182, 201

Rabinow, P., 28, 44, 239, 249
race, apartheid, 39, 95, 254, 267;
    geographical space, 234; racism,
    147–8, 236, 238–9; tensions, 13,
    26, 33, 136; Victorian evolution
    theory, 49
Radcliffe-Brown, A.R., 16, 18, 49,
    52, 67, 158, 177, 272
Ramazanoglu, C., 138, 155
Ramonet, I., 245, 249
rapid rural appraisal, 69
Rath, C-D., 235, 249
Raz, A., 217, 226
Read, Max, 235
Redfoot, D., 194, 201
refugees, 94, 104–5
Reimer, G., 190, 201
Reinhold, S., 85, 89, 92
reintegration, 187

Reinventing Anthropology, 18
relief aid/agencies, 29, 69
religion, 39, 83, 124, 147, 163, 252;
    African autonomous churches,
    75–6; fundamentalism, 22,
    33; geographical space, 234;
    hyper-reality, 173; Islam, 29, 269;
    otherness, 239
Rey, 18
Rhodes-Livingstone, 121
Richards, 18
Riesman, D., 264
risk groups, concept of, 121–4
ritual, 30; old age and definitional,
    209; political, 25
Rivers, W.H.R., 17, 49
Riviere, P., 28, 44
Robertson, A.F., 92, 126, 132
Robertson, R., 13, 44
Robins, K., 242, 249
Roehampton Institute (UK), 193–4
Rogers, B., 137, 156
Roosevelt, President Franklin, 266
Rorty, R., 140, 156
Rosaldo, M., 137, 138, 156
Rosaldo, R., 23, 44, 166, 177
Rosenau, P., 257, 271
Rousseau, J.J., 146
Royal Anthropological Institute
    (RAI), 22, 67, 68, 69
Royal Anthropological Society, 29
Royal Ontario Museum, 85
Rubin, G., 137, 139, 156
Rushdie, Salman, 23, 234, 249
Russia, 115, 183, 231
Rwanda, 255, 256, 260, 263, 269

Sacks, K., 137–8, 156
Saglio, C., 186, 201
Said, E., 15, 23, 44, 76, 92, 133, 262;
    geographical space, 234, 249;
    media and intercultural relations,
    238, 249
Salisbury, R., 79, 92
Sanjek, R., 196, 201
Sarajevo, 242–7, 255, 261
SAREC, 94, 100, 101
Schapera, 116

Scheper-Hughes, N., 127, 133
Schiller, H.I., 230, 249
Schiller, N.G., 123, 133
Schlechten, M., 185–6, 201
Schoepff, B.G., 128, 133
Scholte, R., 239, 249
Schopenhauer, A., 252, 271
Schrijvers, J., 77, 93
Schutz, A. and Luckman, T.,
    206, 226
Schweder, R.A., 116, 133; and
    Levine, R.A., 116, 133
science, 14–16, 74–5, 162, 185,
    207; anti-science branches, 34;
    Knowledge-Based Platform,
    183; paradigms, 14, 16, 46, 56-7;
    representation and interpretation,
    221; scientific ethnography,
    46, 49–53
Segal, L., 138, 156
Seidler, V., 138–9, 146, 156
Seidman, S. and Wagner, D.,
    252, 271
Selwyn, T., 195, 201; and Shore,
    C., 31, 44
Senegal, 186–7
separation, 187
Serbs/Serbia, 254, 259–63, 265–8
sexual behaviour, 19, 36, 85, 126,
    128; promotion, 85–6; *see also*
    homosexuality
sexual imagery, 147–9
shamanism, 126–8
Shapiro, J., 134, 156
Sharma, U., 89
Sherpa tourism, 185
Shire, C., 147, 156
Shore, C., 28, 44; and Johncke,
    S., 73, 93
Shotter, J. and Gergen, K.,
    206, 227
Shweder, R.A., 222, 227
SIDA, 94, 100
Silverman, P., 208, 227
Simmel, G., 264, 271
Singer, A., 137, 156
Slovenia, 242–3, 262
Smircich, L., 83, 93

Smith, V., 181–3, 191–2, 201; and
    Wanhill, S., 192, 201
Snow, John, 121–2
social anthropology, 15–16, 27–8,
    94–107, 119, 203; assessment of
    soundness, 101, 105–7; old age,
    214–15; South Africa, 95
Social Community Work (SASCW),
    71
Social Documentary Film
    Movement, 87
Social Science Research Council, 70;
    Summer Seminar (1954), 184
social sciences, 33, 191, 252,
    260, 272–4
socialism, 75
Society for Applied Anthropology
    (USA), 68
sociology, 193–4, 273–4
Sokolovsky, J., 211, 227
Somali National Academy, 101
Somali National University, 101
Somalia, 98–106, 253
South Africa, 95, 236
South America, 75, 124, 127
Soviet Union, former, 252,
    264, 268–9
Spain, 127, 241
Spencer, Herbert, 17
Sperber, D., 207, 227
Sri Lanka, 77
Stam, R., 236, 249
Star, S.L., 122, 133
Steinbeck, John, 21–2
Stephens, J., 211, 227
stereotypes, 35-6, 189–90, 215, 238;
    of anthropologists, 27
Steward, J., 18
Stirling, P., 68; and Wright, S., 93
Stoler, A., 146, 156
Stoller, R., 143, 156
Strathern, M., 28, 37, 44, 55,
    156–7, 205, 227; feminism and
    masculinity, 137, 140, 149–50,
    152; political discourse and
    keywords, 84, 93
Strauss, A., 217, 227
Street, B.V., 83, 93

structuralism, 52, 137–8, 141, 158,
    205, 274
subjectivity, 34
superstructure, tourism as, 188–91
surrogate concepts, 216–19
Survival International, 94
Sweden, 100–1
symbolic types, 217–18

Tallensi, the, 51
Tamils, 21
Tarlow, Rabbi Peter, 257
Taussig, M., 77, 93, 116, 127, 133
technology, 12, 159–60, 168–9;
    advances in media, 237–8, 245;
    information, 13–14, 20, 69; new
    reproductive, 25, 28; tourism,
    164–5, 173
television, 38, 215, 235–47
Terray, 18
Teski, M., 211, 227
Tester, K., 255, 271
Thaiss, G., 29, 44
Thatcherism, 74, 80, 88
The Golden Bough, 55, 63
theme parks, 167, 169
Thodes-Livingstone Institute, 95
Thompson, M., 165, 178
Thurot, J-M. and Thurot, G., 164–5,
    171, 177
time, restructured, 213–14; time-
    space, 129, 229–30
Todorov, G., 240–1
Toren, 116
tourism, 28, 36, 37, 158–96, 272;
    (1988 conference), 69; post
    graduate degree courses, 193–4
Towner, 192
Townsend, P., 211, 227
traditional societies, 20–1, 79, 204
Trease, G., 162, 178
tribalism, 244, 260
Trinidad, 232
Tully, M., 22, 44
Tunisia, 21
Tunstall, J., 227, 230
Turnball, C., 208, 227
Turner, B., 14, 148, 157

Turner, L. and Ash, J., 159, 178
Turner, V., 187, 213, 214, 227; and
    Turner, E., 116, 133
Tyler, S., 32, 44, 54, 221, 227
Tylor, Sir Edward, 17, 115

Uganda, 126
UK, 21, 25–6, 66, 69, 75–6, 86;
    AIDS/HIV studies, 112, 121–3,
    128; council policies and
    practice, 35, 80–1; feminism
    and masculinity, 146–7;
    Jewish community (East End,
    London), 211, 213–14; media
    imperialism, 230–1; media
    and trauma (Hillsborough
    tragedy), 236; overseas aid and
    development, 95–6, 101, 146;
    post-emotionalism, 262; Soho
    cholera outbreak, 121
Ukranians, 21
unemployment, 33, 80–2
United Nations, 127, 165, 196, 241,
    255, 259, 263–4, 268
United Nations Commission for
    Refugees (UNHCR), 104
United Nations Protection Force
    (UNPROFOR), 259
United States Agency for
    International Development
    (USAID), 35, 94, 101–3, 106
United States State Department, 260
universality v diversity, 209–11
University for the Third Age (U3A),
    Cambridge (UK), 215–16
Unruh, D., 212, 227
Urry, J., 36, 44, 170–1, 178,
    190, 195
US Congress, 101
USA, 18, 22–3, 47, 68, 75–7, 102,
    274; AIDS/HIV studies, 112–14,
    121, 125, 128; apartheid in,
    254; and Eurocentrism, 253–4;
    and feminism, 139; immigrant
    communities, 232; media and
    cultural imperialism, 229–31,
    236–7, 240–2; overseas agencies,
    94; post-emotionalism, 252, 262,

266; right of self defence, 268;
    tourism, 161–3, 167, 172–4, 183,
    188–90
Ustasha regime, 254, 256, 259, 266

Van den Abeele, G., 160, 178
Van den Berghe, P. and Keyes, C.,
    184, 202
Van Dijk, A., 84, 93
Van Gennep, A., 187
Vidyarthi, 95
Vietnam War, 261
violence, 22, 28, 33, 244, 255,
    265; Eurocentrism and post-
    emotionalism, 255–6, 265
Vocational Practice in Anthropology
    course, 70
Voodoo performances, 170
Vukovic, T., 263, 271
Vulliamy, Ed, 22

Wagner, R., 160, 178
Wallerstein, I., 159, 178
war, 22–3, 25–6, 28, 252–70;
    Cold War, 18, 30; Grenada and
    Panama, 268; media coverage and
    otherness, 38–9, 241–7
Watson, H., 56, 64
Weber, E., 257, 271
Weigl, M., 191, 202
Weiner, A., 137, 157
Wenner-Gren Foundation, 71
Westermarck, E., 17
White, L., 18, 158, 178
Wieringa, S., 144, 157
wild animal parks, 172
Williamson, J., 242, 249
Wilson, Godfrey, 95
Wittgenstein, L., 149, 157
Wolf, E., 18, 25, 44, 159, 178,
    234, 250
Wolfe, A.W., 77, 93
women, 47, 56, 77, 102, 106, 128;
    elderly, 210–11, 212; *see also*
    feminism
Woolgar, S., 28, 45
Woollacott, Martin, 22, 23
World Bank, 13, 103, 196

World Health Organization (WHO),
35, 94, 122, 127
World Tourism Organization, 182
Worsley, P., 18, 45
Wright, S., 22–3, 28–31, 35, 45,
65–89, 93; *et al*, 73, 93
Writing Culture, 46–7, 48, 54, 59

xenophobia, 13

Yeltsin, President Boris, 269
Yiannakis, A. and Gibson, H.,
193, 202
youth, images and studies of, 28, 146
Yu-no-kuni-no-Mori, 172
Yugoslavia, former, 193, 242–4,
251–76

Zaire, 128
Zakopane seminar, 182–3, 192–3,
195
Zambia, 95
Zerubavel, E., 205, 227
Zita, J., 144, 157
Zizek, S., 246, 250